THE MEN OF MOBTOWN

THE MEN
OF
MOBTOWN

POLICING BALTIMORE IN THE
AGE OF SLAVERY AND
EMANCIPATION

◆

Adam Malka

THE UNIVERSITY OF NORTH CAROLINA PRESS

CHAPEL HILL

This book was published with the assistance of the Authors Fund
of the University of North Carolina Press.

Manufactured in the United States of America
Designed by April Leidig
Set in Kepler by Copperline Book Services

The University of North Carolina Press has been a member
of the Green Press Initiative since 2003.

Cover illustration: Baltimore's African Americans celebrate the Fifteenth Amendment
at Battle Monument, May 19, 1870. Photograph by William Chase, Stereoview Collection.
Courtesy of the Maryland Historical Society, Image PP1.2.18.

Library of Congress Cataloging-in-Publication Data
Names: Malka, Adam, author.
Title: The men of Mobtown : policing Baltimore in the age
of slavery and emancipation / Adam Malka.
Other titles: Justice, power, and politics.
Description: Chapel Hill : University of North Carolina Press, [2018] |
Series: Justice, power, and politics | Includes bibliographical references and index.
Identifiers: LCCN 2017037708 | ISBN 9781469636290 (cloth : alk. paper) |
ISBN 9781469636306 (ebook)
Subjects: LCSH: Police — Maryland — Baltimore — History — 19th century. |
Vigilantes — Maryland — Baltimore — History — 19th century. | Racism —
Government policy — Maryland — Baltimore — History — 19th century. | African
Americans — Maryland — Baltimore — Social conditions — History —
19th century. | Baltimore (Md.) — Race relations — History — 19th century.
Classification: LCC HV8148.B2 M35 2018 | DDC 363.2/309752609034 — dc23
LC record available at https://lccn.loc.gov/2017037708

To Jennifer

CONTENTS

ILLUSTRATIONS

FIGURES AND TABLES

Figures

Tables

THE MEN OF MOBTOWN

Bird's Eye View of Baltimore City, lithograph by Edward Sachse and Company, ca. 1858. Courtesy of the Maryland Historical Society.

INTRODUCTION

✦

I N THE AUTUMN OF 1864, some months still before the Civil War would come to its final, exhausted conclusion, Maryland lawmakers did something that only a few years earlier had been practically un-thinkable: they liberated the state's approximately eighty-seven thousand enslaved people. Slavery had existed in Maryland from the earliest days of its colonial existence, and the occasion marked a legal revolution for the black men and women in the state. For black Baltimoreans in particular — a group that constituted one of the largest and most important black communities in the nation — the events surrounding the new birth of freedom were greeted with a mixture of hope and despair. The potential for good wages, household respectability, and personal autonomy constituted emancipation's hope. On the other side of the spectrum were policemen and prisons. These, to black Baltimoreans, represented emancipation's despair.

The hope of freedom and despair of policing were often bound together for black Baltimoreans, and at no time was that unhappy bond stronger than during the late 1860s, when municipal officials responded to the state's emancipation decree by arresting and incarcerating large numbers of freed people. Policemen had not, of course, completely ignored black Baltimoreans in the years before the war, but in 1861 African Americans accounted for just 17 percent of all the city's arrests, which was barely higher than their share of the city's population as a whole. After the war, though, the tallies rose quickly. By 1870, when Baltimore's black minority accounted for about 20 percent of the city's total population, black people had come to represent more than 34 percent of all arrestees. The black proportion of arrests thus doubled in under a decade.[1] Nor was that all. Rising arrest tallies among the black community grew the number of incarcerated black people as well.

1

The directors of the Maryland Penitentiary declined to speculate upon the "causes which have operated to produce this increase of crime and apparent demoralization amongst the culored [*sic*] population," yet they did ominously predict that "this class of prisoners, which has so rapidly increased in numbers . . . will for some time in the future continue to increase."[2] At decade's end, nearly seven in ten inmates in the prison were black. That number was all the more remarkable considering that at the decade's start three of four inmates had been white.[3]

At first glance, it may not be obvious why black Baltimoreans' arrest and incarceration rates exploded only after lawmakers excised slavery from the statute books. For although Maryland's 1864 constitution left intact much racially discriminatory legislation, rarely referring to black people at all except to free them, and although the state's constitutional adoption of the Jeffersonian credo that "all men are created equally free" initially rang hollow to the scores of black Marylanders who continued to suffer under what historian Barbara Fields has colorfully dubbed "the rotting corpse of slavery," a liberal sun did rise.[4] During the 1860s, white antislavery officials, attorneys, and activists joined with tens of thousands of black residents to reject older laws predicated upon explicit racial control for a more universal regime of rights, and the legal order they introduced guaranteed all men, regardless of race, the right to possess property, earn wages for their labor, and head their own households. Another state constitution was written and ratified in 1867, and its Declaration of Rights pledged that "every man, for any injury done to him in his person or property, ought to have remedy by the course of the Law of the Land, and ought to have justice and right, freely without sale, fully without any denial, and speedily without delay."[5] Governor Oden Bowie then endorsed the sentiment in his 1868 inaugural address, promising that now and forever would each black man be "protected in all his rights."[6]

The simplest explanation for why so much black policing occurred after the work of emancipation had wiped racial distinctions from the statute books is also the most cynical: perhaps white Marylanders' raceless rhetoric was hollow lip service. After all, most of the authors of the new state constitution, as well as the aforementioned Bowie, were reluctant emancipationists who had to be forced by federal legislation to honor black rights at all. Maybe black policing was just slavery under a different name. Maybe Bowie and his colleagues' true wishes were to reimpose the old order, the same as it ever was.

Cynicism about white motives is not unwarranted here, if only because so many white Marylanders gave lukewarm support at best to black rights, public proclamations to the contrary notwithstanding. Oden Bowie, for one, was a former slave owner. So too were many of the white men who wrote the state's 1867 constitution. In fact, most of these so-called supporters of a deracialized legal order were unreconstructed Democrats who had long opposed emancipation, and we would be wise to regard their sudden paeans to racial equality with a healthy dose of skepticism. And yet questions of timing remain. Why were black arrest and incarceration totals in the early 1860s so comparatively low? Why, conversely, did those totals explode only after the liberal credos of the new order had formally triumphed? And why did the *victory* of a universal rights regime encourage the beginnings of a black carceral state? A comprehensive answer to these questions requires that we resist the urge to succumb to easy cynicism and instead unpack the tangled relationship between liberalism and policing.

To do that, however, we must begin by looking backward in time, to the era when Baltimoreans first introduced the rules and rationales of their rights regime, for it was during the antebellum decades when lawmakers arrived at their beliefs about how to police free people. Slavery, critically, informed these beliefs. White men reared under the old order's racial logic embraced the perverse notion that black people, and black men in particular, could not help but lawlessly abuse their rights, and dismissing the post-emancipation white praise of black rights as mere bluster risks obscuring why so many racist white men felt so comfortable championing black rights in the first place. We might consider instead that Oden Bowie and his colleagues defended the fulfillment of black rights as a framework to condemn the fruits of black freedom. We might even consider that liberal principles, despite the facade of racelessness, were complicit in black oppression. One of the central arguments in this book is that Baltimore's police institutions were from the onset shaped by a liberal order that assumed criminality as the essence of black freedom.

Taking a broader temporal view also reveals which instruments of white supremacy predated — and predicted — the policeman and prison. When the legal codes of slavery overtly constrained black autonomy, it was less state institutions than ordinary rights-bearing citizens — not so much officers and wardens but white vigilantes — who surveyed, attacked, protected, detained, and punished free black Baltimoreans. Hence the (relatively) low arrest and incarceration totals during the antebellum years. Later, after the hard-fought victories of emancipation deracialized the statute books, black Baltimoreans began to confront agents of the state more often. It was racial policing all the same. Instead of inaugurating a new era of racial impartiality, emancipation prompted a more liberal iteration of white power. This book's other primary argument is that the free black experience of the 1850s anticipated the freedman's experience of the 1860s, and that the postbellum policeman and prison were updated versions of the antebellum white vigilante.

Baltimore's system of policing dated to the days of slavery, when a cohort of reformers built new institutions while condemning black freedom, and that system's principles blossomed most fully during the late 1860s, when the agents of the liberal order greeted black freedmen as criminals. One cannot comprehend the mass black policing that proliferated in the aftermath of emancipation without first appreciating the black criminalization and white vigilantism that thrived under slavery. Well before 1864, black freedom and white policing had been closely related. In an important sense, the one had long justified the other. This book concludes that while the post-emancipation legal order codified a number of hard-fought victories for racial justice, not least of which was black men's acquisition of labor and household rights, it also sanctioned state violence that prospered, however perversely, under the very conditions of freedom that African Americans fought so determinedly to secure.

I have organized this story of race, rights, and policing into three sections. The first recounts the emergence of police institutions in Baltimore during the antebellum decades, and it shows that two interrelated systems coexisted between the city's late eighteenth-century incorporation and the start of the Civil War. One system relied upon ordinary white men to guard the city, enforce its criminal laws, and govern in its name. The other, which began to emerge during the 1830s and 1840s, employed policemen to protect property and built asylums to rehabilitate prisoners into the type of individuals (that is, white men) who could possess property. Rather than operating in tension, these two police systems worked in tandem during the late antebellum decades, as complementary police institutions designed to guarantee property rights also protected the rights of white men to police the city as wage earners and householders. Put simply, the birth of the liberal police force and liberal asylum enlarged white male power on Baltimore's streets.

Part II argues that police reform enlarged white male power especially over black people. Staying in the antebellum years, this section narrates the story of white male Baltimoreans policing black people as workingmen, householders, and citizens. Such racial policing was possible because the architects of Baltimore's police force and penal system took for granted that black people were poor candidates for freedom — they presumed that without slavery's compulsions, black individuals would lack the industry, order, and lawfulness that freedom demanded. Seeing crime almost anywhere they saw free people of color, lawmakers empowered Baltimore's citizens to be on guard. Ordinary white men subsequently policed the city's free black community with abandon, working with and sometimes alongside professional police officers. White men drove free black laborers out of the city's worksites, for example; they invaded free black homes; and they arrested, whipped, and sometimes even enslaved free black people. And all of this they did in deference to the law. Baltimore's police system was created in the name of property rights, but the reformers who created it worried that black men's possession of such rights would lead to crime. The result, at least during the antebellum years, was a police system that legitimated ordinary white men's racial violence, rendering it so normal as to make it nearly invisible. From the perspective of the state, most free black people were criminals. From the perspective of free black Baltimoreans, ordinary white men were the state.

Part III moves the story into the post-emancipation period and chronicles the interposition of state power over freed people during the late 1860s. For black Baltimoreans, the years following the Civil War were as tragic as they were triumphant. The triumphs were mostly liberal: as federal agents worked to enforce black men's wage contracts and ratify their marriage contracts, as formerly enslaved black men eagerly asserted their rights to possess both, and as an interracial coalition of activists attacked the stubborn vestiges of slavery, a fully realized property rights regime emerged. Slavery died during the 1860s, and a deracialized legal order predicated upon male rights to workplace and household autonomy arose in its place. But for all of their promise, the changes also brought heartbreak. Black men's acquisition of a fuller bundle of property rights and legal protections brought them into conflict with the very system built to guard those rights and ensure those protections. White commentators scoffed at black men's supposed indolence and bristled at their households' apparent dysfunction; police officers arrested black Baltimoreans for an expanding list of crimes; and black people, black men in particular, were incarcerated at growing rates. During the years immediately following the Civil War, Baltimore's policemen and prisons perpetrated a form of racial violence that was different from yet indicative of the violence inflicted by the old order's vigilantes. Castigated as criminals, freed people's legal victories provoked a form of policing reserved for the truly free.

Policing

This history of racial policing is more focused than sweeping. *The Men of Mobtown* is a comprehensive history neither of Baltimore's police force and prisons nor of the scale and character of crime in the city. It is not primarily a story of how the night watchman became the policeman, how the early "gaol" gave way to the modern prison, or how the various people who either worked for the police or resided in the prisons fared materially from day to day.[7] It is even more insistently not a measure of the authorities' success in combating crime in nineteenth-century Baltimore, if for no other reason than because such an argument assumes that "crime" is an obvious, natural category whose definition is not subject to political debate and does not change over time. Rather, this book is about crime's utility as a political issue and the actions taken to combat its perception.[8]

Such an analytical focus also steers *The Men of Mobtown* away from several other avenues of interrogation. The ways that police professionalization reinforced the domination of poor, ethnic, female, and a variety of allegedly deviant people earn only passing treatment in the following pages, and then mostly in service of the larger argument about white supremacy.[9] Black Baltimoreans' resistance to the police system's racial cruelty as well as the strategies they cultivated to survive that cruelty are largely absent as well. Such elisions should not imply that state policing oppressed only people of color, or that white men were omnipotent and that black people were merely passive victims under a totalistic, oppressive regime.[10] My topical emphases simply reflect a desire to understand the roots of the state's racial violence and how a liberal ideology of freedom cultivated during the age of slavery legitimated the formal policing of black people during the age of emancipation.

What this book does focus upon is the coercive operation of white male power in nineteenth-century Baltimore, and it does so through an examination of the intimate bond between ordinary white men and the police apparatus of the liberal state. One of its primary contentions is that policemen and prisons represented an expansion of white male supremacy. Conversely, one cannot understand the extent of ordinary white men's racial violence without understanding those men's special relationship with the police institutions built in their name. Although it is easy to read the history of policing as part of the state's monopolization of force, the rise of police institutions actually fueled a type of herrenvolk democracy. When it came to policing black individuals, nineteenth-century Americans did not so much replace the posse with the police as build the police in order to strengthen the posse.[11]

One of the conceptual challenges of a project like this one revolves around the slippery concept of "police," a legal construct that has historically defied precise definition. In the truest sense of the term, the "police power" authorizes the state to ensure the public's general welfare and refers to a mode of governance somewhat different from and far more expansive than that with which many contemporary Americans associate it. Police regulations usually encompass a considerable range of issues — religion, morals, health, security, travel, the arts and sciences, commerce, labor, and the poor — whose management typically justifies the state's intrusion into private life.[12] As a legal term, the "police power" is fundamentally illiberal, a manifestation of governmental force that often operates in direct opposition to private rights, and property rights in particular.[13] Insofar as police forces and prisons represent the state's "police power," they represent only a small part of it.[14]

This book uses the tauter, more colloquial understanding of "policing" by focusing upon the enforcement of the criminal law on the streets and the punishment of convicted felons in penal asylums.[15] It also discusses policing in liberal terms and so differentiates the practices of police forces and prisons from the more abstract and illiberal concept of police power.[16] During the nineteenth century, officials who worked for Baltimore's municipality along with legal reformers and commentators who worked outside of it became increasingly wary of threats, both seen and unseen, to individuals' property. Lawmakers' response to these growing fears was to criminalize the threats and empower policemen and prisons to protect against them. By the middle of the century, policing, at least as municipal officials understood it, entailed securing public spaces for the free flow and exchange of property. It also required punishing people who proved unable to hold property responsibly.

Policing thus revolved around property, but "property" demands definition as well. Most obviously the concept refers to a physical asset, something material bounded in space, like a building. If owned, one's home is
one's property. Likewise for land; if marked by borders, it too can be an individual's personal property. But property has another, no less important
definition in that it connotes a legal right regulated by the government and
conferred by a title, a document usually acquired through purchase.[17] And in
a growing city like antebellum Baltimore, individuals not only held titles to
houses and land but also signed contracts for wages and households. In such
a place, labor and household power were properties too.[18] Property mattered
because nineteenth-century Americans defined its possession as freedom itself, which means that policing was a practice by which the state created the
conditions for freedom to prosper. While the new policemen aimed to ensure
that individuals could earn wages for their work and head households full
of dependents, prisons were built to rehabilitate inmates into reliable property holders who would work hard and support wives and children with the
proceeds of their labor. Conversely, the free person who failed to earn wages
for work or head a well-ordered household was a criminal in need of policing.

Because freedom was tied to property ownership, and because property
ownership involved working for wages and governing dependents, gender inequality lay at the heart of the nineteenth-century policing project. In men's
persons lay liberal society's fears: they were the model policers, but they were
also the stock criminals. Women policed, too, to be clear, and women no less
than men were also policed, usually by some combination of salaried officers and the ordinary patriarchs who were their fathers, husbands, brothers,
sons, and neighbors. In the end, however, the liberal subject was male, and so
it was almost always the men of Mobtown whose freedom demanded both
the security and the scrutiny of the state.

This is where race came in: liberals built police forces and penal systems
to promote freedom (that is, property ownership), but they doubted that
black men, when free to choose, would choose to use their property well.
In this sense free men of color were the paradigmatic criminals, the people
most in need of policing. To many white observers, they seemed too indolent
to work hard, too disorderly to head respectable households, too wanton to
abide by the law. The specter of free black men's crime was so frightening
to antebellum white Baltimoreans that local lawmakers curtailed some of
their rights, empowered all citizens to be on guard against them, and attempted to remove them from the state's penitentiary, a space they hoped

to reserve for the truly free. After the war, when both state and federal officials struck down racial inequities in the law, local lawmakers were forced to turn to their last resort, the policemen and prisons that served as coercive instruments for freedom's rule. If one of this book's arguments is that policemen and prisons represented an expansion of white male supremacy, its second related argument is that black autonomy — that is, black men's wage-earning, householding, and property-possessing potential — invited white policing. When policemen began arresting and incarcerating large numbers of black men during the 1860s, their actions represented the culmination of a decades-long attempt to check the perceived excesses (that is, crime) of black male freedom.

Baltimore

Nineteenth-century Baltimore provides a uniquely good setting to tell a history of policing. Labeled by contemporaries as "Mobtown," the city witnessed some of the most prolific street violence of the nineteenth century. It was Baltimore that ushered in a new type of rioting when in 1812 a group of Federalists met their grisly demise defending a press in the center of town; it was Baltimore where Jacksonian democracy's violent impulses found their clearest expression, when the nation's biggest bank riot erupted in 1835; and it was Baltimore where the first casualties of the Civil War were tallied, when Massachusetts soldiers desperately sought to pass through the city on their way to defend the capital and their embattled commander in chief. It was also in Baltimore where Alexis de Tocqueville recorded his thoughts on the American government's lack of administrative power and inability to check the capricious nature of large groups of men. He was thinking of Mobtown when he posited his thoughts on the "tyranny of the majority."[19]

The city was also home to a variety of thinkers, writers, and reformers whose thoughts on racial policing stretched beyond their municipality's immediate borders. Before he penned the Supreme Court's notorious *Dred Scott* opinion, and at a time when the protection of property rights emerged as a legitimate concern of municipal authorities, Roger Taney called the city home. So too did Frederick Douglass, who later made his abolitionist name speaking and writing about his experiences navigating the city's complex police system. Both political economist Daniel Raymond and journalist Hezekiah Niles resided in early Baltimore, where they used national platforms to wax poetic about the importance of criminal justice reform in the

American city — and about the trouble with free black people in any police system geared toward upholding freedom. Any number of prominent Baltimoreans publicly wondered how to fight crime, maintain order, and protect property in a time of legalized racial inequality, and in so doing they helped frame a bigger debate on the subject.

Many Baltimoreans wrestled with how to police race because demographics forced them to confront the issue directly. By 1830, Baltimore was home to the largest free black community in the United States, north or south. That year's census counted almost fifteen thousand free Baltimoreans of color, almost a thousand more than in New York and three thousand more than in New Orleans. By midcentury, the city's free black community had grown to almost double the size of the nation's next largest, with more than twenty-five thousand people, and its 15 percent share of the total population was second only to black Washington's 20 percent. Baltimore was, according to one scholar, the nineteenth-century capital of black America, and the numbers proved it.[20] Yet numbers alone are not the whole story. Because Maryland was also a slave state, the city was home as well to the compulsory laws that everywhere in the slave South compelled black obeisance. And because Baltimore was a thriving port city — by 1810, it was the third-largest city in the nation — a free labor economy was able to flourish wherein many residents signed contracts, earned wages, and participated in economies that brought them into the orbits of western farmers, local factors, and international creditors. Lawmakers were forced to make their police and penal institutions safe for an interracial society where freedom was the norm but where not all free people possessed the same rights. In particular, they had to design institutions to compel free white men to work for wages and head well-ordered households even as many of the men who walked the streets were neither white nor free.

The result, at least during the years of slavery, was the intimate coexistence of two different systems of policing and punishment. Both on antebellum Baltimore's streets and at its firesides, revealing contrasts frequently materialized: a group of white men delivered a free black thief to jail at the very moment professional policemen began walking their beats; a white man proudly protected his home from a veiled intruder even as a lieutenant elsewhere in the city was arresting a black man who had attempted the same; a gang of white caulkers and policemen drove gainfully employed free black men away from a shipyard in the Fells Point neighborhood despite the fact that, nearby, policemen scoured the streets of unemployed vagrants. Before emancipation, neither police professionalization nor penal reform under-mined white men's power over black Baltimoreans. If anything, those devel-opments enlarged ordinary white men's racial authority. A focus upon this fast-growing city sitting both literally and legally upon the border between slavery and freedom helps illuminate the ways that official and ordinary white policing were often mutually constitutive, not exclusive.

An analysis of Baltimore also helps to reveal the ways white male vigi-lantism was reconstituted as professional policing and mass imprisonment after emancipation. Baltimore was both like and unlike other cities in this regard. Northern states underwent the dislocations of emancipation well before the 1860s, and so it was in cities like Philadelphia that arrest and in-carceration rates first began to reflect the criminalization of black freedom in America. To a certain extent, freedmen's criminal condemnation in 1860s Baltimore rehashed the tribulations suffered by newly emancipated black men to the north a generation earlier.[21] At the same time, the widespread arrest and imprisonment of black Baltimoreans during the 1860s anticipated the trials of black southerners during the ensuing decades. It was not long before the black carceral state that arose in post-emancipation Baltimore arose elsewhere in the redeemed South.[22] Baltimore was part of and yet dis-tinct from both regions, a city whose system of policing both mimicked and innovated for others. What its example shows most clearly is the temporal relationship between popular and professional policing. Although elsewhere such a relationship may not have been obvious, in Baltimore one can plainly see how the vigilantes of the 1850s were direct antecedents to the policemen of the 1860s — and how, over time, the latter personified an extension of the former's power.

The history of Baltimore, positioned on the North-South divide, reveals how the racial coercions typically associated with the South overlapped with the liberal coercions typically associated with the North.[23] As in Charleston and New Orleans, ordinary white citizens, by virtue of their skin color, pos-sessed considerable power over black residents. And as in Boston and New York, the municipality established a professional police force and a reforma-tive penal system to protect the rights of property. These two systems simul-taneously converged in Baltimore, and my interrogation of their intimate relationship during the eras of slavery and emancipation shines a light upon the centrality of white male supremacy to liberal policing and punishment in the United States as a whole.

Baltimore consequently offers an opportunity to bridge an analytical divide that, in U.S. historiography, often appears misleadingly as a geographical divide. Ponder for a moment the way region has shaped historical scholarship on criminal justice. Northern locales dominate most histories of the formal institutions of power. Studies of municipal police departments usually focus on Boston and New York and other "free" cities such as Detroit and San Francisco. Meanwhile, studies of penal systems typically concentrate on New York and Pennsylvania, the two states in which the nation's opposing penal philosophies originated. And analyses of the national government's police power almost invariably assume that northern polities, social structures, and market relations offered the critical context of development. As they emerge from the pages of our histories, police and penal institutions were creatures of the North.[24] Then, too, many histories of the South elide these institutional histories altogether from their discussions of crime and punishment. Mirroring the assumptions of northern historians, southern specialists argue that the formal agents of southern policing were weak entities, if present at all. White male vigilantes and lynch mobs, as opposed to policemen and prisons, allegedly governed this "peculiar" region. Historians' focus upon the extralegal techniques of the rural agricultural societies of the South has fed an impression that the region's criminal justice system had little use for the institutions of the North.[25]

There is an understandable logic to such regional distinctions. It is inarguable that the administration of criminal justice in nineteenth-century Boston differed from the administration of criminal justice in nineteenth-century South Carolina. Policing a black-majority agricultural society posed fundamentally separate problems and operated fundamentally differently from policing a white-majority industrial society. Nevertheless, there is also a real danger in drawing too stark a boundary between North and South. Doing so runs the risk of unintentionally juxtaposing ordinary white male power and state power. For in a world policed by the state, white men seemingly had no need to police on their own; and in a world policed by extralegal violence, they seemingly had no need for a state.[26]

And yet most Americans in the early twenty-first century know all too well that policemen and prisons perpetuate white supremacy and that there is plenty of coercive state power in the South. The trouble with our geographic demarcations is that they have obscured the historical sources of these self-evident truths. Indeed, regional demarcations in our historiography have concealed the *national* legacy of both white supremacy and ordinary racial violence to professional policing. From Ferguson to Charleston to New York, from Angola to Attica, black Americans continue to confront the insidious marriage of race and policing all the time. Historians would do well to put studies of informal white power into the same conceptual and geographic universe as those of formal state power.

All of which brings us back to Baltimore, a city whose example sheds light on a story that crossed — and continues to cross — regional borders. Then the country's third-biggest metropolis and easily its largest city with slaves, Baltimore's political culture, social relations, and economic life bridged the nineteenth-century North and South. A racial system of domination most associated with the South underwrote the ideological underpinnings and institutional development of police institutions most associated with the North. Different legal systems, diverse populations, and a robust municipal infrastructure met, providing a contemporary reader with a particularly good milieu to appreciate how liberals feared black freedom and how the police and penal institutions they built buttressed racial hierarchies. If Americans ever hope to understand the way race has shaped the work of police forces and prisons, a look at a historical city with a slave market, many thousands of free African Americans, and a mixed labor economy is a good start. White male supremacy provided a critical context for professional policing and reformative incarceration in much of the nineteenth-century United States, even where slavery was a dead or dying institution. This context was simply clearer where large numbers of black and white people lived among each other, worked alongside each other, and walked past each other every day.

In the Age of Slavery and Emancipation

Retracing the close ties between ordinary white men and the police system necessitates crossing not only geographic borders but also temporal divides. Many works of U.S. history, not to mention U.S. survey courses in college classrooms, either stop at slavery's abolition or begin at emancipation, a choice of periodization that has significant ramifications for the way Americans understand the broader telos of their history. "In its dominant articulation," argues historian Walter Johnson, "the history of slavery exists in a state of civil servitude to the idea of American freedom," with emancipation providing a redemptive endpoint to the nation's original sin. That narrative, however, has wrongly reassured Americans that freedom's triumph was "somehow inevitable rather than contingent, complete rather than unfinished, a matter of the past rather than the present."[27] This book eschews freedom's redemptive arc. Accordingly, it ends not with tales of triumph but with accounts of police brutality aimed at African Americans, high black arrest rates on Baltimore's streets, and the mass incarceration of black Marylanders. Such subjects necessarily demand an examination of how ideologies and practices cultivated under slavery also shaped the possibilities — and limits — of black emancipation.[28]

In particular, those post-emancipation stories demand an alternative history of liberalism, the political philosophy that celebrates the supremacy of the rights-bearing, property-owning, contracting individual. To be sure, Louis Hartz's 1955 claim that Lockean liberalism was the hegemonic American political tradition has not gone unchallenged in the decades since. Hartz famously argued that Americans' faith in the unfettered sovereignty of individuals was so historically tenacious that it was absurd to posit that another tradition could also have shaped American political life — and yet many scholars have done exactly that. Many have done so, indeed, persuasively.[29] Whether arguing that early U.S. politics was more republican than liberal, that the police power has rivaled liberalism as a political tradition, or that racism and sexism have been coequal to liberalism from the Revolutionary period onward, numerous political historians, scientists, and theorists have ably demonstrated that Hartz's version of U.S. history does more to sanitize than to elucidate. Sixty years after the publication of *The Liberal Tradition in America*, it is Hartz's thesis of liberal hegemony, not its numerous challengers, that seems absurd.[30]

For all of their insights, however, many of Hartz's critics have not confronted the violence inherent in the liberal tradition itself, and that is what this book does.[31] *The Men of Mobtown* argues that the very developments that ushered in a new liberal order — the emergence of a rights-centered legal culture, the expansion of property rights across the citizenry, the construction of police institutions to protect those property rights — also played a critical role in subjugating black people.[32] At first white men were ordinary citizens; in time they acquired uniforms. But the effect was similar. Officers of Baltimore's municipality perpetrated a form of racial violence during the late 1860s reminiscent of the racial violence perpetrated by white vigilantes a decade earlier, and we cannot hope to understand how without also accounting for the complicity of liberalism.

Once liberalism itself is subjected to scrutiny, the outlines of a story emerge that should seem familiar to modern-day American observers of news media. It does not stretch the imagination to see traces of black

Baltimoreans' nineteenth-century fates in the modern era's police brutality and mass black incarceration, to say nothing of the waves of white vigilantism that are now finding legal cover under Stand Your Ground laws and the Castle Doctrine. Historical explanations for black Americans' troubled relationship with today's criminal justice system can mostly be found in the more recent past — in histories of the New Right, the drug war, and deindustrialization, to name a few. They also hark back to the lynchings, race riots, and Jim Crow of the first half of the twentieth century. But the sources of today's systemic black policing and incarceration also lie in the violence of the nineteenth century. It was during the age of slavery and emancipation when police forces were first introduced and penitentiaries were first built. And it was then, when Americans so vigorously confronted, debated, and spilled blood over the meanings of freedom, that large numbers of black Americans first confronted the police institutions of the liberal state.

A book about nineteenth-century policing will not fully explain twenty-first-century problems, let alone solve them, but it can expose some of the roots of those problems so that one day, perhaps soon, we can begin the hard work of engaging them more honestly. Only when we fully embrace the racial lineage of American policing practices — and only when we concede that the story of emancipation is as indebted to a history of racial subjugation as it is to triumphant narratives of progress — will we have a chance to address such problems at all. This book is a modest attempt to engage that past. It represents an effort to uncover the debt our police institutions owe to practices and ideologies that most Americans would rather believe are safely confined to the dustbin of history. Yet history, I believe, is not there for comfort, and it remains one of our primary tasks to explore the origins of our ills.

PART I

MOBTOWN

♦

Chapter One

RIOTERS AND VIGILANTES

♦

BEFORE THERE WERE policemen and penitentiaries, there were white men. During the decades following Baltimore's 1796 incorporation, little distinguished the municipal officers who policed for the city from the white male civilians who policed on their own. It is true that night watchmen and daytime constables, as well as justices of the peace, bailiffs, prosecutors, and a host of other municipal officers, participated in the criminal justice system and worked diligently to maintain order with whatever scant resources were at their disposal. They just did not do so alone. The municipality's tiny bureaucracy and its rank incompetence, to say nothing of Americans' broader ideological disdain for standing armies, initially conspired against any monopolization of the criminal justice process by the public authorities. Time and again, the citizenry proved vital to the broader effort to curb assaults, prevent theft, recover lost children, wrestle away hidden firearms, try murderers, protect homes and businesses, apprehend arsonists, fight rowdies, quell riots, and so on. Even if state-sanctioned officers controlled some aspects of criminal justice, white men's popular policing was official policing too.

Baltimore's early municipal government depended upon all sorts of private individuals to interpret and enforce "the law" on the streets, and many of those individuals in turn possessed enough authority to define "order" as they understood it. Occasionally white men earned money for their policing, blurring the line between official and ordinary while giving the lie to any strict demarcation between the two. But they also received far more than financial remuneration for their efforts. By maintaining order and combating

19

crime, citizens enacted a distinctive form of autonomy in an otherwise unfree world. Policing was usually honorable and consistently profitable, and in
an early republican city like Baltimore, it was above all a practice by which
white men affirmed their political inclusion.

Night watchmen depended upon others for help, practicing attorneys and
laypeople alike participated in criminal prosecutions, and governors often
heeded the words of regular citizens when deciding whether or not to issue
a pardon.[1] As seemingly public institutions and seemingly private citizens
functioned alongside each other, and often dynamically with each other,
Baltimore's municipal authorities proved more adept at meeting the era's
policing challenges than would otherwise have been possible. There was policing in early Baltimore — quite a bit of it. It just happened to be performed
by a loose confederation of individuals who would no more have used the
word "official" to describe themselves than they would the word "ordinary."
For these people, for the various white men who counted as citizens, policing
was an important type of political work.

The People and Their Police

During the years following the American Revolution, Baltimore Town transformed into one of the continent's largest cities, and at the heart of its transformation sat a magnificent harbor. Local historians have called that harbor
a "natural haven for ships," which linked the area's inhabitants to an international system of exchange that stretched from the Chesapeake Bay to waters
across the world.[2] Goods passed through Baltimore from the surrounding
countryside to the Atlantic seaboard and then traveled onward to the islands
of the Caribbean, as well as to South America, West Africa, and western Europe. Goods traveled in the other direction as well. Motley crews of workers on the city's noisy docks unloaded cargo recently arrived from overseas
and transported it across a growing urban landscape into the vast expanses
that lay beyond the city's farthest western reaches. This trade provided economic opportunities for a variety of migrants and immigrants — rich and
poor, black and white, male and female among them. Subsequent attempts
to service these new arrivals only produced more demand for labor and the
people who performed that labor, thereby giving rise to a self-perpetuating
process that continued apace for years.[3]

Wheat was the engine for Baltimore's vibrant economic activity, and two
eighteenth-century developments propelled its market. First, German farm-

ers early in the 1700s pushed south from Pennsylvania into western Maryland and there planted wheat, the crop with which they were most familiar. Frederick County's fertile Monocacy Valley shipped wheat not only to the colony's more populated towns to the east but, through Baltimore, to Europe as well. Around the same time, planters on Maryland's Eastern Shore began harvesting cereals on land where they previously had grown tobacco. The tobacco market had always been unstable, particularly when compared to that for wheat: Europeans may have liked to smoke, but they needed to eat. Wheat was also more environmentally sustainable than tobacco; its production put less stress on the soil and promised a more profitable and productive future. Baltimore merchants, after struggling for thirty years in a sleepy, mostly irrelevant tobacco inspection port, suddenly found themselves ideally situated to supply an entrepôt for a blossoming wheat trade — and it was not long before a major road cut through the region's breadbasket, connecting Baltimore with the city of Frederick and its bountiful surpluses. Wheat helped make Baltimore. It created the city, transformed northern Maryland into one of North America's primary export capitals, and built a new industrial hub to boot. By the first decade of the nineteenth century, well over five dozen flour mills operated on the springs surrounding Baltimore.[4]

The city began to bustle. Each year more people walked its streets, labored in its workshops, and lived in its row houses than had the year before. In a sense, Baltimore was an early U.S. boomtown, perhaps the earliest. Fewer than seven thousand people lived in Baltimore Town in 1776; thirty years later, nearly fifty thousand people called Baltimore City home. Although modest by contemporary European standards, such tallies soon earned Baltimore the label of third-largest city in the early United States. No other major American town matched Baltimore's population growth during the early national era.[5] Yet all that rapid growth also had fascinating consequences for the city's demography. Baltimore's population constituted as heterogeneous a mixture of people as that of any city on North America's eastern seaboard.

Most noteworthy was the large size of the city's black community. In the quarter century following the city's incorporation, the black population grew from 12 to 22 percent of Baltimore's population. Whereas in 1790 only about fifteen hundred black people lived there, by 1830 nearly nineteen thousand did. Such remarkable growth owed especially to the expansion of the city's free black population. In fact, even as the black community grew, the city's slave community, never large to begin with, shrank — largely because of the high demand for slave labor in the Deep South and the high prices

Baltimore Harbor View, daguerreotype by Henry H. Clark, ca. 1845–50.
This early photograph shows the Gay Street Dock from Federal Hill, as
well as the ships *Herald* and *Juniata,* the Merchant's Exchange Building (which
was demolished at the turn of the next century), and the Second Reformed
Church. Baltimore's harbor lay at the center of the city's rapid economic
development during the first half of the nineteenth century.
Courtesy of the Maryland Historical Society.

local masters could demand as a result. Visitors observed that "slaves grow
less in number yearly in this State, as agents are stationed to buy up all they
can for the sugar plantations at New Orleans."[6] And while the slave population filtered south and contracted, the number of free black Baltimoreans multiplied eighteen-fold, an increase that considerably outpaced those
in the growing cities to the north. By 1830, Baltimore was the only place in
Maryland where a majority of African Americans were free. With over fifteen
thousand people, the city's free black community was also the largest in the
country, north or south.[7]

So many free people of color lived in Baltimore because Maryland's geographical location, economic system, and manumission laws made the city

an attractive destination for people of color. The state bordered the region of "freedom," or at least the less slave-centered and eventually "free" North. Its heavily industrialized northern region, of which Baltimore formed an important part, demanded enormous reserves of cheap labor to fuel its various sectors. Masters and employers who were cognizant of slaves' propensities to run north promised their bondsmen and bondswomen eventual freedom in the hope of guaranteeing faithful labor for at least a few more years. Individual manumissions proliferated, especially in Baltimore, and the free black population of the city subsequently grew. Slavery in and around the city soon became what one scholar has dubbed a mere "stage of life."[8]

Baltimore was also ethnically diverse. By the turn of the nineteenth century, a substantial number of Germans had arrived in the city by way of Philadelphia, most of them on a route familiar to the aforementioned wheat farmers. French-speaking refugees from Saint-Domingue also flooded Baltimore, much as they did other major American ports during the era of the Haitian Revolution. Mostly, though, it was Irish Catholics who found their way to the growing city. Beginning in the 1760s, the Scotch-Irish began arriving in force, particularly as the town (and later city) emerged as the center of Maryland's indentured servant trade. Not that all Irishmen were indentured, or stayed that way: several of the city's most successful and politically ambitious merchants were Irish. By the time of the War of 1812, Baltimore was a thriving city comprised of different races and ethnicities, dependent upon a mixed-labor economy, and home to remarkable sectarian diversity.[9]

The city's occupational mixture was even more pronounced than its demographic heterogeneity. Baltimore housed a rising, wealthy merchant class, as well as a variety of professional workers, from doctors and lawyers to teachers. It was also home to a more economically marginal population of draymen, sailors, dockworkers, and laundresses, a class usually characterized in city directories simply as "Laborers." By 1815, merchants, professionals, and day laborers combined to form a little more than 50 percent of the city's working population. Largest among all occupational groups were the mechanics, those skilled artisans and master craftsmen who on their own represented, staggeringly, almost half of the city's workforce. Still, the term "Mechanics" overstates the homogeneity of the group; instead of thinking of themselves as a social class, mechanics usually identified with a particular craft — as tailors and dressmakers, shipbuilders, metallurgists, stonemasons, or skilled construction workers. The category also captured men in various stages of life. Master craftsmen qualified as mechanics, but so too did the journeymen and apprentices who in social and economic circumstances more closely resembled laborers than master craftsmen.[10]

Early Baltimore was therefore a racially, ethnically, religiously, economically, and socially diverse city, a vibrant place teeming with life and excitement, hope and possibility. But vibrancy could also breed volatility, and whatever else it may have been, Baltimore was a cauldron of differences that could not always contain the violence endemic to any circumstance in which so many different types of people lived in such close quarters. To numerous residents, the city simply *felt* dangerous. Baltimore's acting health officer spoke for many when in 1830 he deplored the growing number of people who, it seemed, operated under "a false impression . . . that no restraint or restrictions would be exercised in a 'free Country.'" More than a few Baltimoreans believed that a walk on the city's streets was risky at best.[11]

And so we are left with questions: Who policed the city? Who kept the peace and maintained order and protected property? Who helped secure the "free Country" of which the health officer spoke? The answer to all of these questions is — for the most part — the same: it was white men. Irrespective of Baltimore's diversity, the majority of early nineteenth-century Baltimoreans were neither enslaved nor black. Black Baltimoreans formed a significant minority of the population, and they constituted one of the most impressive black communities in the nation. They were a minority nonetheless. The 1820s actually marked the only antebellum decade in which black demographic growth increased relative to Baltimore's total population; in all others the white majority outpaced the black minority. Plus, while many "white people" were immigrants or non-Protestants who endured repeated attacks upon their own racial identities, European immigrants, even Catholic ones, were never confused for slaves.[12] To understand the history of policing, one must understand this racial binary first. Early Baltimore contained a top-heavy, economically stratified society; it was a world in which a large majority of the people possessed a small minority of the wealth. There, as elsewhere, class, ethnicity, and religion helped determine social hierarchy, political power, and cultural capital. Yet during the decades following the city's incorporation, Baltimore's system of policing specifically depended upon the privileges of whiteness and manhood more than upon any others. Whether they were mechanics or merchants, native-born or born abroad, it was usually white men who policed the city.

Historically, policing meant governing, and that ordinary white men policed their city suggests that ordinary white men regularly took an active role in the city's governance.[13] In this sense popular policing was a kind of participatory politics. It was democracy in action, so to speak. Whether it took the form of a citizen's arrest of a suspected murderer or a flight to catch a fleeing thief, popular policing was both a privilege and a responsibility of political membership. But white men policed their communities not only because they could but also because they must. Much like residents of other big cities, Baltimoreans concerned themselves increasingly with crime — with disorderly conduct, larceny, and assault, as well as with other less common though more serious acts such as arson, kidnapping, and murder. Living in a city could be scary, especially for anyone unaccustomed to city life. White men helped assuage the wider community's fears through the protection they provided and the punishment they meted out.[14]

Every time he arrested a murderer or caught a thief, a white man affirmed his racial and patriarchal power. To use the parlance of the time, every time he policed, a white man affirmed his "good citizenship." Mayor Sam Brady congratulated "all good citizens" for their "strong and decisive expressions" against the violence that plagued that year's presidential election. "The lawless disposed were soon made sensible of their folly and madness," proclaimed Brady; "as a consequence, order was soon restored."[15] Other Baltimoreans hailed vigilant white men under much the same rubric. Mayor John Hanson Thomas Jerome directed "all good citizens to exercise their influence" upon any neighbor in the habit of renting property "to bands of profligate boys and youths who congregate therein," while the *Baltimore Sun*'s editors advised "every good citizen . . . to be on the look out" for incendiaries.[16] Mayor Sheppard Leakin was the most direct. After a nativist riot in 1839, he applauded the protectors of a convent for having performed "a duty which every citizen of Baltimore . . . is bound at all times to perform to the best of his judgment and ability."[17] Such language hinted at the importance of vigilantism to civil society. It also suggested that society's most acceptable vigilant members were white men, those "good citizens" hailed by officials and boosters alike. "We do not only ask the police to be vigilant in detecting the ruffians," *Sun* editors rhapsodized after one assault, "but we beg every good citizen to aid them in their search."[18] Another editorial put the matter more succinctly: a good citizen was "one of *nature's police officers*, if not judge and executioner at the same time."[19]

Realizing one's "good" citizenship was important in early nineteenth-century Baltimore because it confirmed for others as well as for the citizen himself that he resided atop civil society and inside an exclusive self-governing body politic that included others just like him. Certain historians have emphasized that a person's legal citizenship (or lack thereof) was just one of several political identities and that a person's office, property, household position, age, and infirmity were as likely if not more so to determine the privileges and obligations one enjoyed.[20] At the same time, the moniker "good citizen," at least when deployed by mayors and newspaper editors, was shorthand for civil society's white male masters and patriarchs. Early Baltimore was, politically speaking, a racially bifurcated, male-dominated society, and just as the vast majority of white men there were citizens, every citizen was also always a white man. To enact "good citizenship" was basically to enact the privileges of white manhood.

"Good citizens" protected other members of society as both an honor and a duty, looking out especially for white women. Mary Pool, to take one example, lost sight of her twenty-month-old daughter on a Thursday morning in May 1819; the girl had only moments earlier been playing outside the house. Pool's cry for help "roused" the neighbors, among them General Heath and Alexander Russell, two white men who quickly embarked on a days-long journey that ended outside Annapolis. "After many fruitless inquiries," Heath and Russell learned that the girl "had been seen on the Annapolis road, and accordingly took that direction in search of her." Their search brought them to a roadside stop where a woman had "dined . . . on Thursday with the child, which she represented as her own." At an inn down the road they discovered where the kidnapper and child had spent the night, as well as which Annapolis-bound stage the two had taken the next morning. Eventually, the citizen-detectives discovered the little girl herself, in bed with a Miss Pomphrey, an unsuspecting traveler, and Nancy Gamble, the kidnapper. Heath and Russell burst into the room and forced Gamble to confess "the whole truth."[21]

More frequently, men attempted to protect women on the city's streets. Observers believed that "it has become imperative upon every father, husband, and brother to use every exertion to ferret out the ruffians and bring them to justice" and opined that it was "the bounden duty of the citizens to arrest the aggressors, and either carry them before a magistrate or detain them before the police officers arrive."[22] Again and again, the term "bounden duty" appeared in writing. "If ladies cannot walk the streets, even in day time, without insult," one editorialist argued, "it is the bounden duty of their male friend to offer them protection, and treat the cowardly blackguards who prowl about the streets with no more ceremony than they deserve."[23] Antebellum Americans were inclined to conflate an attack on women with an attack on men, and the advocates of order were among the likeliest to make the slippage and label a threat to a woman's person "an offence against the male sex, against manly and honorable principles."[24]

As a result, the man who vigilantly defended women on the streets often earned accolades. When Mr. Watkins witnessed John Taylor Starr "commit a rude and ineffably immodest assault on a young lady," he followed him until Starr approached two other young women in a similar manner. At that point Watkins called to a passerby — one Mr. Tilden — for help. Acting quickly, the two men halted the attack, arrested Starr, and conveyed the "scoundrel" to a justice of the peace who promptly committed the offender to jail. "We trust," wrote the editor for the *Sun*, "all the ladies, and every honorable gentleman, will duly appreciate the manly and spirited conduct of Mr. Watkins, and of Mr. Tilden also. A few examples of this kind would give all the ladies impunity in the streets."[25] Other men behaved with a similar gallantry, such as the one who witnessed "a stout, overgrown fellow" knock down an old woman in the middle of a busy intersection. He caught up to the perpetrator and felled him with a stick, dealing a dozen blows to the head and body before his victim scampered into the crowded Center Market.[26] Another "gentleman" aided a young woman, Mary Ann Cooper, when a married shoemaker "of genteel appearance" struck her in the face in the middle of the street. Interfering in the fray, he ensured that Cooper got home safely, without further injury.[27] Still another "gentleman" responded to a botched assault upon a young woman by demanding the assailant give an explanation for his conduct. The assailant scoffed; all the man received was "an insolent threat of personal chastisement"—and so he decided to fight. The "gentleman who espoused the lady's cause, though the weaker man of the two," emerged from the scuffle victorious. "Much as we deprecate the infliction of summary punishment, and abhor the brutality of fisticuffs," concluded one of the *Sun*'s editors, "we cannot but consider the beating this fellow received, as a chastisement richly deserved, and one which no man having a spark of gallantry in his breast could, under similar circumstances, refrain from inflicting."[28]

Good citizens enacted the privilege of their whiteness on the city's streets as well. "I must relate a small transaction to you," A. Robinson wrote to his friend James McHenry in early January 1813. "I know it will give you pleasure."

Robinson and McHenry's mutual friend Colonel Ramsay had recently "lost 80 or Ninety dollars out of his pocket" at the market, and Robinson, suspecting a crime, "instantly" visited the city's markets to interrogate the vendors. After nearly two days of searching for the thief, he finally tracked down a black man named Ned at home, "took him prisoner," and forced a confession out of him. Robinson's whiteness lent him enormous authority over the black man. He took "all the money [Ned] had left, which was $40, and the clothes he purchased," and proceeded to bring his black prisoner, the man's clothes, and the remaining money directly to his "amiable friend."[29]

Robinson did not wait for society to laud him; he boasted and bragged of his good actions too. Only through the heroic narration of his own behavior could Robinson make visible, first to Ramsay and then to McHenry, his good citizenship and, with it, his political authority. That is to say, only through the retelling of past deeds could he prove his greater worth in his friend's eyes. Robinson clearly understood, as surely as McHenry did, that the theft of a friend's money or belongings committed by a black person was as much the ordinary citizen's responsibility as it was that of a passing watchman or constable. White men in early Baltimore looked out for each other, particularly when victimized by nonwhite assailants.

Good citizens thus policed as not just men but white men, but they also policed the city as a mere matter of course. Nowhere was this truer than in their frequent demonstrations of self-defense. William H. Clendenin was a doctor who arrested John Mallory after the latter vainly attempted to force him by gunpoint to help an ailing relative. Mallory, writing later from jail, explained "that the immediate application of medical skills & assistance might perhaps save the life of his nephew," and had desperately begged Clendenin to accompany him home. But Clendenin, for reasons of his own, did not want to be rushed. He did not even want to go. When the obstinate doctor refused a second entreaty, the grief-stricken, distressed man allegedly drew his pistol —"not with any intention . . . of doing any bodily injury to the Doctor," Mallory later assured himself and anyone who would listen, but from the hope that "the doctor, seeing his agitated state of mind, might be induced to go with him." Clendenin saw neither wisdom nor harmlessness in the gesture. He wrested the gun from Mallory's hands and carried the distraught uncle to the nearest magistrate all the while a dying boy waited, in vain.[30]

Good citizens also foiled mail robberies, which counted among the most infamous crimes of the day. "It seems that robbers of the mail are almost universally taken," proudly wrote the newspaper editor Hezekiah Niles. "The public is too deeply interested in its safety, that nearly every man feels bound to lend his aid to detect the robbers of it."[31] One local robber "was seized near Lancaster, by some spirited citizens of that place."[32] Another realized all too late that "the alarm [his crime] had caused was great, and seemed to interest almost every person." The robber dismayingly noted the "great many of the officers and citizens of Baltimore going out to, and near, the place, to assist in discovering who were the perpetrators of so notorious an outrage and offence and crime."[33] The city's most infamous mail robbery (and capture) occurred in 1820. When one day the mail did not arrive in Baltimore on schedule, "parties of patriotic citizens went out immediately . . . to scour the country" for signs of either the mail carriage or foul play. They found both in the nearby woods. Several of these "patriotic citizens" discovered the mail carriage toppled, its bags looted, and its driver shot, stabbed, and tied to a tree. Members of the search party concluded that the "murderers and robbers had retired from the horrid deed towards Baltimore," where "every body" went "on the alert, for all were deeply interested in detecting the flagrant offenders."[34] Catching the robbers did not take long. Later that very day, Morris Hull and Peregrine Hutton "were stopped in Gay-street near the bridge, by three peace officers." The two men had been unable to escape the searching eyes of an entire citizenry alerted to the possibility of their presence.[35] Once imprisoned, they never walked free again.[36]

White men in early Baltimore policed the city in order to be honorable and acted honorably in so policing. "*Valuable Citizens*," one city official wrote in 1830, needed at least to have "a more explicit understanding of the Law."[37] Once a man was imbued with that knowledge, he could not then "look upon the flames of [his] neighbor's dwelling with complacency or inaction." Nor could he, in one reformer's words, "see an innocent fellow-being wantonly murdered without putting forth an effort to save him."[38] Ignoring another person's plight did not make a white man legally liable for that plight, but it did make him morally culpable. He who ignored a neighbor in need violated a cultural code of conduct that for many citizens was not insignificant. For as they guarded against trouble, investigated crime scenes, broke up fights, arrested suspects, and delivered victims to safety, white male Baltimoreans simultaneously enacted their privileges and confirmed their right to hold such privileges in the first place. By policing the city, they transformed themselves into citizens good enough — into citizens authoritative, honorable, and moral enough — to be called "white men."

Acting Like a State

The operation of an early nineteenth-century municipality probably looks strange today. What twenty-first-century Americans understand as clearly delineated "public" and "private" sectors were practically indistinguishable from one another two centuries ago. Ordinary individuals performed seemingly "public" roles all the time, and this proved especially to be the case when it came to policing. White men policed the city in order to assert and affirm the privileges of white manhood. But they also policed in an official capacity.

To be sure, Baltimore's municipality did have paid representatives who worked as guardians of the city. Before any uniformed, professional police officer walked a beat, the city boasted a daytime constabulary and night watch; these were the men who worked the streets during the first half of the nineteenth century. Both constabulary and watch derived from English antecedents, but it was not until 1816, twenty years after incorporation, that city officials organized a system divided between the two. After that, constables and watchmen responded to citizens' cries for help, arrested suspects, and brought suspects to watchhouses for processing. A good watchman patrolled the streets all night, looking out for fires and disturbances; a good constable attached himself to an alderman — a local judge who worked as part of the city's "minor judiciary"— and waited for an opportunity to serve an arrest warrant. Once a constable or watchman delivered his charge to a magistrate, preparations for the trial began.[39]

The daytime constabulary and night watch counted as just one component of a larger municipal infrastructure geared toward controlling crime. Baltimore's criminal court system dated to 1788, at which time the state of Maryland established a criminal court for Baltimore County. Just six years later, the governor responded to growing concerns over property crime in Baltimore Town by issuing a commission for a court of oyer and terminer. This court, which survived the city's 1796 incorporation, had jurisdiction not only in Baltimore City but also in Baltimore County writ large. It did not last long, however. In 1816, the very year that the energetic Stiles administration established the city's constabulary and watch, state legislators in Annapolis concurrently abolished the court of oyer and terminer and in its stead placed the Baltimore City Court, composed of one chief judge and three associate judges. This court oversaw all cases involving "felonies, and other crimes, offenses and misdemeanors ... arising within the city and precincts of Baltimore." The Criminal Court of Baltimore City, which functions today, finds its origin in the Baltimore City Court of 1816.[40]

Someone arrested by a constable or watchman, processed by a local magistrate, and convicted by the Baltimore City Court either paid a fine or went to prison. Getting fined did not mean prison was out of the question; if the offender was unable to pay, he or she was imprisoned anyway. Nor did imprisonment necessarily signal the end of the process. Many men and women convicted of crimes in the city court and conveyed to prison appealed their sentences with the hope of gaining a pardon. The governor, despite the bureaucratic establishment growing beneath him, maintained the ultimate jurisdiction. A holdover from British North America's royal past, the gubernatorial pardon trumped any court verdict in the state.

One may reasonably conclude that as Baltimore developed the institutions and specialized functionaries to police the city, those institutions and functionaries marked an increasingly clear boundary between "official" and "ordinary" policing behavior. It stands to reason that the more stable and self-sustaining state policing became, the more antidemocratic it behaved. But it would be a mistake to believe that state power always grew at the expense of the citizenry, or that state and white male policing became, in all cases, mutually exclusive. In fact, public police functionaries — watchmen, constables, aldermen, judges, and governors — neither replaced nor even necessarily weakened the power of private citizens. When it came to policing, white men remained important actors throughout.

White men insinuated themselves into nearly all facets of the state's evolving criminal justice system. A night watchman and an ordinary white man were in many instances nearly indistinguishable from one another. Consider the circumstances of Benjamin Stewart's murder in June 1838. Nearby, ropemakers Henry Lightner and Alexander Wiley were guarding their ropewalk, a flammable pathway on which hemp lay before being twisted into rope; the previous day someone had set it on fire. "We determined to catch the incendiaries if we could," Wiley later told the court, and "if we could not, we meant to give them a race." When the two men heard "a cry of 'Murder! murder! Oh, Lord,'" they cautiously walked toward the scene "and listened a few minutes, but could not hear anything" else. Deterred, they each returned home. Not far away, George Chariton had also heard the cry and noticed the sound of gunfire in the distance. "I wanted to take my gun, which was loaded, and go in search of the murderer," Chariton recalled. "But my wife and mother would not let me go." Chariton instead waited for morning to approach the crime scene, at which time he was joined by James Hooper, a neighbor who had awakened to rumors that "a man had been murdered" the night before. "I thought I would get on my horse and ride round and see if I could find anything," Hooper later explained under oath. "About one hundred yards west of the body I found a hatchet."[41]

The next day Thomas Stewart, Benjamin's brother, as well as Matthew Drake, a clerk who had sold Benjamin's son William the hatchet that Hooper had discovered, accompanied two constables to one of the city's wharves. There, the four men intended to arrest William, who was returning to Baltimore on a steamboat after a day's trip to Annapolis. Amid a growing crowd the posse approached the suspect. Drake questioned William Stewart about the murder weapon; unwittingly, William confirmed that he had purchased it two days earlier. Thomas Stewart then interrogated his nephew, asking the young man where he had last seen his father, with whom he had last seen him, and where he had been for the previous forty-eight hours. William's responses were, as everyone present fully expected them to be, unsatisfactory. Thomas informed the young man that his father was dead and that he, William, was the prime suspect. Working together, the party arrested and delivered William to a local magistrate for processing.[42]

None of these men — Lightner, Wiley, Chariton, Hooper, Drake, or Thomas Stewart — were night watchmen or daytime constables; none of their job descriptions required them to guard against crimes, investigate crime scenes, and question criminal suspects; none of them were, according to the logic of a strict public-private division, explicitly supposed to enforce the criminal laws. Yet Lightner and Wiley, already standing watch against arson, had investigated the alarming sound of someone screaming bloody murder. Chariton had considered searching for the murderer on his own, only to be convinced at the last moment that, despite his gun, it was too dangerous. Hooper had taken it upon himself to look for clues the next morning and had found the murder weapon. On the wharf a day and a half later, Drake had interrogated William Stewart about the hatchet he had sold him while Thomas Stewart, acting as a concerned uncle and aggrieved brother, had inquired about the suspect's recent whereabouts. Each man separately participated in or considered participating in the policing process by his own initiative. Each did so without coercion or invitation.

As the case suggests, white men supplemented, mimicked, and occasionally replaced the officers who patrolled the city's streets. Yet it was not merely the man on the beat whom the ordinary citizen resembled but also the city's lawyers. The first half of the nineteenth century was also the era of private prosecutions. According to historian Allen Steinberg, the criminal law played a central role in the daily lives of ordinary people, as citizens regularly took one another to court and deployed the criminal law as a personal means for dispute resolution.[43] Let us imagine a fight between two men. If one of the assailants wanted to bring charges against the other, he would have headed to the nearest magistrate's office, complained, and secured a warrant for his opponent's arrest. He or the magistrate's constable, or perhaps the two men together, would have then found, detained, and escorted the defendant back to that office, where the magistrate usually conducted a formal hearing with the two fighters serving as their own lawyers. This process was repeated over and over again. According to Steinberg, private prosecution resulted "in a special kind of incorporation of the citizenry into this pervasive part of the nineteenth-century state."[44]

Steinberg writes about Philadelphia, but his arguments are no less applicable to Baltimore. Victims of crimes routinely took on the role of prosecutor there as well. When in the summer of 1834 James Johnston stole some money from a stranger's trunk, for example, his victim immediately launched an investigation. It was not long before the man discovered "the money" on Johnston's person and "upon the evidence" committed him to jail. At that point, however, the prosecutor decided to forget the matter: Johnston's accuser and victim deemed no trial to be necessary. After all, he had already recovered the money, felt bad about Johnston's desperate economic circumstances, and did not particularly have the energy to wage a legal challenge against his perpetrator. The unnamed stranger dropped all charges and had Johnston released within two weeks.[45]

White men also routinely played the role of defense attorney. Personal incentive aside, a surprising number looked into cases for their poorer friends and neighbors who either personally had been charged with a crime or had family members so charged. This was partly because a governor was more likely to issue a nolle prosequi—the common law term referring to a discontinuance of criminal charges before a trial or verdict—when the petitioner in question had good references. It was also because people in trouble sometimes just needed an advocate to prove their innocence. Single women, much as they might for protection, looked especially to neighborhood elders for official help when facing jail time. "I have taken great pains to make myself acquainted with all the particulars," wrote a confident Walter Farnandes to the governor in 1834. Farnandes had been surprised to learn that a local single mother and her grown daughter had been arrested for theft and so had launched a "thorough investigation of all the facts connected with this painful business" while the two women awaited trial. What he learned had troubled him. He believed that the women's thirteen-year-old domestic worker had been the one who received the stolen goods in question. The girl, according to Farnandes, had merely hidden her spoils in the two women's house without their knowledge. "[I] can conscientiously assure your Excellency that there does not appear to be the slightest grounds for suspecting either of the ladies of any knowledge of the thefts or the deposits," explained Farnandes. "From what has been communicated to me by the parties with whom I have had interviews and from what I have learned from other sources," both women seemed to be absolutely innocent.[46]

It was precisely when a suspect became a convict and was sent to prison that ordinary white men proved themselves most useful to the accused. Farnandes's example indicates the extent to which certain men invested in others' cases well after an arrest had been made. Others worked long and hard to exonerate convicted felons who spent months, and sometimes years, in the Maryland Penitentiary. "Today in company with [the father of a convicted thief] we visited the place where the alleged felony was committed," two men petitioned the governor in 1834. After "a particular examination . . . we are satisfied that young Collier is entirely innocent of the offence charged upon him." The two petitioners were doubly clear about their role and motivations: "In justice to ourselves we will merely add in conclusion that on the present occasion we do not act as professional agents but are actuated by feelings of the deepest and most disinterested sympathy for the distress of young Collier & his most heartbroken father."[47]

Other voluntary detectives delayed making formal "inquiries until this time in order [that] I might make myself fully acquainted with the facts in the case."[48] Such inquiries typically involved speaking with witnesses, as well as to the victims, accusers, and accused themselves. In one case, after Henry Smith was convicted of assaulting and attempting to kill a man named Leckner, an interested outsider involved himself on Smith's behalf. The petitioner argued to the governor that the second charge was too harsh for the deed committed. "I had a long conversation with Smith yesterday afternoon," the man wrote:

> He is naturally very quiet & kind, he would not probably have got into this scrape except thro' great provocation, & even then when he had drank too much. His story about the matter . . . [is] corroborated by Leckner's wife whose house I have just come from. Leckner was not at home. His wife says that he desires very much the release of Smith — thinks he has been punished too much — blames her husband partly about the matter — his temper rather insatiable, Smith's the reverse. . . . I scarcely think Smith's design was to take life, & apart from the use of an instrument calculated to destroy life, (a chisel) would lead me to suppose the case one of aggravated assault & battery, for which he has been sufficiently punished. The instrument was lying beside him when the quarrel took place, & there could not have been any premeditation. He had been badly used by Leckner in the morning.[49]

Pardon petitioners surely sometimes wrote in bad faith, and their motives were not always clear. But the fact that white men could abuse their authority to exonerate actual criminals only further instilled in other petitioners a sense of the seriousness of their actions. White men who had once been on the receiving end of those petitions understood this better than anyone. "My experience, while Governor," related Philip Thomas in a petition of his own, "fully satisfied me that such recommendations were often made without consideration — and, generally, without sufficient knowledge of the facts of the case, whereby the Executive was frequently deceived and exposed to censure." Thomas had no intention of repeating the offense. As a former governor, he was determined not "to aid in procuring the interposition of Executive Clemency on behalf of a convict who might be unworthy of it" and refused to write on behalf of Francis Metz, a man convicted for manslaughter, until he was satisfied that Metz was innocent. Only after having convinced himself "that Metz's guilt, in so far as the actual cause of the death by his hands was involved, was really a question of reasonable doubt," did he deign to write on the man's behalf.[50]

White men attempted to exonerate people convicted of older crimes not only because it was their responsibility but also because their actions were, in the end, an integral part of the system's successful operation. Still, personal motives varied. Perhaps a petitioner just wanted to see justice served;

perhaps he did not trust a verdict or trusted only himself to discover the truth; or perhaps he personally had played a role in the original conviction and over time had changed his mind: for sometimes a citizen felt responsible for the conviction of an innocent man. The foreman of the jury that convicted James Karr for murder felt such pangs of guilt. In the 1850 case, this man alone had convinced his fellow jurors that Karr was guilty of murdering a fellow drinker in a city tavern. All eleven other jurors had entered the recess believing that Karr was innocent of the crime, yet according to the foreman, he had prevailed by taking a stand "based upon the positive & consistent testimony of the German woman who was chief witness against him." Now, however, he realized the witness was mistaken. Once the former foreman had begun to doubt his original conviction, he took the "opportunity of collecting evidence," discovered that the woman "mistook Karr for one Ready Gray, who actually perpetrated the deed while Karr was active in endeavoring to prevent the same," and quickly secured Karr's release.[51]

At every stage in the policing process, from the moment at which a crime was detected to well past the moment of conviction, white men interjected themselves. They searched for clues, arrested suspects, served as prosecutors, defended one another, and helped secure pardons, sometimes after having solved the crimes on their own. White men policed the city, and they did so without apology or regret. One cannot understand the operation of a criminal justice system like the one in early Baltimore City without accounting for the ordinary white men who protected and punished every day. In an important sense, these men embodied state power.

Mercenaries for Hire

The flip side of a powerful and energetic citizenry was an administratively weak municipality. City officials readily acknowledged the importance of white men's popular policing in part because their own functionaries were manifestly incapable of policing the city on their own. This is not to suggest that the city government lacked laws and regulations. As in other municipalities, Baltimore's officials wrote and ratified a prodigious number of statutes that spanned the spectrum of governing interests, from license laws and market regulations to laws governing morality and regulations of the public's health. It is simply to say that the enforcement of all of those laws and regulations relied upon the individual judgments and actions of white male citizens.[52]

Baltimore's oft-imperceptible boundary between popular justice and official policing owed in part to the English Commonwealth (and Revolutionary American) fear of standing armies. In the minds of early nineteenth-century Americans, a strong police force could be dangerous, even "tyrannical." Baltimoreans in the 1820s and 1830s were only one or two generations removed from the Revolution, and many worried that a powerful police force could, like a standing army, pose an existential threat to the democratic "liberty" their fathers and grandfathers had secured.[53] Confirmation could readily be found across the Atlantic. In 1829, the British government established the world's first professional police force in the form of the London Metropolitan Police, and Robert Peel, the system's creator, borrowed heavily from the British military's model: his officers wore uniforms, held ranks, and adhered to a strict chain of command.[54] Such pageantry risked offending American sensibilities. State officers should not act so independently, argued one newspaper editorial, and "an American freeman" should certainly not "strut about . . . in the livery furnished at the public's expense."[55]

A fear of standing armies was inseparable from the democratic ideals that animated early American politics. The world in which good citizens equated vigilantism with their political participation was also a world in which policemen could trample those citizens' rights and responsibilities. Centralized state power appeared to be antidemocratic; authoritative police institutions seemed inherently at odds with liberty. Meanwhile, strong municipal police institutions were likely to undermine any system in which vigilantism was an essential component of good citizenship, and most citizens did not want to surrender their political power. The result was a civil society whose boundary between popular justice and official policing was difficult and sometimes impossible to distinguish, a municipality whose police institutions were weak, and a police system that depended upon the active participation of ordinary white men.

In Baltimore, fear of state tyranny loomed large. Many white male Baltimoreans worried that state-sanctioned officers were as likely to be "harpies who prey upon the prosperity of others" as they were to be "the guardians of the law."[56] An 1837 *Sun* editorial explained that while the night watchman was undoubtedly capable of good, he was also prone to "the most evil. . . . The extent of humanity or cruelty which [he] may exercise, is inconceivable."[57] Even city officials who advocated for a stronger police force (more on them in the next chapter) sympathized with these worries. In 1837, law-and-order mayor Samuel Smith asked the city council to "consider whether further power can *safely* be granted" to expand the municipality's power to police. Emphasizing his concern about his officers' potential behavior, Smith conceded that there was little he could do to guarantee that their conduct would be good. Experience suggested that sometimes it would not be.[58]

In order to address fears of state police power, the law mandated a night watchman to obtain "just cause" before he made an arrest. Every time a morally corrupt officer clothed in the state's authority arrested an innocent man, he subverted "the primary object which the Legislature had in view in establishing the Night Watch." And so, the city's criminal court explained in one ruling, it was equally necessary to "guard against the abuse of authority by so defining [watchmen's] powers as to leave little or nothing to their discretion."[59] Within the gray area that constituted what was and was not "just cause" lay the difference between a suspect's freedom and detention. False arrest essentially made the state a kidnapper, and citizens only recently removed from monarchical rule attached "great importance" to making sure that this did not happen.[60]

Corrupt and incompetent watchmen lent these anxieties a human face. Baltimoreans around the city chafed at night watchmen's propensities to prey upon weaker residents of the city. A tavern owner complained to both his local captain and a lieutenant that John Oldham, a watchman who regularly frequented his bar, had threatened to arrest several prostitutes if they refused to sleep with him free of charge.[61] A group of citizens, meanwhile, were horrified after night watchman Joshua Armacourt abused "an innocent coloured man ... dragging him away from his own door without any provocation on the part of the coloured man."[62] The mayor himself expressed frustrated rage when John Langley, another watchman, beat a prostitute named Elizabeth Burgis "without just cause." Langley had gone to Burgis's brothel earlier in the night to collect some money, presumably a bribe; an hour later he returned in official response to "a great noise and disturbance in the house," at which point "he seized Elizabeth Burgis, dragged her out of the house[,] struck her several times, and once at least with his spear." Then he arrested her. "It is true," the mayor conceded, "that Elizabeth Burgis[,] the individual in this case, is an abandoned young woman and a disgrace to her sex, but however degraded an individual may be, justice demands that they should not be made the victims of cruelty."[63]

Night watchmen did not confine their "cruelty" to "abandoned" women and "degraded" individuals like Burgis. They assaulted, imprisoned, and kidnapped white men, too. In April 1838, a group of them seized Rufus Eachus for passing counterfeit bills. When Eachus demanded to see "the warrant, authority, or legal process by virtue of which he was made a prisoner," the watchmen dragged him to the watchhouse, chained him to the floor, and took several hundred dollars from his pockets. A justice of the peace committed Eachus to jail the next morning. But without, now, financial resources, Eachus was forced to sit in the city's jail for almost a month, the duration of which he stewed over the "violent and unjustifiable taking away from him of his property[,] a palpable Robbery under color of Law."[64]

Alarmed by the specter of wanton watchmen, Baltimoreans were reluctant to grant more authority to public officials, and this reluctance translated into police provisions that were almost comically weak. The city's 1833 budget allocated only $34,000 to watch and light the city, a sum so small that Mayor Jesse Hunt complained the municipality could not own the Western Watch House outright.[65] Nor could he pay the city's twenty-four bailiffs with the $715 available.[66] Budgets during the ensuing years grew slowly. As late as 1850, citizens were asking their councilmen to expand the number of watchmen from several dozen to one hundred, "regardless of expense." Surely, a group of petitioners argued, "the lives of our fellow citizens are not to be sacrificed upon narrow-minded principles of economy." Yet the majority of the Joint Committee on Police scoffed at hiring more than twenty new men, leaving the committee's minority "at a loss to know how it will be possible for our Executive to suppress rioting and violation of City ordinances, so prevalent in our City."[67]

This dearth of municipal funding affected policemen on the street in material ways. During the 1830s, night watchmen earned a miserly twenty-five dollars a month.[68] Those wages were so low that they placed the watchman in economic terms alongside the day laborer, and as a result few men willingly took the job. Among the individuals who did, many had to work elsewhere during the day, when they were supposed to be sleeping.[69] Watchmen's pay was so paltry, and their duties so laborious, that in 1828 one mayor speculated that only the most desperate of men could rationalize such an existence. A watchman reported to the watchhouse no later than 8:30 p.m., began his rounds at 9:00 p.m., worked until 6:00 a.m., and afterward attended to prisoners until well after sunrise. The daylight provided him with but a few hours to sleep, and long before his nightly rounds began anew there were lamps to trim and again, later, the same lamps to relight. "This man's whole time is exacted for the sum of about 75½ cents per 24 hours," complained the mayor, and that sum did not even account for the risks he ran "of being beat and wounded" and potentially made into "an invalid and unfit for service."[70] More than a decade later, the Joint Committee on Police reported that watch duties remained both more laborious and more dangerous than those of any other of the corporation's officers, yet watchmen's "compensation is much less."[71]

Night watchmen, well aware of their own difficult circumstances, demanded raises by using almost identical arguments. In 1835, the city's night lieutenants appealed for higher pay, citing their "duties[,] labours and exposure of health."[72] In 1840, all of Baltimore's watchmen asked collectively for a raise, if only to compensate for the "extra duties imposed upon them," among which they counted lighting the lamps and accompanying prisoners to jail.[73] And in 1846, watchmen whose rounds included outdoor markets asked to be compensated for what they considered a heavier burden than that borne by their fellow officers: they had more lamps to light, more nights during which they had to light them, and "more Lofers and Rowdies to contend with than the other Watchmen."[74] This last point was particularly frustrating; the municipality paid injured watchmen only half of what they made while healthy and working, and that only for two months. As late as the mid-1850s, various watchmen petitioned the municipality to cover their medical costs and living expenses after suffering severe injuries on the job.[75]

To make matters worse, watchmen during the 1830s and 1840s found themselves not only chronically underpaid but also desperately undermanned. Two captains of the 1831 watch, responding to the pleas of a vulnerable wharf owner in the Fells Point neighborhood, informed the man that they were unable to spare a single officer from any ward "without leaving great room for complaint" from other property holders elsewhere in the city.[76] A group of "Citizens" complained in 1838 that their local watchman, John Kirkwood, walked a district "much too large to be properly watched and guarded by one man."[77] Still another group of "Tax payers" wrote in 1839 that their neighborhood's officer nightly patrolled "a space entirely beyond his power to attend."[78] The mayor, for his part, supported a bill authorizing the hiring of additional lieutenants in the eastern district, but the city council refused to approve such a measure.[79] Five years later, in 1844, another mayor called the council's attention to the pitiful state of the watch, which remained "too small for an adequate protection of the property of our citizens, and [one that] has not been increased in the same proportion as the city has enlarged her limits."[80] And yet change still did not come. Subsequent observers noted that Baltimore's population increased annually while "the number of the watch" remained roughly the same, its tallies numbering "little more than when the City contained one half of its present number of inhabitants."[81]

Baltimore's municipality employed so few officers that it could not guarantee their presence around the clock. For decades, constables worked roughly from 9 a.m. to 8 p.m., and night watchmen patrolled from about 9 p.m. to 6 a.m. That left four hours every day in which no officer walked the city's streets. Making matters worse was the city's response to riots. In the case of a civil disturbance, night watchmen could not be called into service during the day, while constables could not help fortify the ranks at night.[82] Critics of the system begged officials to set the watch hours earlier, release the men later, and require everyone to be available at all hours, but a lack of political will combined with a dearth of resources to reject the pleas.[83] One mayor, concerned over the effect that an increase in the watch's hours would have on the watchmen themselves, argued that such changes "would render much less effective (especially during the latter part of the night) that protection to the property of our fellow citizens which is so highly important." In that vein, he advocated hiring more men instead.[84]

Underpaid and overwhelmed, constables and watchmen suffered violent fates. A Captain Willey and Officer Bowman were unable to arrest a man named Jack Downs, guilty of a vicious assault, because on their way to the watchhouse a man struck Willey on the head and allowed the prisoner to escape.[85] Similarly, Constable Augustus Shutt, responding to an Election Day disturbance at the Ninth Ward polling station, arrested the riot's ringleader only to feel his ear "in the mouth of someone behind." Shutt immediately released his prisoner "to save his ear from being bitten off."[86] And yet he, with an ear nearly torn free of its tendon, was actually lucky when compared to Alexander McIntosh, a watchman who crossed paths with Samuel Jones. McIntosh had once attempted to arrest Jones, and the latter, convinced the former had lacked just cause, "meant to have satisfaction out of him." Along with a few friends, Jones attacked McIntosh in late November 1844 and killed him with a blow to the head.[87]

Although murdering a watchman was going too far—Jones went to prison—ordinary citizens could and sometimes did earn a court's nod of approval after violently resisting arrest. In November 1838, for example, Charles Bowen responded to an arresting officer by assaulting the man. Madison Jeffries was the officer in question, and he had held a warrant for

Bowen's arrest for almost six months. Unfortunately, on the day Jeffries finally spied Bowen, he was unable to find the warrant in his pocket. When
Jeffries proceeded to attempt to bring Bowen to the watchhouse anyway,
Bowen refused, "struck [Jeffries] in the eye, and walked for some distance
until he turned a corner and then he fled." The court exonerated Bowen two
days later.[88]

With watchmen outnumbered and undermanned, the city authorities
turned to ordinary white men for assistance. Examples abound: High Constable Mitchell encountered a barroom fight one day in November 1840, and
when in response to his order to "vacate the premises" one of the brawlers
gave him a fight, he asked for "assistance" from neighboring "bystanders."
Upon getting it Mitchell was able to load the man onto a cart and take him
to jail.[89] On another occasion, a night watchman passing a grocery store on
Charles Street noticed a light burning inside. It was after midnight on a Sunday evening. As the watchman peeked through a hole, he saw three or four
men "busily engaged preparing articles to be removed." The watchman immediately "left the place and hastened to obtain assistance." A few moments
later, he returned with a force of six colleagues "augmented by a number of
citizens, who came forward to assist in the arrest." An "assault," a mad dash,
and a series of pursuits later, three of the robbers found themselves in jail.[90]

The moral lexicon of city life often compelled ordinary white men to aid
arresting officers. Officer Duvall, in one instance, demanded considerable assistance when he attempted to arrest the intransigent Thomas Bond in June
1841. Bond had broken open another man's door, and in response the high
constable had dispatched Duvall to arrest him. Duvall did exactly that on
Fleet Street. Once the duo reached the corner of Caroline and Wilk Streets,
however, several of Bond's "associates" arrived. They encouraged their friend
to go no farther, and Bond obediently lay down in the street. Duvall cuffed
him, but Bond resisted forcefully. So Duvall called out to the gathering crowd
for help. Luckily, one man stepped forward — just in time, too: the obliging
bystander saved Duvall from Bond's incoming fist and helped deliver the
resisting assailant to the watchhouse. Interestingly, the newspaper correspondent who reported the story was aghast that only one man stepped forward. When law enforcement officers "known to act with fidelity" demanded
assistance, he wrote, "they should not be resisted."[91]

Mayors mostly agreed with that sentiment, though they recognized that
a policeman rendered weak in the face of criminal intransigence would be

no more effective in coaxing citizens into service. One of their responses was flattery. Mayors routinely praised those onlookers who did actively help night watchmen deliver suspects to jail. "I have the pleasure to acknowledge the receipt of your kind and voluntary offer of your services to assist the police officers in preserving the peace and quiet of the neighborhood in which you reside," Mayor Jesse Hunt wrote to one man in 1835. In the future, should other outrages "be committed during the absence of the officers you will confer an additional service to the community by arresting the perpetrators and taking them before the proper authority."[92] Mayor Sam Brady later dedicated portions of his state of the city address to the citizenry's vigilant behavior. In 1842, after a series of riots instigated by the city's volunteer fire companies, he returned to this theme: "I am happy to inform you, that by the exertions of the great mass of this valuable portion of our fellow citizens, those difficulties are at an end."[93]

Beyond pleas and platitudes, the municipality offered financial fruits to the men who were willing to help police the city. The system depended especially upon informers to alert watchmen and constables to crime scenes and as incentive promised rewards to anyone whose information resulted in a criminal conviction. If someone dug a well within the city's limits, that person owed "two hundred dollars for each offence, one half to be applied to the use of the city, the other to the informer."[94] If someone sold alcohol or sweets or played a "game or sport on the Sabbath day," that person too owed a fine, half of which again went "to the informer."[95] If someone ran a "gaming house," the guilty party had to pay half the fine "to the city and one half to the informer, as usual."[96] Baltimore's municipality was not shy about regulating daily life, but it could not do so without the help of informers.

City administrators also rewarded more vigorous acts of policing, paying, for example, handsome sums to individuals who arrested arsonists. In 1827, Mayor Jacob Small offered "a Reward of Two hundred dollars to any Person or persons who shall discover, and prosecute to conviction, the incendiary or incendiaries who set fire to the said Buildings of the Fountain."[97] Three years later, Small again "approved and signed" a "Resolution offering a Reward for the apprehension of an Incendiary."[98] By the 1830s it had become common for mayors to issue proclamations offering "a reward (of such an amount as he in his discretion may deem proper) for the arrest and conviction" of anyone who "may be found guilty of the crime of setting fire to any building, buildings or lumber yards in the City."[99] Not to be outdone, newspaper editors concerned that Baltimore was "overrun with incendiaries" advised both "police" and "every good citizen . . . to be on the look out for the discovery of the perpetrators of these worst criminal acts."[100] With municipal money for whoever made the discovery, all citizens (and certainly all white men) could consider themselves among the policemen of the city.

Catching a violent assailant, too, could earn an ordinary man a handsome reward. When in 1839 William Franier and five other men arrested "six men who lately committed the outrage upon two young men" in Baltimore, they achieved what the commissioned constables had been unable to do. Franier explained that he had "received information that Messrs. Mitchell and Jeffers were in pursuit of [the suspects]," but, believing that the commissioned officers were following the wrong lead, he assembled his own force and successfully pursued the six men eighty miles away, to the vicinity of Hagerstown. There, Franier and his assembled team captured the fleeing suspects and only later delivered them to Mitchell and Jeffers. "The arrest and punishment of malefactors forms one of the strongest bonds of harmony and well being in society," wrote Franier, and "those who sacrifice their comfort and peril, their lives, towards the attainment of that end, should be liberally rewarded for their services." The city council agreed. He and his friends were awarded $250.[101]

So long as officials publicized crimes and promised rewards for the capture of suspected criminals, ordinary Baltimoreans could become paid policemen on a moment's notice. All they had to do was recognize the person standing next to them as a criminal. One day while waiting for a Baltimore-bound train in Hancock, Maryland, James Watt spied Thomas Evans and Thomas Buckley, two suspects in a Baltimore murder case. Upon the train's arrival, Evans and Buckley boarded in front while Watt, keeping an eye on them, entered a car farther down. When the train left the station, Watt informed three other passengers of his suspicions, and each of them "agreed that the suspicions were strong enough and that [Evans and Buckley] ought to be arrested." In Cumberland, before the train stopped, Watt leapt onto the platform to seek help from a nearby deputy, whom he requested without further explanation to follow him. But Evans and Buckley noticed the excited Watt. They exited the train from the other side of the cars, fleeing "with some haste in an opposite direction to avoid being seen by the passengers or persons assembled at the depot." Watt won the day anyway. In quick pursuit, he managed to have "them arrested and taken before a Justice of the peace and committed to jail." He later wrote to the mayor and received the promised $500 reward.[102]

Good citizenship could pay, and over time Baltimoreans came to expect that it would. Certain individuals demanded that the municipality "liberally reward them for their risk and trouble" regardless of whether a reward had previously been announced or not. One man, having taken off a day from work to rescue "two orphan children from the degradation & disgrace" of "a bawdy house," believed he was due something in exchange, despite the fact that no formal reward had ever been offered for the girls' return. He was adamant that he was entitled to recompense, as his "humanity," however noble, had also cost him a day's wages. City council members tellingly paid the man "one days [*sic*] per diem," confirming the petitioner's belief that a just deed warranted compensation.[103]

The "good citizens" who received fees for chasing and capturing suspected criminals were not unlike many official members of the city's police system, for in Baltimore there was little actual difference between a vigilante and a constable. Although appointed by mayors to bring criminals to justice, constables earned no regular salary and were compensated only with fees and rewards. In this way they were like the white men who arrested suspects and requested compensation ex post facto. The majority of Baltimore's constables spent much of their time pursuing stolen property whose return could bring substantial rewards and waited for victims to offer particularly liberal sums in return for their valuables and the thief who stole them.[104] Unlike the city's night watchmen, they were less preventive of crime than reactive to its committal. They did not patrol.[105]

Constables, in essence, were mercenaries for hire, and in practice they proved indistinguishable from those other Baltimoreans who policed the city as good citizens seeking municipal largesse. Constable Emanuel Stockett traveled in 1847 first to Philadelphia and later to a small town in Virginia in order to find, apprehend, and deliver to Baltimore authorities James Kelly, a murderer who had "abscond[ed] from Justice, [and] for whose apprehension and conviction before Baltimore City Court the Mayor offered a reward of two hundred dollars." Like Franier, Stockett was successful: he arrested Kelly in Virginia. And like Watt, he solicited the help of a local constable to whom he promised "one half of the reward." Back in Baltimore, Stockett sought payment for his travel expenses, for securing the Virginia man's help, and for the success of his mission. He sought payment, in other words, much as any Baltimorean responding to a lucrative reward would have done. It is perhaps easier to think of him less as a functionary in pursuit of a criminal and more as a citizen in pursuit of a reward.[106]

The city's promise of payment and ordinary citizens' sense of entitlement to municipal funds stamped popular justice with an official seal of approval and made seemingly vigilante behavior nearly indistinguishable from formal law enforcement. Sometimes those who successfully pursued suspected criminals were constables like Stockett or John Zell, who tracked down Lewis Cummings well over a year after Cummings had committed a murder.[107] Sometimes the detectives in question were lawyers or doctors or artisans, private citizens like James Watt and William Franier, who voluntarily apprehended violent adversaries after all others before them had failed. Early Baltimore City's political economy of policing made it difficult to distinguish amateurs like Watt and Franier from the functionaries who policed the city under the banner of the state. Blurring the line between official and unofficial policing, the municipality garbed vigilantism with the cloak of formal authority—and so what looked like amateur policing may not have been amateur at all. For white men, policing paid.

Democracy's Tyranny

At the most abstract level, Baltimore's wedding of formal law enforcement with popular justice represented a triumph for democracy. One policed to govern, and that ordinary Baltimoreans regularly policed their city suggests that they regularly took an active role in the city's governance. Of course, the vast majority of those ordinary Baltimoreans who regularly policed the city were white men; this suggests that the democracy in question was more akin to a herrenvolk democracy than not.[108] Yet the racial and gender exclusivity of their system did not trouble most of the city's citizens. The democratization of the policing process, on the other hand, sometimes did. Many white men were comfortable with popular policing, not to mention the white male supremacy that undergirded it, but a growing number were uneasy with the risk to minority rights that a democratic majority seemed to pose.

The downside of Baltimore's police system was rioting, or what contemporaries called mob law. A case in point is the story of Harman Blennerhassett, one of Aaron Burr's accomplices in the failed 1806 military expedition to the Southwest. Blennerhassett and Burr were on the run from U.S. authorities when in 1807 they arrived in Baltimore. There, they met a mob. A circulating handbill representing itself as "the unanimous voice of every honest man in the community" promised the two men's execution "by the hangman on Gallows Hill." Convinced that his life was in danger, Blennerhassett prudently hid in a hotel garret, and from there, secreted away, he watched "the mob pass by the house . . . in full huzza, with fife and drum." More disturbing still were the "two troops of cavalry [who] patrolled the streets, not to disperse the mob but to follow and behold their conduct." The sight shocked Blennerhassett. It was not simply the mob seeking him; it was the militia as well. In a single moment the difference between mob and militia — and U.S. officials and local citizens — dissolved. He learned that in Baltimore, vigilante justice was justice all the same.[109]

A more vivid illustration of the system's riotous potential erupted in the summer of 1812, when a mob consisting mostly of mechanics, many of them of modest means and a few from other parts of the world, violently assaulted several wealthy, native-born white men whose Federalist antiwar convictions clashed with the Jeffersonian beliefs of the city's white male majority. The events of 1812 earned Baltimore the derisive nickname "Mobtown." In the country's as-yet brief national history, this riot was unique in both the tenor of its violence and the nature of its destruction. It was also an exemplary moment in which a mob engulfed the state's power completely, and to devastating effect. All told, several of the victims suffered grievous wounds at the hands of the rioters. One of them, a local Revolutionary War hero, died.[110]

White male Baltimoreans accepted a measure of violence but worried about extremes. They worried especially how under certain conditions mob violence could seem legitimate. Throughout the tumultuous summer of 1812, for example, there were numerous cases where officials either encouraged or acquiesced to the mob. When in June a Federalist asked an officer for help, the latter refused. He retorted that antiwar Federalists deserved to be roped, taken out of town, and hung from "the first tree they came to."[111] More generally, neither of the two city officials who possessed the most political influence — Mayor Edward Johnson and General John Stricker — proved willing to risk the unpopularity (that is, mob violence) that would have resulted from their calling out a large militia to protect endangered Federalists.[112] As a result, various observers in and around Baltimore came to believe that no difference existed at all between the mob and the municipal government. Federalist victims condemned the municipality upon these grounds explicitly. Afterward, one of the survivors of the mob recalled bitterly how "a general with a military force under his command [became] the contemptible fetch and carry messenger of a lawless mob, a Judge [bound] himself to the same gang not to bail men whom he had acknowledged had committed no offence, and police officers [delivered] up their prisoners to be butchered." The angry and frustrated man believed that the "inhuman" and "ferocious barbarity" of the 1812 riot owed to the failings, if not complicity, of the city's own government.[113]

Whatever else it revealed, the 1812 riot exposed the trouble with a democratic police system: at some point, a majority would run roughshod over a minority, and there was little the public authorities could or would do to stop it. Over the years that followed, the 1812 riot loomed larger in the minds of Baltimoreans concerned about the rights of men. "We have no authority outside of and superior to the people," the editor of the *Baltimore American* lamented to Alexis de Tocqueville in 1831, when the Frenchman was visiting Baltimore:

> The militia, itself, is the populace, and is of no use when it partakes or condones the passions of the majority. Twenty years ago we represented a terrible example of this. It was the time of the war against England, a war that was very popular in the South. A journalist allowed himself to attack the war sentiment violently. The masses gathered, broke his presses, attacked the house where he and his friends . . . had taken refuge. An attempt was made to call the militia; it refused to march against the rioters and did not respond to the call. The municipal authorities could rescue the editor and his friends only by sending them to prison. The mob wasn't satisfied. At night it came together and marched against the prison. Again they tried to get out the militia and were unable to do it. The prison was taken by assault, one of the inmates killed on the spot, and others left for dead. An effort was made to prosecute in the courts, but the juries acquitted the guilty parties.[114]

Charles Carroll, the last surviving signee of the Declaration of Independence and one of the richest men in America, was more blunt. Speaking with Tocqueville a few days later, Carroll opined: "*A mere democracy is but a mob.*"[115] Fifty-five years earlier, Carroll had signed the Declaration of Independence, which stated that all men possessed certain inalienable rights. Experience had taught him that not every right could survive a society reliant upon its citizens to take the law into their own hands.

These arguments so impressed Tocqueville that he mused extensively upon them in "The Omnipotence of the Majority in the United States" in his *Democracy in America*. Tocqueville believed strongly that the American state was, contrary to popular opinion, quite strong, and that while "the force behind the state is much less well regulated, less enlightened, and less wise," it was also "a hundred times more powerful than in Europe." By way of example he pointed to the police system of the early U.S. polity:

> In America the means available to the authorities for the discovery of crimes and arrest of criminals are few. There is no administrative police force, and passports are unknown. . . . Nevertheless, I doubt whether in any other country crime so seldom escapes punishment. The reason is that everybody thinks he has an interest in furnishing proofs of an offense and in arresting the guilty man. During my stay in the United States I have seen the inhabitants of a county where serious crime had been committed spontaneously forming committees with the object of catching the criminal and handing him over to the courts. In Europe the criminal is a luckless man fighting to save his head from the authorities; in a sense the population are mere spectators of the struggle. In America he is an enemy of the human race and every human being is against him.[116]

This system was capable of a despotism as great as any posed by a monarch. "When a man or party suffers an injustice in the United States," Tocqueville asked rhetorically, "to whom can he turn?" Not to public opinion, not to the legislature, not to the executive, and certainly not to the police —"they are nothing but the majority under arms." There was nowhere to turn when confronting an angry majority. As Tocqueville himself noted, one need only look to Baltimore's summer of 1812 for proof.[117]

Locals could soon point to an even bigger riot that gave full expression to the violent excesses of majority rule. Erupting out of the fury over frauds connected with the recent closing of the Bank of Maryland, the Baltimore bank riot of 1835 proved to be one of the most violent spectacles of an era well known for its remarkable violence. For several days and nights in August, mobs of angry Baltimoreans ransacked the palatial homes of the bank's managers and trustees. Order was not restored until a group of impromptu soldiers led by an aging war hero gained control of the streets, but by then the rioters had destroyed hundreds of thousands of dollars' worth of property. One man who arrived a week afterward observed the ruins of the city's center. "The military arrangement of cannon and soldiers for the night," he observed with palpable sadness, "looked more war like than anything I have ever yet had the pleasure of seeing."[118]

The bank riot betrayed the trouble with a system predicated upon popular policing: so long as a majority of citizens approved of the mob, there was little anyone could do to stop its violence. And there were plenty of citizens who approved of this mob. The Bank of Maryland's closure in 1834 had simultaneously wiped out the securities of thousands while enriching the few, and the resulting anger that permeated the city translated into widespread support for the rioters. Various witnesses estimated that "there were many thousands present . . . who were, almost to a man, approvers if not instigators of violence."[119] "Not one word of objection was raised!" one man later exclaimed to a friend.[120] In fact, few Baltimoreans raised any objection to the destructive scenes besetting the city because the very people who could effectively do so made up the mob itself. "The mob," one justice of the peace recalled, "was quelled by the simultaneous action of the citizens." The sheriff of Baltimore County remembered it the same way. "The mob was finally quelled by the unanimous turn out of the citizens," he testified. Another witness concurred: "The mob was quelled by citizens generally." It was no coincidence that only when the rioters finally sated their destructive appetites did the citizenry suddenly arise and the mob just as suddenly disappear. A few keen observers noticed the inverse relationship between the pro- and anti-mob forces. "No body knew where the mob was on Monday morning — in fact it had vanished," observed the pseudonymous "Junius" in the Jacksonian *Baltimore Republican*. "Public opinion which had breathed into its nostrils the breath of life, had withdrawn its vitality, and the mob was no more."[121]

Impotent municipal police institutions compounded the problem of an unhinged citizenry. "On Sunday the 9th of August, the mob was permitted to advance in open day in their work of pillage and contempt of the laws," wrote John Morris, one of the bank riot victims. "Until the work of destruction was fully consummated," he continued, "there did not exist or remain a vestige or semblance of a civil authority; the city had been wholly surrendered to the frantic dominion of a mob." The resulting chaos was nothing less than a fearful state of nature. "The civil authorities ceased to exist, and anarchy predominated," Morris concluded.[122] Morris had a point. When a colonel from the militia attempted to call his men into duty, only three responded.

The rest had either already joined the mob or concluded against taking up arms against it.[123] "At no time before Sunday noon," later testified Anthony Miltenberger, the president of the First Branch of the City Council, "do I believe the military would have responded to a call for their services."[124] Another witness reported that "officers and men were ordered out on parade, but refused or neglected to obey the call."[125] Still another testified that "at no stage of the affray, could there be found men enough, trust-worthy and willing, to take up arms to put [the mob] down."[126] In short, the city authorities did not have the "means to disperse the mob before Sunday evening," explained the merchant James Hayman. The mob was only finally "quelled by the change of the current of public opinion. If the same current of feeling could have been aroused at any other time, [the mob] could have been put down."[127]

A prime example of democracy run amok, the bank riot laid bare the trouble with any system that relied so exclusively upon popular policing. It revealed the propensity of ordinary people to riot; it exposed the municipality's institutional weakness; and it demonstrated, perhaps better than any other event in the city's riotous past, the dangers that a violent majority posed to an unpopular minority — even to a minority populated by rich white men. More than a few Baltimoreans walked away from the ashes of the bank riot with the growing conviction that property rights would never be secure unless the municipality was strengthened and the boundary between official and unofficial policing was clarified. By the time the dust had settled, good citizenship had begun to take on a new meaning. White men could soon be heard asking for help from the very government that so many of them supposedly feared.

Chapter Two

POLICEMEN AND PRISONS

♦

WHEN WE TALK of policemen and prisons, we talk of the state. That term, "the state," conjures images of a monolithic actor distinct from the people who constitute civil society. It raises the specter of something external, with a top-down capacity, something more powerful than and in tension with real individuals and the rights they hold dear. When we think of the state, we think of something other than *us*. Yet what interests me in this book is how this notion of a state severed from society fails to capture the complete workings of power. In antebellum Baltimore — to take one example — the police force and penal system were as much products of ordinary white men's actions as they were distinct, autonomous agencies that identified subjects (including white men) for governance.[1] In antebellum Baltimore, white men built the police force and penal institutions. As a result, policemen and prisons represented more an extension of white male power than that power's replacement.

Baltimore City's police system underwent significant changes in the years that followed the bank riot of 1835. The municipality introduced hundreds of blue-clad policemen to the streets in March 1857, completing a process of reform that was decades in the making. These new policemen's collective gaze seemed far greater, and their discipline seemed far stricter, than those of the watchmen who preceded them. Officials also added a host of penal institutions to Baltimore's expanding cityscape. By midcentury, a refurbished prison stood in the city's center while a new almshouse and reformatory school rested at its borders. The professional police force and reformative penal system together institutionalized state power in a way it never had

been, and really never could have been, before. Such change did not mark
the end of collaboration between ordinary white men and municipal officers,
but it did help clarify the distinction between them. In the policemen's case,
this clarification was quite literal: an embodiment of municipal power on
the city's streets, policemen dressed in uniforms so as to distinguish themselves from the many other white men who walked those streets as well.

In Baltimore as elsewhere, police reformers worked alongside the advocates of other forms of governmental centralization, men who at all levels
of government called for better maps and surveys; new roads, canals, and
bridges; modern courthouses, schools, and hospitals; and additional funds
to aid society's growing population of poor, sick, and disabled people.[2] These
reformers' methods were largely liberal, for they designed their new institutions to create self-governing subjects capable of enjoying the privileges and
responsibilities of freedom.[3] Both the police force and penal asylum were
exemplary in this regard; they focused almost exclusively upon the individual. Reformers established the police force to protect the rights of individuals, particularly their property rights, and built penal asylums to remake
inmates into individuals capable of possessing property rights. Police reform
grew state power in the name of liberal freedom.

Ultimately, the fundamental liberalism of police professionalization and
carceral construction had far-reaching implications for a wide range of free
Baltimoreans, particularly the white workingmen who made up the rank
and file of the city's political order. Although lawmakers introduced new
police institutions to protect property holders, more than simple wealth
counted as property in a city like Baltimore. White workingmen were property holders of a different sort: of wages (filling their pockets with the fruits
of their labor), dependents (heading their own households), and whiteness
(in contrast to the black population). And as property owners, these white
workingmen deployed real power under the system of policing that reached
fruition during the 1850s. As we will see, their violence found legitimacy
under the very liberal logic that demanded police reform in the first place.

The municipality's growing strength, the introduction of professional
policemen and reformative prisons, and the hardening legal distinction between "legitimate" and "extralegal" violence all owed to a growing recognition among the citizenry that a police system predicated solely upon white
male vigilantism was inadequate to protect property in the growing city.
That did not mean white men's popular violence disappeared from Baltimore's streets. It just meant that that violence began to prosper under a more

liberal rationale. Property owners both insisted upon building a professional police force and called for the prisons that soon dotted the city's far-reaching horizons. While one result of those demands was a more powerful state, the other result, the one that challenges us to look beyond the familiar binary of liberty and power, was a more liberal state that empowered mobs of free white men in new ways.

Freedom from Fear

Police reform was largely the product of fear. By 1840, more than one hundred thousand people called Baltimore home, and though by modern standards that number is relatively small, it was still large enough to transform most of the city's residents into comparative strangers. The strangeness was novel and frightening. Life in Baltimore increasingly *seemed* dangerous: strangers could pick a man's pocket, vandalize his home, assault his wife or children — any number of upsetting possibilities appeared more likely in the urbanizing world. Actual crime, to be sure, did not keep pace with the city's rapid population growth; urbanization typically leads to lower crime rates per capita, and Baltimore during the nineteenth century was no different in this regard. But the proliferation of anonymity drove a growing impression that both life and property were becoming progressively tenuous.[4]

Confronted by the changing demographics of their city, certain Baltimoreans expressed a far-reaching, almost abstract unease and described the cause of their disaffection simply as "crime." One lecturer nostalgically dreamed of the days of his boyhood, "when the world was glad, and when such atrocities were undreamed of"— and when, presumably, Baltimore was little more than a town in which unfamiliar faces were more exception than rule. As Harry H. Young perused the city of his adulthood, crime felt ubiquitous, and it seemed far more likely to engulf the reformer than it was for the reformer to alleviate the crime: if "you approach too near those who are immured in crime . . . you are not only less able to effect their redemption, but are very likely . . . to bring about your own ruin." The most moral of men could not escape the corrupting influence of "evil communications" that spread through the mundane interaction of seemingly ordinary people.[5]

Men like Young spoke of crime as an epidemic — unseen but present, immaterial yet real. Crime could stand in for all that was lost in a society that had changed too much, too soon. Had he been middle-aged, Young, who gave his lecture in 1853, would have lived through the most rapid urban population growth in American history, the rise of mass and party politics, and an economic expansion so immense that future historians would call it a "revolution." He might well have noticed a decline of social deference and "natural" local leadership and the rise of demagoguery and speculative economic activity, all of which worried clergymen, educators, and moralists, both north and south. The world of Young's youth, a more hierarchical and deferential world of paternal, elite, and religious control, loomed over his present as a safer world, as forces beyond his control had left him and many others like him unprepared to handle the unseen dangers that those forces had let loose.[6]

The type of crime that most unnerved the citizenry was property crime. Beginning in the 1830s, property owners began to write the mayor and city council for help in protecting their homes and businesses. "We respectfully ask you as Citizens[,] as tax payers, as those who would wish to respect and live under civil Law and good government," wrote twelve east Baltimore men to Mayor Samuel Smith in 1837. Without "a degree of safety and security," they explained, their rights, privileges, and property would all be "in continual danger."[7] What these men wanted, what they meant specifically when they demanded "a degree of safety," were night watchmen. Around Baltimore, business and home owners felt increasingly insecure about the ratio of watchmen to city space and population, both of which were growing at faster rates than the city's police institutions, and desired more men and watch boxes assigned to their neighborhoods. In 1833, for example, a group of "undersigned citizens" from the Fells Point area requested a watch box to secure "the safety of their Property."[8] In 1837, another fourteen petitioners protested the nearby removal of a watch box for fear of "the exposure of all the property" and asked for it to be returned.[9] By the end of the decade, legions of others, those hailing from the city's southern, western, and eastern sections alike, feared that someone would not only steal their "valuable property" but also possibly light it afire. Letters routinely arrived in the mayor's and assorted councilmen's offices asking if "your Honors will grant an additional watchman" or at least bestow "such other relief . . . as to your Honor may seem necessary."[10]

"Property" encompassed more than the physical structures that gave form to homes and businesses. In antebellum Baltimore, a man's "property" included his household dependents. "Consider it my duty, as a good citizen to make you acquainted with, all & everything, which might in any degree tend to injure the good name of our city, or disturb the quiet of its citizens," Matthew Drake wrote Mayor William Steuart in 1831. The night before, a mob had attacked his Light Street home as well as the building adjacent to it, yet no watchman ever arrived at the scene, not even after the mob had left. "As mayor of the city," Drake implored, "I apply to you for redress ... if you would send proper officers."[11] Mr. P. Hogan wrote the mayor in the early autumn of 1857 to inform him of the "lawless ... rowdies" who harassed his friends and family on a regular basis. The harassment had recently turned more violent and personal. On the previous Thursday, Hogan explained, a group of young men had attempted to break down his front door. When unable to do so, they had moved behind the house and repeatedly launched bats through his bedroom window, smashing it to pieces and almost "killing my aged mother nearly 80 years old and 3 of my children." As the man of the house, Hogan understood his role to be that of a protector. Now he was finding that responsibility too onerous to achieve on his own. "Sir you are the Chief magestrate [sic] of this City," Hogan signed off, and "I appeal to you as [a] Citizen, to Have us protected as the laws allows."[12]

Fears for property were well grounded, particularly for those who lived or worked at the farthest reaches of the city. In frontier neighborhoods where few or even occasionally no watchmen patrolled, Baltimoreans were too often unable to protect their property personally should a threat suddenly have materialized. Many sought help. A group of "citizens" from the city's northwestern section asked, in 1842, why they did "not enjoy that protection during the night ... in common with our fellow citizens." Home owners had erected more than thirty new houses over the past year, and they needed more of it, and fast.[13] In the eastern section of the city, "the property of citizens within the bounds of Wilke & Gough and Market and Bond streets" lacked any municipal oversight at all. Residents there hoped then-mayor Sam Brady could ensure "better security to the property & citizens."[14] Alas, he proved unable to do so, at least in accordance with the rate of the neighborhood's growth. Four years later another five petitioners explained that "upwards of forty-six new houses have been built within the above District, most of which are now tenanted," and all that within a year's time. Where, these citizens wondered, was their rightful "protection"?[15]

Many people began to seek municipal police assistance for work they had previously done themselves, if only because a more centralized civil authority seemed more efficient. William Carmichael thought "the expense and trouble attending the recovery of lost children" were gradually becoming too much for ordinary men like him to bear any longer. Carmichael first realized the inefficiency of the current system when "one of his own . . . strayed away one morning last summer." "Notwithstanding the united search of himself and family together with about thirty of his neighbours," his child went missing for most of the day and "was not found till 10 o'clock at night and then upon Fells Point." Carmichael advised the city to establish "some control place to which lost children should be taken."[16] Victims of theft also discovered that it was easier to deal directly with municipal officials than to search for lost items themselves. William Robinson of Allegheny, Pennsylvania, "personally appeared" before the mayor in 1833 to ask for help in retrieving "the articles stolen from him" two months earlier, some of which he thought were "now in the possession of [a] pawn Broker" downtown.[17]

Those who decided to eschew vigilantism had usually concluded that even the best individual effort did not always pay. Sometimes the attainment of justice was too cumbersome for any one private citizen to achieve alone. One group of petitioners, for example, claimed to have abandoned their pursuit of a thief after having already caught him. In that case Bartholomew Manning, the thief in question, "without company offered what was discovered and we thought it prudent to let him go to avoid a tedious attendance in court and expose our inability to obtain redress." Some time later, Manning perpetrated a similar crime upon similar victims and ended up in police custody anyway, and his (alleged) earlier victims were glad for the arrest. They had, at least by their own account, recovered the stolen goods on their own, but only the city had time and resources enough to punish the man who had stolen their goods in the first place.[18] "Our preservation," explained another property owner to the mayor, "cannot be attributed to the care of our fellow citizens, though we trust much to a good system of police."[19]

The changing city, and this growing sense of entitlement among the citizenry, led Baltimoreans to look to their municipality to resolve conflicts that in the past they had resolved themselves. A Mr. Legard complained of a chimney "now erected at the corner of Mott and Ensor" that bothered him, his family, and his neighbors.[20] Thomas Hand spoke for his tenant when imploring authorities to deal with two artisans "in the habit of crowding the street with various vehicles . . . not only in front of their own premises, but also that of their neighbors."[21] Another man demanded his neighbor remove an annoying "Stove pipe." When that neighbor refused, he wrote the mayor to make the demand more formal: "He will not attend to it," the petitioner complained, "and I thought it my duty to inform you of the circumstance."[22]

By the late 1830s Baltimore's property owners were writing the city to request and sometimes demand assistance in dealing with the smallest of problems.

The traditional forum of conflict resolution was a magistrate's court, or the minor judiciary. Two men involved in a dispute were as likely to seek resolution through private prosecution as they were to rely upon municipal officers to resolve the problem for them. But even the minor judiciary began to quake beneath the pressures of population growth. Many Baltimoreans grew frustrated with the possibility that wily individuals could manipulate the system and concluded that private citizens acting as prosecutors lied all the time. Thomas Williams, a small businessman in Fells Point, claimed, for instance, that he had purchased six dollars' worth of "common lace" from Charles Starke in 1825, only to witness Starke show up shortly thereafter with a constable, arrest him, and charge him with theft. Williams was flabbergasted at Starke's audacity. Or perhaps his own righteousness was itself a show; perhaps the "zeal of the prosecutor" was justified, and Williams was the liar here. It is impossible to know. But this uncertainty about the validity of such claims is also the point: Baltimoreans were discovering that a man's good name, to say nothing of his liberty, depended in large part upon the designs and calculations of perfect strangers. And that not only was unjust; it was scary.[23]

In response to this rising tide of fear and frustration, city officials began to compensate victims of popular violence — especially after the bank riot. Legislators in Annapolis had followed the events of August 1835 with mortification, and after things calmed down they authored a bill to ensure that future administrations would not be so impotent. The bill had two edicts: the first compelled Baltimore's municipality to repay the riot's victims for the value of their destroyed property; the second placed all of Baltimore's citizens under a broad shield of indemnity, promising redress to anyone who, in the future, lost property to "the lawless wrath" of a mob. The so-called Indemnity Act did not completely repudiate vigilantism as a legitimate means of policing, but it did mandate the city's government to quell destructive riots more effectively than it had during the summer of 1835 — or else literally pay for its failure to do so. By 1836, municipal officers had no choice but to protect citizen from citizen, and the mobbed from the mob, in whatever manner they could.[24]

The Indemnity Act codified into law the growing belief that property rights mattered a great deal and that the state was the political entity best equipped to protect them. Insofar as its dictums necessitated a stronger municipal government, the act clarified the difference between official and unofficial policing, and insofar as those dictums enshrined the sanctity of property rights in the law, the act also distinguished legal from extralegal violence: now, any violence that violated property rights was by definition lawless or extralegal. The bank riot and its aftermath cast the growing importance of property rights and the state's active role in protecting them into sharp relief and was an important part of the larger process by which reformers retooled the social contract in a way that strengthened state power in the name of property. In law at least, Baltimore's municipality after 1836 was to be a liberal state. Its focus was to be increasingly upon the protection of property rights.

It was not long before the city's citizenry began to feel entitled to compensation for the damages they incurred at the hands of a mob. When the newspaper editor Isaac Munroe learned, for example, that a Baltimore Street building he owned was to be the target of an angry mob, he quickly alerted the authorities of what was to come. "Notwithstanding said notice," Munroe later recounted, "the said building was attacked by a riotous assemblage." With no one to quell the disturbance and repel the rioters, his property had been badly damaged. Now he wanted satisfaction. Munroe knew the law, and he knew that his injuries entitled him to a claim upon the city. Citing the Indemnity Act, a law that in his words affirmed "the well established principle, that those who live under & submit themselves to the laws in a civilized community, are entitled to be protected in the unmolested enjoyment of their property," Munroe contended that the "authorities who have failed to protect him shall indemnify him for his losses, out of the public treasury."[25]

Munroe's claims — both his initial request for help and his later demand for remuneration — revealed the growing importance of state policing to liberal freedom. They mirrored those of the bank riot's victims, who had also argued that "protection" was the "foundation of every free government."[26] A man's "rights as a citizen of the state under the constitution of the state" gave him "a clear title to protection from the injury for which he seeks redress," explained Reverdy Johnson, one of the bank riot's victims.[27] To ignore his injury would be akin to violating his property rights. It would be as if the state were denying him freedom itself.

Intrinsic to such arguments was a biting criticism of the police system that historically characterized Baltimore's governance. What increasingly frustrated property owners was the blurry boundary that heretofore separated official from unofficial policing. As many saw it, the government that failed to protect property was itself a threat to property. Reverdy Johnson likened his situation to that of a victim of state violence. "If by an act avowedly official, the authorities of the city had expressly directed the destruction of the property of your Memorialist — if each individual citizen had joined in the perpetration of the outrage," reasoned Johnson, "your Memorialist supposes that no one would be found to deny that he would have a clear claim to indemnity from the city itself, which ought to be enforced." In a way, that was precisely what had happened: "Is there any distinction between the cases supposed, and that which occurred? On the contrary, are they not in principle identical?"[28] Johnson believed that officers of the state might well have been the very individuals who demolished his home and set fire to his belongings; in either case, his demands for redress would stand on equally sound legal rationale. In either case, too, the story was of municipal failure to secure property rights.

It was not just the victims of the bank riot who believed that the city's inability to protect property violated "the duty of protection which the State owes the citizen," "subvert[ed] the plainest principles of freedom," and "trample[d] upon the declaration of rights" that formed the basis of the social contract.[29] Increasingly, municipal officials also hoped to use their vested powers "at all times and under all circumstances ... for the protection of persons and property, and for bringing to punishment all violators of the laws and ordinances of the city."[30] Unfortunately, for decades the corporation lacked the revenue streams and officers to protect property rights adequately, let alone completely. In his 1848 message to the city council, Mayor Jacob Davies nodded to this reality while pondering the unnerving "extent and population of the City." As mayor, Davies was perhaps better situated than anyone to understand how the city's ever-increasing numbers of houses and people translated into too much for a small administration to protect, protect against, and punish.[31] His colleagues in the city council generally agreed with him. Conceding that "the protection of person and property is essential in all cities, of necessity the lives and property of the community are under its care," the Joint Committee on Police, writing less than two years later, concluded that Baltimore needed a more "efficient night watch."[32]

As it happened, over the course of the next decade officials would introduce the city's first professional police force. State legislators in Annapolis would meanwhile fund, build, and refine a penal system that they located almost entirely within Baltimore. Once large numbers of property holders began demanding a more efficient municipal government, and once public officials, in response to those demands, began to grapple with their offices' lack of efficient and powerful police institutions, real reform was probably inevitable. "Every citizen is entitled to protection," read an 1850 city council report, "both in person and property. . . . It is the duty of the City Authorities to afford that protection."[33] And so, in time, they did. The citizenry's embrace of state power gave rise to new conceptions of good government, as well as to the very institutions that constituted such power. By asking for help and expressing fear — by sending "petition after petition, remonstrance after remonstrance to the Legislature"— a diverse collection of property holders helped call into being a new police force and penal system.[34]

Policemen

The Indemnity Act was mere prelude to the creation of a professional police force in Baltimore. Generalized anxieties expressed during the 1830s and 1840s created the conditions under which police reform could occur, but fear alone did not give rise to innovation. To understand why Baltimore lawmakers introduced major police reform in 1857 — as opposed, say, to a decade earlier or a decade later — we must also grapple with the local political context of the 1850s as well as with the movement by major American municipalities toward bureaucratization. Only in the most general sense did the birth of the policeman and prison owe to property holders' fear. More proximate factors also played a role.

One of those factors was partisanship. Democrats and Whigs dominated Baltimore's politics for a generation, but that dominance began to dissolve during the late 1840s when several major voting blocs grew dissatisfied with the two parties. Most important among these constituencies were native-born white wage earners. This politically enfranchised group was struggling mightily in the face of industrial and demographic change, and neither the Democrats nor the Whigs proved able (or willing) to meet its demands to aid strikes, provide relief jobs, and stem the tide of immigration. More generally, neither party proved effective (or interested) in helping to soften the rough transition that skilled workingmen endured from the world of artisanal workshops to that of industrial factories. The result was the dissolution of the prevailing political order, with Whigs folding in the early 1850s and Democrats hemorrhaging large numbers of native-born workers every passing election season. Into the ashes of the city's Second Party System stepped the Know-Nothings.[35]

In Baltimore, they called themselves the American Party. Such an appellation was telling because the Know-Nothings' most important constituents were American-born, wage-earning white men who demanded more attention to the city's unpredictable labor market and more restrictions upon foreign immigration. These angry and frustrated white working-class "Americans" helped nativist politicians win the mayor's office and a majority in the city council in 1854. Two years later, Know-Nothings did even better, sweeping local races and securing a stranglehold upon the municipal government that they would not relinquish until 1860. Pulling both disillusioned Democrats and Whigs into their coalition, American Party leaders used their power to reward the rank and file in much the same way that machine politicians have always repaid their supporters: by giving them jobs. In particular, the Know-Nothings put their working-class supporters on a new police force. Police reform in Baltimore was not only the offspring of fear but also the product of patronage.[36]

Baltimore's police reformers operated in a more national context as well. By the 1850s, other large American cities had begun to introduce professional police forces, and whatever were the local conditions in Baltimore, the Know-Nothings who dressed the city's first policemen were also just following a trend. First in New York and Boston, and later in cities like Cincinnati, Philadelphia, and Detroit, reformers eliminated the distinctions between day and night police, consolidated their respective departments under a single chain of command, and substantially enlarged the size of their forces. The process of reform followed its own logic in each city. Sometimes officials introduced uniformed policemen in response to growing perceptions of crime, sometimes as an antidote to riots, and sometimes in an attempt to control strangers, particularly immigrants. Occasionally police forces emerged out of some combination of these fears, or out of altogether other ones to boot. Yet while reasons varied, police reform occurred in multiple cities at roughly the same time, suggesting that Baltimore was part of an urban network in which innovative ideas flowed back and forth. Reformers in Maryland's flagship city were always in conversation with others and imitated them accordingly.[37]

Whether in Baltimore or elsewhere, police reformers confronted a dilemma simultaneously theoretical and practical. It was one thing to proclaim, as many officials were wont to do, that "every citizen is entitled to protection, both in person and property."[38] It was quite another to provide that protection without jeopardizing another citizen's person and property in the process. Policemen were necessary, but policemen were potentially dangerous. What was a *liberal* police force supposed to do? The answer lay in a spatial distinction that lawmakers made: they intended for the policeman to help mark a clearer boundary between public and private spaces. That is, reformers wanted policemen to secure the streets from "assaults with intent to kill, riots, and street fights, and palatable programmes of rowdyism," and to eliminate the "murder, theft, incendiarism, and vandalism [that] stalked freely abroad in open daylight."[39] Only once policemen had cleared the streets of their prolific violence could citizens be properly equipped to govern freely, as sovereign subjects, within their own properties.

Baltimore was by no means the only city where lawmakers aimed to transform the shape of governance on the streets so that property owners could continue governing off them. New police officers — more numerous, professionally uniformed, and occasionally armed — embodied a growing consensus across the industrializing world that cities should be free for property owners to govern. From London and Paris to New York and Baltimore, reformers coupled their introduction of new police forces with a plethora of ordinances condemning behaviors that prevented the "free" circulation of people, goods, and ideas. New laws outlawed "standing," "loitering," and "remaining" and prohibited street sellers from "jostling" and "annoying" passersby. New laws abolished anything that could impede the progress of carts on the roads and people on the walkways, from clotheslines to garbage to projectiles. New laws even sought to control traffic, manage language and speech, and eliminate any behavior or demonstration that seemed "riotous," "indecent," or "profane." By the middle of the nineteenth century, regulations in cities like Baltimore had become so widespread, so ubiquitous, that they touched upon almost every conceivable practice of public life. The policeman lent institutional muscle to this broader attempt to secure freedom for the self-governing individual to think, work, and trade without encumbrance.[40] "Law and order, order and law, these are the two cornerstones of empires," wrote the editor for the *Baltimore Sun*. "They are especially the main pillars of republicanism."[41]

Police reform in Baltimore reached fruition by the middle of the 1850s. Flour merchant and Know-Nothing mayor Samuel Hinks's administration oversaw its initial phase. Elected in 1854, Hinks helped grow the size and scope of the city's administrative reach in a number of areas, and at the end of his term he and his allies transformed the police system. Working closely with the nativist-dominated city council, Hinks signed into law an 1856 bill that created a police force consisting of 400 officers in total: a marshal, his deputy, 8 captains, 8 lieutenants, 24 sergeants, and roughly 350 officers to patrol the city's ample territory. The modifications to Baltimore's police institution produced in the broadest sense a more disciplined, bureaucratic, and powerful system. In the narrowest sense, police reform allowed Know-Nothing political bosses to compensate hundreds of rank-and-file working-class supporters with new jobs.[42]

On March 1, 1857, the new police force took the streets for the first time, and to even a casual observer the officers seemed to represent real change. As insurance that policemen would patrol more of the city's space for longer periods of time, the police bill increased manpower, ordered roll to be called six times a day, and disallowed any officer from leaving his beat until a replacement appeared. It also established a more rigorous chain-of-command structure. Patrolmen reported to sergeants, sergeants reported to lieutenants, and so on up to the marshal. Moreover, by placing all 400 men under the same organizational umbrella, reformers hoped to guarantee that each officer would be available in a moment of crisis, no matter the location or time of day.[43] They also subjected every policeman to the same strict code of conduct. If an officer behaved in a rowdy, lawless, or generally criminal fashion, the marshal was to fire him.[44]

Professionalization took several forms, and one of those was plainly visible. Uniforms were adopted so that the officer on his beat could socially distance himself from the city's other citizens. "Single-breasted cloth frock coat, nine buttons on the breast and four behind, two buttons on the sleeves," one journalist breathlessly reported after surveying the new duds. And all that blue! The city's policemen clothed themselves completely in blue, with woolen pants and overcoats (during winter) made of a "blue cloth" to distinguish them as they walked their beats. Otherwise, the buttons lining their summer and winter coats were perhaps the uniform's most noteworthy characteristic. These consisted of "superior gilt army style, having a wreath like the dime coin has, and a German text 'P' in the centre." According to the correspondent, "It is a handsome uniform."[45]

Police officers also began taking home regular salaries. In contrast to their predecessors, they were not to receive supplemental rewards for providing information, catching arsonists, and arresting murderers. Such acts were simply to be part of their job description and warranted no additional pay. The corporation subsequently made it illegal for any salaried officer to pocket money as an "informer" and began denying policemen who asked for monetary rewards after arresting incendiaries. One joint committee report from the city council, speaking to the latter point, argued that "it is the duty of police officers to make such arrests, and that they are only entitled to their weekly salary for so doing."[46] The uniforms were perhaps uncomfortable, and the loss of certain types of remuneration was possibly costly. But these marks of professionalization were vital in the effort to distinguish professional policemen from the ordinary white men who wore no uniforms and still claimed municipal largesse for their mercenary acts of vigilantism.

Most important, Baltimore's new policemen were to prevent crime, not simply respond to it. City officials wanted to avoid indemnifying citizens for lost and destroyed property, and that required the preemption of crime. This, above all, is why they mandated uniforms and salaries. In theory, each served to deter wrongdoing. In the case of the uniform, Baltimore's reformers followed the logic of James Gerard, the New York attorney who had first advocated dressing policemen in blue. Gerard had argued that the power of the policeman "in preventing crimes lies in his coat," largely because that coat, as a symbol of state power, would strike fear and uncertainty into potential criminals.[47] Consistent wages would also discourage future crime because they liberated policemen from the old constabulary system, which incentivized officers only to recover stolen goods. Now robed in state's attire, those officers were incentivized to prevent such thefts from occurring in the first place.

In conjunction with the introduction of a uniformed police force, the city council passed new legislation instructing worried property holders to notify authorities the moment they sensed trouble afoot. A few did: "Having reason to believe that our store 239 Balto. st will be broken into," wrote one Morrill Thomas, "we hereby notify you that we hold the city responsible for any damage done."[48] Employees of a newspaper who espoused unpopular political beliefs highlighted an upcoming "exhibition of mob violence . . . in order that the city may be held responsible for any damage that may be done, and that you may take such action in the premises as you may deem necessary and proper."[49] Individuals worried about their homes also gave officials advance notice. Jacob Myers informed the mayor of an imminent "attack" on his east Baltimore residence and requested "such measures . . . to prevent any such occurrence" from happening.[50] The new police force's preventive agenda hinted at an enormous shift in the municipality's obligations. Whereas during the early 1830s they recognized no responsibility to deter attacks, by 1860 the city's leaders were authorizing policemen to protect property holders as their primary responsibility.

In theory, these changes made for a less democratic system. Lawmakers wanted the new police force to protect property rights from large mobs, even when those mobs were able to claim the people's will and engulf the civil authority. Uniforms, standardized beats, regulated procedures, and a bureaucratic chain of command all reflected a desire to liberate police officers from the whims of the populace, as well as an attempt to create the impression that policemen worked out of professional obligations, not political persuasions. Police reform thus sought to solve Alexis de Tocqueville's conundrum: to whom could an imperiled minority turn in a democracy? The answer was the undemocratic policeman, the one white man whose loyalty extended strictly and solely to the law, the one citizen who patrolled the streets in the face of intolerance, fanaticism, and the "lawless spirit that gives vitality and concert of feeling and action to the mob."[51]

And yet, frightened as they were of crime, Baltimore's citizens did not abandon their fear of centralized state power, either. Myriad people, including many officials, continued to worry about a tyrannical state, and in particular about policemen armed with too much power for their own (or anyone else's) good. Right up until the 1856 passage of the police bill, Baltimoreans were warily writing officials about night watchmen who harassed civilians.[52] No code of conduct or chain of command could fully eradicate the risk such men posed to the very rights they served to protect. Consequently, the willingness to bestow more power and authority upon the professional policeman went only so far. Baltimore's new police force was not to be a standing army. Reformers urged police officers to secure "individual rights" by employing the most "conservative means" at their disposal and insisted that police officers walk their beats armed with batons, not firearms.[53] Even in times of riot, restraint was necessary: the marshal issued his men revolvers or something similarly suitable, but those men had to provide receipts for their weapons once the trouble had passed.[54]

Still, whatever the citizenry's persistent fear of the tyrannical officer, police reform did introduce meaningful change. Professionalization signaled a movement away from the era of informal policing, when white male Baltimoreans had policed their city in uncertain and often partial ways. If robbed, perhaps a man would have apprehended the thief himself; perhaps he would have caught the thief but on a whim let him or her go, as one man claimed he had.[55] Now, however, "with firmness and without partiality," policemen were supposed to walk their beats as the primary enforcers of a criminal code whose central purpose was to liberate the city's streets from crime and to protect property rights.[56] It was supposed to be their job alone to catch thieves, and the choice was not theirs to let those thieves go. And, perchance, should a policeman enforce a law that upset popular opinion, the problem, reformers argued, would lie not with him but with the law. "It is made expressly their duty by the law creating the Board to 'enforce all the ordinances of the city, which may be property enforceable by a police force,'" explained one police report, "and this they must do in all cases alike."[57] An editorialist added, "This is their duty, and they are bound to do it."[58]

The introduction of a larger and more organized police force by the Know-Nothings had numerous effects. For one thing, the upsurge in policemen walking the streets dramatically expanded the city's budget during the 1850s. Municipal expenditures on policing more than tripled, growing from a paltry $70,000 at the decade's start to almost $260,000 at its end.[59] That increase reflected not only the growth in the number of officers but also a rise in their activity, as more policemen arrested more people. In 1853, the year before the American Party took control of the city government, law officers delivered just over 2,200 arrestees to jail. By 1859, the final full year of Know-Nothing control, that number had ballooned to more than 5,500. Further regime change did nothing to slow those tallies down, either.[60] In 1861, two years after the Democrats had recaptured control of the municipality, policemen committed close to 7,500 people to jail.[61] All told, the number of arrestees committed to jail grew 240 percent in eight years. The increase in arrests was not as large relatively as it was absolutely — the city's population also grew during these years — but both the police budget and the number of jail commitments outpaced demographic growth by considerable margins.[62]

Prisons

By the late 1850s, more police officers armed with more power were arresting more people. Such was the price of freedom in antebellum Baltimore. But reformers did not stop with policemen. Around the time property holders and officials were coming to accept the necessity of state policing, reformers in cities like Baltimore were beginning to embrace state punishment as well, and the prison in particular. Much as the uniformed, round-the-clock patrolling of a policeman marked a shift away from older methods of protection, the secretive incarceration of a penitentiary introduced a meaningful break with earlier methods of punishment. "It may not be urged that Governments have nothing to do with all this," declared a defiant city council report in 1854. If, however, "the perpetuity of our free political institutions depends on the virtue and intelligence of the people, then too, it were most wise to provide these means of reform or prevention."[63]

The policeman walked a beat to prevent the unlawful from inhibiting the free, and the penitentiary incarcerated the unlawful in the hope of transforming him into someone worthy of freedom. Only upon teaching criminals to be property holders — to be men, citizens, and autonomous, self-governing individuals — could the state successfully protect the rights of other property holders. Nineteenth-century liberals increasingly understood incarceration to be an appendage to the larger preventive policing project. Effective punishment necessitated not only cleansing the streets of criminals but also schooling them in the values of property. Effective punishment, in short, demanded the rehabilitation of souls.

To understand how the nineteenth-century penitentiary came to mirror the professional police force, and how Baltimore's robust penal system came to be, we must first look backward in time and an ocean away. Punishment before the era of reformative incarceration was both cruel and capricious. Officers for the early modern state relied upon gory spectacles to terrify the populace into submission, frequent pardons to demonstrate the mercy of those in charge, and intermittent executions of prominent members of society to reassure subjects that justice was impartial. Yet so much pain and so much death was troubling, and the system's excesses began to fall out of favor in the eighteenth century when critics began questioning their efficacy, if not also their legitimacy. Perhaps the most notable skeptic was an Italian philosopher named Cesare Beccaria. A Milanese aristocrat, Beccaria published his *On Crimes and Punishment* in 1764, wherein he asserted that punishment should be proportional to the crime, without consideration for the character or status of the criminal; mild, or at least milder than death; and certain, with no possibility of a pardon.[64] These were radical ideas, especially in a world characterized by monarchy and the divine right of kings. But the times were changing, and Beccaria's arguments soon found a welcome reception across the Atlantic in the former colonies of British North

America. There, Americans would adapt them and develop a new site for punishment, one that by the middle of the next century had become the paradigmatic institution of liberal state power in the United States.

American reformers concluded that imprisonment was the best means to achieve the Beccarian principles of proportionality, mildness, and certainty. Whereas traditional sanctions were severe and crudely applicable for a broad range of crimes, a prison could incarcerate criminals for periods proportional solely to their specific crimes. And whereas older policy depended upon the ruling class's exertion of maximum discretion, penal reformers believed that the prison, with its comparatively lenient model of punishment, could help de-emphasize discretion in sentencing.[65] Cesare Beccaria would have been gratified to know that in nineteenth-century cities like Baltimore, a growing contingent of boosters believed that nothing was "more essential to the peace and good order of our great cities, [than] that [the law's] violation should be *punished* with *certainty*."[66] It was as if the long-dead Italian had written the words himself.

Some of Americans' interest in incarceration was homegrown, born out of the very discomfort with mobs that helped facilitate the establishment of professional police forces. The Philadelphia physician, politician, and social reformer Benjamin Rush provides an illustrative case in point. Rush's medical thinking about the human body led him to a series of conclusions about the body politic. Having lived through the Revolution, Rush saw irrational and unrestrained moblike excesses of liberty — rioting, essentially — as a contagious disease that endangered citizenship for everyone and worried that the spectacle of public punishments encouraged observers to feel sympathy for the criminal. He also was concerned that gratuitous displays of punishment provoked hostility for the law that condemned the criminal to suffer. Rush's solution was twofold: separate criminals from the public, severing the citizenry's potential sympathy for them, and transform them into what he called "republican machines." Reformed inmates, Rush hoped, would be independent, rational, self-governing subjects fit for a free world.[67]

In the late eighteenth century, these and other ideas like them began to inspire new penal projects in the more populous states. The idea was to separate the criminal from all contact with the outside world, isolate him, and put him to work. Unfortunately, early prisons failed on most counts: prisoners lived in large groups and took their meals in a common dining area; discipline was nonexistent; and whatever innovations administrators introduced were quickly abandoned. By the late 1810s prison reformers con-cluded that they needed a new path forward, and they settled upon two com-peting models. One was in Auburn, where New York State's new penitentiary opened in 1818. The other was in Philadelphia, where in 1823 construction began upon Pennsylvania's Eastern State Penitentiary. The Auburn system favored group labor during the day and solitary confinement at night, while the Philadelphia system advocated the total separation of inmates through-out the day and questioned the utility of prison labor at all. Differences be-tween the Pennsylvanians and New Yorkers helped frame a wider argument over penal forms that erupted during the 1820s on both sides of the Atlantic, and regardless of its outcome — the Auburn system eventually gained more supporters in the United States — the debate showed how by the late 1820s most liberal reformers had reconciled themselves to the necessity of state discipline and punishment.[68]

And the penitentiary, at least in concept, was indeed liberal. Penal re-formers argued that inmates — supposedly lawless, wanton, and unworthy of holding property — needed to become lawful, restrained, and industrious laborers worthy of possessing property before rejoining civil society. If the criminal imperiled the rights of property, the penitentiary was to teach the inmate to appreciate it. Foreigners fascinated by American institutions vis-ited the young nation's asylums to observe the institutions most emblematic of liberal democracy's values. "What is the principal object of punishment in relation to him who suffers it?" Alexis de Tocqueville asked after his 1831 tour of American penal institutions. He had no doubt as to the answer: "It is to give him the habits of society, and first to teach him to obey."[69]

Maryland's prison was part of the first wave to appear in the early nine-teenth century, and its ethos was thoroughly Beccarian. Passed in 1809, the state's Penitentiary Act stated that "a mild and justly proportioned scale of punishments" was "the surest way of preventing the perpetration of crimes, and of reforming offenders" who had violated "the lives, liberties or property, of others." It then delineated that scale in great detail: first-degree murder mandated the death penalty, kidnapping incurred a sentence of two to nine years, theft of goods worth less than five dollars garnered a maximum sen-tence of one year, and so on. But the 1809 law not only inscribed the prin-ciples of proportionality and mildness into a penal code but also increased the likelihood of punishment itself. As the theory went, more prescription for juries reduced the possibility of acquittal while more prescription for gover-nors reduced the potential for pardons.[70]

Like the early prisons in neighboring states, the Maryland Penitentiary also attempted to transform inmates into industrious individuals well suited for wage work and domestic leadership. Prison reformers reasoned that rehabilitation could be achieved only through a twofold approach of confinement and labor. The former would allow convicts to reflect upon their crimes, and the latter would instill in them the values of industry (that is, wage work) and responsibility (that is, oversight of dependents). Reformers steadfastly believed that the state could inculcate a faith in the values of freedom and individualism through coercion and that discipline was integral to the valuation and protection of property rights. Hezekiah Niles, the national newspaper editor and one of Baltimore's most vocal supporters of the prison project, advised "citizens of the state, and especially gentlemen honored with the power of making or administering the laws," to visit the state's penitentiary as often as possible in order to see just how important it was to the preservation of their own propertied freedom. "Every citizen," he argued, "has some part in [the penitentiary's] general reputation and success," and that was because every good citizen needed to bear witness to the production of others just like him.[71]

The liberal bona fides of the Maryland Penitentiary were most evident in who did not reside there. Reformers wanted their prison to function as a space for free people, and one of the ways to ensure that result was to ban slaves. In February 1819, nearly a decade after the penitentiary opened its doors, the General Assembly passed a law preventing any enslaved person from being imprisoned by the state. In case a slave committed a capital crime, he or she was to be "sentenced to receive on his or her bare back, any number of lashes not exceeding forty." Slave owners were to maintain control for all other slave crimes.[72] This was the theory, anyway. Reality was messier, and despite the 1819 law a handful of slaves did end up in prison during the ensuing years, a conundrum that often led to gubernatorial pardons. "In lieu of the punishment to which the said negro Charles was adjudged as aforesaid," proclaimed Governor Joseph Kent after an enslaved man had received a murder conviction in southern Maryland, "he [shall] receive publicly thirty lashes."[73] Not all slaves were pardoned and whipped, however, and the prison was only rarely empty of their presence entirely. As late as 1854, about 4 percent of all prisoners there were enslaved.[74]

Maryland's penitentiary opened in November 1811 to poor reviews, and not just because enslaved people occasionally ended up there. An 1823 special investigation launched by the House of Delegates produced a total denunciation of the institution's practices. John R. Pitt, the report's primary author, lamented that the prison "is not only the receptacle, but the nursery of crimes." He worried that "unless some very important changes can be made, so as to effect the object of its establishment, the prevention of crimes, and the reformation of offenders," then the entire penal project deserved to be scrapped. Problems of space concerned the House committee in particular. Investigators had learned that the warden did not have nearly enough cells to impose solitary confinement and in any event made little or no effort to separate prisoners by age, offense, or duration of sentence. "Every night the murderer, the robber, the counterfeiter, are locked up with prisoners, whose light offences, by a ruinous policy, has consigned them to the same abode with the most infamous of mankind," complained Pitt. "Every effort of returning virtue is checked, every struggle of reviving honor is paralysed, all the suggestions of sensibility to shame, and all the resolutions of retrieving a character are overwhelmed by the nightly communications of confirmed depravity and narratives of successful vice."[75]

Vice, like a disease, seemed contagious. Once inside the prison's walls, anyone, even the mildest and most gentle of inmates, could become infected by the character of a hardened criminal. Juries increasingly petitioned the governor to release convicted felons for fear that incarceration in the penitentiary would only make matters worse. "We are induced to make this application for his pardon," one jury foreman wrote for a young thief in 1824. "We believe, that confinement in the penitentiary instead of being any service to the prisoner would on the contrary be attended with consequences injurious to him and society hereafter."[76] Niles himself grew disenchanted. "I have rather abandoned a hope I once entertained, of the general *reformation* of offenders, through the penitentiary system," he lamented in an 1829 resignation letter from the prison's board of directors. His worries sounded a familiar refrain: "Many badly-disposed persons, are, surely, rendered more wicked, by their associations here, and others seem to *calculate* on indemnifying themselves for their involuntary labor within the penitentiary, by fresh depredations on the public, when their periods of service shall have expired," he wrote. "Others leave the prison with what they suppose a fixed determination to live an honest life thereafter; but too many of these slide back into their old habits, return to intemperance, and again become violators of the law."[77]

Other penal advocates did not so easily give up hope. In 1828, a delegation consisting of one of the penitentiary's directors as well as its keeper and chief

clerk began a tour of northern prisons. The men sought ideas for how to improve their institution's system of discipline, and what they saw confirmed
suspicions that "the police regulations of the Maryland Penitentiary have
been inadequate to much improvement of morals." Auburn especially impressed the Marylanders. Its plan of "labour by day and solitary confinement
at night," concluded the delegation's final report, "is the best system that has
been devised for the punishment of criminals."[78] But adopting the Auburn
plan was easier said than done. The implementation of such an ambitious
agenda called for enormous resources, as Maryland's current penal architecture was ill suited to place prisoners in isolation from the outside world
and in complete silence for twenty-four hours. A new 1829 dormitory did
allow the keeper to segregate "the juvenile, the adult, and the incorrigible"
at night, yet he remained at the mercy of "the original disadvantages in the
arrangement and construction of the buildings," particularly in regard to
daytime discipline in the workshops.[79] As it existed before 1830, the Maryland Penitentiary simply afforded too many "opportunities of association"
between inmates.[80]

Reformers responded by crafting a new floor plan modeled on Auburn
Prison, which they hoped would direct "every Incitement . . . to the task of
reformation."[81] Currently constituted, the "scattered location of the buildings" in the prison rendered "constant supervision impracticable." The new
plan, in contrast, subjected convicts "wherever situated . . . to the same disciplinary influence." It called for a "concealed supervisor" lodged in "a central
position, with avenues radiating from his office," who could see all prisoners
at all times. This man, the warden, would act as "an apparent omnipresence,
an invisible all-seeing eye, whose gaze cannot be shunned, whose detection
cannot be avoided"—thereby preventing "mutual contamination," promoting "habits of industry and order," and assuring the "certainty of moral improvement" through a "rigid and constant surveillance."[82]

It took reformers almost a decade to build, but build it they did. In 1835,
after years of wrangling, state legislators approved construction on new
workshops in "three radiating buildings" as well as on "a central octago-
nal tower." The tower served as an "inspection lodge and keeper's office,"
and it connected to the three buildings by corridors that, at a "specified distance from the lodge," became "continuous with inspection avenues." Prison
guards, once the shops opened, watched the inmates through "loop holes
or apertures of observation." Inside the workshops were "lateral branches"
upon which other guards stood, "elevated above the level of the floor, so as

to afford an advantageous longitudinal view." Crews completed the north-ernmost of the buildings in November 1835, and in January of the next year they finished the westernmost. By early 1837 the prison was "in complete occupation throughout."[83]

As in Auburn, discipline was the centerpiece of the new prison's agenda. Aiming to instill in inmates the practices of good industry and patriarchy, the redesigned program called for continual surveillance to prevent prison-ers from speaking, physical labor to teach them proper work habits, and sex segregation to ensure that they understood the difference between the public and private spheres. Incarcerated men performed the type of manual labor that one day could earn them wages, while incarcerated women performed the type of housework that could one day make them good wives. The ad-ministrators of the Maryland Penitentiary joined other penal reformers who saw their work as the vanguard in enlightened liberal progress. To them, the prison represented the best means to ensure that all people, even the most wayward and wanton, could one day worship at the altar of property. Theirs was thus a hopeful task. "It is to be remembered," one set of directors reasoned, "that the great object of establishing the Maryland Penitentiary, was not to make it a source of revenue to the State, but an instrument for punishing the violators of our laws, and, if possible, converting them into better and useful citizens."[84]

Other asylums expanded upon the broader project of reformation, bring-ing disciplinary techniques to more than just criminals. The two most notable were the city's almshouse, which housed "paupers," and the state-run House of Refuge, which incarcerated "friendless and vicious children."[85] Each institution incorporated the punitive practices, reformative ideology, and preventive program of the penitentiary. Both attempted to create in-dustrious wageworkers and respectable heads of households. Together, the almshouse and House of Refuge gave "to the innocent that protection which they should be entitled to receive" all the while affording inmates an "op-portunity for reflection, and the formulation of resolutions for future good conduct."[86]

Opened in 1823, the Baltimore almshouse evolved over the next few de-cades into a reformatory concerned with remaking inmates into good wage earners and house workers. Its original purposes were myriad: the alms-house initially provided work for the unemployed, medicine for the sick, treatment for the mentally ill, discipline for the vagrant, and sanctuary for the homeless. And unlike inmates of the penitentiary, residents of the almshouse generally arrived willingly, albeit often out of desperate necessity. To gain entry, a potential resident needed to convince a local "ward manager for the poor" that his or her case was compellingly dire enough to warrant admission. Once safely inside he or she gained a place to sleep, three meals a day, and new undergarments to boot. Administrators charged inmates thirty cents for each day in residence, but nearly a quarter of the people who entered the almshouse walked away before paying off their debts. Administrators typically wrote off these costs as the unfortunate though unavoidable price of charity.[87]

During the 1830s, almshouse administrators grew as dissatisfied with their program as their police and prison counterparts grew with theirs. Their response, like that of penal reformers elsewhere, was to expose their residents to a regimen of systematic surveillance, physical labor, and social punishment. Upon the arrival of a new inmate, a clerk cataloged his or her personal information, including birthplace, length of residence in Baltimore, religion, and circumstance. Officials then forced that person, insofar as he or she was capable, to work. Such work routines were sex-segregated, as usual. The object, increasingly, was to teach men to earn wages and head households and to help women learn housework and be obedient dependents. According to one 1840s report, male residents worked as carpenters, tailors, weavers, stonemasons, wood sawyers, farmers, and hospital attendants, and female residents worked as washers, ironers, knitters, sewers, cooks, maids, and nurses.[88] Officials also hoped to secure a treadmill for those able yet unwilling to work but in the meantime satisfied themselves with the shower bath, a torturous water chamber used to punish inmates who had once absconded but recently returned.[89] Whereas coercive labor helped reform paupers into "useful and respectable members of society"— into good wageworkers and homemakers, in other words — disciplinary punishment blurred the line between pauper and prisoner. "The perpetuity of our free institutions depends upon the virtue and intelligence of the masses," argued another report. Because all people's "morals, for good or for evil, are coeval with [the] existence of the Republic," the almshouse, by making residents work, sought to transform indolent people into industrious men and women well served to participate in society.[90]

Such arguments about the state's capacity to create industrious workers and well-ordered households culminated with the House of Refuge, whose first stone was laid on October 27, 1851. For decades various Baltimoreans had argued for such an institution, if only to "take cognizance of vice in its embryo state" and "to anticipate crime, by arresting the first drawings of immorality."[91] As early as 1823, Baltimore-based political economist Daniel Raymond could be found arguing that "when a child or youth, under sixteen or eighteen, commits a crime, instead of inflicting that punishment provided for men, I would have them taken from their parents and placed under the care of some good master."[92] Two decades later reformers were still wondering, "How long shall it be until we have such an establishment where juvenile offenders may be punished?"[93] There were, after all, penal institutions to match up with other existing ails of society, such as pauperism and crime. But while "Alms Houses may be provided for the first and jails and penitentiaries may confer the older or more expert criminal," there was no "sufficient and infallible remedy found for the prevention or reform of juvenile delinquency."[94] Judges were forced to sentence youthful convicts into general prison populations, subjecting them to what contemporaries called the "baneful" and "corrupting" influence of hardened offenders.[95] "When a child is convicted of theft or other felony, and thrown into the common prison among the veterans in crime," surmised one editorial in 1838, "he is placed in a hot bed of villainy, where he soon loses all sense of moral rectitude, and becomes an adept in every species of roguery."[96] "Numerous cases, during the recent session of the city court," argued another, "demonstrate the importance of establishing an institution for the recipiency of juvenile violators of the law, where they will not be permitted to mix with old offenders, and thereby become confirmed rogues and vagabonds."[97]

Yet still the authorities dallied. Despite the many members of Baltimore's city council who were convinced that there was no "object more deserving the fostering protection and encouragement of the Corporation," the municipality possessed too few funds for a new penal institution dedicated exclusively to children.[98] Not until the 1850s, when the institutionalization of professional policing was in full swing, did the political will arise. By that point officials in Annapolis had grown so exhausted of Baltimore's stories of badly behaved boys and girls that they opted to fill the financial void themselves. State legislators hoped that a House of Refuge would be "not only *remedial* but *preventive*" and that it would serve both "the moral good of juvenile delinquents and the protection of the community."[99]

The House of Refuge opened its doors in Baltimore on December 5, 1855. Focusing "upon the very germ of crime," its officers gained the power to hold "all such children as shall be taken up and committed as street-beggars or vagrants, or shall be convicted of criminal offences."[100] They hoped, in the process, to provide for unruly youths "a parental sway and friendly guard-ianship" and desired greatly not to replicate "the repulsive appearance of a prison."[101] Discipline was nevertheless still paramount, and the architects adopted the prison's floor plan anyway, which revolved around "a main or central building, with radiating wings."[102] Guardians separated young law-breakers from society and classified them "according to their grades of char-acter," forcing each to perform manual labor while in residence. Supposedly "idle, willful, truant" when they arrived, inmates were to be "systematically educated, taught . . . some useful trade, or kept in regular employment, their old habits thoroughly broken up, and . . . taught to find even a pleasure in steady occupation."[103] The House of Refuge thus worked to ensure the rights of property by raising new property holders altogether. "We save men for so-ciety," exclaimed the institution's chief patron, Charles F. Mayer, "by raising [them] into government . . . through changed pursuits and engaging forms of industry."[104]

Just like the penitentiary and the almshouse, the House of Refuge wedded the liberal values of individualism, self-government, and property ownership to the disciplinary techniques of concealment, compulsion, and coercion. This seemingly paradoxical union was conceivable because a growing num-ber of property owners believed that reformative incarceration was the best means of punishment for a society predicated upon the preservation, and sanctity, of their property rights. As a growing number of Baltimoreans saw it, no other type of punishment could achieve that end. Prisons protected citizens by separating them from lawless people, and those institutions then attempted to transform those lawless people into good citizens. Prisons pro-tected wage earners and householders by transforming criminals into wage earners and householders too.

Nineteenth-century reformers in a variety of states used the penal sys-tem to target a wide range of people, and in Baltimore that project reached its zenith during the 1850s. The prison population expanded rapidly in that decade (see table 2.1). So too did the number of people admitted to the city's almshouse (see table 2.2). Meanwhile the House of Refuge, which did not exist at the decade's start, was accommodating close to three hundred inmates by its end. Dotting Baltimore's growing horizon, the penal system came to full fruition in the very years that the city introduced its new police force.

Such timing was hardly a coincidence. In concept, a reformative prison was a companion to the uniformed policeman. Both responded to the

TABLE 2.1. Maryland Penitentiary population, mid-nineteenth century

Year	Number of prisoners
1849	229
1851	282
1854	394
1857	415
1860	422

Source: Calculated from 1849, 1851, 1854, 1857, and 1860 Annual Reports of
the Maryland Penitentiary, Government Publications and Reports, MSA.

TABLE 2.2. Average annual Baltimore almshouse admissions,
mid-nineteenth century

Year	Number of admissions
1846–48	1,652
1856–58	2,211

Source: Table A in 1846, 1847, 1848, 1856, 1857, and 1858 Reports of the Trustees
for the Poor, appendices to the Ordinances of the Mayor and City Council of
Baltimore, DLR.

growing belief that "individual welfare is inseparably connected with . . .
the power and office of the constituted authorities," and both conferred new
power upon those authorities in the name of property.[105] If the policeman
worked to liberate the streets of disorder so that rights-bearing free men
could govern their properties as they wished, prisons taught inmates how
to bear rights and be free. The state's power to police rested upon a bedrock
of liberal values: together, the protective policeman and reformative prison
attempted to strip wayward people of their liberty so as to promote freedom
for all. "The citizens subject to the law are protected by it," observed Gustave
de Beaumont and Alexis de Tocqueville after their 1831 tour of American
prisons. "They only cease to be free when they become wicked."[106]

Mobtown in the Age of Reform

It is easy to read the introduction of a municipal police force and reformative penal system as part of a larger story in which public agencies grew at the expense of popular policing. The story seems obvious enough. Citizens who had traditionally participated in the policing of society alternatively restrained themselves and begged for help, while officials who once relied upon ordinary citizens to police the city and punish assailants gradually took over those jobs in the name of property rights. Thus did the popular justice of the early republican period give way to the professionally policed society of the late antebellum period and the policeman and prison replace the vigilante. In this reading, the days of Mobtown seem to have been numbered once police reform began in earnest.[107]

Events in the twentieth and early twenty-first centuries have only further reinforced this declensionist narrative of popular policing. Early professional police forces, many historians concede, were mostly incompetent and entirely corrupt, however new were their uniforms and regular their beats. Historians likewise observe that the utopian visions of penal reformers set early asylums up for failure. Individual reformation was far easier to achieve in theory than in practice, especially as state budgets grew tight and inmate populations exceeded the capacity of prisons to house them. In the early going, solitude was impossible to maintain, industry never touched enough prisoners, and recidivism remained high. But our histories often portray these early missteps as mere hiccups. Police forces in time became almost armies unto themselves. Prisons eventually abandoned the more naive strains of reformers' hopes for rehabilitation and settled into their status as the public authority's most visible specters of power. The American criminal justice system ultimately became, to use one scholar's words, the "sharpest weapon of oppressive government" conceivable in any society, let alone one predicated upon the consent of the governed.[108] These latter-day developments have made it almost impossible to read the story of state policing as anything but a fait accompli, a process of becoming whose only notable caveat was the halting and uneven nature of growth itself.

I would like to suggest a different narrative. The trouble with declensionist histories of popular policing — and, really, with all arguments that treat official and unofficial policing as if the two were mutually exclusive — is that they obscure why certain acts of popular policing persisted long after police institutions arose, as well as how the new institutions extended and even augmented some of the practices that preceded them under newly liberal logic. In fact, police forces in cities like Baltimore often looked very much like mobs, and that was not simply because the progress of reform faltered. Property holders helped author the police force and penal system as a bulwark to their own authority, but in nineteenth-century urban society, white wageworkers and householders counted as property holders too. As a result, the liberal police system empowered white workingmen to police and riot in fascinating ways.[109]

This was true from the outset. The Know-Nothing administrations that first implemented reform used police officers to support their own rowdies. Policemen arrested Democratic gang leaders, disarmed immigrant militia companies, and participated in the violence near voting windows. Sometimes they led mobs themselves. Democratic partisans regularly complained of "ill treatment" at the hands of the police and were not shy about expressing frustration when "the police beat me." It is no stretch to say that in 1850s Baltimore, the Know-Nothings' hold upon municipal power depended in large part upon these "legitimate" uses of brute force.[110]

Not all policemen joined the mob outright, but most stood aside while their plainclothed allies attacked civilians. Police indifference to the plight of political rivals manifested most obviously on election days, when policemen did little to halt nativist attacks upon Democratic voting rights. Consider, for instance, a November 1859 Election Day postmortem from the *Sun*:

> In the first ward Edward Cockey was badly stabbed with awls, and several persons seriously beaten. About half past ten o'clock a man named Kelly started up the hill to the polls, when about a hundred yards distant he was assailed by five men, one of whom dealt him a blow which felled him to the ground.... In the second ward the rowdies interfered with the election, compelled many naturalized citizens to vote their ticket. Wm. P. Preston, Esq., democratic candidate for Congress from the third district, was brutally beaten.... In the third ward Mr. Henry Herring, Jr., lumber inspector, No. 82 Bond street, went in behind the barricade to vote, and being pressed and jammed by the roughs, he staggered outside and fell dead.... A man named Dan Crothers was badly beaten.[111]

This was only an excerpt. According to the paper's correspondents, rowdies attacked Democratic voters and politicians in all twenty wards, and a few of the polls descended into "a scene of carnage." Insofar as policemen interfered at all, they usually arrested the Democratic victims.[112] Moreover, such incidents were common, as uniformed policemen fostered conditions for popular violence to flourish on days without any election. "A number of disorderly persons" destroyed William Pendergast's house on York Street a mere eight months after the introduction of the new police force, and no officers deterred the attack.[113] Elsewhere, Jacob Voglesang's store on the corner of Cross and Johnson Streets "was Surrounded by a gang of unlawful men" who demanded entrance, and when Voglesang refused, they commenced "breaking the transom over the door & throwing Bricks and other missiles and Smashing and demolishing all within their search." Again, no policemen helped turn back the assault.[114]

For all of the denunciations of disorder that propelled professionalization and reformative incarceration, police reform helped legitimize certain mobs. At first, to be sure, those mobs were mostly nativist. Both the Hinks and Swann administrations brazenly dressed their rowdies as policemen, and the ensuing fluidity between the police force and the political gangs lent the latter's violence an aura of legitimacy. Victimized Democrats argued that neither the nativist rowdies nor the Know-Nothing policemen were heroic guardians of the law — to say nothing of property rights — but in the process they confirmed just how similar the two groups were to each other. One Democratic witness to an 1859 riot testified with palpable disgust that "the police appeared to head the rowdies openly."[115]

Democrats, however, were not much better, as their frustration with rowdy policemen was soon revealed to be more political than principled. In late 1859 a group of "Reformers"— Democrats all — successfully lobbied the state's General Assembly to pass "the Baltimore Bills," a set of statutes that (among other things) transferred administration of Baltimore's police force to a new state-appointed board. The result was more patronage hiring, only now for the nativists' opponents. The Democratic police commissioners almost immediately replaced the Know-Nothings on the force with their own men, many of whom just happened to hail from Democratic gangs. And so the script flipped: if the Baltimore police force looked like a Know-Nothing mob during the late 1850s, it began to look like a Democratic mob by the early 1860s. Democratic policemen wasted little time arresting nativist gang members who had terrorized immigrants for the previous few years and happily joined sympathetic mobs when the opportunity arose. Meanwhile, the Democratic politicians who had spent the better part of the

1850s bemoaning the city's partisan police force now turned that same force against their political enemies without a qualm.[116]

Perhaps the clearest embrace of popular violence by the Democratic police occurred in April 1861, when a riot erupted over the arrival in downtown Baltimore of seventeen hundred Union troops. The soldiers hailed mostly from Massachusetts and were among the first responders to President Lincoln's April 15 call for volunteers. In order to get to Washington, they needed to change train stations in Baltimore — and the walk between the President Street Station where they arrived and the Camden Street Station from which they would depart was more than a mile along Pratt Street. It would be a long, hard walk. For several hours on April 19, thousands of Baltimoreans, a large majority of them Democrats, pelted the Massachusetts boys with cobblestones, beat them with clubs, and shot at them with pistols. The soldiers began running and only stopped to fire their muskets at whomever they suspected of having shot at them first. When they finally arrived at their station, they were greeted by another mob. "The scene was indescribably fearful," reported a correspondent for the *Sun*. Hundreds if not thousands of Baltimoreans charged the train, pressed their faces to the glass, and shot out the windows. By the time the soldiers were safely on their way to Washington — some three hours after they had arrived in the city — thirteen volunteers and twelve civilians were dead. Many more were injured.[117]

In the tense days that followed, the conceptual boundaries that separated the police force from the mob broke down completely. Hoping to forestall the passage of any more troops through the city, Baltimore's police commissioners ordered their men to burn the railroad bridges and fell the telegraph wires, effectively garrisoning the city as an enclave apart from the North. Meanwhile, rumors spread that additional soldiers from Pennsylvania and New York were on the way, and in an emergency session the city council appropriated half a million dollars "for the defense of the city."[118] Policemen helped enroll nearly fifteen thousand citizens into armed companies, a large number of whom had both participated in the riot and belonged to Democratic gangs. These citizen-soldiers were soon patrolling the city side by side with the uniformed officers. "By this means," wrote Mayor George William Brown years later, "the police [force was] supplemented [and] the disturbers of the peace became its defenders."[119]

So much ambiguity between police officers and gang members hints at how police reform derived from — not superseded — the extraordinary power of ordinary white men. The wealthiest Baltimoreans most clearly benefited from the added presence of officers on the streets and prisoners in the penitentiaries. This held across party lines. Many prominent Democrats, for instance, enjoyed police protection of both property and rights despite the Know-Nothings' hold on municipal power in the late 1850s. Likewise for respectable Know-Nothings after the Democrats regained control of the police force: they too benefited from police protection personally, even when they suffered politically.[120] Less obvious were the working-class white men who also profited under the aegis of reform. It was these men who policed the city in the age of police reform. Sometimes they did so as uniformed and paid professionals, working directly for the city; sometimes they did so as gang members and vigilantes. But however they policed, whether in the form of popular violence or as an expression of legitimate force, white working-men were critically invested in a police system dedicated to the protection of property, and that was because they were property holders too.

The rationalizations that rowdies used to explain away their violence all centered upon property, broadly conceived. Nativist gang members justi-fied the riots by decrying the immigrants who had depressed their earn-ings, stolen their jobs, and taken what was rightfully theirs. They portrayed themselves as respectable patriarchs who strove to put "a smile of approba-tion on the face of the mothers and daughters of the present day."[121] They also belittled their opponents as "black Democrats" who refused to vote a "white man's ticket." To hear certain Know-Nothings describe it, the distur-bances of the 1850s were mere expressions of the rights of industrious white men motivated by home and hearth. For their part, Democrats made simi-lar arguments. They frequently denounced Know-Nothings as racially sus-pect "black Republicans" and characterized their own violence in domestic terms. Speaking in support of the Pratt Street riot, one Democrat proclaimed that the attack upon the Massachusetts soldiers was intended to protect "our firesides, with all that is dear and valuable around us. We have every right to invoke the sanctity of the domestic altar."[122]

Such assertions of liberal victimhood were absurd considering the vio-lence wrought by the political gangs. A neutral observer would have scoffed at the notion that the rioters, to say nothing of the policemen who permitted their behavior, were property-protecting citizens who wanted only to up-hold the property rights of white men. After all, many white men numbered among the rioters' victims: thousands surrendered their rights, hundreds incurred terrible injuries, dozens lost their lives. The *effect* of rowdyism in

1850s Baltimore was illiberal by almost any definition of the term. But that does not make the professed motivations for the rowdyism illiberal too. No matter how much victims decried them, and no matter how reasonable were those victims' claims of loss, the people who enacted popular justice on Baltimore's 1850s streets were typically property holders seeking to protect what they believed was rightfully theirs. As historian Frank Towers has shown, Baltimore's political gangs (as well as their professional policing counterparts) consisted predominantly of skilled laborers who worked for wages in the manual trades. Most of them were married and heads of households. And all of them were white, born in either America or Europe. These men may not have been conventionally wealthy, but they were rich in other ways.[123]

The history of American policing is in a fundamental sense the history of an intimate, mutually reinforcing relationship between popular and professional policing. To view the two practices as always mutually exclusive is to miss the numerous ways that the state empowered property holders of all types to police, as well as how policemen themselves often behaved like rioters. It is true that the police force and penitentiary almost always served the interests of the very wealthy, sometimes to the detriment of everyone else. Yet when municipal and state officers built new police institutions, they opened the door for a wide range of individuals, especially white workingmen, to police as property holders as well. That policing has been rendered nearly invisible by its very legitimacy, by the sanctity of the public institutions erected in its name. It should be invisible no longer.

PART II

BLACK LIBERTY,
WHITE POWER

♦

—————— Chapter Three ——————

SECURING THE WORKPLACE

♦

INETEENTH-CENTURY Americans called Baltimore "Mobtown"
for good reason. The derisive nickname actually dated to the
early days of the War of 1812, when an angry crowd of Jefferso-
nians attacked a group of antiwar Federalists inside the city's jail, but the
moniker seemed no less appropriate over four decades later, when during
the 1850s mobs terrorized unsuspecting victims on the city's streets. In
those days triggers for violence were myriad, and the actors involved could
be diverse: Protestants and Catholics routinely fell into brawls; partisans
regularly assaulted members of the opposing party; rival fire companies frequently waged war outside of burning buildings.[1] And occasionally white
workers attacked black workers whom they accused of stealing their jobs.
This last display of collective violence — white workingmen assaulting black
workingmen — often occurred under the watchful eye of Baltimore's new
professional policemen.

A good example occurred in the summer of 1859, when work began on a
new brig in the east Baltimore neighborhood of Fells Point. White men were
hired to do the caulking for the vessel, but the company in charge of the construction had also contracted with black men to do the coppering. The choice
angered some among the local white community. Shortly after lunch on June
27, 1859, a handful of white men appeared at the dock and threatened the
black men there with summary justice if they did not halt their work. They
did not, and two hours later a much bigger group arrived. One of the city's
leading nativist rowdies, the president of south Baltimore's Know-Nothing
Tiger club, Joseph Edwards, stood in front of the crowd and ordered the black

men to stop working at once. Again, the men ignored the order. But this time, Edwards and his compatriots "fell upon them and beat several severely, and finally drove them from the work." A white witness to the fracas attempted to intervene but earned a harsh blow and several kicks to the abdomen for his trouble.[2] It was this attack on a white man that led to Edwards's arrest, but in the end the charges did not stick. Eight months later Edwards was again leading white workingmen's quest to monopolize Baltimore's shipbuilding industries for white men alone.[3] Edwards never stood trial for inflicting "severe wounds on several of the colored men."[4] In fact, he never faced any meaningful state-sanctioned punishment of any kind, for the policemen present at the tumultuous scenes on the docks did little to dissuade the aggressors from launching their assaults. Baltimore could not be Mobtown without police collusion.

The 1859 incident at a Fells Point shipyard revealed not only the political power of certain white workingmen but also the political weakness of most free black workers, particularly after the introduction of a professional police force. By the late 1850s white workingmen were commonly chasing skilled black workingmen from the docks and rail yards with the police's complicity. This was because the law did not treat all workers equally, even in an industrializing city where employers held much of the leverage and the vast majority of the people of color were free. Black workers were prolific in Baltimore, and the wages black Baltimoreans earned were meaningful evidence of their freedom, but from both legal and cultural perspectives they were also at a remarkable disadvantage when confronted by white rowdies. More times than not, policemen confirmed the disparity.

White gang violence owed its success to many different factors, but two of the most important were the advent of the wage doctrine, which defined wage earning as one of the primary bases for freedom, and the criminalization of black liberty, which most often materialized in the white majority's inability or unwillingness to view black people as industrious wage earners. These two trends together helped facilitate an alliance between white workingmen and the police force during interracial disputes in the labor market. Not all white workingmen could call upon favors from the police. In 1850s Baltimore, however, more than a few could, and that this was so meant that it was not employers alone who could deploy the violence of the municipality on their own behalf. What follows is an excavation of the roots of white workingmen's racial power and the unusual alliance that made it possible.

Wage Freedom

To understand why racial policing plagued Baltimore's late antebellum labor market, one must first understand the inclination of liberal thinkers and policy makers to commodify labor — one must grasp the growing tendency, that is, to define labor as a form of property that could be exchanged for money. "Labor is a commodity," wrote the Baltimore newspaper editor Hezekiah Niles in 1835, "and persons may dispose of, or purchase it, at [their] discretion, the same as bread and meat."[5] In the years to come, U.S. senators standing on the floors of Congress would echo Niles, as would lecturers speaking in lecture halls in front of large crowds.[6] By the middle of the century it had become almost axiomatic among economists, boosters, jurists, lawmakers, editors, and employers across the country that wages were subject to the rules of supply and demand and that "labor is a commodity in the market the same as anything else that is bought and sold for money."[7] The idea seemed simple enough. Governed by the laws of contract, labor was allegedly like any other tradable good. One could exchange it for a price. But this simple idea was also fraught with enormous meaning, for if the possession of property was a precondition for freedom, and if wages were a form of property, then the act of working for wages was nothing less than freedom itself.

The argument that wages equaled freedom relied upon several social fictions: employers and workers were akin to buyers and sellers who met in a marketplace; that market was fair; both groups were legal equals; all workers were male; and so on. But none of those was more fictive than the argument itself.[8] Like all ideas, wage freedom had a genealogy. Until the first few decades of the nineteenth century, most Americans considered wage earning to be a decidedly *un*free way to live. Eighteenth-century republicans in particular had argued that wage work signaled dependence, an absence of autonomy, the submission of one will to another. Well into the nineteenth century one could hear certain Americans decrying the commodification of labor as a "slavish doctrine, which reduces man to the condition of a brute.... [It] destroys individual independence, and makes the many dependent upon the few."[9] For a very long time, labor had not been a commodity.[10]

Yet social and economic changes during the nineteenth century rendered it increasingly necessary to recast wages as the basis for freedom, particularly in a growing city like Baltimore. Although in 1800 the majority of laboring Baltimoreans were either white skilled craftsmen (and their apprentices) or black slaves, free people of color and European immigrants flooded the labor market over the next sixty years. Large-scale factory production and the unskilled wage labor upon which it depended quickly caught and then surpassed the volume of Baltimore's skilled artisan production. In 1833, small workshops consisting of fewer than ten employees still produced 70 percent of the city's manufactured goods; by 1860, over half of the city's industrial workforce labored in factories that employed fifty or more employees. The workshop, in essence, became the factory, as many shops expanded in size. At the same time, Baltimore's small craftsmen began to disappear, leading to a decline in the total number of producers. Artisans continued to work in and around the city, but by the 1850s a laborer was more likely to be unskilled and working in a factory than skilled and at work in his own shop.[11]

Factory production did not entirely account for the growing ubiquity of wageworkers — not in Baltimore, and not elsewhere either. An 1829 essay written by the Bostonian Joseph Tuckerman suggests that there were many Americans, not just those toiling in large manufactories, who found themselves reliant upon wages for sustenance:

> The classes are very numerous, of those who are wholly dependent upon wages. They would, indeed, be numerous, if we looked for them among those only who have no trade.... This large division includes shop, market, and other porters; carmen; those who are employed in lading, and unlading vessels; wood-sawyers; hod-carriers; house servants; those employed by mechanics in a single branch of the business; and multitudes, who are men and women of any work, occasionally required in families, as washing, scouring, &c.; or on the wharves, or in the streets of the city. Besides these, the number is great of those, who are journeymen, and many of whom will never be anything but journeymen, in the various mechanic arts.[12]

The growing scale of wage work forced Americans in cities like Baltimore to confront the conundrum born of republican assumptions: too many white men were dependent upon wages. It was in this context that political economists and boosters began to redefine freedom.

The commodification of labor conversely made it necessary to eliminate bound wage work. Laws gradually decreed that it was an individual's right not only to choose an employer but also to quit a job. In England, the American iron manufacturer Abram Hewitt testified that "I have never known a master to go to court" in order to force a worker back to a job and argued that any legislation that purported to inflict such coercion was neither po-litically feasible nor legally desirable. Hewitt surely exaggerated, considering the stubborn persistence of apprenticeships and indentures in the American countryside, yet his words did highlight a trend: both apprenticeship and indentured servitude were disappearing from the statute books. Reformers worked with haste during the first half of the century to expunge any law held over from the British common law that imposed criminal sanctions against workers who left their employment without an employer's permis-sion. By the logic of wage freedom, the employee who needed such permis-sion was less an employee than a slave, and any employer whose permission was required was more a master than a boss. It was just this faith in the liberating potential of the wage contract that led one Maryland federal judge to categorize bound wage labor as "opposed to the principles of our free in-stitution and . . . repugnant to our feelings."[13]

Crucially, it was not just employers, policy makers, and boosters who de-fined wage work as freedom. Many of Baltimore's workers did too. A large number of these people were native-born white men, the individuals who formed much of the city's small yet growing middle-class workforce as well as a significant minority of its diverse working classes. A smaller number consisted of members of other groups—unskilled white, immigrant, and black men, as well as perhaps a handful of women. These workers' embrace of the wage doctrine was balanced by the myriad workers who continued to see the act of working for wages as a type of dependence. But there were nevertheless many working Baltimoreans who during the antebellum years began to consider themselves uniquely free in what was otherwise an unfree world. For these people, wage earning was less servile than empowering.

Male workers were best positioned to profit from the logic of the new political economy. In the abstract, the wage provided all men, and not just white men, with a rationale to head their own households full of dependents. Classical theorists had built the very idea of wage freedom out of a grammar of manhood. When Adam Smith waxed poetic about "liberal wages," he was thinking of an income large enough to allow a husband to support his wife and children. "A man must always live by his work, and his wages must at least be sufficient to maintain him," explained Smith. "They must even upon most occasions be somewhat more; otherwise it would be impossible for him to bring up a family."[14] Decades later John Stuart Mill argued pretty much the same thing. In the best-case scenario, wrote Mill, "the man's wages must be at least sufficient to support himself, a wife, and a number of children."[15]

Classical political economists like Smith and Mill believed patriarchy was a necessary precondition for the "freedom" of a cash-based economy and presumed that the free laborer was a male laborer.[16]

American boosters, commentators, and lecturers followed in the British theorists' footsteps by associating the husband with cash earning and the wife with dependency. "The more severe manual labors, the toils of the fields, the mechanics, the cares and burdens of mercantile business," espoused one Boston minister, all "devolve upon man." Women, meanwhile, were not supposed to work for wages at all. "The power of woman is in her dependence," explained a group of Congregational clergymen in Massachusetts. If she hoped to help her husband — and every woman was supposed to have a husband — a wife needed to devote herself to "those departments of life that form the character of individuals" while chastely demonstrating "that modesty and delicacy which is the charm of domestic life." By the standards of the day, a good man worked for wages and supported his family, and a good woman nurtured him after he returned home from a hard day's work.[17]

The wedding of wage earning with men's work was common across the nineteenth-century United States, especially in cities like Baltimore where growing numbers of people were forced to rely upon wages for subsistence. Trade unions, for example, routinely conflated "a new scale of prices" with a family wage.[18] The Beneficial Society of Journeymen Hatters sought not just "a fair compensation for labor" and an end to "that cruel injustice which wrings wealth from the brows of industry"; rather, its members also aimed "to be useful and meritorious citizens," to occupy "the position of men," and to demand "men's rights." In these workers' eyes, wages were "men's necessities" and the wage earner was obviously a man.[19] Other associations adopted similar language, such as when in 1844 the journeymen caulkers struck for a return to the wages they had enjoyed before the Panic of 1837, $1.50 per day. "We are poor men and want no more than enough to make a decent living for our families," the membership resolved.[20] Nine years later, when the society was again at odds with the master shipwrights of the city, little had changed in the way its members defined an acceptable wage. "The high price of all necessary articles of consumption, and the rise of rent, with that of our lost time in the course of a twelvemonth, render it nearly impossible for us to afford to ourselves and families the very poorest comforts of life," wrote James Jones, the association's secretary.[21] Only wages could guarantee subsistence, and in Baltimore, men were seen as the primary wage earners.

Early trade unions helped render the deeply gendered language of free labor ideology to workingmen. Most of them delivered a simple message: "We have a disposition to work whenever we can... and we will work for any man that will pay us, and it is well known, that we are trying to make an honest living for our families as well as for ourselves."[22] In theory, a trade association's enemies were monopolies and their political enablers who "combined to prevent labor and skill from receiving an adequate reward and a fair compensation for their services," and its friends were those decent employers who allowed hardworking men to earn "an honorable sustenance for themselves and for those whom God has placed in this world dependent upon them."[23] There was no in-between. A good employer paid men wages high enough to support a household; a bad employer did not. Yet there was more at stake than household subsistence alone in wage disputes between employers and employees. The boss who denied a worker his "manly and respectable" wage was treating that man like a slave or a servant— by denying that workingman a living wage, he was denying him the material basis for freedom itself.[24] Thus striking workers could simultaneously celebrate "America, commerce and freedom" and present themselves "not as the beggars come, imploring [potential employers] to give them bread without labor," but as "freemen and workmen" who sought good work for fair prices.[25] Wage work was evidence of freedom, and the men who earned good wages for their work were, by definition, free men.

Numerous women did work for wages in Baltimore. By the second decade of the nineteenth century, women headed almost a fifth of all households in the city's two biggest working-class neighborhoods, Old Town and Fells Point, and were well represented as householders in several others as well. In a dynamic city like Baltimore where so much labor was performed and so many different types of people worked for wages, anyone could be a breadwinner, women included. Propertied widows represented a sizable minority of the city's female householders, but most female-headed households belonged to poorer women like Margaret McNichols, a poor peddler who sold "a few trinkets" in support of "herself and two small children."[26] Women performed jobs ranging from keepers of boardinghouses, taverns, and shops to nurses, midwives, and teachers; from glove makers and cigar makers to distillers and fishmongers; from sausage dealers to seamstresses. And these were only the women with enough means for the directory compilers to notice. Still others, probably a majority, lived and worked out of official sight, beyond the margins. As historian Seth Rockman notes, hardworking, wage-earning women "were neither unanticipated nor invisible" in the growing city.[27]

The ubiquity of laboring women in nineteenth-century Baltimore did little to undermine the broader belief in female dependency, however. Patriarchal beliefs grew only more ingrained with time, often in direct tension with the reality of female wage earners. This was bad news for both female wage earners and the households that relied upon women's paid labor for subsistence. Society's larger presumption that Woman embodied the antithesis of the industrious, wage-earning Man helped justify wage inequality between the sexes. Women who worked in the same sectors as men typically earned substantially less than their male counterparts — a female teacher, for instance, took home half of what a male teacher earned — while the city's female-dominated fields, like sewing, generated wages so low that they would have been comical if the consequences were not so tragic. Since women were not supposed to be working for wages anyway, few labor radicals felt obliged to speak out on behalf of the countless numbers who did. On a related note, an overwhelming number of labor radicals were men.[28]

Wages allowed male workers to gain a new form of social authority from that of the preindustrial era. Whereas in the eighteenth century men generally claimed the resources upon which future generations depended (that is, land), in the nineteenth century they began to claim the resources upon which the present generation subsisted (that is, wages). The living wage replaced the family farm, and the breadwinner superseded the patriarch, but the end result was largely the same. It should therefore come as no surprise that so many skilled male workers embraced a wage regime that helped destroy the craft system upon which they had once relied for independence. In a man's world, a good wage provided a new form of power.[29]

Working Baltimoreans also embraced wage freedom for religious reasons. Evangelical Protestantism was an effective transmitter of liberal tenets, albeit in ambiguous and occasionally ambivalent ways. In Baltimore, evangelicals of all stripes, especially Methodists, preached the merits of self-discipline and hailed workers' capacity to transcend material circumstances through spiritual self-help. In one sense, such arguments indicated an uncertainty about liberal capitalism among people who called for the individual to subordinate himself or herself to something larger. They also implied an understandable hesitation among Christians to adopt the agenda of an economic system that provoked social dislocation and economic privation among hundreds of thousands, perhaps millions of people. Yet in another sense, exhortations of discipline fused easily with pleas for industry, and these pleas firmly placed the city's growing number of Protestants within a still faster growing cohort who believed that a man's labor demanded a breadwinner's price and that working for a wage counted as meaningful freedom. Evangelical Baltimoreans were not often unrepentant advocates of laissez-faire economics; their gospel was usually not the gospel of wealth. But neither were most of them communitarian radicals. Although they preached against the commodification of laborers, they felt comfortable calling labor a commodity.[30]

Protestant values mapped well onto craft unions' rhetoric, and in fact there was significant overlap between the membership of Baltimore's trade associations and the constituency of its various Methodist congregations. A large number of wage earners identified as Methodists, attended weekly church, and understood their economic agenda (that is, their fight for higher wages) in theological terms. The city's coopers cited scripture when in 1833 they struck for a breadwinning wage. Its hatters, led by Methodist Sabbatarian John H. W. Hawkins, did too. The Typographical Society included numerous active churchgoers as well as a few religious leaders whose print work brought them together in the name of better wages. But it was the butchers of Baltimore who most explicitly personified the wedding of evangelical morality and labor activism. Both the Baltimore Hide and Tallow Association and the Butchers' Association of Baltimore formed in the 1830s, and for the next decade groups like these followed Lewis Turner, an active Methodist, in fighting to protect the price of their labor — and with that price, the principle that labor was worthy of being called property. Shipwrights, carpenters, and tailors, too, all largely agreed with the local evangelical organ that argued that "justice between man and man" relied upon all men receiving "adequate compensation" for their labor.[31] At the same time, neither a pious nor an industrious man would ever "support the indolent and lazy."[32]

Leading evangelicals frequently weaved liberal ideals through their theological beliefs. A preponderance of local itinerant preachers focused, for instance, upon the salvation of individuals, for whom self-restraint was crucial. That was why Methodist preacher and former chair maker Henry Slicer expended so much energy criticizing individual sin when, on his circuit, he visited the factories and mill towns that surrounded Baltimore. It was also why he balanced calls for conversion with appeals for order. Preachers like Slicer believed earnestly in the importance of internal empowerment, in the ability of individuals to overcome obstacles through hard work and

moral living, and they regularly urged listeners to take a more active role in
controlling their own fates. Never mind the fact that most economic forces
operated outside any single individual's control and that no one, not even
the wealthiest of citizens, lived beyond the vicissitudes of the market. In the
evangelical lexicon, no one was destined to stay poor; in Slicer's sermons,
any man was capable of making his own luck. Championing discipline over
docility and autonomy over submission, a number of Baltimore's evangelical
religious leaders responded to the changing circumstances of the material
world with encouragement for congregants to find spiritual salvation within
and to develop the skills to survive life's hardships on their own, without
anyone else's help.[33]

The privileges of manhood and the ethos of evangelicalism combined to
make wage freedom attractive to large numbers of working Baltimoreans.
For these people, the wage purchased liberty and independence. Conversely,
the dependency endured by those who could not support themselves—
those who failed "to earn something more than what is precisely necessary
for their own maintenance," to use Adam Smith's words—seemed akin to
servitude.[34] Wages increasingly ensured *freedom* and precluded *slavery*. And
in Baltimore, a place with actual slaves, such reasoning could be extremely
powerful.

I do not mean to suggest that all wageworkers in Baltimore wholeheart-
edly accepted the liberal doctrines espoused by Adam Smith and others. A
great number of working people surely rejected the theory that their wages,
however generous or secure, made them as "free" as those who employed
them. Many skilled craftsmen also probably maintained the producerist
ideals of an earlier generation, when artisans proudly called themselves mechanics and celebrated the economic, political, and cultural independence
of their shops.[35] But people working for wages in Baltimore and elsewhere
confronted a remarkable set of obstacles if they wanted to upend the wage
regime altogether. The logic of wage freedom structured their lives; few
workers would willingly roll back the real advantages of the new economic
order. Wageworkers of all types rejected the label "servant," abhorred corporal punishment, and objected quite loudly to most of the disciplinary tac-
tics reminiscent of a bound labor regime.[36] In the process they also gave the
system their stamp of approval. The five hundred Irish laborers brought to
Maryland by the Chesapeake and Ohio Canal Company clearly saw utility
in the wage doctrine when, in 1829, they left the construction site for better
wages in Baltimore. The company angrily attempted to prosecute them as

runaways, but no jury would convict free people for choosing a different employer. It was a "free" country, after all.[37]

Indeed, many working people took wage freedom seriously, and among those who took it most seriously were black workers. Black workingmen especially embraced the notion that wage work epitomized the ideal of a free life. They were men, after all. "There was *no* reason why I should be the thrall of any man," wrote Frederick Douglass in his narrative autobiography. For months as a young man in 1830s Baltimore, Douglass had been "living among *freemen*" despite being enslaved. The jolting realization that one could work like a freeman for wages and yet not possess any right to enjoy those wages made Douglass's bondage feel all the more degrading. "I was now getting . . . a dollar and fifty cents per day," wrote Douglass. "I contracted for it, worked for it, earned it, collected it; it was paid to me, and it was *rightfully* my own; and yet, upon every returning Saturday night, this money — my own hard earnings, every cent of it — was demanded of me, and taken from me by Master Hugh. He did not own it; he had no hand in earning it."[38] Here, Douglass was highlighting one of the great indignities of slavery: that slave masters could claim their slaves' rightful wages. This made them lawful thieves. As the vexed Douglass remarked, "The right to take my earnings, was the right of the robber."[39]

It was all Douglass could do to restrain himself when each week he faced his master Hugh Auld and, through gritted teeth, forced himself to "pour the reward of my honest toil into [his] purse." Auld added insult to injury when he occasionally doled "out to me a sixpence or a shilling, with a view, perhaps, of kindling up my gratitude; but this practice had the opposite effect — it was an admission of *my right to the whole sum*." Despite Auld's best efforts, or partly because of them, the weekly pilfering was not lost on Douglass. It may not have been lost on Auld either. "The fact . . . that he gave me any part of my wages," Douglass later speculated, "was proof that he suspected that I had a right *to the whole of them*."[40]

Black workingmen like Douglass also subscribed to the gendered assumptions of the wage doctrine. Douglass himself attributed his political awakening to having lived in Baltimore "among *freemen*," employed the masculine language of rights, and wrote about the iniquities of slavery from a male perspective. Nor was Douglass the only Baltimore-bred race rebel to frame his argument that way. In 1859, as a re-enslavement movement erupted in Maryland, opponents mocked the measure's sponsors for being so frightened of a group of people "deprived of almost every right pertaining to manhood." Underwriting the argument was an axiom: black men lacked the rights of men. Racial egalitarians, as rare as they were in nineteenth-century Baltimore, wanted that to change. Douglass and his ilk believed that black redemption should look a lot like male wage freedom.[41]

At the same time, no group in Baltimore was as evangelical as the free black community. In church on Sundays, black congregants listened to preachers extol discipline, thrift, and industry and heard regular reminders of the importance of hard work and self-control. No less than in white churches, the theological message imbibed by worshippers in black churches cohered well with the values of the wage system. Free black men who sought entry into Baltimore's more respectable ranks recognized that social acceptance, insofar as such a thing was possible in a slave city, required that they conform to the industrious image of white liberal fantasies. Black Christians celebrated industry and hard work, too.[42]

Black workingmen, in other words, were probably as likely as white workingmen to equate wage work with freedom. They were men, and they were often evangelical. But we do not need to study their words alone in order to glean their ideologies; their actions are also open to scrutiny. In this case, their actions speak loudly: an overwhelming number of black Baltimoreans worked for wages as soon as they became free, and sometimes even before then. Slavery had initially defined the city's black population. At the time of the first federal census in 1790, enslaved black people in Baltimore Town outnumbered free black people by nearly a four-to-one margin, 1,255 to 323. Yet over the next ten years the free black population increased to 2,771, making it almost equal in size to the city's slave population. When combined with the stagnation of the slave population, such growth soon helped sever the ties between blackness and slavery in Baltimore. By 1830, when nearly 19,000 black Baltimoreans were counted among the city's 80,000 people, the large majority of them were free.[43]

Baltimore's large number of free black people were deeply embedded in the wage economy. While visiting Baltimore in 1835, the northern lexicographer and educator Ethan Allen Andrews remarked with some surprise that free black Baltimoreans were not "excluded from any trade or employment which may be practised by the whites."[44] Andrews was observing no less than capitalism in action. Although there were various statutes designed to regulate black economic activity, employers readily hired black workers so as to swell the labor market, drive down wages, and maximize profits.[45] The result was an urban workforce saturated with free black labor. Both black men and women performed some of the most thankless tasks in the dirty, industrializing city — digging ditches and cleaning streets, repairing gutters and sewers, dredging the harbor — and also entered skilled and semiskilled trades in large numbers. A passerby walking on Baltimore's bustling, noisy streets would have witnessed black people carting, draying, driving, brick-making, boot blacking, cigar making, potting, stonecutting, glue making, dyeing, rope making, sawing, rigging, and doing any number of jobs that required at least a modicum of skill. Depending on where he or she looked, that onlooker would also have noticed black workers, and black men especially, who labored as blacksmiths, tanners, barbers, coopers, shoemakers, carpenters, and butchers. Some black Baltimoreans ran oyster houses and diners; others oversaw their own retail shops; still others provided domestic labor in white households, workshops, and inns. Free black Baltimoreans worked all the time, and they usually did so for wages.[46]

Free black people were most prominently represented in the city's maritime industries. On the wharves, a black laborer who lacked a definable skill set might toil as a lowly stevedore, helping to unload a ship's cargo and carry it to market. In the shipyards, a skilled black craftsman might earn a more handsome wage as a caulker or carpenter. But whichever was the case, whatever the type of work they did, free black Baltimoreans frequently made their livelihoods near the water. Sometimes they found a wage on the water itself: more than a few functioned as seamen, cooks, and deckhands aboard the boats that arrived and departed daily from the city's harbor. So ubiquitous were black workers on the wharves and at the shipyards that these sites provided excellent cover for fugitives looking to escape slave catchers and survive away from home. Nowhere else in Baltimore could a black person so easily find wage work and pass as a free person.[47]

Much of this work was permissible under the cover of law. When he decided *Hughes v. Jackson* in 1858, the chief justice of the court of appeals, John Carroll LeGrand, was explicit about free black rights to make contracts, hold property, and earn wages in Maryland. "From the earliest history of the colony," LeGrand wrote, "free negroes have been allowed to sue in our courts and to hold property, both real and personal," and therefore deserved "means of defending their possessions" and protecting "their earnings." State law stripped free black people of their legal personhood in only two instances: when testifying against white people, which they could not do under any

circumstance, and in freedom suits, during which the presumption of servitude outweighed the presumption of freedom. In all other cases the statute
books took black freedom seriously. LeGrand certainly did.[48]

The justices on the court of appeals knew that people of color commonly
functioned as economic agents, especially in Baltimore. That much was obvious to anyone who spent time at the city's courthouse, where black Baltimoreans conducted a wide range of economic activities, from property
proceedings to licensing applications to estate planning. They frequently
secured gun, dog, and travel permits, conducted bankruptcy proceedings,
recorded property titles, indentured children, and incorporated churches.
Many got married. In one case a group of black caulkers formed a trade
union. In short, black Baltimoreans earned wages for work, however humble,
and with them built free lives worth living. The thousands of black Marylanders who poured into Baltimore during the first half of the nineteenth
century found meaningful freedom in the cash they earned for labor.[49]

Freedom for black Baltimoreans, then, amounted to the right to earn a
wage no less than it did for white Baltimoreans. And many from the city's
black population proudly worked for wages as free people. But this endorsement of the wage system, be it active or implicit, was also fraught with risk,
especially for black people in an age of institutionalized racism — for the
very system that championed wage work was also designed to punish failure.
In the wage economy, those individuals who failed to earn enough for themselves and their families confronted forms of compulsion that were as new as
the ideas that transformed labor into a commodity. So what was to happen
to the black people who did not manage to lift themselves seamlessly from
slavery to prosperity? What would the city do with its poorest population,
a group who faced more barriers to success than anyone else? What would
become of a people whose every autonomous economic act was greeted, it
seemed, with doubt and derision? Wages provided black Baltimoreans with
the currency of liberty, but in a world where race still mattered greatly, the
"free" labor market could also be an arbiter of black crime.

The Crime of Black Poverty

Beneath the wage system, supporting it and allowing it to thrive, there was
freedom. Many black Baltimoreans were free, at least in the economic sense.
For the most part, they worked as diligently for wages in nineteenth-century
Baltimore as did everyone else, filling the city's docks, rail yards, factories,

streets, and households with their labor. But the very act of paid labor perversely also subjected them to a malicious form of white scrutiny reserved for the free. Whether they worked in skilled professions or scrapped for work, whether they made good wages or bad, whether they even headed their own households, free black workers often looked like unreliable workers to white Baltimoreans. One of the reasons why the city's white workingmen acquired the power to police free black workers was because the architects of state policing criminalized black economic freedom.

In theory, any worker who, under the wage regime, failed to sustain himself or herself ran the risk of being labeled a criminal. According to the logic of the wage system, all workers were to rely upon themselves for survival regardless of seasonal patterns in the work cycle, structural changes in the economy, or sheer bad luck. Workers had no excuse if they failed; all explanations came back to them. Indeed, Baltimore's policy makers and boosters were adamant that mere "courage, patience . . . [and] mutual acts of charity and forbearance, alleviate the sorrows of the most difficult seasons in the life of labor" and that "time, by restoring trade and industry to their ordinary channels and avocations, does the rest." Anyone who suggested that poverty could be endemic was a liar. Anyone who argued that an industrious nature did not always guarantee a good wage was propagating "false theories of political economy."[50]

Fears of failure thus accompanied celebrations of the wage contract's liberation potential. It was quite common for advocates of the new political economy to lament that "a great portion of the pauperism of this country arises from a reluctance to labor."[51] In Baltimore as elsewhere, liberals accepted as a truism that "vagrancy and mendacity had become an art."[52] One story in the *Baltimore Sun*, for example, opined how "it cannot have escaped the observance of any one who reads our watch reports, that a very large majority of those who are taken in at night are white men who call themselves for lodgings." Although "humanity" mandated that night watchmen provide these impoverished souls with a place to sleep, the editor demanded that there be "some provision made to prevent [policemen] from being so continually plagued by the applications of loafers and vagrants — men who have no visible means of obtaining a livelihood."[53]

What most concerned boosters and economists, to say nothing of lawmakers and government officials, was that the wage regime would increase not just indolence but also crime. Too much freedom could be a bad thing. "This fearful increase of pauperism and crime under which our land is groaning," complained an 1836 report from a Maryland House of Delegates subcommittee, "*may* and *must* be found in the increased temptations which are thrown in the pathway of common life." To the committee members, freedom offered any number of enticements — from taverns and gambling dens to con men and prostitutes — to men who should otherwise have been working industriously. Freedom, in other words, was wonderful, but it made the appearance of loafers, vagrants, and criminals more likely.[54]

City officials did make occasional reference to the "worthy poor" but only as a rhetorical cudgel to highlight the inadequacy of most impoverished Baltimoreans. One almshouse report after another decried the ubiquity of "the worthless vagrants" relative to the "unfortunate poor" and begged for financial and other types of remedies to prevent the two groups from being housed together.[55] Insofar as they existed, members of the "virtuous poor" were the "insane white women," "the '*little children*' with their mothers and nurses," and "the most respectable aged women," a group of people they tenderly labeled "poor Old Ladies."[56] Almost all other poor people were, apparently, slothful. "The vagrants under commitment are mingled indiscriminately among the poor," moaned one 1844 report.[57] Ten years later, little had changed: "Another subject to which the attention of the Council is respectfully called is the bringing together in the occupancy of the same rooms, worthy paupers . . . with those who are at best vagrants, in many instances criminals unpunished, and rogues supported by the public benefaction."[58] This distinction between "worthy paupers" and "worthless vagrants" hinted at a potential recognition among elites that the capriciousness of an uncaring market could overcome any person, including the most industrious of workers, but it also suggested the frequency with which commentators, policy makers, and observers were prone to blame material misfortunate on any worker who failed to earn enough to thrive. Simply by being impoverished, the poor person was a "loathsome vagrant whose nature is so debauched by vicious excess as to make him a 'pest to society.'"[59]

So pervasive was the condemnation of poverty, and so obvious was society's fear of the "lazy pauper," that prisoners in the Maryland Penitentiary — and male prisoners especially — began to decry indolence in order to gain pardons. Any inmate who demonstrated that he once was or would now be "an industrious mechanic, following a laborious business," could potentially earn back his freedom.[60] James Curtain claimed he was "by profession a Victualler, and is and has been uniformly engaged, in that avocation." James B. Manner alleged that he was one of the "Mechanics of the city of

Baltimore." Richard McLean's "occupation is, and has been for many years that of a printer in said city." Frederick Kines promised that "if discharged never to engage in the like business — but to continue faithfully at his trade which is that of a victualler (*called Butcher*)." On it went, with petitioner after petitioner sounding the same paean to honest labor: Henry Williams was "a mechanic and an orderly citizen." John Thompson, "a practical mechanic," aimed to return to the "laborious business of a Blacksmith." All of these men and others to boot not only promised to continue the paths from which they had strayed but also assured officials that they would work industriously, correctly, and honestly "for a subsistence" if released from prison.[61] These petitioners were survivors who did what they needed to do to win back their freedom, but in the process they contributed to a belief system that equated poverty with criminality and unemployment with the committal of a crime.

There were two groups of workers whom Baltimore's lawmakers primarily associated with laziness, mendacity, and crime: immigrants, especially from Ireland though also from Germany, and free black people. In regard to the former, reformers focused intensely upon the supposedly "large proportion of paupers from other places."[62] City councilmen were not above speculating "that it has been the practice for some years in some of the parishes in the thickly inhabited countries of Europe, for all the inmates of their Alms Houses, to be sent to this country at the expense of the public."[63] Others fretted about ship captains who unloaded "paupers or such persons as are unable to provide subsistence for themselves" and deplored "the facility with which Emigrants of bad character may be thrust into this community."[64] Such assertions were almost always unfounded, but officials and commentators needed no evidence to make their claims. The impoverished nature of most newcomers, groups of people who were almost necessarily poor — why else emigrate? — provided evidence enough. Even Baltimoreans sympathetic to the immigrant's plight found themselves forced to confirm the assumption. In 1837, a member of the German Society responded to xenophobic concerns about his countrymen by assuring the city council that all recent German arrivals were neither convicts nor paupers but rather "Farmers, the other Mechanics, artists."[65]

More, though, than they worried about European governments sending them "all the inmates of their Alms Houses," lawmakers agonized about native-born free black people. That was because many white Baltimoreans believed blackness signified a constitution resistant to normal incentives. As early as 1819, newspaper editor Hezekiah Niles was asserting that "free negroes are necessarily without the *moral force* . . . to elevate their condition."[66] Elsewhere, he explained that "we, in the United States, are so accustomed to moral restraint, or moral force, that we do not appreciate its value as we ought." While "we live under a government of *laws*, we reverence their majesty, and at the call of the law, rally round its standard," black individuals, apparently, did not.[67] As far as Niles was concerned, people of color made "a thousand shifts rather than seek employment," preferred stealing to working, and found motivation solely from the slave master's lash, not from their own personal will.[68] He argued that the "simple liberation of the person of the negro does little for him — in many cases, we seriously believe, that he is injured by emancipation, and the condition of society is not advantaged in the least."[69]

Remarkably, Niles opposed not only slavery but colonization as well. The former he considered barbaric; the latter, impractical. His antagonism toward slavery and colonization nevertheless failed to translate into a faith in free black people themselves. He assumed that people of color required some form of police regulation; otherwise they would sink into abject poverty and be lost forever. "Too many will not work unless of daily necessity, hence they are commonly destitute of means," Niles intoned after an 1832 cholera epidemic wrought havoc on the city's free black community. A proponent of wage freedom and an opponent of racial slavery, Niles believed that black wage earners were degenerates, "more thoughtless and dissolute" than "the poorest class of whiter persons."[70]

Other commentators also questioned free black Baltimoreans' capacity to govern themselves, earn good wages, and live happy lives. Daniel Raymond was one of Baltimore's biggest proponents of wage freedom as well as the one-time president of the Maryland Abolition Society. He was a liberal, through and through. And yet he denounced people of color by reasoning that "nine out of ten" manumitted slaves, "so industrious and moral before" their liberty, "become vagabonds."[71] Another of the city's early abolitionists, Elisha Tyson, lectured black Baltimoreans about the lamentable "reflection that the misconduct of some amongst you . . . should afford ground for the assertion that you are unworthy of liberty."[72] The abolitionist publisher Benjamin Lundy meanwhile rationalized that "any slave who failed to save enough" to purchase his or her own freedom "is scarcely entitled to the enjoyment of civil liberty."[73] And the leaders of the state's colonization society estimated that freed slaves' "previous habits disqualify them often for proper exertions here for their own support."[74] Many of the city's professed opponents of slavery and believers in the "free" market doubted black Baltimoreans' capacity to work industriously for wages despite the fact that so many of them already did so.

Various white property owners joined the chorus by bemoaning the ubiquity of African Americans in Baltimore's economic sphere. Residents of the neighborhood surrounding the Lexington Market, for example, complained about disruptions "by parcels of Negroes and others, who are constantly making fires and cooking victuals during Market hours." Such irritations were particularly bothersome when "a Squabble ensues, and the whole neighborhood is disturbed."[75] Most of these annoyances were simply the result of people of color selling wares to make ends meet. But white Baltimoreans alleged that their black neighbors were breaking the law. Black people, according to some whites, were lecherous pests who were attracted to illegal hucksters. "The subscribers have been much annoyed of late … by the introduction of a class of hucksters" who had been selling used clothing without the requisite permits, announced one group of petitioners. To the great annoyance of everyone else, they were also attracting "drunken disorderly persons and crowds of people of color."[76] These complaints nourished broader assumptions that black people upset commerce, undermined hard work, and damaged society's productivity. Fears about black unworthiness for a wage economy focused upon black men in particular, which makes some sense; the discourse of wage freedom was also a discourse of manhood. A concern over black laziness would necessarily, almost naturally, manifest as concern over black men's laziness. Baltimore's newspapers regularly reported on the free black men who roamed the streets as vagrants, beggars, and loafers, that "most unfortunate class of all in a community" who refused to work and depended instead upon those who did. They portrayed the black male community as if it was populated almost entirely by gamblers, thieves, arsonists, and drunkards.[77]

Black Baltimoreans and their allies attempted to combat charges of their unfitness by imploring critics to account for the various burdens they bore while living, working, and saving in slavery's long shadow. "Give us the same stimulus to honesty, industry, and virtue," beseeched "A Colored Baltimorean" in Benjamin Lundy's *Genius of Universal Emancipation*. "If we fail," he allowed, "then brand us with epithets of thieves, vagrants, &c."[78] Another tactic was to direct appeals inward. Each spring the religious leaders of Baltimore's black community gathered together in conference, where they pledged their commitment to the principles of temperance, education, and spiritual uplift.[79] Both rhetorical methods, however, conceded black inferiority under present conditions, as well as the possibility that black men really were unfit for a wage economy. A more direct route was to challenge the notion that black people were inferior at all, notwithstanding the economic burdens they already bore. "The worst that can be said of them, as a class," railed a writer in the *Maryland Colonization Journal*, "is that they are idle and improvident — as thievish, perhaps, as others in like circumstances." Black allies suggested that insofar as there was anyone to blame for black poverty, it was dishonest employers: "How often too are their wages withheld, even by those claiming a respectable standing, or payment made in worthless trash, contracts broken with impunity?"[80]

Such pleas were like cries in a wilderness. Whatever the protestations of black Baltimoreans and their allies, a large number of white Baltimoreans saw black indolence, not industry. Workers who were "highly intelligent, honest, industrious, and obedient," wrote one skeptical white man in 1854, counted as part of a "class of colored servants rapidly decreasing and never numerous."[81] It did not help that black Baltimoreans were overwhelmingly poor. In the 1850s, black real estate owners accounted for less than half a percent of all black people in the city and less than one-tenth of a percent of the city's total population. Other numbers paint a bleaker picture still. In 1860, the average white person was worth almost $700; the average black person was, on the other hand, worth less than $25.[82] Black Baltimoreans worked hard and worked often and formed an important part of the city's labor market, but they were poor even by the standards of other black communities. The free black populations in both Philadelphia and Charleston, as well as in cities like New York and New Orleans, were richer both in aggregate and on a per capita basis than Baltimore's. In fact, of the fourteen biggest free black communities in the 1860 United States, free black Baltimoreans were the least likely to own property at all.[83]

Various factors explain why black Baltimoreans were so poor relative to white Baltimoreans, and one of the biggest was slavery. Although the institution was by no means omnipresent in the city — there were few slaves in Baltimore relative to the general population — its tentacles helped shape black life under freedom anyway. Acts of manumission, for instance, frequently took money from black Baltimoreans and gave it to whites, imposing a regressive redistribution of wealth out of the black community. That is because a large number of black people paid for their own freedom, while an even larger number helped purchase friends and family members. Such totals added up: too many free black Baltimoreans used their prime working years to earn wages that they later sent to white slave owners for their own and others' freedom.[84]

The experience of one working black family demonstrates the barriers to prosperity that slavery subtly inflicted upon Baltimore's free black community. Noah Davis was a shoemaker-turned-preacher who met his wife while both were still slaves, and over twenty-eight years the couple birthed nine children, seven of whom were born into slavery. In a family like this one, money was scarce. All available workers sent all available wages to white slave owners and creditors. "My wife's mistress agreed to sell to me my wife and our two youngest children," recounted Davis in his memoirs. "My salary was only three hundred dollars a year; but with hard exertion and close economy, together with my wife's taking in washing and going out a day's work, we were enabled by the first of the year, to pay the two hundred dollars our dear friend had loaned us" for the children's purchase.[85] Later, Davis managed to buy one of his sons with the help of an entire community:

> I thought it was possible, that I might find three hundred persons among my friends in Baltimore, who would contribute one dollar each to save my son, and that I might then obtain some friend in Baltimore to advance four hundred dollars, and let my son work it out with him: and give this friend a life insurance policy on the boy, as a security. This plan seemed practicable, and I wrote to his owners, asking for ten days to raise the money; which they granted me. I now got my case made known publicly to the different colored congregations in the city — and was very much surprised to find how many friends I had, and how kindly they engaged in helping me. The result of it was, that I obtained the three hundred dollars, and also a kind friend to advance the four hundred dollars, within the ten days, and recovered my son; who is now doing well, in working out the money advanced on him.[86]

Noah Davis and his wife confronted financial desperation on a daily basis as they scrapped, saved, and paid to liberate their children from slavery. And yet, like so many other black families in Baltimore, they were not completely successful. Despite a lifetime spent sending almost every resource to slave owners, the couple purchased just "five out of the seven in slavery. . . . Two are still in bondage." And they never escaped poverty.[87]

Noah Davis's story hints at how, despite the fact that so few slaves lived in Baltimore, the broader slave economy converted black wages into white capital. Free black Baltimoreans also confronted more obvious barriers in the labor market itself, where an occupational hierarchy that earmarked skilled positions for white men hampered black men's ability to accrue savings. "Just as free blacks appear to have been able to find ready employment in the city," writes historian Christopher Phillips, whose work on Baltimore's free black community remains one of the best accounts of any antebellum black community, "so did whites begin to restrict them to the most unskilled positions in Baltimore's work force." During the early decades of the nineteenth century, thousands of white sons from the countryside poured into the booming port in search of opportunity, and many of them already knew trades. The white proportion of the unskilled labor force subsequently dropped, and the proportion of white skilled labor increased in kind. Large numbers from among the city's unskilled white laborers meanwhile learned new skills in order to improve their lot, and they too entered trades — many of which were racially exclusive. A combination of white ambition and racism helped relegate many black workers to the meanest and poorest jobs in Baltimore.[88]

There was also the matter of immigration. As mentioned, Irish and German immigrants faced considerable hostility of their own, but their presence exacted a heavy toll upon black economic prospects all the same. As early as the mid-1830s, one visitor noted how "the Irish are fast encroaching upon the territory of the blacks."[89] A decade later, the proslavery John L. Carey observed that "here in Baltimore there are no ordinances excluding free negroes from particular occupations. The competition of white labor, however, mostly Irish and German, has driven the free negroes from many sorts of employment on Fell's Point, especially from the wharves and coal yards."[90] The colonizationist Robert Steuart agreed. "White labor has driven the black from many employments," sighed Steuart, "in consequence of the late rapid increase of German and Irish emigrants."[91] By the early 1850s, the steady trickle of immigrants arriving in the city had become a heavy flood, and each new arrival was, to use John H. B. Latrobe's words, "a sign and a warning" to free black workers. "In Baltimore, my home, ten years since, the shipping at Fell's Point was loaded by free colored stevedores," recalled Latrobe. "The labor at the coal yards was free colored labor. In the rural districts around Baltimore, the principal city of a slave State, free colored laborers, ten years since, got in the harvest, worked the mine banks, made the fences, and, indeed, supplied, to a great extent, all agricultural wants in this respect." Everything changed with the onslaught of European-born workers. Now "the white man stands in the black man's shoes; or else, is fast getting into them," concluded Latrobe. "And where, fifteen years ago, nearly all the signs above shop doors on Fell's Point showed English names — now two-thirds of them are German."[92]

Liberal commentators who ignored structural factors when it came to explaining black poverty compounded the error by ignoring black prosperity, too. One of the biggest silences in accounts of black economic ignorance is a lack of any reference to the real black wealth that existed in Baltimore — for not all black Baltimoreans were poor. Garrison Draper, a cigar maker, was worth around $1,200 in 1850, and when he died in 1864 he had $4,600 in stock and more than $2,500 in cash; the tailor Peter Dode opened a clothing store in which he employed seven people and had merchandise valued at $4,000; Robert Ross was a huckster who reported $2,000 in real estate; and so on. Black teachers, cabinetmakers, ministers, caterers, brickmakers, barbers, and store owners acquired capital during the antebellum decades, but to read men like Niles, one would think they did not exist.[93] Many white people simply saw the inadequacy of black economic behavior, full stop. If recently manumitted slaves were poor, it was because they had been thrust too soon into a world with "few inducements to good conduct; where they are surrounded by a thousand incentives to indolence and vice."[94] If Irish and German workers were stealing black jobs, it was because "of the physical inability, or to the comparatively idle habits of free blacks, who, in general, will not labor regularly."[95] And if individual black persons had worked hard for good incomes, they were the exception, not the rule.

The extraordinary discipline of black Baltimoreans who liberated themselves and their loved ones from slavery, to say nothing of the vibrant community they built once free, revealed the stereotype of black laziness for a pernicious lie. Yet although absurd, the stigma was tenacious. Free black people personified the workers about whom Baltimore's liberals most worried. In white eyes, they seemed more indolent than even the Irish, which was no small thing in a city where nativists would seize control of the municipality for several years. When the Baltimore Whig John Pendleton Kennedy bemoaned in 1821 to his colleagues in the House of Delegates that the "free black population [was] too high for communion with slaves[,] . . . too low for the associates of freemen," and incapable of competing "for work with . . . whites," he was merely expressing a popular sentiment that would grow stronger with time.[96]

Such a sentiment grew so strong, in fact, that lawmakers eventually acted on it. City councilmen spent the 1830s and 1840s passing new laws that prevented free black Baltimoreans from buying alcohol without a special permit, from trading with white people in a variety of sectors, and from selling specified commodities — such as corn, wheat, or tobacco — even to other black folks.[97] They also implemented a 10:00 p.m. curfew that had a distinctly economic bent; after the given hour, free black pedestrians had to carry passes that confirmed their industry when indolence would otherwise be assumed. By the 1850s, legal checks on black economic autonomy had intensified to the point that state lawmakers were requiring free persons of color to serve the full term of written contracts or else risk forfeiting the entire sum of their wages.[98] Such legislation sought to control free black workers, not re-enslave them. Black labor remained too important to the health of the local economy to eradicate completely, and in any event most of these "black codes" were only selectively enforced. Even the most racist of policy makers were forced to confront that which lawmakers in other southern cities had realized: attempts to collapse the legal distinction between free and enslaved black people were impossible without full re-enslavement, and free black labor was too valuable to do that.[99]

Instead, what these police regulations achieved was the creation of the separate legal category "free negro." Free people of color soon became what one *Sun* editorialist called "the creatures of the law — the beings of special statutes."[100] They possessed certain rights, deserved protection under the law, and collected wages for their work like other free people. At the same time, their rights were constrained, their protections were far from absolute, and their wages, at least when compared with the wages of whites, were considerably more insecure. Baltimore's criminal court judge Nicholas Brice put it well when he complained to Governor Joseph Kent about the anomalous status of so many black Baltimoreans and called them "a sort of middle class, neither slave nor free."[101]

It was no accident that the same white men who built freedom out of wages and celebrated the virtues of an open labor market worked to circumscribe black rights in the marketplace. Many of them were liberals, and they never stopped believing that they were working toward "a wise and necessary policy."[102] In their eyes, free black people were just too different to abide by the same legal code as white people. "The free negro population should be well and thoroughly controlled by efficient laws, to the end that it may be orderly, industrious and productive," proclaimed state senator James Alfred Pearce in the majority report of an 1859 "Slaveholder's Convention" that met in Baltimore. Pearce's report rejected re-enslavement. In the abstract, he and his colleagues advocated black freedom. Yet while they believed free black people deserved some legal protection from aggressive slaveholders, they argued that all people of color, even the free, required "well-regulated subordination."[103]

In short, free black people were disparaged, though not enslaved; free, but constrained. In Baltimore, they occupied a category unto themselves — and that mattered, if only because such an anomalous legal status perpetuated a disparity of legal power upon the streets. During the 1850s, when a uniformed police force appeared for the first time, the new policemen strove to keep the wage economy functioning smoothly. White workingmen often worked closely with police in this regard and frequently profited from the association. Black workingmen were not so fortunate.

Neither Slave nor Free in the Age of Free Labor

Toiling for wages in a place like antebellum Baltimore was hard work. It sometimes meant leading the type of life that could fall apart at a moment's notice, whether because of something as general as an economic downturn or as specific as a capricious supervisor; it usually meant performing arduous labor for little compensation; it always meant hoping against all odds that employers would resist the urge to exploit a crowded marketplace to their advantage. Many of Baltimore's employers did not resist that urge. They treated laborers as interchangeable parts, driving down wages in the process, and proved more than willing to allow people of different ages, ethnicities, sexes, legal statuses, and races to compete for a handful of positions. Nor did they always discriminate about which workers performed which labor so long as the work in question got done quickly and cheaply. Employers' willingness to flood the labor market with as many people as possible plunged numerous wageworkers into desperate economic circumstances, for the supply of labor almost always outstretched its demand.[104]

That said, employers' devotion to a large and diverse labor force did not make all workers in Baltimore the same — not in city officials' eyes, not in liberal commentators' eyes, not in their own eyes. Real differences divided the city's multitude of wage earners from each other, and one of the most important markers of difference was race. Race often helped determine whom the police protected and whose plight they ignored. White workingmen, particularly the native born, benefited from a close relationship with policemen, not only enjoying their approval during strikes but also exploiting their allegiance during job-busting actions. Black workingmen, in contrast, suffered mightily as policemen turned a blind eye on growing levels of white violence in the workplace. Race had long divided workers in Baltimore. What changed during the 1850s was the municipality's alliance with white workingmen through police reform.

Recall that many workingmen espoused the principles of wage freedom no less than did liberal boosters. Such an embrace was more than a rhetorical ploy to rationalize a tough existence. It was not uncommon, for instance, for white workingmen to enlist the municipality's help during their work actions. The most notable incident occurred during the Seal Strike of May 1857, when conductors for the B&O Railroad blockaded the tracks west of the city in the hope of dissuading the company from holding them liable for all theft from the cars. In that case, policemen resisted management's call to disperse the picketers. Many of the strikers were members of the same Know-Nothing gangs that helped supply the police force with its men, and the police's sympathy lay with the workers. Another strike occurred two years later, and this time two hundred white workingmen who wanted higher pay walked off a track construction job. Once again, the city's police officers ignored management's appeal to intervene. In the first action the state militia broke the strike without the city police force's help; the second ended with the employers' capitulation and a pay hike. Whatever their outcomes, however, both cases provide a glimpse of the close and mutually supportive relationship between white workingmen and city policemen.[105]

Certain workers were thus capable of marshaling state power on their own behalf. Conditions had to be right for this to happen, of course. The workers in question needed not only to be wage earners worthy of being called "free" but also to share ethnic traits with the policemen in question. Baltimore's Know-Nothing police force accordingly helped native white workingmen, not Irishmen, during the labor strife of the late 1850s. But even under these precise conditions the relationship between workers and policemen is notable, if for no other reason than because it reveals the police to be something more than the weaponized arm of capital. Policemen were supposed to arrest paupers and vagrants, but we would do well to remember that many white workingmen were neither paupers nor vagrants.

Put another way, those workingmen who most successfully hailed themselves as independent wage earners were capable of deploying considerable power under the aegis of the state. This was why labor leaders desperately described their ranks "not as the beggars come, imploring you to give them bread without labor, but ... as freemen and workmen."[106] This too was why pious Protestants defined justice as good wages and proclaimed that they would never "support the indolent and lazy."[107] Workingmen who spoke in liberal terms were submitting to the logic of the wage system, but they were also reaching for power. And power, during the age of slavery, was overtly racialized.

By the time Baltimore's municipal authorities introduced a new police force, the collective desire among skilled white workingmen to monopolize the trades for themselves was quite old. White attempts to overtake free black workingmen dated to the 1830s, when "riots" erupted episodically along the B&O Railroad line. In August 1831, a group of Irishmen attacked black workers in New Market, Maryland, about thirty-five miles west of the city. Authorities arrested twenty of the alleged ringleaders, but some four hundred Irish workers freed their friends from jail and authorities sought no convictions. Three years later, near Georgetown, armed German rail workers on the Washington branch of the B&O assaulted black laborers "who were content with the wages paid to them." The Germans, evidently, were less content with the pay, and they blamed their black coworkers for driving down the price of labor.[108]

That decade, violence also exploded in the city's shipyards, where a mixture of free and enslaved black workers, a few of them quite skilled, labored alongside a motley crew of white ethnics of varying skill sets. Frederick Douglass was one of the black workers in 1836. Apprenticed as a caulker to William Gardiner, a master Fells Point shipbuilder who was operating under a tight deadline to produce two large vessels for the Mexican government, the teenage Douglass found himself overworked and at the beck and call of seventy-five different white men. "My situation was a most trying one," recalled Douglass.[109] It was also a dangerous one. "All at once," Douglass continued, "the white carpenters knocked off, and swore that they would no longer work on the same stage with free negroes. Taking advantage of the heavy contract resting upon Mr. Gardiner ... they swore they would not strike another blow for him, unless he would discharge his free colored workmen." Douglass was a slave, and the carpenters' demands should not have concerned him. Yet "the spirit which it awakened was one of malice and bitterness, towards colored people *generally*," and so he suffered along "with the rest, and suffered severely." One day, four white apprentices attacked Douglass in broad daylight:

> The attack was made suddenly, and simultaneously. One came in front, armed with a brick; there was one at each side, and one behind, and they closed up around me. I was struck on all sides; and, while I was attending to those in front, I received a blow on my head, from behind, dealt with a heavy hand-spike. I was completely stunned by the blow, and fell, heavily, on the ground, among the timbers. Taking advantage of my fall, they rushed upon me, and began to pound me with their fists. I let them lay on, for a while ... but, finally, getting tired of that sport, I gave a sudden surge, and, despite their weight, I rose to my hands and knees. Just as I did this, one of their number (I know not which) planted a blow with his boot in my left eye, which, for a time, seemed to have burst my eyeball. When they saw my eye completely closed, my face covered with blood, and I staggering under the stunning blows they had given me, they left me.[110]

What most shocked Douglass was the "not fewer than fifty white men" who stood by, watching, doing nothing to help. Insofar as they did anything at all, these onlookers yelled encouragement to his attackers: "Kill him — kill him — kill the d —— d nigger! Knock his brains out — he struck a white person." This was the third incident in which Douglass almost lost his life at Gardiner's shipyard, and by that point he had learned that the best recourse was to run. To fight back, he wrote, "was death, by Lynch law. . . . The whole sentiment of Baltimore was murderous." So he ran.[111]

Such incidents were more harbingers than signifiers, as few employers allowed their labor forces to become exclusively white during the 1830s. During the 1850s, however, police reform helped spur white workingmen to violently close ranks against their free black competitors.[112] In one case, thirty or so white men in 1858 assaulted the black men employed at two local brickyards. According to a witness, the white rowdies resorted to this action "for the purpose of driving out the colored employees, and supplanting them in their places." In this they were successful: the mob forced the black bricklayers "to run for their lives — pistols, and in several instances guns being fired upon them." Henry Thomas, an owner of one of the yards, called upon the recently established police for help, but the policemen took their time in arriving, and by the time they finally did the black workers had scattered. "So much were their fears exercised," reported a *Sun* correspondent, "that it was with the greatest difficulty they could be collected again." The next day both yards lay completely idle, "the demonstrations of the former day having deterred many of the colored hands from resuming work."[113]

More sustained was the violence at the nearby Federal Hill shipyards, which employed mostly black workforces in what was otherwise a white working-class neighborhood. The problems revolved around caulking. In early Baltimore, caulking was one of the few skilled trades dominated by black men. This bothered white workingmen, and for years they agitated to earn entry into the trade. By the end of the 1850s their efforts began to bear fruit. The first shipbuilder to capitulate to white demands was J. T. Fardy, who advertised in May 1858: "WANTED — Several good (white) CAULKERS."[114] Fardy's advertisement was a spark. In the days that followed, "a number of dissatisfied white men" attacked black caulkers at other south Baltimore shipyards, all in the hope of driving the workers from the trade, or at least out of the city where they plied said trade. Also notable was the rowdies' political affiliation: the riotous white workingmen were led by south Baltimore's Tiger gang, a nativist club whose currency was violence and whose allegiance was to the city's then-ruling American Party. "Several of the caulkers belonging to the ship-yard of A. J. Robinson, Esq., (late Hoopers,) have been attacked going to and from their work, and severely beaten," reported the *Sun*.[115]

Robinson and his fellow shipbuilders remained disinclined to allow laborers of any race to determine the constitution of their workforces, let alone to dictate (however implicitly) the price of labor. And so, like many property holders before them, they applied to the municipality for help. Mayor Thomas Swann agreed with the angry shipbuilders, at least superficially. He announced that his police marshal would deploy a group of officers to serve as the black caulkers' protectors, as well as to secure the yards (and rights) of his petitioners. But Swann was a Know-Nothing, the shipyard owners were Democrats, and the white men clamoring to expel the black caulkers constituted Swann's rank and file. Several of the neighborhood's policemen, meanwhile, were actual members of the Tiger club. Perhaps, then, it should be unsurprising that the policemen whom the authorities deployed did not secure the yards: "At 6 o'clock, however, as the workmen were giving in their

Fardy and Auld's Shipyard, oil canvas by William Hare, ca. 1854.
The scene shows the city's harbor, and on the Federal Hill shore a building
identified as Fardy and Auld's Shipbuilders, which by the late 1850s
had begun to transition to all-white caulking crews.
Courtesy of the Maryland Historical Society.

time at the office, they were assaulted by a party of men between forty and
fifty strong, and most unmercifully pelted with stones, and beaten with
clubs," read the report the next morning. Several of the caulkers sought refuge in the office, where they locked the door and sealed the windows. But no
matter—"they were forced open by the mob outside, and the refugees beaten
like the others and compelled to run for their lives. One was followed and
beaten down with a club, and another was badly stabbed, and last evening it
was feared that he would bleed to death."[116] This was on June 9, 1858. At Robinson's site the following morning, none of the black workers showed up for
work. Robinson was compelled to hire white caulkers in order to complete a
vessel whose contract was soon due.[117]

White caulkers intended to make Fardy's exclusionary exception the general rule. "For several months past," explained an observer, Fardy and his
associates "have employed none but white caulkers. The object of the attack
on the yard of Mr. Robinson is avowed to be the expulsion of the colored

caulkers, and the substitution in their places of white workmen." Expelling black caulkers, however, also necessitated attacking white men. During the excitement, a gang surrounded Robinson's white foreman, threatening to lynch him. One of the members of the crowd actually brought a rope. The group decided against using it only after the foreman begged "in piteous and humiliating terms for his life." Other rowdies chased one of the shipbuilders who deigned to hire black workers through the yards, stoning and insulting him "with almost every vile epithet" as they went.[118] What began as an attack on black caulkers ended as an attack on white shipbuilders and eventually proved disastrous for the shipbuilding industry in south Baltimore as a whole.[119] One of the largest shipbuilding companies in the area suspended operations, removed all books and papers from the premises, and turned its operations over to the municipality until the violence subsided. As for the black caulkers, so great was their fear — and so pitiful was their police protection — that most of them left Baltimore to seek work elsewhere.[120]

These and other workplace assaults reveal the power that certain white workingmen possessed on worksites in 1850s Baltimore and the stigma that free black men bore as workers. Not all policemen protected white vigilantes and ignored free black rights, but in general the introduction of a professional, uniformed police force empowered particular white workingmen to attack skilled free black workers with impunity. The reason why was twofold. On the one hand, native-born white workers allied with the political party in power during the late 1850s, the Know-Nothings. Indeed, the group most responsible for the job-busting riots was south Baltimore's Tiger gang, a nativist collection of white men who also counted ten policemen among their ranks. Many of the caulking jobs abandoned by black Baltimoreans eventually fell to Tiger club members, or to their relatives and friends. Political alliances between the Tigers and the Know-Nothing city government prompted the police to ignore black workers' calls for help and allow white rioters to take control of multiple shipyards.[121] On the other hand, black workers were at a considerable disadvantage because of their legal status and cultural stigma. The former prevented them from testifying in court against any of their white attackers, while the latter justified their violent removal from the labor market. Native-born white workingmen attacked other types of workers during the era of police reform — the Irish come to mind — but no group suffered more at their hands than did free black men.

The impact of the 1850s job-busting riots upon the free black community was significant, as the violence on the docks and railways helped drive black workers from well-paying jobs and install white workers, predominantly native-born men, in their place. Whereas before 1850 black skilled labor was scarce, it became even scarcer by the end of the decade; and whereas in 1850 black semiskilled labor had been somewhat more common, it was less so by 1860. Not only did the number of black caulkers in the city decline from 75 to 63, but also the number of black butchers fell by 7, carpenters by 13, sawyers by 99, shoemakers by 13, and shopkeepers by 8. Baltimore's unskilled occupations also witnessed a drop in black employment; there were 228 more black laborers and 118 more black washers in 1850 than in 1860.[122] All told, the data show a reduction in overall black employment during the 1850s despite the growth of the city's population by nearly 50,000 people. Of the twenty-five leading black occupations in the city, only seven saw a gain in black workers. In each of the other eighteen trades, black participation dwindled. More than 500 black workers left the labor force during the 1850s, bringing the total number of black people employed in the city's twenty-five leading black occupations down from 2,554 to 2,024. [123]

It was no coincidence that native-born white workingmen launched their assault upon free black workers just as police reform reached full fruition. The uniformed officers who began patrolling the streets in the 1850s served not only to ensure that people were working but also to ensure that the *correct* people were working. White workingmen were evidently the correct people. However much free black Baltimoreans cherished the wages that made them free, liberal lawmakers and politicians generally interpreted their work lives as failures, undermined their rights, and oversaw a police force that turned a blind eye on the gangs of white men who attacked them. Racial discrimination and violence in turn triggered a vicious cycle: black poverty confirmed black indolence, which authorized legal discrimination, which legitimized white workplace violence, which exacerbated black poverty. The new police force was created to protect property rights, yet its officers primarily protected the rights of those white workingmen whom members of the city government considered political allies. As such, Baltimore City's new policemen played a critical role in making the city's workforce whiter.

The combination of legal discrimination, white violence, and police indifference did not drive free black Baltimoreans from the labor market entirely. Black caulkers, albeit in lower numbers, continued to work on the north side of the harbor through the war years, and most of the city's free black residents continued to toil as laborers, carters, porters, bricklayers, and barbers, just to name a few. Whatever the reasons free people of color stayed in Baltimore — perhaps their work was still lucrative; perhaps loved ones lived nearby; perhaps children or spouses remained enslaved; perhaps their communities were in Baltimore; perhaps white benefactors promised help; perhaps, even, the unknown specter of a new life in a strange place proved too frightening — they continued to try "quietly and diligently... to make an honest livelihood."[124] Black work was usually hard and hardly glamorous, but for those who lived in a world of racial slavery, the wages were something to cherish, however small and insecure they might have been. Even constrained freedom was meaningful, and in 1860 nearly twenty-six thousand black Baltimoreans were free.

Yet the events of the 1850s were also worrying, for they portended a troubled relationship between black people and the police. Reformers saw the uniformed men on the beat as a solution to popular violence and a salve to imperiled property rights, but from black Baltimoreans' point of view policemen promised little relief at all. If anything, the policeman seemed to empower the white vigilante, not curb his excesses. Still more concerning was the logic that underwrote this system in the first place. Despite the presence of thousands of black wage earners in Baltimore, many whites, including numerous white liberals, derided black workers as lacking "the *moral force*... to elevate their condition."[125] By the 1850s the free black worker looked to many whites like the paradigmatic "lazy pauper," and that stigma helped to justify the official apathy that greeted white workplace violence against an otherwise free group of people. White power and black condemnation ultimately went hand in hand. The very stigma that rationalized free black Baltimoreans' legal disabilities also gave white Baltimoreans the power to push them out of their jobs. And that, in the end, was a tragedy.

——— *Chapter Four* ———

PROTECTING THE
HOUSEHOLD

◆

FREE BLACK MEN'S violent expulsion from the labor market was particularly visible because contemporaries were most inclined to define black inferiority in terms of industry. "Freedom with them," explained one of Maryland's leading critics of black liberty, "is synonymous with idleness, [and] idleness begets vice to an alarming extent."[1] Many white Baltimoreans thus believed that black men's supposed indolence legitimated violence in the workplace. But racial policing also extended to the household. When white vigilantes attacked black Baltimoreans, they drove not only allegedly lazy paupers from their jobs but allegedly irresponsible patriarchs from their homes. Black men who hoped to earn a living wage faced a growing set of violent hurdles in the city's labor market. Those who desired to protect their households as husbands, fathers, and brothers confronted obstacles as well.

While police reform heightened free black wageworkers' exposure to white job-busting actions, it also helped render free black householders vulnerable to white home invasions. Highlighting such vulnerabilities does not require overstating them. Most black households in Baltimore survived the antebellum years without a burglary, kidnapping, or assault. Nor were free black householders ever completely without rights, even in the face of white male aggression. Yet for those who did endure such violence, the very policemen introduced to protect property rights sometimes ignored their plight — or, worse, participated in the crimes themselves. And that is telling, if only because it underscores the dominant legal culture's ambivalent treatment of black freedom. Black Baltimoreans' home lives were vulnerable because professional policeman did not, and usually could not, treat free black householders as truly free.[2]

Police reform was implemented in the name of property, and households often counted as male property. Free black households, however, fit into this system somewhat uncomfortably. Ordinarily poor, they bore a stigma that was not unlike that borne by other poor households, and so one may be forgiven for assuming that in antebellum Baltimore black householders endured the typical poor person's fate. They did not. Police regulations targeted specifically at black families combined with the prohibition of black testimony against white people not just to undermine black household autonomy but also to heighten white male power over black households. When a white person entered a black home, there was not much the policeman could do, even if he wanted to. There was not much that the householder could do.

The policing of black households in antebellum Baltimore relied upon informal white power no less than it did upon formal state power, a curious fact that owed to the law's treatment of the free black population as a people in-between. Black patriarchs engendered no shortage of contempt. They were often poor, and like other poor men they relied upon alternative household arrangements to survive a wage economy that paid little mind to bourgeois norms of respectability. But they were also black, and for them elitist contempt manifested in special ways. During the antebellum years, Baltimore's free black householders found themselves uniquely susceptible to white violence.

Household Autonomy

Understanding the fraught relationship between policemen and black households in antebellum Baltimore first requires appreciating the importance of household autonomy to liberal definitions of freedom. For many Americans, the right to head a household was equally important as the right to earn a wage. Historically, in fact, earning a wage and heading a household formed two sides of the same conceptual coin. The famed English jurist William Blackstone equated the two, identifying those contracts "for any valuable consideration" to be those conducted "for marriage, for money, for work done."[3] Early American political economists likewise blurred the line between the wage and marriage contracts by distinguishing them from all others: these, in preindustrial times, were the two contracts that constituted the basis for domestic relations.[4] In liberal theory, the free individual maintained what Blackstone called "despotic dominion" over both his labor and dependents.[5]

Many antebellum Americans similarly defined freedom as the right not only to earn a living wage but also to head an autonomous household. It did not matter whether those Americans opposed or supported slavery, either: for anyone schooled in the language of nineteenth-century freedom, wage earning and householding went together. Abolitionists like Angelina Grimké denounced slavery, for instance, by equating wives with wages. "The Code Noir of the South," she wrote, robbed slaves "of wages, wives, children, and friends."[6] Frederick Douglass made the same connection in an 1849 speech, cataloging these horrors of slavery: "To buy and sell . . . human beings, to rob them of all the just rewards of their labor . . . to blot out the institution of marriage."[7] Opponents of slavery like Grimké and Douglass defined the slave's condition as being "shrouded in the midnight ignorance of the infernal system . . . compelled to toil without wages," as well as being a "husband, powerless; no right to his wife."[8] Interestingly, proponents of slavery did much the same thing when responding to the abolitionists. They asserted, for example, that emancipation would inevitably lead to the liberation of wives from their husbands' patriarchal control. That made white men's ownership of black men's wages the bedrock of white male household authority. In the proslavery worldview, to control the terms of other men's labor necessitated the control over those men's households.[9]

Slavery was crucial to the nineteenth-century American definition of freedom, for describing what the freeman must have and always be able to do necessitated identifying what the slave did not have and never could do. And no slave could lay claim to wages and a wife. Americans across the United States, across the political spectrum, across even the slavery debate, embraced a gendered vision of freedom that wed ownership of labor to ownership of a household.[10] Proslavery ideologues would not have disagreed with Grimké's assertion that slavery "robs the slave of all his rights as a man." In their view, that was precisely slavery's point: they called it a "domestic institution" for a reason.

Contemporaries called the ideal household "respectable," but that was just another word for patriarchal, as the respectable household brought together a group of people under a single roof and subsumed their identities under the male household head. Wives, children, apprentices, servants, and slaves were all, in this ideal household, legally dependent upon the man. In turn, that man was a free individual who participated in the polity as a good citizen. Freedom was increasingly predicated upon a unique set of privileges to own property, cast votes, and coerce dependents to do one's bidding. The respectable household ideal built the citizen's political independence and property rights out of a man's patriarchal power: having dependents effectively made the male householder a sovereign individual. Not just Baltimoreans subscribed to this fantasy of household order, either. Everywhere in America, in one way or another, members of a growing middle class endorsed some form of it as well.[11]

The rise of the respectable household ideal was not unrelated to the gendered definition of the wage doctrine. From economists to ordinary men and women, early Americans depicted men's cash earning as the whole of the economic system and wage work as the whole of the labor system. As both a visible form of labor and a vital component of the market economy, housework gradually disappeared behind the domestic veil and took its dependent practitioners with it.[12] Meanwhile, laws in every state, including in Maryland, limited voting rights to white men and restricted married women from owning property. These laws essentially codified the common-law system of coverture, which absorbed a woman into her husband's legal and economic persona and granted him the civic presence that, upon marriage, she lost.[13] The respectable household thus vested adult men with considerable power. Gendered divisions of labor, separate spheres, and a domestic realm into which dependents disappeared and out of which householders emerged as autonomous, rights-bearing individuals were its most defining characteristics.

And in Baltimore, few groups were as invested in the respectable household ideal than free African Americans. One need only look at the actions taken after manumission to see how important black Baltimoreans thought household autonomy was. During the first few decades of the nineteenth century they started families, purchased property, and put down roots in prodigious numbers. The households they established were overwhelmingly male-headed, too, and became more so over time. Whereas in 1790 two-thirds of the city's free black householders were male, by 1830 three-fourths were. Such a ratio compared favorably to the numbers from other free black communities; even in Philadelphia, home to one of the most vibrant black communities in the nation, men headed just over seven-tenths of black households during the 1830s. The same could be said for two-parent house-

TABLE 4.1. Value of property held by Baltimore's blacks

Year	Black property holders	Total value of black property	Average value of black property holding
1813	59	$7,843.00	$132.93
1836–38	307	$157,100.00	$511.73
1860	348	$449,138.00	$1,290.63

Source: J. Wright, *Free Negro in Maryland*, 184.

holds. By 1850, more than four-fifths of Baltimore's black households were two-parent affairs, a higher figure than that of Philadelphia, where during the late 1830s just under four-fifths of black households were overseen by two parents. The growth of two-parent, male-headed households in ante-bellum Baltimore spoke not only to the importance that free people of color ascribed to family relations but also to the power of bourgeois social norms. Almost immediately upon gaining freedom, black Baltimoreans embraced the family structures that characterized the respectable household ideal.[14]

Black Baltimoreans were eager to create independent home lives rooted in marriage and property ownership, and the city's religious institutions helped with the former. No sooner had certain couples acquired freedom than a clergyman would marry them in a Baltimore church. Some couples did not even wait for both members to reach freedom. So tenacious were black Baltimoreans in their desire to start families, and so liberal were certain congregations in the city — particularly the Methodists — that ordained ministers occasionally officiated the marriage ceremonies for enslaved people too.[15] Wages, in the meantime, helped many black Baltimoreans purchase property. In their various trades, free black workers slogged, saved, and sacrificed, and as they did the value of property holdings within the black community grew (see table 4.1).

The city's most typical black home owner resided in a brick two-story row house that sat somewhere along the city's outskirts to the east or west. Although modest, these homes marked a step up from earlier decades, when the majority of Baltimore's tiny class of black home owners lived in smaller, less sturdy frame dwellings.[16] Home ownership among black residents became more common as the years passed: by the 1850s, there were hundreds of black Baltimoreans who owned their own homes. Fifty years earlier there had been merely dozens. Still, not unlike in white society, a handful of people began to consolidate this wealth, particularly by midcentury. At the start of the 1850s, 338 black people possessed a total of $289,492 in property—an admittedly small sum by white standards, but a sum nonetheless. By decade's end, 348 black Baltimoreans held $449,138 in property. A 3 percent increase in property holders accounted for a 55 percent upsurge in property holdings.[17]

Black men's attachment to household autonomy was exemplary but not unique. White men also defined freedom in such terms, and so too, crucially, did municipal officials. One can see the municipality's desire to create independent and free households most clearly in the actions of its police officers. When a father proved unable to keep his dependents safely at home and out of sight, a policeman could provide a stabilizing influence. In one late 1857 case, a Baltimore County resident named Helmsteter "called upon" Officer King of the middle district of police, whom he implored to help find his daughter. The girl had recently run away, and Helmsteter feared that she had become a prostitute somewhere in the city. In fact she had: Helmsteter and King soon found her in a brothel on Fell Street. The father, weeping at the sight before him, begged the girl to return home, but she was unimpressed and refused, "apparently happy in the miserable career of life she had chosen." King then involved himself. Cloaked in official authority, the policeman proved much more persuasive. At the appearance of a uniformed officer the girl abandoned her resolve and within minutes chose a new path "on the way to those who mourn her error." Her example showed that what a father could not achieve, a police officer sometimes could.[18]

More often policemen protected householders from external attacks like the ones William French endured. For several nights in January 1859, rowdies stoned the French home, breaking most of the windows. One evening, French's wife went to the door in response to a call of fire. She "was saluted by a shower of stones, one of which struck her in the back, and another knocked one of her children down." The middle district police captain dispatched three officers to defend French and his family, and after several frustrating evenings during which they detected but could not catch the offenders, the officers "went in disguise." When the attacks resumed, "they sallied out in different directions, and arrested three men." Nobody in the neighborhood understood why the assailants had chosen the French household, but the reasons did not matter to the police marshal. His job was simple, and he did it. Having given "orders to guard the premises, and arrest all parties who are suspected of being engaged in the attack," he saw to it that household order was restored.[19]

One of the ways that policemen acknowledged male power in the home was by deferring to patriarchs once they stepped inside a patriarch's front door. Certain policemen transgressed this norm only to discover the limits of their authority. In September 1861, police officers Foard and Sutton responded to a call at the Strausberger home on Harrison Street and confronted Strausberger's two sons. For reasons unknown, one of the policemen drew his gun, and in response one of the boys drew his; the two policemen then quickly disarmed the boy and arrested him. Several days later, however, both officers found themselves in custody "on warrants issued by Justice Bayzand, charging them with assault on two youths . . . at the residence of their father." Behind the doors of his own house, Strausberger was the only man garbed in the authority to discipline his own sons. Once the officers entered his home, they had become guests compelled by law to abide by his power. And when they did not, they became intruders.[20]

While policemen were charged with protecting householders from unseen threats, the criminal court employed equally coercive measures in the name of patriarchy. Sometimes jurists actually compelled men to become patriarchs. In one remarkable instance, a judge forced Patrick Quinn into a marriage he did not want. Quinn's story, as it were, had begun with a pledge: he had promised to marry a woman soon after the two had settled in Baltimore. Unfortunately, instead of fulfilling his commitment he had soon fled, with one of the woman's shawls disappearing with him. Suspicion pointed to him, and his former fiancée offered him an ultimatum: either agree to marry or go to jail. Quinn refused to marry. In response, the girl visited a justice of the peace and asked him to issue a warrant for theft, and not long thereafter "Patrick was arrested and in due form of law committed to jail for trial." Patrick Quinn suddenly underwent a change of heart. He concluded that life as a husband was less burdensome than life as a convict, repented of both his theft and flight, and uttered a confession so convincing that the judge substituted a marriage license for the arrest warrant and married the couple right there in the jail. Once the two had become one, Mrs. Quinn no longer possessed a right to bear witness against Quinn. The couple departed, "he with the promise to love, cherish, and protect her, and she happy in the knowledge that by the loss of a shawl she had gained a husband."[21]

Quinn's case illustrated how the state's investment in patriarchy could work for as well as against men, sometimes at once. The court bullied Quinn into an unwanted marriage even as it endowed him with considerable power once within it. Conversely, the law both provided opportunity for the scorned woman to coerce her delinquent beau and stripped her of rights through marriage. There was real power here for patriarchs: power over dependents, power over women and children, power over their own households. But that power was available only to those who subscribed to a very particular vision of household order.

Patrick Quinn learned this the hard way, but he was not alone. Inmates in the city's penal asylums were forced to adhere to a disciplinary regimen designed to teach them the values of respectable household order as well. The Maryland Penitentiary, for example, incorporated an exclusively female department, headed by a "matron."[22] "No men can visit the women, unless they're in the company of the inspectors," read the rules, "and no women can visit the men, unless it is for religious instruction."[23] Housed separately, female prisoners were also dressed differently. They wore gowns, for one thing, which distinguished them from the male prisoners, who sported trousers, shirts, and overalls.[24] Also in contrast to the male inmates, who worked in manufacturing shops, female inmates learned to spool, bind shoes, sew, knit, and wash clothes.[25] Whereas men were trained in the practices of wage labor, women learned housework and piecework — and that they learned such work at all in a prison system that financially sustained itself through inmates' paid labor speaks to the centrality of the institution's patriarchal ethos.[26] The penitentiary aimed to mold female prisoners into good domestics. If their labor earned none of the financial rewards that male labor brought, so be it. Such a division of labor was crucial to the development of well-ordered households, respectable householders, and the dependents who helped make them free.

Likewise, the House of Refuge sought to combine the punitive program of the penitentiary with the domestic stability of the family. More than other asylums, the refuge emphasized the respectable household ideal, incorporating sex segregation into all facets of daily life.[27] Boys and girls each received their own school, complete with their own classes.[28] In 1860 they received their own dormitories, too.[29] From its 1855 opening onward, male inmates labored primarily as artisans — shoemakers, tailors, bakers, and so on — and as engineers, farmers, and police attendants in the church, classrooms, and dorms. The few girls in the institution sewed.[30] Because its basic objective was "the reclamation of the young delinquent and his restoration to society, where in manhood he may take his place among the good and virtuous

TABLE 4.2. Percentage of boys in the House of Refuge, mid-nineteenth century

Year	Total residents	Male residents	Percentage male
1857	173	156	90.2
1858	219	212	96.8
1859	281	258	91.8
1860	318	281	88.4

Source: Calculated from table 1, Superintendent's Report, Seventh (1857), Eighth (1858), Ninth (1859), and Tenth (1860) Annual Reports of the Managers of the House of Refuge, EPFL.

and become a useful and honest citizen," the House of Refuge also sought to re-create actual households for its still-impressionable, mostly male inmates by attempting to color its punitive discipline with domestic nurture.[31] The directors organized a "Ladies Committee" to provide the maternal influence supposedly missing from the inmates' lives, not to mention from other penal institutions' disciplinary regimens. Like good mothers, these women were supposed to exhibit "a desire to be present with . . . a sympathizing heart whenever the occasion may require it."[32] In the meantime, when an inmate was sent to a new home, he received not only a new father but a mother and siblings as well so that he could be "quite domesticated in the family," a prerequisite for his later becoming "a good citizen."[33]

This emphasis upon "manhood" and "good citizens" underscored the fact that, for all of its sex segregation, the House of Refuge was primarily a male project. When it opened, the refuge initially held 19 children, 6 of whom were girls. But a year later, when 185 children resided there, 147 of them (about four-fifths) were male.[34] Boys' preponderance among the residents actually increased in the years to come, and by 1860 the House of Refuge was unequivocally, overwhelmingly, a male institution (see table 4.2). Indeed, it was the boys whom the institution's architects most wanted to reform. Their goal, and really the penal system's broader goal, was to create good men whose own future sons would be as respectable as their fathers were once corrupt.

And the prisoners knew this. To prove that they were fit to rejoin society as productive citizens, inmates in Baltimore's various penal asylums usually

begged for pardon using a vocabulary of fatherhood. One Frederick Warner, a delinquent father and husband, assured the governor that he would
never again shrug his patriarchal obligations and that if released he would
perform his duties and perform them well.[35] Other men took a similar tack
by invoking their dependents in their pardon petitions. Stephen Deaver's
jurors appealed for the murderous assailant's pardon in the name of "his
large family and his general good character."[36] Petitioners portrayed David
Holmes, a convicted thief, "as an honest industrious man, with a large family
to support."[37] Others appealed for another thief, twenty-three-year-old William Wilkinson, "in consideration of his young wife, now in a most delicate
condition, and his aged and respectable mother."[38] It did not matter what
the crime was; the inmate and his allies almost always sought release on
these grounds. James Wright wrote on behalf of his good friend Charles Torrey, the New England abolitionist imprisoned after helping Maryland slaves
escape north. Torrey deserved his freedom, argued Wright, not because he
had committed no crime but because he must return "to his amiable and
respected wife & his two lovely children. . . . It is very desirable on account
of his lonely *family* that he should be set at liberty." Like others, Torrey could
restore the order of his household if he was released.[39]

Prisoners wanted to be free, and there was no better way for them to re-
gain their freedom than to speak the language of fatherhood. Whether or not
public officials successfully stabilized existing households or created well-
ordered new ones was, however, beside the point. Simply by subscribing to
a gendered vision of freedom, police officers and penal institutions together
underwrote a legal culture in which patriarchs possessed remarkable power
within their households, in the privacy of their own homes. One temperance
editorial beautifully articulated the importance of private power in liberal
society. "The distinction we take to drunkenness, we take to be this," explained the writer. "That in the *public streets* it is a *public* offence — that in a
man's own dwelling it is a *private* affair."[40] And therein lay the significance
of official devotion to respectable households: a man's business inside his
domicile, where he was armed with the power of the state itself, was his own
concern. At home, he could do almost anything he wanted.

A man's household authority was precisely what liberals designed the police system to protect in the first place. They wanted fathers, husbands, and
brothers to maintain order at home and discipline their dependents when
the situation called for it. And so this is what householders did: whether
through corporal punishment, confinement, or some other means, male

Baltimoreans forcibly maintained their households' internal peace. Legal historians have made clear that "the power to protect the family's welfare against threats from the inside, through discipline," was long a critical component of household governance, while women's historians have made clear that nowhere else was a man's power more important and complete under the liberal law than within the household inside of which he crafted his political independence. For a man, to surrender power over one's household was akin to surrendering freedom itself. Male power was a primary expression of household autonomy.[41]

Statistics from police and penal institutions hint at how big a role internal household policing played in the maintenance of Baltimore's late antebellum social order. Dependents rarely appear in these institutions' annual reports. For instance, in the state's penitentiary, the vast majority of prisoners throughout the 1850s were men. New male arrivals usually constituted 90 percent of all convicts sent to prison. Women never accounted for more than a tenth of the prison's population, and they often accounted for significantly less than that (see table 4.3). To a lesser extent, men also constituted most of the prisoners in the city's jail. In any given year between 1840 and 1858, women usually accounted for under a fourth or fifth of the number of people committed (see table 4.4). In Baltimore, it was primarily men who went to jail.

Perceptive observers noticed women's absence from the penal system. After having visited the country's various penal asylums, including the Maryland Penitentiary, Alexis de Tocqueville and Gustave de Beaumont surmised that "this fact must be ascribed above all, to the small number of crimes committed by [women]."[42] It could have been that. More likely, though, the explanation owed to women's social inferiority and political exclusion, not to their natural goodness. "There may be times and cases in which husbands are very strongly provoked," wrote one court reporter after witnessing the exoneration of an abusive husband.[43] As it happened, at the city's jail the admissions officers did not even use domestic abuse (or anything approximating the term) as a category when they recorded the crimes of incoming inmates, suggesting that few men were ever actually charged with assaulting their wives.[44] The absence of both abused women and abusive men from penal records hinted at an ugly truth: while the state punished many husbands behind prison walls, many husbands punished their wives behind front doors.

Men's domestic power also looked outward. The corollary to the maintenance of internal household discipline was the protection of households

TABLE 4.3. Men in the Maryland Penitentiary, mid-nineteenth century

Year	Total	Male share of new prisoners (%)	Male share of total prisoners (%)
1851	282	91.47	92.55
1854	394	88.81	92.39
1857	415	90.58	90.84
1860	422	93.55	94.79

Source: Calculated from 1851, 1854, 1857, and 1860 Annual Reports of the Maryland Penitentiary, Government Publications and Reports, MSA.

TABLE 4.4. Male Baltimore city jail commitments, mid-nineteenth century

Year	Total jail commitments	Male share of commitments (%)
1840	1,730	80.75
1846	2,173	76.30
1852	2,031	82.27
1858	4,952	77.50

Source: Calculated from 1840, 1846, 1852, and 1858 Jail Reports, appendices to the Ordinances of the Mayor and City Council of Baltimore, DLR.

from external threats, and men in Baltimore dutifully guarded their homes from "all such scamps" who threatened to destroy their property.[45] At night, they looked "to the security of the fastenings of their premises," often armed and primed to kill the burglar whom they could detect but not catch.[46] They fought for their dependents, from their wives to their children to their slaves, repelling anyone from their homes whom they labeled a threat.[47] They received "intruders" in the usual way: as "the gentleman of the house [who] took up a pistol."[48] Not to be outdone, commercial property owners vigilantly protected their establishments as well, treating their stores like castles. Shopkeepers chased, caught, and reprimanded suspected shoplifters while bar owners defended their premises from drunken, violent customers.[49] In one case, the proprietor of a Light Street tavern shot at a group of seven or eight young men who had refused him payment, broken his windows, and threatened the other people reveling inside. Afterward, the marshal of police expressed his determination "to arrest every one of the assailants of the house." He approved of the aggrieved man's actions and was only sorry that he could not do more.[50]

Men also retaliated for wrongs done to their dependents, and it was in these moments that the state's investment in patriarchy became most evident. Richard Wheeler, for instance, was exonerated after castrating a ten-year-old black boy whom he accused of assaulting his six-year-old daughter. Members of the grand jury, although compelled to vote for trial, petitioned the governor for a nolle prosequi on the grounds that the father's act represented not a crime but "exemplary vengeance upon the miserable culprit." Wheeler's neighbors and friends also expressed "unspeakable indignation at the act of a wretch whose crime was appropriately punished." To use the words of one of Wheeler's petitioners, "vengeance was an attribute of sovereignty"—and in Baltimore vengeance often belonged to fathers. We will never know what happened between the ten-year-old and the six-year-old; what we do know is that Wheeler never went to trial.[51]

John Stump, on the other hand, did go to trial, but he was acquitted for killing the man whom he alleged had raped his younger sister. The girl was mentally disabled, explained defense attorney Coleman Yellott to the jury, and for years she had been Stump's "especial object of affection." When Stump discovered the (alleged) rape, he had become "agonized—maddened—phrenzied," and with blood "on fire" and images of his aging, tearful parents dancing before his eyes, he killed "the monster who had committed the awful crime." Someone soon afterward found the dead body of Stump's uncle in the garden, and Stump *was* the killer, conceded Yellott. But the circumstances rendered the killing "justified by the laws of nature and the laws of man." The lawyer laid out the case:

> When an individual enters into society—there is a compact made between him and society. He stipulates to surrender up a portion of his natural rights. He gives up the right of self-redress. This is his part of the compact. In consideration of this,—society contracts to protect him in the enjoyment of his social and natural rights, and to give him adequate redress in all cases where those rights may be violated. Here

then is the compact. Where it is faithfully performed by one party, then the other has no right to violate it. But if one party fails to perform the compact in any particular, in so far the other is released from the obligation of a strict observance. If society has failed to protect one of its members in his natural rights, — he has a right to that extent such member may resort to his natural right of self-redress. In such event, the compact between him and society, is *pro hac vice* dissolved, and he falls back upon his natural rights.

... She — society — having committed the first breach of compact — having failed to protect, has no right to punish.[52]

Translated, Stump's sister was Stump's property, and the crime against her was a violation of his property rights. The act of vengeance was hence legal. Yet such an act could be legal only because Stump was a free man whose property rights rested upon a bedrock of male domestic power: "Whatever may be the common law of England," concluded Yellott, "this is the common law of American freemen." The members of the jury, twelve freemen themselves, readily agreed. Acting "as husbands, as fathers, as brothers," the jurors returned a not guilty verdict in just under fifteen minutes.[53]

Internally, household power was almost as available to black men as it was to white men. Data from the jail show, for example, that the authorities committed black women on criminal charges only slightly less rarely than they did white women, which made the inmates in that institution overwhelmingly male. Women of both races usually faced discipline, whatever it was and whatever it was for, at home (see table 4.5). Black children also went to jail infrequently during the antebellum period. In the typical year, fewer than two dozen black juveniles would end up in jail, a considerably smaller total, in fact, than the number of white juveniles usually committed. These numbers suggest that black men no less than white men punished (and policed) their dependents behind closed doors.[54]

For their part, black patriarchs took their roles as householders quite seriously. They believed with some validity that their right to an independent household, while not always absolute, gave them the voice "of an American citizen, and a freeman of Maryland."[55] The black community's most eloquent opponent to colonization actually used his household as evidence for why free black Baltimoreans should stay home and forsake the uncertainty of a life in Liberia. Writing under the pseudonym "A Colored Baltimorean" in the antislavery *Genius of Universal Emancipation*, William Watkins asked,

TABLE 4.5. Female Baltimore city jail commitments,
mid-nineteenth century

Year	White female (%)	Black female (%)	Male-to-female ratio
1840	7.6	10.4	2.4
1846	8.3	10.0	2.3
1852	4.1	7.3	2.2
1858	10.1	8.5	1.5

Source: Calculated from the 1840, 1846, 1852, and 1858 Jail Reports, appendices to the Ordinances of the Mayor and City Council of Baltimore, DLR.

"Why should we abandon our firesides and everything associated with the dear name *home* . . . and expose ourselves, our wives, and our little ones . . . for the enjoyment of a liberty divested of its usual accompaniments?" Watkins worked as both a teacher and minister, and at the time he wrote these words he headed a household of seven people. As a patriarch, and as a man who surely considered himself respectable, he trusted that access to "many of the comforts of life" in Baltimore was more than merely tolerable. Why leave, Watkins wondered, when one already had a free life with its "usual accompaniments" in Maryland?[56]

Watkins was more financially comfortable and politically notable than most other black men in the city, but his faith in the importance of home life was not an exception within the black community. Household autonomy was one of the primary symbols of freedom in the nineteenth-century United States, and many thousands of black Baltimoreans were free. Free black men built lives, families, and homes out of the opportunities that the city afforded them and formed a community that revolved as much around kinship ties as it did around wage earning. They had rights, too. That is to say, many a black patriarch governed his own domain, as most of the city's freemen sought to do.

My larger point is that to be a freeman in midcentury Baltimore, regardless of one's race, one needed not only to earn cash for labor but also to support a family with that cash. One needed to head a household, protect and punish dependents, and defend against intruders and assailants. "I was only doing my duty when I defended my wife," explained one man after he attacked a neighbor who had allegedly harassed his wife. "I would think myself below the level of a man if I did not do so." Here was an individual who spoke the language of liberty in the age of coverture. By his own account, he had done only what he had had to do to preserve the autonomy of his household. He had attacked a threat to his household, and his power — male power — was the price of freedom.[57]

The Crime of Black Disorder

There was, however, another side to this story of respectability and patriarchal power. The respectable household was only an ideal, and in practice ideals are almost always illusory. And so it was with this one: however desirable, both well-ordered households and the gender roles that underwrote them were difficult for most people to sustain, particularly in a city where so many people depended upon such paltry wages. Male Baltimoreans of all races toiled in the harbor, or in the city's factories, or at sea, and in those capacities they frequently earned too little to support an entire household on their own. Many of these men accordingly depended upon their dependents to work for money, which meant that they organized their households around material necessity, not kinship. In antebellum Baltimore, respectable households were actually quite rare.[58]

It was not uncommon for women in Baltimore to bear children out of wedlock, but even when a family formed within the legal boundaries of marriage its dependents might have worked. Numerous wives scrimped, borrowed, and scavenged their way through their days, doing what they could to contribute to the household economy and forsaking the housekeeping done by their "respectable" counterparts. Poorer children meanwhile helped provide for their families rather than going to school and on average began their working lives around the age of twelve. Sons proved valuable in this regard, particularly within households headed by women or by a set of parents incapable for one reason or another of supporting themselves. One of the main ways that lower-income households deviated from middle-class norms was in the visibility of dependents as economic actors.

Children of the working poor were especially visible in a growing city like Baltimore. By 1820, more than two-fifths of the city's population was under fifteen, and many of these children came from impoverished homes. There was a sound economic logic for the proliferation of so many young Baltimoreans, for they made their families more financially viable. While their parents worked, they often dealt with utilities or ran errands. They toted water up the stairs and slops back down them; they fetched wood for fires and threads for sewing and potatoes for dinner; they made various purchases, often piecemeal, often by credit. But while this work was critical to the survival of poor families, it was also, by necessity, visible. Lower-income children's work took them out of the home and into the world that lay beyond it, putting them onto the streets and in plain sight.[59]

Once outside the home, these children elicited attention, most of it negative. If lazy workers were one group of people who concerned liberals, rambunctious boys who congregated on the city's street corners were another. "Bad boys" seemed to be everywhere in antebellum Baltimore, and wherever they were they seemed to cause trouble.[60] "Their name is legion," seethed a reporter for the *Baltimore Sun*.[61] Witnesses reported on "riotous" and "overgrown" boys frequently enough for correspondents to bristle about how "scarcely a day passes that we do not receive complaints from some quarter, of the peace and quiet of the neighborhood being disturbed by the congregation of boys of a riotous character."[62] Newspapers regaled their readers with tales of boys who gathered on street corners and compelled pedestrians to walk in the streets, which during winter were knee-deep in mud; of boys who cursed, swore, and uttered "the most blasphemous oaths" at unsuspecting people; of boys who stole clothes, threw stones, and set fires at city intersections, coercing the volunteer firemen out of their repose and into the streets, where the same boys could, in turn, trigger a riot between the rival companies.[63] The most alarming anecdotes depicted indiscretions of youthful violence. In one story, recurring so often as to constitute a genre, a young offender "wantonly and without the least provocation deliberately took up a stone and severely wounded a most peaceable and inoffending citizen."[64]

Private property holders complained incessantly about the annoying presence of "young men," "Boys and Lads nearly grown up," "Boys from 14 to 19 years of age," or the "large number of grown boys" who, "from their appearance, we might suppose to be gentlemen, but from their conduct we should judge to have not a spark of good breeding."[65] These young men were superficially indistinguishable from all other boys, and they seemed to assemble daily and riot nightly across the city's various neighborhoods. Many residents began to see in the shadows of every dark alley and unlit street corner the faces of the young and male looking back at them. Mayors and councilmen also took notice. In his 1837 annual address, Mayor Samuel Smith lamented the number of "unruly boys" who roamed the city's streets, day and night.[66] The Joint Committee on the Almshouse issued a lengthy report that detailed the municipality's inadequate system in regard to its "misguided youth."[67]

Liberals worried that the proliferation of misguided youths across their city foreshadowed a dark future, and newspaper editors proved only too happy to furnish examples of bad boys who had grown up to become criminals. The *Baltimore Gazette* reprinted one story about a boy whose short career apprenticing at a Philadelphia newspaper furnished "striking evidence of the miserable consequence of boys indulging in irregular practices." Guilty of an "inveterate fondness for running out at nights," he made an "acquaintance with vicious boys of his age, such as are witnessed every night, lounging about the corners of our streets, often swearing and drinking."[68] The *Sun* warned of the more dire consequences of living lawlessly while young: "William H. Dews, convicted of the murder of McKeever, explained his crime upon the gallows, at Jacinto, Mississippi.... He attributed his ignominious death, in a large degree, to the fact that in early life he was a bad boy. He said he was an instance of what bad boys come to."[69]

The hysteria over bad boys mirrored commentators' similar concern with bad workers, two related ills that could both be explained by a lack of character among the lower ranks. Indeed, just as they were wont to blame poverty on a worker's indolence, liberals tended to blame deficient patriarchs for the so-called disorder of their households. Policy makers lamented the influx of fathers "lost to parental instinct as well as moral feeling."[70] Newspaper columnists likewise decried "*the decay of parental discipline*," a critique of poorer men who no longer seemed able to keep their children in line. "There can be no just parental discipline when there is no character to back it," explained one editorialist. "How can a man effectually warn his son against bad company... when the example is bad?" The existence of so many children on the streets suggested that depravity, not purity, reigned inside that man's "family circle, the domestic hearth." As the editorialist understood it, "most people become what they are made at home," and a home on the streets was no home at all.[71]

Critics aghast at a city overrun by unruly and lawless children, and by unruly and lawless boys in particular, concerned themselves with two different forms of bad parenting. On the one hand, they fretted that too many patriarchs were abandoning their parental responsibilities. "The number of boys who are subject to little or no parental control ... [or] who are without parents and guardians to assume control of them," complained one editorial, "is in the aggregate very great."[72] Then, too, a group of missionaries who sought to educate the young and impoverished reported that more than half of the boys they tutored "are orphans by one parent. Some are entire orphans left to the care of indigent relatives."[73] Left to fend for themselves, such unattended children had little chance in a city like Baltimore. Another missionary report observed that "a considerable proportion of the population, are growing up in ignorance and becoming accustomed to vice in its most formidable features." It warned that young boys often spent day and night "on the streets, unrestrained by parental authority.... Truly they are receiving their education in idleness, and are preparing for its baleful companion — crime."[74]

Detractors also agonized over the possibility that fathers were actively corrupting their sons. "It is very rarely, if ever, found that simple destitution of itself is a cause of crime or even of street begging in the young," asserted one report from the House of Refuge. Crime proved "in nine cases in ten . . . to be the educated result of bad home-government if not actual home example."[75] Time and again, city officials cited "bad home example," "pernicious domestic influences," and "parental indulgence" as the sources of their city's youthful lawlessness. Bad men made for bad fathers, and bad fathers raised bad boys.[76] By the 1830s, it was commonplace for concerned onlookers to decry not only the spectacle of so many boys in the streets but also the likelihood that those boys' fathers had "reared" and "instructed" them to live wickedly.[77]

Baltimoreans disturbed by boys' wickedness often complained about "the neglect and bad influence of careless and criminal parents" in the same breath.[78] Both negligence and corruption mattered because boys were especially impressionable, a "morally exposed" group "ready for infection."[79] Without appropriate boundaries and with few or no good examples, a young man would frequent the "haunts" of strange characters where he would be "steadily educated for all species of daring impiety and blood-guiltiness" and thereafter "ripen" into a criminal.[80] One writer urged the city's citizenry to visit the penitentiary and ask its inmates about their upbringings. The vast majority of residents, contended the editorialist, would prove to be men who "had been in early youth permitted to associate with the depraved, and frequent the grog shop and the brothel, to become street brawlers and early drunkards."[81]

Those who complained about bad boys, negligent or corruptive fathers, and a breakdown in household order were often brazen in their elitism. "Sir, I beg leave, very respectfully to represent to you," wrote one man to the mayor, "that my own family, & all the other residents in Lloyd street . . . have been — for about three weeks past, annoyed, our privacy broken in upon, our rest disturbed, and our property endangered, by crowds of white boys and young men." He speculated — tellingly — that most of the boys were sons "of the refuse of the town."[82] This elitism in turn shaped the nature of policing. Only a small fraction of the city's children ever found their way into a penal institution, but those who did generally came from poorer, immigrant families. More than two-thirds of the House of Refuge inmates in 1857 had parents who came from somewhere other than the United States, with nearly half coming from Germany and Ireland alone.[83] Those numbers declined somewhat over the ensuing years, yet future reports nevertheless indicated a relatively high concentration of children born to foreign parents (see table 4.6). Immigrant children's prominence in the House of Refuge may have owed to anti-Catholic animus among the native-born population, but it also owed to the poverty of the foreign-born — for immigrants were typically poor. Their children were counted among the likeliest to work for wages, wander the streets without supervision, and harass passersby.

But they were not the very likeliest, at least in most middle-class eyes. For all of the concern that immigrant households garnered, and for all of the ways that fears of household disorder were generally elitist, the households that most alarmed liberal Baltimoreans were black ones. Black Baltimoreans *were* poor. Although a few hundred of the city's black residents resided in their own homes, thereby forming a small but real black middle class, many others resided in narrow alleys and courtyards where pools of water lay stagnant and garbage rotted throughout the year.[84] Disease spread readily in these areas, and black Baltimoreans' death rates were almost always higher than whites' as a result. Black residents suffered especially during the epidemics that plagued the city during early summer months. In an 1832 cholera outbreak, 28 percent of the victims were black; in an 1849 outbreak, 33 percent of the victims were.[85] Authorities also tended to blame black households for spreading disease. The city's physician, Thomas Buckler, suggested that the cause of the 1832 epidemic lay in "a number of pig styes [that] were kept by some free negroes, whose houses were only accessible by narrow alleys running into St. Paul street. The filthy condition of these places beggars description."[86] Buckler concluded that to fight epidemics, the municipality would

TABLE 4.6. Inmates of foreign-born parentage received in the
House of Refuge, mid-nineteenth century

Year	Total inmates	Inmates with foreign-born parents	Percentage of inmates with foreign-born parents
1858	127	65	51.18
1859	135	76	56.30
1860	145	79	54.48

Source: Calculated from Superintendent's Report, 1858 (table 5), 1859 (table 5), and 1860 (table 6), Annual Reports of the Managers of the House of Refuge, EPFL.

need to evacuate "dilapidated dwelling[s] occupied by negroes," and so in 1849, as the signs of another cholera outbreak were starting to present, he sent police officers into a black neighborhood to do just that. In one location, the officers "were astonished to find such a scene of misery." They removed the occupants, "all of whom were aged, were in the most wretched condition, suffering from various diseases which flesh is heir to," and proceeded to "rid the building of its contents, consisting mostly of old clothing, or rags, litters of pigs, dogs, filth, and broken furniture." They burned everything.[87]

Antebellum black households were also overcrowded. One of the costs of independence was space, as economics forced many free black Baltimoreans to live in multifamily units where the various breadwinners could help the whole survive without outside help. Sometimes close relatives clustered together; in other instances friends found sanctuary with each other; occasionally mere strangers huddled beneath the same roof. Some groups of black Baltimoreans lived in separate quarters located to the rear of an already occupied house, while others rented out rooms in other people's homes. And boardinghouses, of various types, were not uncommon. But whatever the chosen method, black Baltimoreans did what many working people have so often been forced to do: they adapted their living arrangements to survive. The size of black households increased over time, especially as greater numbers of ex-slaves made their way to Baltimore from the surrounding countryside. Before 1830 the average black household in the city had actually been smaller than the average white household, but afterward black households began to outpace white ones. None of this was unusual. Free black people's households in many of the nation's cities became more noticeably crowded by the middle of the nineteenth century.[88]

Black poverty earned unwanted white attention. In much the way that they historically associated sexual rapacity with black masculinity, white Baltimoreans grew increasingly disposed to view black men as poor patriarchs and their households as disordered.[89] One need not have been a militant antislavery activist to recognize the multitude of explanations for free black poverty in a slave city, as well as the structural hurdles to respectability that Baltimore's black families confronted, but white observers frequently blamed black people for their own plight and concluded that disarray was normal in, if not natural to, their households. They blamed black men in particular. The "idea of acquiring property, real or personal, beyond [a black man's] immediate wants, rarely crosses [his] mind," wrote Hezekiah Niles in 1819. "The notion that he is to become a *man* is never entertained by him."[90] White men like Niles believed that black men were unable or unwilling to work for wages of their own accord, and they extended the logic to black households: the wealth a black man failed to accrue was by definition wealth he was denying to his wife and children. His laziness as a wageworker led to a disordered household.

To white eyes, free black households looked like prototypical dysfunctional households where lazy men, licentious women, and wanton children cohabitated. "In [my] all[e]y, within a few feet of my fence, is located a family of free coloured persons, who keep a house of ill fame," explained one Mr. Murray in a letter to the mayor in 1831. "There coloured men collect, in considerable numbers, day and night, drinking, cursing & swearing, fighting and crying murder to the alarming of the neighborhood." Murray claimed that on numerous occasions he had "been deprived of sleep during the whole of the night" because of the noise. That noise symbolized the problem with black households in antebellum Baltimore, at least from this point of view. Black households seemed unruly and chaotic, headed not by men but by "wretches."[91]

Certain observers were so dismissive of the concept of black manhood that they compared black men to children. "Children are not the only species of annoyers to be met in our streets," wrote an editor for the *Sun*. "Strong, stalwart and healthy negroes" were too.[92] Another of the newspaper's stories lauded the foresight of a druggist who refused to sell arsenic to a young black girl without, first, "an order signed by a responsible person," as it was "a general rule with druggists, never to sell deadly poisons to children, or blacks, without their exhibiting a proper voucher that they are authorized to receive it."[93] This girl was both young and black. Had she been an adult, her race would have disqualified her from the ranks of the "responsible" anyway. Her dependency, and thus her unreliability, stemmed from both youth *and* race.

Black households were so apparently concerning that in the end they provoked a form of policing different from even that inflicted upon the Irish. Lawmakers passed several regulations that targeted them specifically. One 1830s law required black householders to seek the municipality's permission before hosting a gathering at their homes. In essence, it forced black householders to prove that they were extraordinarily suited to enjoy the ordinary right of assembly. Black men began appearing at city hall hoping to earn back the right. Mr. Ross wished "to have a Company this evening" and justified his claim by explaining that he had "a very quiet family." Daniel Kobourn's Bond Street ball was certain to be peaceful since he "invariably kept a decent and orderly house." Samuel Grayson's party would disturb no one; he was "a good and Peacefull Neighbour." Taking black household disorder for granted, the statute rendered black householders (and especially black men) dependent upon white people who could vouch for their internal affairs. Petitions from white men describing the excellent nature of black men's household governance poured into the mayor's office: Jacob Hamer imparted "good morals to the children under his care"; Abraham Williams's home life approached "the style of his white acquaintances"; Simon Coalman's household operated under "good order."[94] White householders did not have to request the city's approval before having a party, nor did they have to prove that their household's "good order" was an exception to a rule. Only black householders had to earn others' signatures and beg for municipal permission before having over guests.

Another series of laws compelled free black householders to surrender their children to the local orphans court if they could not demonstrate self-sufficiency. Dating to the eighteenth century, Maryland's orphans courts bound out parentless children to manufacturers, mechanics, and farmers as apprentices. Boys' terms typically expired when they turned twenty-one; girls' terms ceased at sixteen. But in 1808 the state legislature ordered the courts to apprentice any child of "lazy, indolent or worthless free Negroes" as well. Ten years later, the legislature broadened the charge, mandating that any black child not already learning a trade was to be bound out. By 1825 court officials in every county in the state were seizing the children of free black parents who appeared too poor to clothe and feed them. The result was an annual pilfering of young black Marylanders from their families and black children's entrance into a system designed to replace disorderly householders with respectable ones. Although the apprentice system admittedly burdened masters with providing their wards with room and board, its actions represented a clear rebuke of the household authority of black men: the law essentially took for granted that they were unlikely to provide for and govern their own children effectively.[95]

Unsurprisingly, free black men chafed at the rebuke. One delegate at the 1852 Maryland Free Colored People's Convention angrily denounced the legislation "by which the children of free colored persons, whom the officers decided the parents were unable to support, were bound out." Another lamented that "the hog law of Baltimore was better moderated than that in reference to colored people." At least that law "said at certain seasons [hogs] should run about, and at certain seasons be taken up; but the law referring to colored people allowed them to be taken up at any time." Delegates at the Baltimore convention likened their status as householders to animals so as to highlight the wide legal gulf that divided free white families from free black families. They did not like that the state could intervene between them and their children and thus divest them of one of the most fundamental rights of freedom. They intensely disliked the fact that "they were men, but not recognized as men."[96]

The orphans court did not serve exclusively as a site of black policing. Sometimes black parents apprenticed their children of their own free will. Apprenticeship was particularly useful for those black Baltimoreans who worried about the lack of education options in a city where only white children could attend public school. Indenturing one's offspring was a good way for an unskilled householder to impart knowledge of a useful trade, whether such skills came from a white person or another black person. That is what Benjamin Cook did with his son. Cook indentured Benjamin Jr. to a white farmer named George Lynch in 1838, hoping that the boy — not yet five — would learn to support himself as an agriculturist instead of burdening the family with one more unskilled mouth to feed.[97] Cook's actions were probably born of financial desperation, but they hinted at how black parents could use the legal system's racial animus to their advantage. The law's presumption about black household disorder opened a window of opportunity to train their children through other means.[98]

Baltimore's orphans court actually dealt rarely with black children. During most terms, the court approved few more than twenty new indentures, and many of those it did approve were for white children who went to live with relatives after their parents had died.[99] At no point did the court's proceedings on black children approach the panoptic. What the orphans court example shows — and for that matter, what other police regulations of black households suggest more generally — are the legal constraints on black patriarchal power in antebellum Baltimore. Put simply, free black Baltimoreans' household rights were incomplete.

The court case *Hughes v. Jackson* perhaps best illustrated how the state's legal system could simultaneously acknowledge certain forms of black patriarchal power and yet also undermine the integrity of black households. The Jackson in question was Samuel Jackson, a free black laborer in the Eastern Shore county of Dorchester who one day in March 1851 appeared before a circuit court clerk to swear out a complaint against another free black man, Josiah Hughes. Hughes, Jackson informed the court, had broken into his house and kidnapped his five children, and now Jackson wanted them back. He also wanted financial redress: in addition to charging Hughes with trespass, assault, and breaking and entering, he demanded $1,000. The case persisted for years, and only in 1856, some five years after the initial claim, did the circuit court uphold Jackson's claim and rule that he was entitled to $750 as well as his children. This in turn prompted Josiah Hughes to appeal to the Maryland Court of Appeals, the state's highest court, on the grounds that the case should be dismissed because the plaintiff lacked legal standing to sue at all. Jackson was black, Hughes's lawyer asserted, and that disqualified his claim. In 1858, the court handed down a decision that for Jackson — and, by implication, other free black people in the state — was something of a mixed blessing.

Writing for the court, Chief Justice John Carroll LeGrand ruled that Samuel Jackson indeed could sue under state law, contra the federal *Dred Scott* decision from a year earlier. "The courts have never decided," LeGrand argued, that "all negroes should be regarded as slaves. . . . To deny to them the right of suing and being sued, would be in point of fact to deprive them of the means of defending their possessions."[100] Under this logic he affirmed the lower court's ruling and ignored Roger Taney. But LeGrand's decision did not return to Jackson all five of his children. Two of them, his daughters Lilly and Mary, returned home, but three others, sons Theodore and Dennis as well as daughter Ellen, remained in another man's household as slaves. Historian Martha Jones has pieced together roughly what had happened in the preceding years to trigger Jackson's suit and by extension why his legal victory was only partial in the end. It appears that William Hughes, Josiah's wealthy father, had in 1840 come to an oral agreement with Jackson to purchase the latter's enslaved wife and daughter from a white woman. Jackson in turn agreed to work for Hughes in order to pay off the debt. Over the next decade, he toiled on William Hughes's land all the while living with his wife, Mary, with whom he had four more children. But then William died in 1850, and his death precipitated the crisis. William Hughes's son and legatee, Josiah, denied that there had ever been an agreement between his father and Jackson and proceeded to seize all five of Jackson's children as his rightful property. Josiah Hughes subsequently sold Theodore, Dennis, and Ellen to a local white farmer, Alward Johnson. For all that it said about Jackson's right to sue, LeGrand's ruling in *Hughes v. Jackson* did not overturn the three children's sale to Johnson. They remained enslaved until 1864, when a new state constitution overturned slavery in Maryland once and for all.[101]

Hughes v. Jackson was notable for many reasons, not least because it exposed the practical limits of Roger Taney's argument in *Dred Scott* that free black Americans lacked all standing under the law. In Maryland, at least, free black men like Samuel Jackson did possess a meaningful bundle of rights that entitled them to some legal protections, particularly from black interlopers. But the case also exposed the limits of black household autonomy in a slave state and indicated just how difficult it was for free black householders in Maryland (and by extension, Baltimore) to hold their families together. Jackson surrendered three children to another man despite having the rights "to sue in our courts and to hold property, both real and personal."[102] His story illustrated that whatever their free status, black men's households could be broken, and however extant their rights, their patriarchal authority was still constrained. In the end, Jackson was unable to gain control over all of his dependents. Victory in court did not liberate him from having to defer to another patriarch for years to come.

Neither Slave nor Free in the Age of Coverture

To recap: the free black men of antebellum Baltimore were not unlike the other free men of their time and place. They too sought control over their households. And many of them did indeed head households. It was neither uncommon to see free black men governing and supporting families nor strange to find black men who, like other aspiring patriarchs, built a type of freedom out of the bodies of their dependents. But as they did with black men's wages, white liberals harbored doubts. Many expressed skepticism toward black men's ability to head well-ordered households even as they confronted a reality in which such households actually existed. The very fact of black households, their very existence, was often greeted with white disdain, and in the age of slavery, white disdain could be quite powerful. For black patriarchs, white disdain translated into legal disabilities.

The result was a fraught relationship between free black householders and Baltimore's policemen. In some circumstances, police officers protected black households from aggression, much as they did white households. In other circumstances, they did not. Ignored at times by the authorities and stifled in court by the prohibition of black testimony against white people, free black householders often learned that their properties, "both real and personal," were vulnerable to white violence against which they could not always defend. They could fight to protect their own on their own, but they also occasionally needed police help that failed to materialize.

Sometimes the police did come through. Every so often an officer would track down a kidnapper who attempted to sell a free black child into slavery. Solomon Sanders was one such potential kidnapper whose best-laid plans were foiled by law enforcement. In August 1860, Sanders was the legal guardian of "a free colored boy" named Jordan Murray who, he claimed, had run away. And Murray *had* run away. But he had done so not to shirk his duties to Sanders but to escape the clutches of a man who wanted to transport him to Virginia "for the purpose of disposing of him or selling his time." Sanders eventually recaptured Murray, convinced the local orphans court that his ward's flight merited a two-year extension to his term, and made his way for the docks — and he got as far as the steamer *George Peabody* before Officer Chisholm stopped him. Tipped off, somehow, the southern district policeman boarded the ship "and there found Sanders and the colored boy, the latter handcuffed." Chisholm promptly arrested Sanders, and soon thereafter the orphans court canceled the extension it had recently imposed.[103] Not every policeman could or would preempt a crime against a black family. More frequently officers simply responded to distress at black homes and duly tracked down the perpetrators. Policeman Pearce, for example, arrested Andrew Haggerty in May 1860 "on the charge of beating a colored man in his own house."[104]

Yet however helpful a particular policeman could be, his colleagues were as likely to be uncooperative. Take the officer who arrested Theodore Denny. Denny, a black man, argued that he had no more than protected himself at home before the police hauled him to jail. His story was alarming. One day, claimed Denny in a pardon petition, he had answered his door and found his landlord's son standing there, demanding rent money Denny claimed to have already paid. "The mere expression of my doubt of his having been authorised to call on me in this manner," continued Denny, "led to his attack upon me, which was repelled only by my shoving him down on a bed to prevent injury to myself." The white man obtained an indictment against Denny and had him arrested for assault. There were no other witnesses, and all we have are Denny's words — a petition whose motivation was clear enough. But although it is impossible to say what really happened in that house, we can say this: a white man entered a black man's household and had him arrested. Denny's race prevented him from testifying on his own behalf. Whatever happened that day, his power to keep his household's peace had been compromised.[105]

Black male Baltimoreans could also get into a serious legal mess when courage made them audacious enough to fight back. Thomas Harris's mother ran "a shop" where, one night, Robert Gamble and two other white men came in for a drink. The "very respectable colored woman" informed her visitors that they "could not get it there," to which Gamble, feeling provocative, responded with a demand "for cakes, with which he was furnished." It was soon clear that Gamble had neither the money nor willingness to spend it in a black-run shop. So he asked Mrs. Harris "to trust him" for future payment. For her part, the black woman took back the cakes and retorted that she would do no such thing. This seeming impudence provoked a barrage of cursing from the white men, and it was at that moment that Thomas Harris walked inside. Angered and under the assumption that the men had eaten the cakes in question, Harris requested that they pay. To which Gamble, now fully enraged, responded by striking Harris "a violent blow alongside the head, under the ear," setting off a full-blown fight. At some point during the fray Harris knifed Gamble's arm from shoulder to elbow. Gamble had initiated the fight, but Harris was arrested for knifing an unsuspecting victim. His stand ended with a criminal charge.[106]

Harris's and Denny's examples suggested that free black men's rights as householders and patriarchs were hindered when dealing with white aggressors. Their tales also hinted at the danger of relying upon policemen during interracial conflicts. But even policemen who wanted to protect black households from white encroachment could be checked. Night watchman William Evans, for instance, claimed that his interference in a quarrel between a white woman and a black woman had unfairly resulted in his own arrest. According to Evans, the white Mrs. Shoak had approached him with a martyr's tale one day in 1852, explaining that a "black woman had assaulted her, and requested his aid to make an arrest." Yet when Evans repaired to the scene, he found the black woman "in her own house with her door locked, and not committing any breach of the peace." Evans informed Shoak that he had no authority to make an arrest upon someone in her own house. This, however, would not do. The white woman flew "into a rage in presence of the officer[,] striking at the black woman through her window, and behaved in such a disorderly manner that the officer felt himself bound to arrest her." But by arresting Shoak, Evans made a mistake. The criminal court released the woman and charged the officer with assaulting *her*. The doors to black homes did not provide inhabitants with sanctuary from white violence, and Evans, by his own admission, had violated his oath by assuming they did.[107]

The law rendered Evans nearly useless to the unnamed black woman, yet uselessness was a virtue compared to the actions other policemen took. Certain police officers not only ignored the defense of black households but also participated in the violence against them. In one case, a white man looked to a policeman for assistance after "a small black boy, named Cushing," allegedly struck his six-year-old son in the head with a brick. The attack had left the child injured and the father fuming, and white fury, in Baltimore, could beget vengeance: "The father preferred giving the black a whipping rather than the law," recorded a police reporter, "and officer Teal tanned his hide in the latest style." Teal's participation in the flogging revealed the routine nature of his act. White men were well within their rights to punish black children who acted out. They were especially within their rights to act on their own when, as in this instance, the child of a black man attacked one of their dependents, allegedly or otherwise. What made this violence so frightening — what made it so frighteningly legitimate — was its acceptability in the eyes of the police. Here, a policeman acted as a literal instrument of a white father's wrath.[108]

Policemen also invaded black people's homes themselves. Night watchman Howard, for example, was "induced to enter the House of a coloured man residing in Pine St at about 11 o'clock" one night in 1834. According to a report filed by mayor Jesse Hunt, he did so to assist "an individual to whom it appears the coloured man owed a small debt for which he had procured a warrant." Night watchmen, recall, were not supposed to either collect debts for other men or enter other men's homes without cause. And they certainly needed a good reason to use force when they did enter a private residence. Hunt explained that although in this case "all was peaceable, and the family were preparing to go to bed at the time," Howard went inside anyway, seized the black man, and dealt "several severe blows" with his spontoon. Hunt believed that it was impossible to justify such conduct, for policemen "in the discharge of their duty are not to use violence unless it is unavoidable." Not even the mayor could enforce that standard, however. Howard's commanding officer excused his action as a one-off, concluding that "his improper conduct was not the result of a disposition to do wrong," and let him off with a warning.[109]

Black householders' legal disabilities and fraught relationships with the police were obvious enough to constitute common knowledge. "You are liable to insult and contumely at every step," explained colonizationist James Hall in an 1859 address to Maryland's free black population, "and even your private dwellings are not sacred from intrusion and violence of lawless ruffianism; for, however aggravated a case may be, and ample the testimony of your own race, legal redress you have none."[110] In one sense, Hall was exaggerating for effect. He wanted to convince free black Baltimoreans to leave the country, and he conveniently ignored the fact that they could sometimes find legal redress despite their formal incapacity in court. William Watkins had argued specifically against colonization by invoking "our firesides and everything associated with the dear name *home*."[111] Black households' insecurity was nevertheless quite real, and colonizationists like Hall took an almost perverse pleasure in pointing it out. "It cannot be denied that the humble tenements of these poor people are often entered by the lower class of whites," wrote the editor of the *Maryland Colonization Journal* a few months later. As long as black men remained in Maryland, he argued, they would suffer the indignity of "the persons of their wives and daughters insulted, if not violated," and they would fail to find adequate "means of redress" against white intruders.[112]

What protection black householders did receive from the attacks of white "ruffians" often came from other white householders. In 1844, a white man called upon officials "to disperse from the corners the youths who assemble nightly." The boys, he explained, not only disrupted local "business" and annoyed people at night with "their vulgar songs" and "obseen [*sic*] language" but also struck "coloured persons[,] taking off their hats or caps and keeping them and committing such acts as should be deprecated amongst the most vulgar of the human race." His demand for help incorporated antiblack assaults alongside disruptions to white business and disturbances to white sleep, framing racial violence as a violation of his own property rights. In the process, the petitioner affirmed his status as a householder and, implicitly, confirmed the weakness of "coloured persons" whose status denied them a comparable legal standing. His act of benevolence was really an act of authority.[113]

In still other instances white men acting as householders petitioned for black men's exoneration from criminal charges. John Garrettson was a free black Baltimorean charged with assault. His neighbor Elisha Harrington took up his case: "I have known them about six years," wrote Harrington of Garrettson's family. "They have lived in sight of my dwelling during that time, and if they had been of a disorderly character I certainly should have known it." The white man had no doubt that Garrettson had committed the assault for which he was charged, but Harrington also believed that Garrettson "had great provocation, and that he believed he was acting in preservation of his own life" as a man should be able to do. Garrettson knew that the law did not grant him the same presumption of manhood as it did to a white householder. He accordingly sought Harrington's endorsement, lending credibility to the appeal and demonstrating his high character, orderly household, and correct conduct.[114]

Baltimore's growing police institutions were introduced to create, reestablish, and sustain respectable households full of dependents — wives, children, apprentices, servants, and sometimes slaves — out of whom men were to build their independence as citizens, over whom they were to govern as patriarchs, and for whom men were to fight as protectors. Men were introduced to serve male power in the home. But in a place like antebellum Baltimore, not all householders were created equal. Frederick Douglass captured the peculiar nature of black male status when in 1847 he told a New York audience about his recent sojourn to England, where he "saw in every man a recognition of my manhood, and an absence, a perfect absence, of everything like that disgusting hate with which we are pursued in this country."[115] Douglass's experience as a young man in Baltimore had taught him the racialized meaning of manhood and how rare it was for lawmakers to treat black householders as bearers of a full arsenal of rights. He yearned for the respect he received in England. Indeed, he yearned to have the power of the state behind him.

One final incident deserves mention. During the summer of 1838, white rowdies attacked the Sharp Street African Methodist Episcopal Church in west Baltimore. Although not a home, per se, the church was a private meetinghouse within whose walls worshippers were supposedly shielded from threat. The events of Sunday, August 26, exposed such safety for an illusion. That night, "a considerable mob . . . commenced an attack on the house, by throwing stones and breaking the doors and windows." Inside, the congregation panicked. Many parishioners escaped the melee "by rushing through the doors, jumping out of the windows, &c." Many more were injured.

What makes the Sharp Street assault so revealing is the dual role that the police played in it. On the one hand, policemen were their typical ineffective selves. "By the time the police had collected in sufficient force to avert the disturbance, the mob had concluded their work and dispersed, so that no arrest took place," reported a newspaper correspondent.[116] Days later the authorities were no closer to finding the responsible parties, and local white Methodists, upset about the attack, had resorted to begging for "the city Police [to] be directed to afford the necessary protection to the Coloured congregation who Regularly assemble for publick worship in the evenings."[117] The authorities had proven useless, or nearly useless, once again. But law enforcement was more than just ineffective during this affair: it was also implicated. The precipitating event for the riot had been an altercation between a night watchman and a group of black men. The white rowdies, in attacking "the innocent and unoffending attendants at the church," were retaliating for what they considered an unprovoked attack upon an officer. Rioters during the affair essentially acted as an arm of the police, inflicting a legitimate form of violence. It is telling that even those who decried the mob also conceded that it "had a right to chastise or inflict punishment upon those who committed the outrage upon the watchman."[118]

Although many white Baltimoreans disavowed the violence at the AME Church, and although other religious groups, particularly the (largely white) Catholics, suffered assaults during the period as well, the events on Sharp Street exemplified the unique vulnerabilities of private black spaces in antebellum Baltimore.[119] So long as the rights of black men remained incomplete — so long as free black people occupied a legal middle ground between slave and free — police reform had the perverse effect of heightening ordinary white power over black households. Even the most respectable black householders lacked a full array of responses when defending their homes and dependents from the city's growing list of mundane horrors. To their dismay, they could rely upon neither the police nor their own fists with complete confidence. If under siege, they were hamstrung.

Chapter Five

POLICING THE
BLACK CRIMINAL

✦

NY HISTORY of policing is also a history of criminality. Who gets to police, and how, often depends upon who is policed, and why. Those two identities — policeman and criminal — are wedded to each other conceptually and prove particularly inextricable in the history of American policing, where the police forces and penal system were erected to preserve freedom while the freedom of an entire race of people was stigmatized as criminal. Many nineteenth-century white people believed black people were inferior to them and that black men in particular were unwilling to work industriously for wages, support well-ordered households, and abide by the criminal law as free people. White skepticism about black self-control fed a similar skepticism about black lawfulness, and during the age of slavery that skepticism justified black codes and ordinary white policing.

One cannot fully understand the mutually constitutive relationship between ordinary white men and official police institutions without also considering the association of black freedom with criminality.[1] The preceding two chapters hint at a working definition of crime in antebellum Baltimore. As they showed, liberal elites increasingly interpreted the failure to earn a living wage and head a respectable household as the telltale signs of crime itself. This assignation normalized the typical criminal as male: the man who did not work consistently for cash was more likely to beg or steal than the man who consistently earned good wages; the boy whose father was either drunk or absent was more likely to riot than the boy whose father governed sternly and fairly. Such a definition also rendered the type of "crime" that most concerned the authorities as that of free men. Whether in public office or private practice, most elite Baltimoreans believed that freedom above all guaranteed men the opportunity to earn wages and head households. Those who were either unwilling or unable to do so seemed unfit for the freedom whose fruits they were squandering. In the eyes of elites, the failure of freemen to be industrious and orderly made those men criminals.

These liberal meanings of "crime" and "criminal" implicated many different antebellum Baltimoreans, particularly poorer freemen who could not find regular work and oversee respectable households. Yet no group of men was as implicated as free black men. Racism long predated the founding of Baltimore, and Europeans had spent centuries — not years, but centuries — dismissing black nature on the grounds that darker skin signified an inferior mental, emotional, and intellectual capacity.[2] For as old as racial ideologies were, though, the rise of liberal ideals also provided white people in places like Baltimore with a new vocabulary to understand black inferiority. It was almost self-evident for people in a political culture that championed autonomy, industry, and order to discuss black incapacity through a language of crime. Many white Baltimoreans simply presumed that without slavery's shackles black men would refuse to work, ignore their household responsibilities, and break the law. And not only proslavery zealots and colonizationists believed such things; certain antislavery activists did too. The typical white person in pre–Civil War Baltimore believed that black freedom begat crime and that free black men were more likely to become criminals than almost anyone else.[3]

Baltimore's system of policing was created in the name of freedom. We must appreciate, however, that the men who designed that system also believed that whenever black Baltimoreans were free to choose, they would choose indolence, licentiousness, and crime over industry, respectability, and lawfulness. White Baltimoreans acted on these fears of black freedom all the time, sometimes impulsively, often violently, and almost always with the municipality's approval. As a result, the compatibility between white professional and popular policing materialized not only in job-busting attacks and home invasions but also in more traditional forms, such as when an ordinary citizen arrested a black man for theft or protected a black victim from harm. The public authorities were nominally engaged in a broader project of seizing legitimate force for the state alone, but free black Baltimoreans did not possess all of the rights that white Baltimoreans did — not during the age of slavery, in any event. Just free enough to warrant concern, black

Baltimoreans posed a specter fearful enough to put all citizens on guard. When it came to policing black people, white male vigilantes were the police.

The Crime of Black Freedom

Freedom for black Baltimoreans increasingly became the rule during the nineteenth century. The relative anonymity of city life combined with the sheer size of the city's free black community to obliterate the close association of slavery with blackness that still prevailed most everywhere else in the slave states, including in the Maryland countryside. By midcentury nearly 90 percent of the city's black community had been born free, and a good number of that generation's parents could say the same. When a white observer spied a black person on a Baltimore city street, he or she was far more likely observing a free person than an enslaved one, and that white person knew it. Blackness in antebellum Baltimore carried the presumption of freedom.[4]

Such freedom presented in myriad ways, and one of the primary ways was social. Members of the city's black community founded a plethora of fraternal, benevolent, and relief organizations during the middle decades of the antebellum era and through them performed the work of uplift and improvement. Certain societies provided aid to the poor as well as to the family members of sick or disabled workers, while others promoted forums for intellectual engagement, political debate, and various lectures. Black fraternal associations did both: they buried former members and assisted their widows and children while training a new generation of black leaders to speak in front of and organize large groups of people. Historian Christopher Phillips has documented the enormous breadth of these associations in Baltimore, which began officially with the Freemasons' Friendship Lodge in 1825. Within a quarter century, the city's black men were liable to belong to one or more of such organizations as the Zion Lodge No. 4, the Prince Hall Lodge of Free and Accepted Masons, the lodges of the Royal Arch Masonry, the Good Samaritans, and most especially the Order of Odd Fellows, which in Baltimore was the most popular lodge of them all. There were also black literary lyceums, sewing circles, temperance groups, Bible societies, and a trade union. And in almost all of these, free people of color, and especially free black men, constituted the membership.[5]

Black freedom was also evident in the black community's high literacy rates. Although state law did not formally prohibit slaves from learning to read, many masters did, as Frederick Douglass learned after his master Hugh Auld discovered Douglass's lessons with Auld's wife, Sophia. Incredulous, the white man lectured his wife about the risks of literacy. It was a skill for free people, he believed, and "it would forever unfit [Douglass] for the duties of a slave."[6] Auld undoubtedly recognized, as Douglass soon did, that freedom and literacy were related. As it happened, a sizable minority of Baltimore's free black population — just under 37 percent — was literate by 1850, and that number skyrocketed during the next decade, jumping to about 75 percent.[7] By the start of the Civil War, nearly 19,500 black residents of Baltimore claimed some degree of literacy. Most literate of all were the younger African Americans, who benefited from the community's maturation during the antebellum years. Many attended church schools run by black ministers like William Watkins where they could take advantage of opportunities not previously available to persons of their status and race. Watkins himself made the connection between freedom and literacy. "Give the rising generation a good education," he claimed in 1836, "and then when liberty, in the full sense of the term, shall be conferred upon them, they will thoroughly understand its nature, duly appreciate its value, and contribute efficiently to its inviolable preservation."[8]

Perhaps the most notable signifier of black Baltimore's free status was its political power. No black Marylander could vote, but there was more to politics than the franchise. There was even more to politics than citizenship.[9] Like their brethren in Philadelphia who also confronted formal exclusion, black Baltimoreans cultivated alliances with powerful white men so as to influence a political culture that treated them as inferior, and they won real political battles in the process. In January 1842, a group of the state's slaveholders convened in Annapolis to discuss the problem (as they saw it) of free people of color in a slave society. The convention recommended new laws that would increase the state's regulatory power over free black people, more obstacles to private manumissions, and better methods of preventing fugitive slaves from escaping their owners. Black Baltimoreans reacted angrily to the publication of these recommendations, as did a number of their white allies. A biracial and interdenominational group of protesters in Baltimore decried the proposed legislation as a violation of both black and white men's rights. The bill died in the state Senate.[10]

Black Baltimoreans defeated other racist programs in the years to come. In 1850, the Eastern Shore planter Curtis Jacobs, along with other pro-slavery ideologues, attempted to seize control of that year's state constitutional convention and eliminate the free black population entirely. Initially, the delegates approved Jacobs's call to form a committee that sought to colonize free black Marylanders in Liberia, but under political pressure the majority voted down the committee's subsequent recommendations to prohibit free black people from acquiring real estate, ban all manumission, compel all free black people to register their names with a local court, and prevent any free black person from ever entering the state again. Jacobs was undeterred, and he reemerged nearly a decade later as the leader of a re-enslavement movement. Propelled by the white terror provoked by John Brown's recent raid on Harpers Ferry, Jacobs and his House Committee on the Colored Population proposed a new law that would have forced free black Marylanders to leave the state or return to slavery. "Free-negroism throughout this State must be abolished," Jacobs believed, and the state legislature, following his lead, opted to turn the measure into a referendum in the fall, when the presidential vote was occurring. Black Baltimoreans rose up en masse to defeat the bill. Aided by white Methodist leaders, they held prayer days, gave lectures, and organized a massive petition campaign against the proposal. In November 1860, more than 70 percent of Marylanders voted against Jacobs's dream. Baltimoreans of both races opposed re-enslavement by an almost eight-to-one margin.[11]

The large number of black organizations, the relatively high black literacy rates, and the successful campaign against re-enslavement indicated both the vibrancy and power of the city's black community. Each reflected the fruits of black freedom. Such freedom, however, came with a price. For all that white Baltimoreans accepted their black neighbors as free people who deserved protection from rapacious whites who wanted to re-enslave them, many also believed that black freedom begat black crime. One group of white petitioners was emblematic when they described the city's black community as "less fearful of the operation of the law than the white population."[12] Another white petitioner called free black people "a shameful influence" who "hang like dead weights upon the advancement of our institutions and are a burden of great expense to every county and town. Without the control of masters and too weak to protect themselves their sufferings are sometimes intense."[13]

As such words suggest, white Baltimoreans sometimes expressed their anxieties about black lawlessness by unfavorably comparing free people of color with slaves and lamenting the absence of mastery to keep the former in line. "You may manumit the slave, but you cannot make him a white man," explained colonizationist Robert Goodloe Harper in a well-publicized 1817 letter to American Colonization Society secretary Elias Caldwell. "He still remains a negro or mulatto."[14] Although not a colonizationist, Hezekiah Niles agreed with Harper's diagnosis of free black wantonness. "The free blacks in Baltimore are not only less abundantly supplied with the necessaries and comforts of life than the slaves, but they are also much less moral and virtuous," wrote Niles in an 1825 edition of his *Weekly Register*.[15] Religious leader John Hersey went so far as to conclude that "if our slaves could be delivered from a state of bondage at once, and compelled still to dwell among us, it would not better their condition, or cause them to be more respected, happy, or independent."[16] Tellingly, none of these commentators believed in slavery or re-enslavement; Harper and Hersey favored removal, and Niles considered himself a gradual emancipationist. And each, for the most part, argued that free black lawlessness was habitual, not biological. It was just that that supposed lawlessness troubled them. They worried about turning loose "an idle, worthless and thievish race" of people who lacked what Harper called "the restraints of character."[17] Perhaps Niles put it most clearly: "The mere liberation of the *person* from slavery may just as likely be a curse as a blessing to the individual, unless he has been taught to *think* for himself."[18]

Many white Baltimoreans worried that black Baltimoreans could not think for themselves and that without the habits of self-reflection they lacked the industry, order, and restraint so vital to the maintenance of freedom. These fears hardened with time. When delegates to Maryland's 1864 constitutional convention debated emancipation, for example, opponents of the measure expressed concern about free black men's "natural aversion to labor" and the likelihood that they "would refuse to work, and with their families, sink into the lowest depths of destitution and wretchedness." Proslavery delegates likewise worried that "the jails, almshouses, and penitentiaries" would be freedmen's "only refuge from starvation" and feared that those freedmen "would become an intolerable burden, and all classes of society would rise up to expel them." The nightmare of a supposedly "idle and thriftless population," of a "non-producing class" catapulted from slavery into freedom, conjured for many lawmakers a dual spectacle: "jails, almshouses and penitentiaries" filled with black men on the one hand, and white taxpayers financially burdened with policing and incarcerating tens of thousands of suddenly free black criminals on the other.[19] Black liberty was by this logic an invitation to crime. Ostensibly, it left black men "without a guide or protector in the midst of a society where they can possess no rights; where they have few inducements to good conduct; where they are surrounded by a thousand incentives to indolence and vice."[20]

Not all white Marylanders, particularly in Baltimore, associated black freedom with crime, and many of those who did followed Harper, Hersey, and Niles by blaming structural inequality, poverty, and the legacies of slavery (material or otherwise) for the problem. But even the white commentators who derided biological explanations for black behavior conceded that free black people were prone to break the law if only because their options were so circumscribed. And — crucially — they were not alone in doing so. White northerners in free states could also be heard likening black freedom to crime. New Yorkers, for instance, frequently did so when they deliberated giving black men the vote at the state's 1846 constitutional convention. A majority of delegates opposed suffrage on the grounds that there was "a criminal disposition in the race." These men pointed to a recent state census for proof, arguing that its results demonstrated "the relative proportion of infamous crime is nearly thirteen and a half times as great in the colored population as in the white." One criminologist described a black man imprisoned at Blackwell's Island as having "the capacity to be made a very useful or a very desperate and dangerous man." What truly petrified white liberals was the belief that people of color did not take advantage of their capacities for good. If permitted to do so, they too often seemed to choose the dangerous path.[21]

The criminalization of black freedom in Baltimore often manifested as derision of the very behavior that connoted said freedom. Take black assembly. As the years passed and the number of free black Baltimoreans grew, the sight of black people congregating in public became more common. Visitors to the city remarked upon the "crowds of coloured people" who assembled on streets and sidewalks to say hello, exchange pleasantries, and pass along information about mutual friends and distant relatives. One English observer noted the "series of giggles and shakings of the hand, interspersed with questions about uncle Johnson, cousin Jackson, and twenty other darkeys of their acquaintances, whose history and welfare seem to afford to both a vast deal of merriment." Another foreigner, this one a Hungarian woman touring with Lajos Kossuth's delegation in 1851, remarked that "none but the coloured people loiter about corners of the avenues," clustered "together, talking and glancing around, obviously delighted."[22] White Baltimoreans frequently expressed frustration with these spectacles. One group of petitioners complained of being "disturbed by parcels of Negroes and others, who are constantly making fires and cooking victuals" nearby. They wondered why there were no "officers" to disperse the gatherings, particularly when fights erupted and "the whole neighborhood is disturbed."[23] Another group railed against the sight of "drunken disorderly persons and crowds of people of color" on Harrison Street.[24] Specters of black people assembling in public unnerved whites to the point that some likened black assembly to rioting: "There are certain portions of the city where the blacks appear to have taken the law into their own hands, and attempt to riot as it best pleases them," reported one *Baltimore Sun* correspondent in 1840.[25]

White Baltimoreans also described black churches as incubators for lawlessness, and rioting in particular. This was notable if for no other reason than because black churches provided the institutional bedrock for free black life in the city, from spirituality to recreation to politics. By 1850, black Baltimoreans had more sectarian diversity than any other black community in the nation, and by 1860 there were sixteen black churches and missions in the city representing six denominations, with nearly one-fifth of all people of color attending church on a regular basis. Several of these congregations were affiliated with white umbrella organizations and remained under the jurisdiction of white leaders; others were more independent. Whatever the racial makeup of their respective clergy, black churches both reflected and promoted black autonomy. With classrooms, libraries, meeting halls, rec centers, and graveyards, religious institutions provided the schools, concerts, associations, fairs, pageants, lectures, exhibits, and funerals that were the hallmarks of black freedom in Baltimore.[26]

And many white people were wary of them. White Baltimoreans worried about black religious congregations for much the same reason that they worried about black assemblages on street corners: large black crowds just *seemed* riotous. "I take this method of informing you that the Negroes which visit sharp st. meeting on Sunday are a great nuisance to our citizens and particularly to those who are under the necessity of passing that way," wrote one white man to the mayor in 1831. As the petitioner saw things, not only were the crowds outside the church unnecessarily large but also many of its members were "ungentlemanly," making it impossible for "Ladies" to pass by. "I merely suggest this to you hoping you will have it altered," he implored.[27] Whites also associated the behavior inside black churches with rioting. A letter to the editor of the *Baltimore Clipper* complained that the worshippers at the Bethel AME Church regularly made "night hideous with their howls, dancing to the *merry* song of some double-lunged fellow, who glories the more his *congregation* yells." "Is an entire neighborhood to be disturbed day after night after night by these *rioters*," he wondered, "because some well meaning persons choose to say they are free to worship?"[28]

The association of black worship with lawlessness (and riotous conduct in particular) helps explain the 1838 attack upon the Sharp Street church. As I mentioned in the last chapter, the alleged trigger for the maelstrom had been a fight several days earlier during which "a watchman named Lawton was severely beaten, by a party of negroes." The subsequent assault upon the church was a white mob's retribution on Lawton's behalf, leading many outsiders to conclude that the watchman's assailants had belonged to the church in question. But the Sharp Street parishioners had had nothing to do with Lawton's beating. So confusing was the relationship between the watchman's black assailants and the target of the mob's subsequent anger that the *Sun* was forced to clarify for readers that "the negroes who assaulted the watch" were "by no means connected with the church or its concerns." To the members of the white mob, however, that difference was inconsequential. The black people "in the vicinity of the church, standing about the doors," seemed little different from the congregants who prayed inside: in the eyes of the white mob, both groups were akin to violent rowdies, and both deserved summary punishment.[29]

White criminal condemnation of black autonomy extended to slaves and shaped conceptions of what historians would one day call "slave agency." Contemporaries tellingly called runaway slaves "fugitives." So long as enslaved persons submitted to a slave owner's control, they legally affirmed their status as a political nonentity, or what Aristotle labeled "a living instrument" of another, "the reverse of independent." Once a slave escaped from bondage, however, he or she became a "fugitive" from justice who had stolen from someone else — he or she became a thief of another's property. A flight for freedom, a demonstrably political act, legally transformed the dependent slave into the consenting criminal.[30] Years later, when Congress was debating the Thirteenth Amendment, Baltimore representative John Creswell made this point explicitly and eloquently. "To seek his freedom by flight made the slave a felon," he explained.[31]

This criminalization of slave resistance was made even more pernicious by the law's presumption that all free people of color were slaves until they could prove otherwise. Free black people could and did prove otherwise, to be sure. A black man named Joe won his freedom in 1834 after heirs of his mother and grandmother's former masters claimed him as their own. Joe successfully argued that for three generations his family had been living as free within the vicinity of, and without objection from, those masters, and that it therefore did not matter that no manumission deed was ever filed. Both a lower circuit court and the Maryland Court of Appeals upheld Joe's claim to freedom, deciding that the former slave owners, William and Elizabeth Mackubin, had manumitted the black family through action if not deed. But Joe's case also underlined how — to use words from the court's decision —"a negro in this State is presumed to be a slave; and on a petition for freedom, must prove his descent from a free ancestor, or that he has been manumitted by deed or will."[32]

Free black Baltimoreans' legal stigmatization as potential *slaves* marked them as potential *fugitives* even when they had done nothing wrong. Most black people were well familiar with white looks of suspicion and displays of harassment, particularly on the public roads that led out of the city, despite the fact that an overwhelming number of them were already free. A black Methodist preacher observed by the New Englander Ethan Allen Andrews illustrated the point in a telling analogy on a summer's night in 1835. Speaking to a Sunday congregation, he delivered a sermon about the difficult road to spiritual salvation. "He warned his hearers against supposing that they could enter heaven without love to Christ in their hearts," recounted Andrews. "This he told them was the only 'free pass.'" The preacher then continued with his analogy: "If they wanted to go from the south to Philadelphia or New York, they knew very well that they would be stopped on the way if they had not a free pass, and so it would be if they should try to enter heaven without a pass containing the name and the broad seal of Christ."[33]

With its reference to a pass system that touched all black people regardless of their status, the minister's analogy hinted at the complex position from which white Baltimoreans approached the question of black freedom. Many understood that free black Baltimoreans were not going anywhere, whatever their wishes to the contrary. Many also believed that free people of color — and free black men especially — deserved a limited bundle of rights and legal protections and greeted re-enslavement movements with some measure of hostility. Andrews himself noted that most of the white people he met in the city were "not bound to [slavery] by any interest, either real or supposed, and are in reality longing for its final extinction." But these same people, he explained, often also expressed a "belief that the situation of the slaves is not in fact improved by their emancipation" because black people possessed "indolent and improvident" characters that led them to shirk hard work, ignore household order, and break the law. White Baltimoreans, in other words, acknowledged black freedom but worried about its results. They took it for granted that black men were poor candidates for liberty, yet many also believed that those men had a right to fail. Indeed, white Baltimoreans disliked racial slavery and accepted black crime as the price of its absence.[34]

White Vigilantism in the Age of Slavery

One might reasonably surmise that white fears about free black lawlessness would have led Baltimore's authorities to police black Baltimoreans with a vengeance. After all, this was the era of police reform. Just as white Baltimoreans were expressing their concerns about free black men's indolent dispositions, disorderly households, and criminal behavior, liberal reformers were erecting new institutions to guard against and incarcerate the indolent, disorderly, and criminal. What else were policemen and prisons for, if not to check the lawlessness of a people who seemed uniquely unprepared for freedom? Reformers embarked upon their grand projects because laws alone were not enough to stop the wanton from running wild, and to many white observers, black men seemed like the most wanton free people of all.

And yet: police professionalization did not give rise to a dramatic increase in black arrests in antebellum Baltimore. Consider the data from the 1850s city jail reports (see table 5.1). We can glean three different conclusions from these numbers. First, black Baltimoreans were overrepresented in jail relative to their share of the city's population. The 1860 census, the first that treated Baltimore City as a separate corporate entity from the county, counted 25,680 free African Americans out of 212,418 total residents. Such numbers made free black people only 12.1 percent of Baltimore's population, and black people in general (counting slaves) only 13.1 percent.[35] Even at the nadir of black arrest totals — 1861 — black individuals accounted for about 17 percent of the jail's commitments, which outpaced their share of the city's total population. Clearly, black people's reputations as indolent, disorderly, and criminal informed their treatment by the public authorities. Second, we can also see that the absolute number of black arrests grew after the new police force hit the streets in March 1857. The directors of the jail reported that 42 percent more black people had been committed in 1858 than had been just two years earlier, before the reforms had been implemented. But these numbers also show a decline in black people's *relative* numbers over

TABLE 5.1. Black share of Baltimore city jail commitments, mid-nineteenth century

Year	Total	Percentage black
1850	621	27.7
1852	490	24.1
1854	923	29.4
1856	802	24.6
1858	1,141	23.0
1861	1,288	17.3

Source: Calculated from table B in 1850, 1852, 1854, 1856, 1858, and 1861 Jail Reports, appendices to the Ordinances of the Mayor and City Council of Baltimore, DLR.

time, leading to our third takeaway: although still overrepresented among those who entered the jail, black people became less so during the 1850s. If anything, the immediate effect of police reform was to reduce black Baltimoreans' proportion of city jail commitments, a curious fact considering white fears of free black crime.

The best explanation for the relative diminution of black commitments to the jail lies with the law's racial inequities. Although the vast majority of black Baltimoreans were free, they still stood apart legally. Unlike everyone else, free black people lacked a full array of rights. The result was that ordinary white Baltimoreans maintained remarkable power over black lives despite police reform and the state's supposed monopolization of legitimate force. If anything, professional policemen increased ordinary white citizens' power over black Baltimoreans, protecting white property rights while ignoring those of their black victims. The solution to black crime in antebellum Baltimore was not, during the late antebellum years, more professional policing. It was more popular policing. So long as free people of color occupied their peculiar legal status and the law treated them as neither slaves nor truly free, white vigilantism in Baltimore was ubiquitous.

To understand why white popular policing was not only coherent with the onset of police reform but in some ways complemented by it, we must return to the matter of free black Baltimoreans' legal constraints under slavery.

Terrified of black freedom, lawmakers were explicit about wanting to place free African Americans "beyond the reach of temptations to crime, which a life of idleness readily embraces."[36] They wanted, that is, to prevent free black people from becoming full "members of the body politic" who benefited from the rights and privileges that other people enjoyed.[37] To preempt free black lawlessness, they believed it necessary to curtail black rights.

In white eyes, Nat Turner's revolt in nearby Virginia hinted at the nightmarish possibilities of unregulated black behavior. The story was well known in Maryland. During the early morning hours of August 22, 1831, Nat Turner and several other black Virginians banded together in rural Southampton County, hoping to seize control of the small town of Jerusalem. They planned to gather forces along the way and kill any white person who got in their way. Which is what they did: Turner and his followers, a group that included more than a few free black people, went from one house to the next murdering the white people they found. By the time they were finished, nearly sixty whites, most of them women and children, lay dead. Although local white militiamen eventually killed or captured most of the rebels, Turner himself escaped, disappearing into the woods. Well into the autumn months he remained at large.[38]

Over two hundred miles away, white Baltimoreans digested rumors of race war and feared for their lives. They read that slaves in North Carolina had burned Wilmington to the ground; they heard about possible uprisings on Maryland's Eastern Shore and in nearby Baltimore County; they learned, from an anonymous letter to a local newspaper, that in the very heart of their own city, on Saratoga Street, "a number of Blacks have been in the Habit for several night[s] past, of Assembling" in military dress, performing military exercises.[39] Two other letters found their way to the mayor's office, the first purporting to be from one black conspirator to another. It explained that Turner himself was coming "from Philadelphia on the morrow to get the men you have in muster ready ... which will end in the overthrow of the whites and our freedom." The second, in reply, assured "that there was eight hundred people in town that were going to help murder the damd white people."[40]

News of Turner's uprising filtered into Baltimore at the very moment that white residents were coming to grips with their city's unusually large free black population and just when mainstream beliefs were hardening toward them. The Virginia rebellion confirmed for many whites that people of color were as unlawful as they had feared. White Baltimoreans had spent years attempting to reconcile their skepticism of black nature with the multitude of free black people in their midst, and when they heard about Nat Turner and his murderous band of followers, they reacted poorly. No black-led revolt ever came to Baltimore, or to anywhere else for that matter. What came instead was a legal backlash that consisted of what one compilation of state law called the "most important of the numerous acts" regarding black Baltimoreans before the Civil War.[41]

By the time Nat Turner rampaged through the Virginia countryside, the state of Maryland already mandated newly manumitted individuals to register their names and carry written proof at all times of their status and prevented any free black person from testifying against any white person in court, voting in any state or local election, or owning and using a firearm without a special permit.[42] The events in Virginia convinced legislators in both Annapolis and Baltimore that more laws were needed, if only to reduce free black people's actual numbers. In Baltimore, councilmen spent the better part of the next decade trying to figure out how "to prohibit the introduction into this city of free negroes from other cities and states."[43] New laws pouring in from Annapolis animated those hopes by prohibiting any more free people of color from entering Maryland, legalizing the sale into slavery of those who did, and barring those who left from ever returning. Other statutes simultaneously made "emigration to Liberia, a condition precedent of obtaining freedom on the part of a slave."[44]

Hindsight informs us that the number of free black Baltimoreans continued to grow after the 1830s and that the vast majority of the state's manumitted slaves did not end up in Liberia. For this reason alone one should avoid confusing antiblack legislation with its enforcement. The gulf between the law on the books and the law in action was no less wide in Baltimore than it was anywhere else: a program to extradite all freed slaves and halt all free black immigration was farfetched and doomed to fail. But such laws did get enforced occasionally, a circumstance that mattered to free black people. In the summer of 1832, for example, members of a local chapter of the Colonization Society had the Philadelphian Charles Gardner arrested after the black Methodist pastor overstayed his visit to Baltimore. He had been in the city for more than ten days, which was a crime. Eventually, Gardner did avoid prosecution on a technicality, and he quickly fled the city after leaving police custody.[45]

Legislators were not content to limit their attention to absent free black people or those not yet free. They also directed legal dictates at those who already were free and promised to remain in Maryland. In particular, law-makers sought to limit black people's right to assemble. To some extent, laws prohibiting free African Americans from entering the state already did this: they limited Baltimore's robust free black community from hosting national black conventions.[46] Legislators now stripped free black people of the right of praying together without a white clergyman or proxy present. In places like Baltimore, where the size of the free black population made such pro-hibitions difficult to enforce, new state laws also authorized ordinary white citizens to halt services when they deemed it appropriate.[47] Municipal au-thorities took their cue from Annapolis and quickly approved a 10:00 p.m. curfew for all black Baltimoreans, which forced black religious gatherings to break up earlier than usual. City officials also obligated black people to request written permission from the mayor if they wanted to gather at all, at any time.[48] Black people, the law implied, were unable to control themselves when congregated together. Those who petitioned had to prove they were not lawless so that they could enjoy a privilege of assembly: Basil Savoy was "quiet and peacible" and "a woman of good Character"; Enols Chase was "a very peaceable man"; Samuel Grayson was "sober, honest & industrious."[49] Assumptions about black Baltimoreans' criminal dispositions hailed those black individuals who proved they were "peaceable" and "industrious" as exceptions to a larger rule.

These laws ultimately divided free Baltimoreans along lines of race. That did not make free black Baltimoreans into slaves, despite the wishes of cer-tain proslavery ideologues. Even in the 1840s and 1850s, Baltimore's free people of color continued to enjoy opportunities to work for wages, belong to autonomous households, and exercise a variety of rights. But neither were free black people, even free black men, legally equal to white people, and the racial disparities in law translated into racial disparities in power upon city streets. This, then, is what black constraints had to do with policing: while lawmakers checked free black mobility and assembly, limited black economic behavior, and restricted black testimony, the subjects of such laws were no less white than black people. Legal discrimination not only codified racial inequality but empowered white vigilantes.[50]

Sometimes it seemed as if a white man could do almost anything he wanted to a black person under the cover of law. He could assault. He could kidnap. He could shoot. When a white man shot a black woman in July 1844, for instance, the victim possessed little legal recourse to have him punished. "Circumstances pointed to McArdee as the offender, and he was arrested," reported a court observer. But since the woman was black and the offender was white and no other white person was present to testify on her behalf, there existed "no direct evidence against" McArdee. He was soon "discharged on his own recognizances."[51] Sooner or later, the poor woman must have lamented that justice was often fleeting for the black victims of white assailants. Those assailants could act beyond the law. They could act at times as if they embodied the law.[52]

McArdee's example notwithstanding, white power was not absolute. Francis Schaeffer, a white man "determined to take the law into his own hands, and punish persons as he thinks just and proper," twice attacked the black tailor William Hanoe in January 1841. In both cases he was quickly arrested and required to give $200 bail.[53] The saloonkeeper George Ulenburg also discovered the limits of his racial authority when in 1860 he assaulted a black customer, Isaac Downs. According to Ulenburg, Downs had ordered and consumed whiskey for which he could not pay, and the German victualler had attempted a "settlement by striking Downs alongside of the head with a bottle and afterwards with a club, inflicting two very severe wounds." The black man, "nearly blinded by the blood which flowed from his wounds," made his way to the western district station, where he lodged a complaint. Two policemen answered his call.[54]

Hanoe's and Downs's stories underscore that black Baltimoreans were not without legal voice and that they were capable of making successful claims for redress from white aggressors, insofar as redress meant those aggressors' arrest. White Baltimoreans could overreach. In the eyes of the law, white Baltimoreans *did* overreach. No less important, black Baltimoreans could act as policing agents themselves. In July 1852, when black Marylanders convened a statewide convention in Baltimore to discuss immigration to Liberia, black protesters gathered outside the building that housed the proceedings, harassing entrants and raising a "considerable excitement." Certain members of the crowd got inside, where they booed the proponents of removal. Some of the protesters actually took the stage. Policemen had to protect one of the leaders of the convention, the Reverend Darius Stokes, as a crowd chased him through the streets. Either out of fear for their persons or personal principle, most delegates expressed opposition to any scheme of removal, voluntary or otherwise.[55]

But even if white Baltimoreans' power was not absolute and black Baltimoreans were not absolutely powerless, inequality was still the rule on the streets, and it frequently manifested in white popular policing. White people occasionally intervened in interracial fights in which their own had lost the upper hand. In one case, "several citizens" arrested James Brian for having committed "a violent assault" upon a white boy. Brian, who was black, argued that he had been defending himself from "a gang of white boys" and that the crowd had misjudged his act of self-defense as an act of provocation. His argument went unheeded. With no sympathetic white witnesses present, Brian's word on the street proved no more audible than his testimony in the courtroom, and so he found himself at the mercy of the judgment of white passersby. The white crowd delivered Brian to jail, where he was to await trial.[56]

White men also took it upon themselves to arrest black people whom they considered to be rowdy and riotous. Take this case: on a Sunday night in the autumn of 1837, "several gentlemen" attending to a sick friend in northwest Baltimore became annoyed by "a large collection of negroes" who had gathered across the street. As far as these "gentlemen" saw it, the black people constituted "a gang" and were acting "riotous and disorderly." And so they did what white men in antebellum Baltimore felt empowered to do: they ordered the assemblage to leave the area. The black Baltimoreans refused and a brawl ensued, by the end of which "two of the negroes (Jim Topman and Henry Cook) were shot, though not dangerously wounded," and in the whites' custody. A white crowd then spent the next day locating and seizing five more of the alleged black rioters and committed the whole for trial. "We trust the remainder of these daring desperadoes will be brought to condign punishment," concluded a newspaper correspondent. He was not talking about the white men with guns.[57]

Black Baltimoreans suspected of being thieves confronted watchful white men as well. One black man writing from jail in 1854 complained that he had stolen "a set of castors of little value" before being "arrested by citizens, not officers." Now he was anxiously awaiting his punishment, which was re-enslavement, and hoped for a reprieve.[58] In another instance, a black man named John Fields took a box of raisins from Daniel Thomas's store before Thomas, a white man, "pursued him about one hundred yards, and overtook him with one box of raisins in his possession, in less than a minute from the time the property was missed." Thomas delivered his charge to jail, testified before the criminal court, and — eventually — witnessed Fields's conviction.[59] Few if any lawmakers questioned the legitimacy of these ordinary citizens arresting black people. In a city with both large numbers of free people of color as well as legalized racial inequality, citizen arrests of black persons were merely part of the normal machinery of the municipality's police.

White male Baltimoreans also were in the protection business, and it was not unusual to see them fight for black men. This did not always end well: on a winter's afternoon in early 1844, for example, a mob of white rowdies violently assaulted a white jeweler after he stood up for a black man they were chasing. Members of the mob had dragged their victim into the street, knocked him down, and repeatedly kicked him in plain view when a number of passersby begged that they "not . . . kill the nigger." "Do you take his part?" several of the attackers replied. Frightened, none of the passersby did. The black man, however, took his own part and used the distraction to run away. As the parties came around the corner of Gay and Front Streets, the aforementioned jeweler stepped out of his store and confronted the pursuers head-on, demanding to know what so many men wanted with a single person who had, in all likelihood, done them little or no harm. The jeweler misjudged. He was quickly "seized by two or three of the party, dragged almost headlong into the cellar beneath the house . . . and there struck by the party in so violent a manner as to cause very serious injury to the head."[60]

The jeweler made a mistake in confronting an angry gang without help. Others who intervened in fights on behalf of black victims acted more carefully. Appreciating that an angry gang was also always a dangerous gang, some sympathetic white men formed their own gangs when attempting to protect the black targets of white wrath. In 1841, "a party of young fellows" in northeast Baltimore seized a black man named Joseph Green and "commenced a violent assault upon the unoffending creature." Nearby, a few "citizens" who took notice combined forces, halted the fray, and took the beaten man "into custody." Once Green was out of harm's way, the group of citizens turned their sights upon the offending party and managed to detain one of Green's assailants. They then waited with their charge until the arrival of constables, who delivered the man to jail.[61]

Citizens arrested and protected black Baltimoreans often enough to blur the distinction between vigilantes and policemen. Consider the reaction to James Dent's arrest by James Musgrave, H. Kennedy, and Frederick Willar in early March 1861. The three white men had been walking in their northwest Baltimore neighborhood when they noticed a black man, Dent, carrying eight dead chickens. Suspicions aroused, one of the cohort asked Dent to stop, but he opted, instead, to run, and he hurled stones at his pursuers as he went. After a small scuffle, Dent "plunged" into Gwynn Falls and therein "a desperate struggle ensued" during which the suspect allegedly attempted "to drown his captors." At last, one of the white men struck Dent with a piece of lumber, which knocked him down and left a "deep gash on his forehead, from which the blood flowed freely." The three men managed to secure their suspect "with his plunder," brought him to the city center, and delivered him into the custody of Officer Pumphrey, from whose care Dent eventually went to jail to await action from a grand jury.[62]

The difference between "ordinary" white men and "official" policemen was almost imperceptible to someone like James Dent. Musgrave, Kennedy, and Willar took it upon themselves to stop him for questioning and acted aggressively once he refused to be questioned. The municipal government sanctioned such behavior through silence. No one, not the "official" police-man Pumphrey nor the processing magistrate, protested the vigilantism that brought Dent to jail. Nobody suggested that such behavior was lawless or extralegal, extraordinary or exceptional. In fact, Musgrave, Kennedy, and Willar merely delivered Dent as a matter of course, acting on their suspicions once those suspicions had been confirmed.

In other cases the municipality more explicitly sanctioned racial vigilan-tism. It did so particularly when citizens protected private property from black arsonists, an act for which white men frequently asked and expected municipal redress. "The undersigned beg leave to state to your Honourable Body that they on the 7th day of November 1839 arrested Sarah Young a Woman the property of John B. Morris Esq., charged with setting fire to the back Building of the Dwelling House of Elizabeth Rouge in German Street," Andrew Kellor and P. Allright wrote the city council. "You will be pleased to take their case into your consideration and grant them such compensation as the Services rend. the city."[63] Peter Kreis and Benjamin Horn likewise wanted compensation for their "services." But their case was special, too: they not only had "discovered" Amelia Thomas setting fire to a tannery but had discovered her setting fire to *Horn's own tannery*. Not content with merely having prevented the destruction of his own property, Horn wanted municipal compensation as well for his act of vigilance. He was, after all, a white man who helped arrest a black woman, deliver her to jail, and assure her conviction. That was work that usually entailed compensation. As a re-sult, Horn felt "entitled to the reward of His Honor the Mayor for such arrest and conviction."[64]

Well into the era of police professionalization, mayors kept offering rewards for catching arsonists while white men, in response, kept arresting black men for committing arson. "In consequence of the many fires that have recently occurred in our city, doubtless in many instances occasioned by the hand of the incendiary," Mayor Brown wrote in 1853, "I hereby, by virtue of Ordinance No. 31, approved June 3rd 1850, offer the reward of *three hundred dollars* for the arrest and conviction in any court of any person or persons who may be guilty of setting fire to any building, lumber yard, or ship yard, in the City." Five years later the offer still stood. In 1858, a Baltimore man named Urich Muir petitioned Mayor Swann with Brown's original resolution attached. Following protocol, Muir also attached written evidence of "the Arrest and Conviction of Robert Queen (col'd) for burning the stable of Bartus Wilkins," of Queen's subsequent indictment, and of Queen's guilty verdict. "The Boy was arrested by me," Muir signed off. "I most respectfully ask your honorable body for the reward as offered under said resolution, and in duty bound will ever pray."[65]

The supposed professionals acted (and were paid) like mercenaries while ordinary white men acted (and were paid) like professionals. After the police force began to professionalize, and after night watchmen were disallowed from receiving monetary rewards for making arrests, certain officers continued to collect supplemental rewards for arresting black suspects.[66] Night watchman Nicholas Pamphilon's case is instructive. In 1851, Pamphilon petitioned the city council for $131 after arresting a black man for larceny. In Maryland, Pamphilon explained, a free black person convicted twice for larceny was usually sold into slavery out of state, and because this arrest resulted in such a sale, part of its proceeds rightfully belonged to him, the arresting officer.[67] Baltimore's city registrar was not so sure. He thought Pamphilon's request was "contrary to law" on account of the fact that an arrest counted among a night watchman's paid duties. But an attorney for the city explained that according to an 1838 state law, Pamphilon was correct. That law sought to "encourage *all the officers in the State* to enforce the law against free negroes who had been convicted a second time," effectively transforming salaried officers like Pamphilon into mercenaries entitled to a reward.[68]

Such a system of compensation blurred the line between white vigilantes and city officers by lending popular policing an air of formality and coloring the officers' actions with an aura of vigilantism. In a variety of ways, the distinctions between official police officers and ordinary white men were stark and growing starker with each passing year. The city's registrar who argued Pamphilon should not be paid like a private citizen understood those distinctions. What he missed was how race troubled the easy demarcation between official and ordinary: when it came to policing black people in antebellum Baltimore, all white men possessed some degree of authority, deployed real power, and wore a type of uniform. At the moment Pamphilon arrested the black larcenist, his position as a police officer mattered less than did his identity as a white man. Black suspects were in this way transformative for white policers: their blackness rendered the differences between professional and private white men almost obsolete, adorning the latter with some of the powers and responsibilities of the former. Pamphilon collected his money.

None of this is to suggest that the municipality absented itself from policing free people of color; the law instructed salaried officers, for instance, to "arrest and convey to the Watch house, all negroes or persons of colour" who violated the city's curfew.[69] The larger point, rather, is that any white male Baltimorean could have been any black Baltimorean's "policeman" on any given day. It did not matter whether those white men were policemen paid to guard against and respond to crime, or whether they were ordinary citizens taking a walk on a sunny day. When it came to policing Baltimore's free black population, a vigilante and a policeman possessed similar powers. And this was notable because Baltimoreans were increasingly reliant upon and policed by the city's official representatives. Only in this one critical area did white men retain their right to act as though police power was still dispersed across the citizenry. Popular policing persisted in Baltimore amid police professionalization because racial inequities in the law empowered ordinary whites to police black criminals too.

So let us return to the numbers in table 5.1, which showed a relative decline of black commitments to the jail during the 1850s. Whereas in 1850, 27.7 percent of all the people committed to the Baltimore jail were black — about twice the black share of the city's total population — in 1861 just 17.3 percent were. That drop cannot be explained entirely by black Baltimoreans' decreasing share of the city's population, for the free black population's relative decline in the city's overall population was nowhere near as steep as the relative decline of black inmates in the city's jail.[70] And it surely cannot be explained by growing comfort among whites toward free black people, as these very years also witnessed some of the most stringent antiblack laws of the entire period.[71] What accounts for the decline of black commitments was instead, and perhaps perversely, legalized racism: by the 1850s municipal authorities were nearing completion of a decades-long blitz on black rights, during which they charged ordinary citizens to handle the problem of black crime on their own. As for the new police force, officials mostly used it to combat their political enemies, be they Know-Nothings or Democrats, as well as other "criminal" people who counted among the truly free.

The 1850s was a decade of police professionalization *and* racial panic. The bundle of rights possessed by free black Baltimoreans entitled them to certain protections under the law, but increasingly both state and municipal authorities constricted those rights and empowered whites, and white men especially, to police the black community with vigor. White men arrested black suspected criminals, protected black victims of white mobs, and generally behaved in a manner that seemed to dispute the notion that the city's authorities held a monopoly upon legitimate uses of force. Police reform was coherent with white popular policing. The professional and uniformed policeman who walked an 1850s Baltimore beat did not seize power from white vigilantes; he supplemented it.

Black Punishment in the Age of Slavery

There was another side to this story, one that played out off the streets in the city's various asylums. Just as white vigilantism was proliferating under the watchful eye of the new policeman, penal officials were attempting to limit their intake of black inmates. To some extent, they succeeded; during the 1850s, prison populations across Baltimore grew markedly whiter. The white prison population was the corollary to the white vigilante. Both trends — the proliferation of white vigilantism and the decline of black inmates — epitomized solutions to (the perceived problem of) free black crime during the age of slavery. With an institutionalized system of racial control already in existence, state and municipal officials worked to reserve the prison as a site of punishment for whites alone.

From the prison's inception, reformers had imagined it as a white space. The ideal prisoner, the political subject most capable of looking inward, becoming penitent, and redeeming one's self, was both white and male, for it was only white men who were legally entitled to the full privileges and immunities of citizenship. Black prisoners thus presented reformers with something of a dilemma, even in northern states where African Americans possessed a greater number of rights and white liberals were less inclined to associate black people with enslavement. "It is not by remorse and anguish that he is affected, so much as by intellectual and mental weakness and decay," wrote Dr. Benjamin Coates after observing black prisoners in Philadelphia's Eastern State Penitentiary in 1843. According to Coates, the black inmate was "constitutionally free from that deep, thoughtful anxiety for the future, so conspicuous in his paler neighbor." The consequence was that "gloomy confinement becomes thus to him, mentally as well as physically, a nearer approach to the punishment of death."[72] State officials in Maryland readily agreed with Coates's diagnosis of black nature. In his 1858 farewell address, Governor Thomas Ligon explicitly stated that incarcerated black inmates were "not reformable by our prison discipline, and . . . [their] confinement in the prison . . . seems to be attended with such unprofitable results."[73]

Because penal reformers doubted the utility of incarcerating black people, blackness increasingly presupposed a series of fates for the alleged criminal that did not involve imprisonment. One of those fates was simply release: sometimes policemen sent black suspects home without charging them with an offense or processing them for court. "Among the arrests made by the officers of the western district for Saturday night and yesterday, were twenty four colored individuals 'jerked' for offences as varied as their sex and age," read one newspaper account. "A few were fined because they had money to pay it with . . . and the rest were let off with a promise to behave better in the future."[74] Black people "jerked" off the streets may well have been let go because in Baltimore the newly uniformed policemen wanted to spend more time monitoring those people who could better perceive the difference "between right and wrong": free white men.[75] In fact, by 1860 nearly three out of every four people arrested by city policemen were white men.[76] Black inmates, on the other hand, merely took up space. According to one watch report, the black individuals arrested over the previous weekend were "too humble to be honored with a place in our reports."[77] According to another, the grand jury released a black arsonist after the jurors concluded that she "was not more than half-witted."[78]

White arresting parties also sometimes let black suspects go after administering a beating. "On Tuesday night," informed one weekly watch report, "a few vagrant negroes were taken up, kept all night and reprimanded, i.e. 'beaten with many stripes.'"[79] Another reported how "a lady of color . . . was brought to the watch house, and *reprimanded*."[80] And yet another, in summarizing an uneventful week in the various watch districts, generalized that "a large, very large proportion of those received into the 'lock-ups'

are miserable negroes . . . [a group] usually *reprimanded*."[81] Police reporters
were so familiar with "the peculiar way the officers of the watch" abused
free black arrestees that they began to describe such beatings with glib eu-
phemisms.[82] "In the Eastern District, a few disorderly negroes were brought
in, and received their deserts in the shape of a cow-hide, well laid on," one
journalist recounted.[83]

The public authorities reserved corporal punishment for black Baltimoreans. While policemen "reprimanded" black suspects, and as the criminal
courts sentenced black convicts to receive "nine and thirty lashes," and
despite the fact that governors pardoned black prisoners on the condition
that they "receive publicly thirty lashes" or "twenty stripes" in lieu of serving
time in the penitentiary, most liberals looked upon corporal punishment
in the abstract with horror.[84] One *Sun* editorial went so far as to condemn
"corporeal punishment" as "only suited to the atmosphere of Algiers and
Tripoli, and is by no means to be tolerated in any section of the country. We
presume that it would long since have been stricken from the laws of the
commonwealth, had it been *known* to exist."[85] And yet corporal punishment
did exist in Baltimore and was reported in the very newspaper whose editor
railed against it. The *Sun*'s pages were so littered with reports of black "rep-
rimands" that its stories presumed that "readers know what [reprimand], so
frequently used in this connection[,] means."[86] Outrage over corporal punishment was for whites alone. "The populace would never permit the flag-
ellation of a *white* man," concluded the "Algiers and Tripoli" editorialist.[87]

Of all noncarceral punishments that suspected black criminals endured
in antebellum Baltimore, however, enslavement was the worst. Sentences
of re-enslavement provided a remedy for both growing penal populations
and the problem of black incarceration.[88] Lawmakers began excluding free
people of color from prison in 1836, when state legislators approved a statute
ordering criminal courts to sell any black freeperson twice convicted of a
crime into slavery; twenty years later, another law mandated all criminal
courts sell into slavery any free black person convicted of larceny—petty
or grand, for the first time or not.[89] Singling out property crime was not
coincidental: throughout the antebellum period, black inmates made up
a higher proportion of charged thieves than they did of any other class of
criminal. In 1850, for example, black arrestees accounted for more than 36
percent of all people committed to Baltimore's jail for theft; meanwhile, they
accounted for about 20 percent of all people committed for assault and 30
percent of those committed for public drunkenness.[90] Black Marylanders,

despite their minority status overall, occasionally formed an outright majority of thieves in the penitentiary. In 1837, 162 of the 297 people incarcerated for theft were black.[91] After 1858, free black people convicted of theft began to become slaves, not inmates.

It was not uncommon for criminal court judges to sentence free black convicts into slavery for having committed the same offense that whites, present in court the very same day, had also committed. After a jury found James Peters, a white man, guilty of stealing a trunk from Mr. James George's storefront, the judge ordered him to serve eighteen months in the penitentiary. The court immediately thereafter heard the cases of Philip Frisby and James Henry Williams, two black men accused of stealing exactly that which Peters had stolen — a trunk. Upon conviction, the judge ordered that Frisby "be sold out of the state for the term of ten years" and Williams "for a term of fifteen years, having been before convicted."[92] A few months later the same court administered differential justice yet again after James Buffalo, "a rare specimen of the genuine white loafer," stole a twenty-two-dollar cassinette off a wagon, and a black woman named Charlotte Williams stole twenty dollars in specie from a neighbor. While "Mr. Buffalo was sent to graze for three years in the penitentiary," Williams, "this being the second time she was found guilty of a like offense . . . was ordered to be sold out of the State for seven years."[93] In this case, the "rare specimen" deserved imprisonment; the more common black convict, enslavement. And so the beat went on. Alexander Wilson, convicted of stealing a hat and piece of cloth; Eliza Smith, convicted of stealing a piece of flannel; and Hyson Williams, convicted of stealing two bushels of corn: the Baltimore City Court sold each of these people into slavery out of state rather than incarcerating them.[94]

Selling black convicts into slavery was remarkably uncontroversial in mid-nineteenth-century Baltimore. No high tribunal ever heard a case that challenged the legality of the practice, nor did any court ever undermine its ubiquity. The only element of criminal re-enslavement that garnered judicial challenge at all was the question of the black person's ultimate destination: should the court send the individual somewhere beyond the state's borders, or should it sell him or her to someone in Maryland? Certain judges preferred to send black convicts as far away as possible, which usually meant deeper into the South, but state law did not give them discretion to do so for "simple larceny." Murder, arson, and rape were exportable offenses. A theft of five dollars was not. So when the Baltimore City Court sentenced Thomas Watkins to be sold out of state for stealing a silver watch, Watkins appealed to the Maryland Court of Appeals and won. "Under the sentence prescribed by the law, the convict may be purchased and held by a citizen of Maryland, or he might be purchased by a non-resident," the court ruled. Watkins stayed in Maryland. He did not, however, stay free. What was not in question was whether he could be "purchased and held" by someone at all.[95]

Insofar as penal reformers questioned the efficacy of re-enslavement, they lamented its leniency. "We would call your attention to the laws for the punishment of slaves or free negroes committing crimes, less than capital," read one penal report in 1845. "In the case of a free negro, who is convicted of a second offence, the only punishment inflicted on him is to sell him out of the state." The prison's directors wondered if this was punishment enough — whether, that is, "his case is made better or worse by this, though his offence may be one for which the severest punishment, short of death, should have been inflicted."[96] For their part, free black people thought differently. When someone was sold away, family members did not have the ability to visit their kin, as they would have if he or she was incarcerated nearby; they may not have been able to see their loved one ever again, in fact. "My Brother has been arraigned before the Criminal Court of Baltimore and Sentenced to be sold out of the state for five years," a desperate Rachel Jones wrote the governor in 1854. Jones had been informed "that persons sold hence for a term of years are never likely to recover their liberty at the end of the term, they go South into Speculators hands who unjustly take from them the copy of Record given them for evidence of right of discharge at the end of the term." She worried about what might become of her brother and what might become of the family he left behind.[97]

The result of these actions — the consequence of police officers releasing black suspects from custody and courts selling black convicts into slavery — was a transformation of the racial makeup of penal populations. In a word, they grew whiter. During the 1830s and early 1840s, for example, the majority of incoming prisoners to the Maryland Penitentiary went from black to white. The numbers were striking: in 1836, about 57 percent of new prisoners were free people of color, yet in 1845 about 40 percent were (see fig. 5.1). That trend accelerated during the 1850s, the same decade during which police reform reached fruition and racial vigilantism expanded under the aegis of the new police force. Although in 1857 some 43 percent of convicts sent to the penitentiary were black, just four years later only one convict committed to the institution — a single, solitary man — was an African American (see fig. 5.2).

FIGURE 5.1. Incoming prisoners to Maryland Penitentiary, by race, 1836–1845

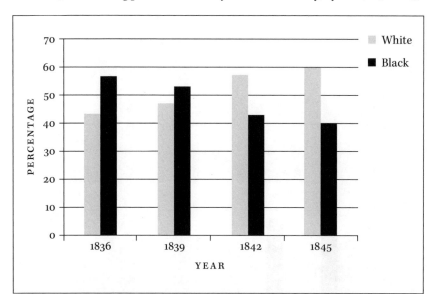

Source: Calculated from 1836, 1839, 1842, and 1845 Annual Reports of the Maryland Penitentiary, Government Publications and Reports, MSA.

With fewer black prisoners arriving, the prison's inmate population grew overwhelmingly white. During the mid-1850s, black people were still over-represented, with white people representing slightly more than half of all prisoners; by the early 1860s, white prisoners accounted for more than three-quarters of the total prison population (see table 5.2). People noticed the change, too. Among officials, the decline in black prisoners elicited praise, if for no other reason than because those officials wanted fewer inmates and saw racial exclusion as the best means to achieve that goal. In 1842, for instance, the penitentiary's directors attributed "a reduction of the number of prisoners in confinement" to "the law of 1836, ordering that negroes, upon a reconviction of crime, be sold out of the State."[98] Seven years later, the prison's warden again singled out "the law passed some years since, and now in existence, which authorised the sale of free persons of color out of the State, for second offences." He described the reduction of inmates "gratifying."[99]

The number of black people at the almshouse also fell over time, particularly during the 1850s. As early as the 1820s, black Baltimoreans were somewhat underrepresented there, at least relative to their actual need; they appeared in the almshouse's ledger at roughly the same rate at which they

FIGURE 5.2. Incoming prisoners to Maryland Penitentiary, by race, 1857–1861

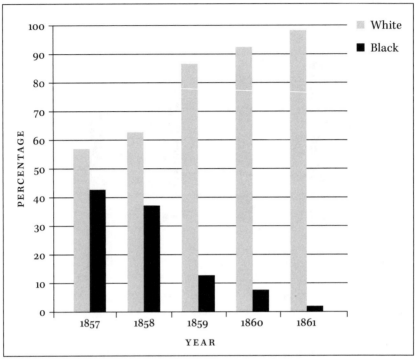

Source: Calculated from 1857, 1858, 1859, 1860, and 1861 Annual Reports of the Maryland Penitentiary, Government Publications and Reports, MSA.

resided in the city, despite the fact that they were overwhelmingly poor. Over the next four decades, African Americans' presence in the institution grew scarcer still, so much so that by 1861 they accounted for less than 13 percent of the almshouse's population. Once we take the relative poverty of Baltimore's black population into account, the dearth of black inmates in the almshouse becomes more apparent (see table 5.3). Almshouse administrators claimed to house any individual who proved unable to support himself or herself. This, after all, was the institution par excellence for reformers who hoped to make wage freedom a reality. Its segregation of men from women, its implementation of work routines, and its methods of surveillance all formed part of a disciplinary program designed to transform paupers into reliable wageworkers. Yet almshouse administrators welcomed white inmates far more frequently than they welcomed black ones, much like their colleagues in the nearby Maryland Penitentiary.[100]

TABLE 5.2. Maryland Penitentiary inmate population by race, mid-nineteenth century

Year	White	Black	Percentage black
1857	235	180	43.4
1858	247	178	41.9
1859	288	134	31.2
1860	320	102	24.2

Source: Calculated from 1857, 1858, 1859, and 1860 Annual Reports of the Maryland Penitentiary, Government Publications and Reports, MSA.

TABLE 5.3. Baltimore almshouse inmate population by race, mid-nineteenth century

Year	White	Black	Percentage black
1846	5,121	1,260	19.7
1852	6,464	1,348	17.3
1856	6,356	1,123	15.0
1861	8,261	1,214	12.8

Source: Calculated from 1847, 1853, 1857, and 1862 Reports of the Trustees for the Poor, appendices to the Ordinances of the Mayor and City Council of Baltimore, DLR.

But black people did end up at the prison and the poorhouse, whatever their decline over time; the same cannot be said for the House of Refuge. The most rehabilitative of the penal system's disciplinary institutions, the refuge was, at least in theory, a *"reform school"* whose inmates intended to "take [their] place in the world, with a manly bearing and an honest sentiment of self-elevation and self-reliance."[101] It existed to create lawful, hardworking men who would be well equipped to govern their own households one day. Yet when it opened its doors in 1855, the House of Refuge's inmates were all, to a child, white.[102] Despite the scorn and derision that white commentators heaped upon black households, no black boy entered the refuge to "take his place among the good and the virtuous and become a useful and honest citizen."[103] No black boys were deemed worthy enough to be "systematically educated, taught ... some useful trade, or kept in regular employment, their old habits thoroughly broken up, and ... taught to find even a pleasure in steady occupation."[104] The House of Refuge was from its inception a white institution, with only white children coming in and out of its rooms and workshops.

These trends might seem surprising to twenty-first-century Americans accustomed to growing inmate populations driven by black prisoners. Many modern-day Americans justifiably associate the criminalization of black-ness with the incarceration of black people.[105] But in the United States, the criminalization of blackness began as the criminalization of black *freedom* in a world of racial *slavery*. Free black people during the antebellum years were unable to escape slavery's long legal shadow, especially in a city like Baltimore where bondage was still on the books, numerous laws codified racial inequality, and fears of black crime manifested in white vigilantism. Although not slaves, free black Baltimoreans were not fully free either, mak-ing them poor candidates for a system of punishment built in the name of freedom. It was no accident that white males dominated the ranks of Balti-more's initial prison populations. The architects of the city's penal asylums wanted their institutions to house the truly free.

We can better glean slavery's influence upon the racial demography of pris-ons, and better understand the attempts by Maryland lawmakers to whiten their inmate populations, by comparing the Maryland Penitentiary to its peer institutions in the slave South. Penitentiaries in states with large slave populations for the most part contained few or no free people of color. During the 1850s, free black people represented about 8 percent of Kentucky's prison population, about 4 percent of Tennessee's, and about 1 percent of Alabama's and Mississippi's. Georgia's state prison housed no black people at all, while South Carolina did not even have a prison. States with robust slave econo-mies and small free black populations were able to outsource black punish-ment to slave owners while reserving their penitentiaries for white people exclusively. Of the slave states, only Virginia's prison population looked any-thing like Maryland's, as white inmates accounted for just over two-thirds of its prisoners.[106] Not coincidentally, Virginia was also home to the nation's second-largest free black population; in 1860, more than fifty-eight thousand black Virginians were free. Only Maryland contained more.[107]

Maryland's officials wanted their prisons and asylums to look more like those of the deep southern states, but short of re-enslavement — which the

majority of white Marylanders opposed — they struggled to stop incarcerating free black people, a group they considered culturally inclined (if not
inherently predisposed) to commit crimes. The Frenchmen Gustave de
Beaumont and Alexis de Tocqueville captured the fears and frustrations of
the state's prison directors when, in their 1832 survey of the nation's various
penal systems, they noted that

> Maryland is that state the settled population of which commits most
> crimes. This fact is explained by a cause peculiar to the southern
> states — the colored race. In general, it has been observed, that in those
> states in which there exists one Negro to thirty whites, the prisons
> contain one Negro to four white persons. The states which have many
> Negroes must therefore produce more crimes. This reason alone would
> be sufficient to explain the large number of crimes in Maryland: it is,
> however, not applicable to all the states of the South; but only to those in
> which manumission is permitted: because we should deceive ourselves
> greatly were we to believe that the crimes of the Negroes are avoided
> by giving them liberty; experience proves, on the contrary, that in the
> south the number of criminals increases with that of manumitted per-
> sons; thus, for the very reason that slavery seems to draw nearer to its
> ruin, the number of freed persons will increase for a long time in the
> south, and with it the number of criminals.[108]

In such words we can see the twin maxims of state-sponsored punishment
in antebellum Maryland. On the one hand, prisons were for free people. On
the other hand, black freedom was criminal. These two "truths," taken together, foretold a world of large prison populations unless free people of color
could be eliminated altogether, and as the various laws passed during the
antebellum era show, Maryland lawmakers did try to eliminate at least some
of them. The re-enslavement of black criminals beginning in 1858 was only
the boldest in a long line of attempts to divert free black convicts from prison
to plantation.

And the ploy worked, at least partially. Both the penitentiary and the
almshouse housed much whiter populations in 1861 than they had in 1851,
and the House of Refuge opened its doors in 1855 to white youths only. Yet
some version of the prophecy advanced by Beaumont and Tocqueville must
have haunted Baltimore's white liberals, particularly during the 1860s as
slavery collapsed under the combined weight of civil war and black resistance. White vigilantism and black re-enslavement could check perceived

black crime so long as the lawbooks codified slavery and institutionalized racial inequality, but what would happen if the lawbooks were to change? What would happen if Baltimore's large free black population outlived slavery's law? And what would happen — this was the scariest question of all — if all the slaves in the state suddenly became free? To state officials, city officers, and white jurists, reformers, and commentators, the answer was both obvious and unnerving: black inmates would flood their prisons.

In a world with slavery, however, the desire to combat free black crime could materialize beyond the typical bounds of formal state power. The proliferation of white vigilantism and the whitening of prison populations represented different iterations of the same impulse to fight black crime with the whole of the citizenry. On Baltimore's streets, white men policed the black minority with abandon, and they often worked with the city's paid policemen to protect, and protect against, black Baltimoreans. Off the streets, penal asylums geared toward rehabilitation weeded out black inmates, leaving policemen to release black suspects (sometimes with a whipping) and judges to sentence black convicts into slavery. Such was the peculiar response to the perceived ubiquity of free black crime in antebellum Baltimore. It was a solution indebted to the legal inequities of an illiberal institution.

Uniformed protection and carceral punishment had promised to bring security to insecure streets. Reformers had argued that the city's citizenry deserved the right to pursue their dreams, enjoy their liberty, and hold their property without worrying about the violence awaiting them around the next corner. Triggered by fear, police reform had been intended to bring hope. Yet the introduction of new protective and carceral institutions had brought more than hope: police reform ultimately perpetuated the racial inequality that had defined life in Baltimore long before anyone imagined a policeman on a beat or an inmate sitting alone, penitent, in quiet contemplation. Free black Baltimoreans did possess certain rights and protections, but legal constraints also rendered their relationships with the new institutions fraught at best. Police officers did not always protect them. Prisons did not always house them. In the age of slavery, Baltimore's officials preferred to leave the fates of free people of color to the capricious whims of the truly free, those white men and good citizens of the growing city.

PART III

EMANCIPATION AND ITS DISCONTENTS

✦

Chapter Six

THE RIGHTS OF MEN

◆

RACIAL SLAVERY in Maryland did not survive the Civil War. Unlike elsewhere, where the institution's demise owed to an on-coming Union army, federal action, or some combination of the two, slavery collapsed in Maryland because of measures taken at home, in the state itself. Elite white Marylanders gathered in Annapolis during the summer of 1864 and wrote a new constitution that was quickly ratified in the various counties. This was how the border state that stayed in the Union liberated its eighty-seven thousand slaves: while the war raged on in neighboring Virginia, Governor Augustus Bradford proclaimed a new con-stitution operational at 12:01 a.m. on November 1, 1864. Many black Mary-landers rejoiced. Anywhere they could be found, former slaves greeted the announcement of their liberation with jubilation. Crowds in Baltimore fired five hundred cannons and rang church bells, hung flags, and made speeches throughout the next day, as well as in the weeks to come. Frederick Doug-lass came back to celebrate the occasion. Having fled in the late 1830s as a fugitive from slavery, Maryland's most famous native son returned home in triumph, finding the city of his youth fully transformed and finally free.[1]

Not all Marylanders hailed emancipation with revelry, however. Many white people opposed it, particularly in the southern and eastern counties of the state where the plantations were more numerous and the slave pop-ulations had been more extensive. In fact, many of the very men who con-vened in Annapolis in June 1864 had dedicated their time there to fighting the emancipation clause with all of their rhetorical might. Daniel Clarke of Prince George's County spoke for many planters when he called the proposed

measure an illiberal violation of the U.S. Constitution. It impaired "the obligation of contracts" and divested "the rights of creditors," he insisted.[2]
Richard Edelen of Charles County made a similar argument: "If the General
Government cannot take the slaves of Maryland without compensation," he
complained, "the State has no right to do so." And yet here was "the majority
of this House impelled by a zeal" to destroy slavery "without providing the
smallest compensation for the loss of thousands and millions of dollars invested by the people in slaves."[3] Were slaveholders "not liberal" too? asked
Chapman Billingsley of St. Mary's County. In Billingsley's mind, they surely
were, just as the article under consideration was surely not.[4]

The proslavery arguments not only focused upon the sanctity of contracts
and the threat emancipation posed to slaveholders' property rights but also
warned that emancipated black men would be poor keepers of contract
and possessors of property. "The scheme proposed by the abolitionists of
Maryland," argued Edelen, would inevitably "turn adrift upon the white
population of the State an idle unthrifty, nonproducing class to pray upon
their substance." It would "give liberty to the slaves, which for many will be
the liberty to starve." And it would, in the end, turn loose a population who
"would refuse to work, and with their families, sink into the lowest depths
of destitution and wretchedness."[5] Angry slaveholders like Edelen articulated a nightmare scenario as indebted to the values of property as to the
belief that black people were best understood as property. According to the
slaveholders' zero-sum view, white men's property rights were incompatible
with black men's property rights, and society was better off honoring solely
the former.

Proponents of the emancipation clause took the opposite tack, arguing
that black men were as motivated by economic incentives as were any other
race of men, and undoubtedly more so if the alternative was to work for
whips and chains. "I need no other evidence than my own eyesight to convince me that [black people] work better when free than they do as slaves,"
argued Joseph Pugh in response to the proslavery delegates. "The greatest in-
ducement to toil, and the only relief to the heavy burdens of life, is the reflection that thereby we secure our own happiness and that of those around us;
and fulfill to that extent the destiny for which we were created."[6] Pugh hailed
from Cecil County, in the far northeastern corner of the state. Insofar as geography and demography mattered, it was unsurprising that a resident of a
mostly white county bordering Delaware would support emancipation. His
constituents had less to lose than the others. But in one crucial sense Pugh

agreed with his proslavery colleagues, much as he did with everyone else gathered in Annapolis. The delegates may have differed over the prospects of black success in a post-emancipation world, but, to a man, they all believed that freedom in 1860s Maryland meant working for "wages adequate to the support of his family."[7]

All of the delegates to Maryland's 1864 constitutional convention believed that true freedom meant male self-sufficiency, and in this, other Marylanders concurred. Federal officials subscribed to the notion that emancipation's success hinged upon the freedmen's ability to lift themselves and their families out of poverty. Edgar M. Gregory, commander of the Maryland District for the Freedmen's Bureau, believed that in time black men would show that they were "hard working, temperate & frugal" while demonstrating "industrious and manly behavior."[8] Reverend J. W. Alvord, the inspector of schools and finances for the bureau, wrote that the state's new birth of freedom required black men to rely entirely upon their own "individual elevation" for success. He too was confident they would. "They have settled down with the calm and firm resolution to make this work the one great & earnest effort of their lives," concluded Alvord, "demonstrating their manhood in the face of oppression & despite the prejudice and accumulated wrongs of many years."[9] Another official was no less explicit: "The Colored People will lift themselves [out of] the depression of Bondage and Proscription, to the light, the duties, and the privileges of intelligent freedom."[10]

This emphasis upon "intelligent freedom" from emancipation's friends and foes alike underscores how, in white minds, black freedom would rise and fall upon black men's success in demonstrating self-reliance. Such beliefs led federal officials to resist providing handouts to impoverished freedmen. "Republics," wrote one assistant commissioner for the Freedmen's Bureau, "dependent on the labor, integrity, and intelligence of the individual, cannot for a moment afford to empty their treasuries, or degrade the self-respect of any of their individual members, by any such disbursement of supplies as will encourage beggary, or foster idleness, or other crime."[11] Federal officials believed that black people, and black men in particular, needed to support themselves without anyone else's help; otherwise they would become beggars, rising up from slavery only to become wards of the government. Intelligent freedom precluded state handouts.

Even those white individuals who were most sympathetic to freed people's plight echoed this conviction in freedom as self-reliance. The pages of the strongly antislavery *American and Commercial Advertiser* were littered with admonitions for freedmen to "depend mainly upon their own exertions."[12] When promoting the Civil Rights Act, the editors assured readers that "it is not an act of charity."[13] The only type of assistance that black men could reasonably expect was a basic education to teach them to stand on their own. One white man rationalized that "if we are to employ the African in our midst, in any way, and expect him to render service for his wages, he must be educated in order to render an intelligent service." On the other hand, "if the States are to be relieved of the dishonest and vagrant negroes, which is much to be desired, they must be educated."[14] When a member of the Baltimore City Council sounded a similar refrain, reasoning that "if we must have [black people] among us, we can have them fitted to render the most useful services," his words were telling.[15] Black freedom was to be "useful"; it was to be "intelligent." If not, it would fail.

Many newly emancipated black Marylanders conceived of freedom in more nuanced terms, especially those in the countryside who yearned for the land on which they had worked for so long but which belonged, as before, to white planters. But a large number of freedmen also considered their emancipation as an opportunity to stand alone. "The colored people ought to learn to make the best of the present opportunities," implored Henry Highland Garnet, the chair of a large meeting of freed people some weeks after the new constitution became operational. They must, he continued, "use the hands made free by endeavoring to get homes for themselves, wives, and children, and show that they can and will do for themselves."[16] In the months to come, thousands of black men, most of them former slaves, joined a temperance movement dedicated to individual responsibility and personal uplift. "The Temperance movement has commended well among them, and they seem disposed to sustain the cause, and prosecute the good work," wrote one Maryland-based official in a report back to Washington. Black men throughout the state were recognizing "the great necessity for Temperance and Morality to fit them properly for their condition."[17]

All of these sentiments — by conservatives and radicals, by white and black men alike — suggested a liberal mindset that in the post-emancipation world defined freedom as self-sufficiency and self-reliance. What follows is the story of that philosophy's implementation in Maryland during the mid-1860s. Before the war, local lawmakers had singled out black subjects as deserving of their own set of laws, and the statutes they passed helped shape black life and empower white men to police free people of color in the city. But then, pressured by national legislation, monitored by federal agents, and compelled by many freed people themselves, lawmakers after the war grudgingly struck down the most explicitly discriminatory laws left on the books, both locally in Baltimore and more broadly in Annapolis. The post-emancipation story was one of the legal code's deracialization. It was the story of black men's acquisition of what one group of freed people called "the rights of which they have for a long period been unjustly deprived."[18] And, in a certain kind of light, it was a story with a happy ending.

Acquiring the Wage

When Henry Highland Garnet implored Maryland's freed people to "show that they can and will do for themselves," he was essentially telling them to show that they could work industriously for wages. Sympathetic white onlookers thought about emancipation in the exact same way. "The great object in view," asserted an army colonel stationed in southern Maryland, "is to afford these freedmen a means of subsistence by procuring for them good homes at fair wages, and by securing to them the legitimate fruits of their labor."[19] Unlike former slaveholders, the federal officials who arrived in Maryland after the war were quite confident that freedmen would work hard and make money in short order. One officer happily noted that in his district "no well grounded complaints against Freedmen for violations of contract or lawless behavior of any kind, has been received at these Head-quarters and it is very evident, that they feel desirous of doing right, if given the opportunity."[20] This faith in the liberating power of the wage also shaped local Republican support for the 1866 Civil Rights Act. According to the bill's advocates, it ensured for black men *"the right to labor,"* namely by protecting their "right to choose their occupation and employer, to contract for wages, and to appropriate [for] their own use the results of their labor. . . . Liberty for work surely means liberty to be paid for work."[21] As understood by federal officers and Republican partisans, the success of emancipation rested upon a bedrock of black men's wages.

Both black activists from the North and black workers from the city also judged emancipation as an opportunity for all black men to earn a living wage. "Slavery means shirk and liberty means work, and to work for your-self," intoned the black Ohio lawyer John Mercer Langston in an 1867 lecture at Bethel Church on Saratoga Street. At the time, Langston was serving as inspector general of the colored schools in the South, and he saw things the way Garnet saw them. "The secret of success is self-reliance," he explained, and self-reliance meant one primary thing: "Get money and property." To do otherwise, to be lazy, was "to make a sad mistake."[22] A group of Baltimore's black tradesmen meanwhile gathered at the local Douglass Institute in 1869 to demand fair prices for their work. Echoing the northerners who preached the liberative potential of wages, the mechanics contended that "the bestowing even of the franchise upon the colored men would benefit them but little if they did not organize and protect themselves and their families in this manner."[23] Without an opportunity to work for a living wage, in other words, black freedom was a false promise.

Antislavery activists believed deeply in the power of industry to lift freedmen from the muck of slavery, yet former slaveholders and their allies were just as intent on keeping them in it. Most glaringly, Maryland's 1864 constitution had left unperturbed the criminal courts' authority to sell black convicts into term slavery. Two judges scandalized local activists and, in time, Radical Republicans in Congress by selling black individuals convicted of petty theft into bondage. Sometimes the alleged stolen object in question was worth less than one dollar. In the eyes of Judges W. H. Tuck and D. R. Magruder, that did not matter: they insisted upon putting the alleged black thieves up for auction anyway.[24] In 1866 the state's governor, former Baltimore Know-Nothing mayor Thomas Swann, made mention of these injustices in his annual address, deploying a sort of logic that must have nauseated freed people and their friends. "In relation to that feature of your Code, relating to the colored population, adopted years ago, giving to the courts the power to commute criminal sentences, by selling the offender into slavery for the period of his sentence," explained Swann, "I would commend it to your notice, not in the interest of the colored race, to whom it is a benefit, but as making an unfair discrimination under the new order of things, against the white man, from whom the same privilege is withheld."[25] Upon those grounds Swann called for repeal.

Black Marylanders' other "privileges" during the immediate aftermath of Maryland's emancipation included legal incapacitation in court. The state's slave code had banned all black people from bearing witness against white persons in any court of law, and antislavery activists had hoped that the new constitution would end that indignity. It did not, at least not explicitly. As a result, many local judges continued to refuse to hear black testimony.

"Our manner of securing justice among Freedmen has been by bringing their complaints before the civil authorities, but such a course I am convinced is inadequate, owing to the refusal of Justices of the Peace, in many counties, to take the evidence of colored people," wrote one federal official. Magistrates' denial of black testimony in turn encouraged "whites to continue in the commission of acts of injustice and oppression upon the colored people."[26]

But as pernicious as re-enslavement and legal impotence were, white attempts to maintain black servility manifested most commonly in simple labor disputes. Former slaveholders, and for that matter numerous white people who had had nothing to do with the slave system, refused to honor their contractual obligations toward freed people. Sometimes these employers had the law on their side. For example, the post-emancipation legislature let stand a provision that punished free black workers who left employers to whom they had hired themselves; after 1864, more than a few employers took advantage of the rule.[27] Other times, however, these employers ignored the law altogether, and instances of breach of contract abounded: many employers paid their nonwhite workforces erratic wages and insisted that it was their right to decide how much to pay whom when payday arrived; others drove black laborers from the premises instead of paying what they owed; still others decided to withhold wages on a whim. "My idea of the actions of these people," wrote one federal officer about white employers, "is that they wish to hold out as long as possible with the hope that the freedmen will be . . . reduced to that state of dependence from which they have just emerged."[28] Both in Baltimore and in the counties, white Marylanders manipulated the contract regime in order to perpetuate the black population's economic servility.

The most typical complaint among freed people referred to white employers driving them from a worksite — a farm, a factory, a dock — without payment. In one case, a trio of freedmen who had contracted to work for a Cecil County man were run off the property after refusing to go to Washington "to recover some things left there by him." Such a charge was usually just a pretense for an employer to avoid paying his workers. "It seems from their statement that the contract was not violated by either one of them," wrote a federal agent to the white man, Dr. J. H. Cunningham. "You had no cause given you for driving them off; and that by doing so you have taken the responsibility on yourself" before the law. Unfortunately, more times than not the law was unenforceable without sympathetic local magistrates, a group hard to find outside of Radical Republican circles. Throughout the state, black wage earners could be thrown "out of employment almost penniless" on a moment's notice.[29]

Employers violated the terms of their contracts most commonly when the workers in question were black women. James Parkes promised Mary Jane Monck, a freedwoman, that he would pay $7 a month for four months of labor; in the end, he paid only $19 and threatened her with assault if she complained to anyone about the overdue account.[30] In another case, a white woman from the city named Annie Watts declined to pay the freedwoman Phillis Jones for services rendered.[31] And then there was William Bain, a white home owner on the corner of Eutaw and Lombard Streets, who dismissed Judy Davis after she had arrived late for work one morning. Adding insult to injury, Bain also rebuffed Davis after she asked to be paid for the work she had already completed.[32] White employers took special advantage of black female householders. Jane Wright hired her son to a white man in Baltimore County named Abraham Baldwin, but after three years the latter had paid only $15 of the $150 he owed her for the boy's labor. Baldwin well understood his power in the relationship. He was a white man, Wright was a black woman, and there was little she could do about the paltry sum regardless of her position atop a household.[33]

Black women's gross disadvantages in the labor market intermittently materialized in physical violence. The aforementioned William Bain had beaten and strangled Judy Davis before firing her.[34] In another instance, Susan Spicer suffered awful physical conditions while working for a white woman on Charles Street. Spicer's employer, who obviously ignored the 1864 emancipation edict, treated her "in the most cruel manner, keeping her for twenty-four hours at times without food." The poor black woman was also "kept at work under servilence [sic], and as soon as she is done she is confined in a room and no one is allowed to see or speak to her."[35] It was no coincidence that both Davis and Spicer were domestic workers, laboring under a white person's roof away from the eyes of potential onlookers. For the black women who worked so often in other people's homes, the immediate post-emancipation labor market looked quite a bit like its pre-emancipation predecessor.

The federal government eventually responded to these and other troubling conditions by establishing an office of the Freedmen's Bureau in Baltimore. But it did so cautiously and gradually. Unlike most other slave states, Maryland had stayed in the Union and fought against the Confederacy, exempting it from the rules of federal Reconstruction. Not until late September 1865, some six months after Congress approved its creation, did the bureau decide to extend its operations into northern Maryland at all, and only then because complaints in the area had grown too loud to ignore. Oliver Otis Howard, who headed the bureau in Washington, first appointed William P. Wilson as acting assistant superintendent for Maryland. Wilson served until March 1866, when George J. Stannard replaced him and became the first assistant commissioner for the newly established Maryland District. Stannard's command included all of the state, with the exception of the southernmost counties (Calvert, Charles, Montgomery, Prince George's, and St. Mary's), that fell under the D.C. jurisdiction. By August, a new commander, Edgar M. Gregory, oversaw most of Maryland plus six counties in Virginia and two in West Virginia. It was not long before Gregory oversaw all of Delaware as well. The bureau's Baltimore office operated until late summer 1868, at which time Howard reassigned its affairs to the assistant commissioner for the District of Columbia.[36]

In its three years of operation, the Freedmen's Bureau strove to supply "somebody to have care for [the freed people], to protect them, to show them the way to the freedom of which they have yet but vague and undefined ideas."[37] Such words betrayed a paternalistic program, as well as a presumption that freed people were ill prepared to meet the circumstances of their freedom. Yet those words also revealed a *liberal* program, for "the way to the freedom" to which the bureau referred was one predicated upon wages. Federal officials wanted the newly emancipated to learn to work for wages in a harsh, uncaring world. And that, federal officials believed, required an education of sorts.

The bureau acted in a number of ways to school freed people in the values of industry. For one thing, its agents endeavored to secure certain freedmen's release from prison. Jerry Dorsey had been convicted for stealing a horse from his master while enslaved, but he insisted that he "only took the horse and wagon to convey his family, then slaves, to a free country." He also claimed that "it never was his intention to appropriate the horse." Federal officers agreed, and Dorsey soon went free.[38] More generally, the bureau provided legal assistance in a wide variety of civil and criminal cases across Maryland, usually when the officials felt that a black person had been wrongly accused, charged, or convicted. In 1868 alone, the Baltimore office handled nearly nine hundred such cases.[39] But the converse was also true: officials sided only with those black persons whom they believed to be falsely accused. After John Wyatt was arrested for stealing four pairs of pants in the city, for instance, he requested money to travel to Philadelphia, alleging his innocence. An agent for the bureau declined the request on the grounds that "this is a suspicious case, including the guilt of the applicant."[40] Education demanded rewarding the industrious and ignoring the criminal.

In much the same vein, federal officers sent as many impoverished freed people away from Baltimore as possible. Federal money conveyed Alex Moore's children to rural Virginia.[41] It transported the "destitute" Joseph Lacey's to Richmond.[42] It dispatched the "indigent" Ephraim Smith to Frederick.[43] As much as they were able, and for as long as they could, assistant commissioners for Baltimore's Freedmen's Bureau granted passage for penurious freed people, a majority of them men, to anywhere there were friends or family who could "prevent suffering" or where they could "gain a support."[44] That the bureau oversaw the removal of individuals to cities as close as Washington and as far away as Little Rock, as large as Philadelphia and as small as Winchester, Virginia, revealed a strong desire to rinse the black population of those who were in "ill health, destitute, and unable to do any hard work."[45] The rationale was that if emancipation's success hinged upon black industry, any black worker incapable or unwilling to perform such labor increased the likelihood of its failure. And so off these poor people went.

While federal officials sought to exonerate the industrious and send the indigent away, they provided black workers with precise instructions for surviving a labor market organized by contracts. "Labor contracts should be in writing," Howard counseled Gregory in early 1867. "If possible, persuade laborers and employers not to rely upon mere verbal agreements. They occasion much confusion." The bureau sought to police deceitful employers too, with agents acting diligently "to secure fair contracts for the freedpeople" free of charge.[46] Yet the bureau's power was circumscribed when it came to controlling employers; except for a handful of rural counties near the District of Columbia, federal agents did not exert direct influence over labor agreements. "All contracts between the white and colored population in the state are regulated by mutual agreement between themselves," lamented one official. That confined the officers in Baltimore "to the investigation of complaints made by colored persons against their employers."[47]

Of those, however, there were plenty, and the office always had much to do. Freed people either wrote for help or showed up in person requesting the same. In response, a clerk would attempt to "settle said complaints by correspondence." If that method proved unsuccessful — which it often did —

an agent would investigate the situation and report back, awaiting a decision on what action to take. In most cases, that action obliged the investigator to bring the case before the civil authorities, a Republican magistrate if possible, thereby providing legal counsel for the complainant in a lawsuit.[48] Between the summers of 1866 and 1868, this process repeated itself time and again, with freed people arriving at the Baltimore office and federal agents investigating their claims over the ensuing weeks. Many black men and women acquired their wages during the mid-1860s through these means.

Not every complaint found a successful resolution. Sometimes, such as in Anthony Armstrong's suit, a delinquent employer could not be found, leaving the freed person aggrieved, dissatisfied, and possibly hungry.[49] Other times it was the black complainant who disappeared. Despite her claim that Sarah Wallace owed $11.44 for seven weeks of domestic work, Maria Hamilton never appeared for trial.[50] Phillis Jones issued a complaint against her former employer Annie Watts, who, she alleged, had failed to pay her for domestic service work. Jones failed to show up for a hearing as well.[51] So too did a man who dug two wells on the Frederick Road: he argued that his employer owed him a balance of $78.50 for the work. When the time came to appear before a magistrate, he never arrived.[52] There were also occasions when the complainants themselves dropped the charge. Amie Augustus left no evidence for why she suddenly withdrew her allegation against Lizzie Lucy, who owed her compensation for a day's worth of washing. Perhaps Augustus settled outside the purview of federal agents; perhaps she became frightened of Lucy's response or grew exhausted from the case. Either way, the bureau never confirmed that she settled the debt.[53]

Among the questions the bureau's investigators pursued was whether or not a complainant merited payment in the first place. Worried about encouraging indolence, federal officers strove to avoid compensating freed people unnecessarily. Jessie W. Ames, for example, failed to persuade the bureau's investigators that an attorney owed him an extra $45 after settling a claim against the "Schooner Burgen." The lawyer, S. D. Smucker, had helped Ames collect the $125 to which he was entitled for work aboard the ship, but— as per his usual contract—had pocketed one-third of the sum. Officials noted that Ames had agreed to the contract, and, considering their ideological commitment to the sanctity of such documents, they were disinclined to help him break it.[54] In another example, Hannah Snow unsuccessfully sought $250 from the Baltimore storekeeper James Lister. Snow claimed that in 1858 her late husband, then free, had paid that amount to Lister, who was then her slave owner, "with the intention of buying Hannah." Unfortunately, the black man had died before fulfilling his obligation, and the unfortunate woman remained enslaved until the 1864 constitution liberated her. Now, having "repeatedly asked [Lister] for the money, who does not deny having it," she turned to the bureau for help. The bureau refused. An agent "carefully examined the case and [saw] no redress for [the] complainant." Snow's late husband had agreed to pay Lister a specific amount of money and had failed to fulfill his end of the bargain, albeit unintentionally, by dying.[55]

Ames and Snow each discovered the reluctance of federal officials to assist anyone they believed had violated a labor contract. In Ames's case, he had consented to surrender a third of his wages to a lawyer. In Snow's case, her late husband had agreed to pay her former slave owner his wages for her freedom but had also consented to surrender the payment if he failed to complete it. Federal agents were dedicated to helping freed people receive only the wages to which they were legally entitled, and nothing more. By the same token, those freed people who broke a contract were on their own.

More times than not, though, it was the white employers who violated labor agreements. Ship captains were specifically likely to shirk their responsibilities: the skipper of the *Roanoke* declined to pay Charles Williams the month's wages he earned as a servant; the captain of the *Diamond State* failed to pay Robert Prackston following the man's service aboard the ship; he also did not remunerate Jane Gardner for her service as a chambermaid; another ship captain did not reimburse John Whitney for his monthlong stint; still another never compensated John H. Butler for his two weeks of labor.[56] Domestic employers were frequently unreliable, too, regardless of whether they were men or women: a housewife on Pratt Street refused to pay Harriett Whittington for a week's worth of labor; another housewife on North Street denied Louisa George after her week's worth of labor; a householder on the corner of Eutaw and Lombard Streets ignored the pleas of Indy Jones despite her two weeks of labor; a colonel deprived Amanda Buchanan of her wages after his wife fired her; one householder forsook Lydia Duvall despite her having worked in his home for eight months; a different householder gave Sarah Nichols nothing for a month of her labor.[57] Nor could all municipal officers be trusted with black people's wages. Officer Moore collected the twenty-eight dollars that a local restaurant owed Rebecca Parmelia for storage fees yet gave her just five dollars.[58]

In most of these cases the Freedmen's Bureau facilitated favorable outcomes. Williams, Prackston, Gardner, Whitney, and Butler all received their money from the delinquent ship captains. Whittington, George, Jones, Buchanan, Duvall, and Nichols all secured their wages from their employers. Parmelia collected her fees. Federal officials did not successfully resolve all of their cases, but they did resolve quite a few of them, and it was not uncommon to hear them express optimism about former slaves in a wage economy as a result. "Work is very plentiful," proudly wrote an assistant commissioner in mid-1867, "and as a general thing, wages are good. Contracts between Freedmen and Planters are faithfully carried out by both parties."[59] Other federal officials were no less sanguine. "The moral effect of the presence of a Bureau officer is good," explained one agent in October 1866, "and that [the Bureau] exercises a powerful influence in preventing abuses is beyond question." In R. G. Rutherford's eyes, the state's "freed labor system is satisfactory," with the freedmen having become "an industrious and well disposed class of people." Everywhere they seemed to be "generally at work" and receiving "a fair remuneration for their labor."[60] To hear the federal agents tell it, Maryland's story was beginning to look like a triumph. Commissioner Howard observed in 1868, around the time the bureau shuttered its Baltimore office, that freedmen across Maryland were showing themselves quite "capable of securing their own rights in labor contracts and before the courts."[61]

Freed people themselves lacked the privilege to indulge in so much optimism. From their point of view, the mounting bullishness of federal officers belied a sadder truth. The large numbers of people who flooded the Freedmen's Bureau office to its last day, to say nothing of the sheer volume of complaints it accrued in its three years of operation, told a different story of progress. What is more, white employers and planters probably violated their labor pacts as often in 1868 as they had in 1865. The problems may have even grown worse over time. Dishonest proprietors surely felt more comfortable breaking contracts, convincing illiterate workers to sign exploitative contracts, and agreeing only to oral (and thus often unenforceable) contracts once the federal government departed for bloodier fights abroad.

Still, the pervasiveness and persistence of deceitful employers could not alter a fundamental truth about labor relations in post-emancipation Maryland: for many black people, the world had turned upside down. There was no more slavery. All black Marylanders were subsequently free to choose their employers and seek the best terms available. And many did. Freed people grew increasingly adept at finding higher wages elsewhere, infuriating former slave owners and exasperating federal agents who wanted to establish economic stability in the roiled region. Many more were steadfast in their drive to support themselves and their families through paid labor. Ex-slaves who began to work for wages in the aftermath of emancipation did not always conform to the classical economist's fantasy of rational workers — in the countryside, large numbers formed a subsistence-based peasantry wherever possible — but they did leave the uniquely coercive measures of a slave economy behind. Before 1864, almost ninety thousand black Marylanders labored out of fear of lash and sale. By 1868, most of those people were laboring for very different reasons.[62]

Creating the Household

The attainment of the wage was but a prelude to the oversight of the household. Although freed people never conquered the labor market to the extent that federal officials believed they had, they did fight openly and earnestly to enjoy the financial fruits of their labor. And in this, at least, many of them succeeded. A large number of ex-slaves across the state began to collect money for work they theretofore either had performed for free or had been unable to perform because they had been unfree. Slavery met its demise because enough white people in the state bowed to antislavery activism and wartime exigencies that insisted black people be allowed to work for wages too, and the very forces that had led to this fight for wage freedom now encouraged freed people to procure household autonomy as well. Among the friends of emancipation — among black and white liberals alike — success hinged upon the creation of black families no less than upon the acquisition of black wages.

Practically every celebration of the wage was accompanied by a salute to the household. Federal officials aspired to help freed people secure both good wages *and* good homes and so advised their agents to ensure that black men received wages high enough to support dependents. Sympathetic white northerners as a whole accepted it as self-evident that so long as freed people cultivated respectable households, "their desire to remain [would] be permanent and their labor cheerful."[63] Black northerners did not argue the point. The aforementioned John Mercer Langston ardently believed that emancipation provided freed people with a remarkable opportunity to work on their own and for black men in particular to support themselves. But such self-sufficiency also translated into patriarchal responsibility, for black men owed "it to their wives and children to stand on their own soil, to make their homes beautiful, and thus render them citadels of virtue." Langston urged his audience, which numbered three thousand strong, "to feed, [and] clothe ... those dependent upon you."[64] In Congress, John Creswell made a similar point, only in the negative. Arguing in favor of the Thirteenth Amendment, the Baltimore representative explained that the slave "could not say my home, my father, my mother, my wife, my child."[65] But now, the freedman could.

For their part, most black Marylanders attempted to reunite with their loved ones and establish their own households on their own terms. The demands of war had scattered tens of thousands of people, slaves among them, and before long large numbers of freed people could be seen crisscrossing Baltimore in search of missing family members. Black women were particularly noticeable in this regard; many of them sought news about husbands (as well as fathers, brothers, and sons) who had enlisted in the U.S. Army but never returned. Anna Bishop's case was only one example, though an exemplary one. In the summer of 1866, she arrived at the newly established office of the Freedmen's Bureau asking about her husband, Thomas, who fought with the Seventh Regiment of United States Colored Troops. Bishop had written him five times without response and feared the worst.[66] Frequently, the worst actually came to pass, and in those circumstances a widow requested her husband's military back pay or pension.[67] For a struggling black family absent its male householder, that money could be a godsend. It allowed certain freedmen to support households beyond the grave.

Nowhere was freed people's desire for household autonomy so clear as in the value they placed upon acquiring control over their children. For most black Marylanders, freedom meant parenting. One black man believed that emancipation finally afforded him the chance to demonstrate that he was "a sober and industrious man, a good husband and kind father ... fully competent to take charge of his children."[68] Freedom meant parenting because black people, like white people, loved their children, but parenting also came down to the question of consent: now that the slaves were free, they insisted that no one, neither other citizens nor the state, be allowed to seize their children without their consent. A black man named Robert Wilson made exactly this point when speaking with a military officer two weeks after the state's new constitution became operational. He alleged that the orphans court of Kent County had bound out his two children to a white Baltimore man "without the approbation and against [his] consent ... the father."[69] That was unacceptable, he alleged. By ignoring his wishes, the court had undermined his rights as a man and his freedom as a freedman. "We were delighted when we heard that the Constitution set us all free," declared Lucy Lee, a black Baltimorean, "but God help us, our condition is bettered but little [if] free ourselves, but deprived of our children." For many ex-slaves, "the only thing that would make us feel free and happy" was control over their children.[70]

Black Marylanders' intense desire to control their own households derived almost as much from the circumstances of want as it did from the sentiments of love. Children could work, and in the 1860s they usually did work, with the cash they earned helping to sustain entire households. "A good many of these children are old enough to hire for good wages and can get a plenty of labor," remarked Bartus Trew, a deputy provost marshal for the U.S. government in 1864.[71] In fact, children's wages were often essential to black families struggling to survive in the aftermath of emancipation. This was principally true when single black women headed those families. The black Baltimorean Jane Wright, for instance, needed most of the wages her son Alexander generated while working for a doctor in Baltimore County just to stay afloat.[72] And women like her were not unusual, especially in Baltimore. But it was not just black women who depended heavily upon "the services of their children, with which they can make a good living."[73] Black men frequently did too. A freedman named Perry Riley noted that once he hired out his two children, "one I can get twenty dollars for, and the other I can get victuals and clothes this year." Sometimes the two motivations for black parental control — love and want — converged into a single rationale. "I have four children," a black woman from the Eastern Shore wrote a federal official. "I can by their assistance maintain them." Many freed people believed that with their children's wages, their parental love could find fulfillment.[74]

The trouble was that after emancipation, thousands of black parents could not actually claim their children at all. Many white Marylanders moved in late 1864 to seize black children's labor under a section of the 1860 Maryland Code of Public General Laws that authorized orphans courts to indenture the children of allegedly indolent "free Negros." The new constitution had failed to repeal the clause. Never mind that the term "free Negros" no longer made sense in the post-emancipation world; within hours of the governor's proclamation on November 1, ex-masters from all over the state began applying to have their ex-slaves' children bound to them. One federal officer recorded that in Annapolis the orphans court grew so busy that it threatened "to take every able bodied negro boy without regard to age."[75] Other witnesses told of former masters bringing black children to courthouses in "ox-cart loads" and "wagonloads, with or without the consent of the parents."[76] In and around Baltimore, white applicants appeared in prodigious numbers to have black children bound to them. It made no difference that the city was by then a Radical Republican stronghold.

Friends of emancipation knew that forced apprenticeship was slavery under another name. Assistant Commissioner Edgar Gregory did not mince words when describing it as such in a report to Washington. Apprenticeship "is in fact a phase of slavery," he wrote in November 1866. "Parents are deprived of those who are able and willing to support them, while children are deprived the blessings of education and doomed to spend long years in toil and servitude, without an adequate compensation."[77] Elsewhere Gregory described black children's treatment as apprentices as "worse than in the days of slavery."[78] A black Baltimorean who lost his children to the system was similarly blunt when lamenting their being "bound down in slavery to their former owner." The former owner, for his part, "said that he considered the children the children of his negro woman, and he meant to keep them and do by them as he has done by his slaves in the past, and no better than he done by them."[79] Emancipation had failed to topple the state's archaic apprenticeship system, and the result was the survival of unfree labor for several more years. As of March 1867, nearly 2,300 black children remained bound out to white masters across Maryland's sixteen counties.[80]

To freed people, the return of their children was imperative, a necessary prerequisite of their emancipation. The fracturing of families was a characteristic of *slavery*, not of freedom. In March 1866, Baltimore's black leaders petitioned President Andrew Johnson about their plight and about how much their children meant to them: "Because everywhere throughout the state our homes . . . [have been] invaded, and our little ones seized at the family fireside . . . give us the right to a home or guarantee to us the safety of our children around the hearth while we are at labor, or their support in our old age."[81] Such sentiments capture the import of household autonomy to black conceptions of freedom and mark a measure of the tragedy that the apprentice system wrought upon black lives after emancipation. Freed people's stories read like a catalog of parental horrors: Martha Brown lost her children to a white man in Caroline County; Lydia Garret lost her young sister to a white man in Howard County; Mrs. Hill lost her children to a white man in Somerset County; Ann Jones lost her daughter to another white man in Somerset County; Edward Dorsey lost his son to a white man on Deal Island; Caroline Anderson lost her son to a white man in Baltimore; Henrietta Wright lost her son to a white man in Baltimore County; Mary Bacon lost her daughter to a white man in Baltimore; Ann Broome lost her daughter to a white woman in Calvert County; Harriet Mason lost her niece to a white man in Kent County; Mary E. Darr lost her son to a white man in Calvert County; A. Mason lost his son to a white woman in Dorchester County; Stephen Wright lost his son to a white man in Kent County; Annie Cornish lost her niece to a white man in Dorchester County; Sarah Harris lost her son to a white man in Queen Anne's County.[82] On and on the reports came, from the city as well as from the counties, together forming a record of slavery's enduring shadow. The slaves were free, but that freedom would not be meaningful until they got their children.

The apprenticeship system represented a strategy by slavery's stubborn advocates to nullify the spirit of the new constitution. For if household autonomy made people truly free, the loss of black parental consent made freed people something else entirely. And make no mistake: the orphans courts around the state typically apprenticed black children against their parents' will. In the frantic weeks and months following emancipation, numerous judges declined to hear testimony that exonerated black parents from the charges of indolence. Those courts, to be sure, preferred to have one of the parents present for the hearings so as to provide proof that the apprenticeship was nominally consensual. But it was rarely consensual. "They sent for me to come to the courthouse," recalled Maria Nichols, "and they sent high sheriffs after me and taken [me] by force." Once in court, the judge proceeded to ignore Nichols's cries as he bound her son to a white man.[83] These and other instances like them amounted to theft. Sympathetic observers certainly thought so. "Little is done in the state courts to help these poor people who have been robbed of their children with but the shadow of law," Gregory sighed in a note to Washington.[84]

Insofar as they did anything at all, local law enforcement officers were more likely to abet the appropriation of black children's labor than to stop it. The freedwoman Lucy Lee lost her thirteen-year-old daughter to a white woman who "brought two police and took her away."[85] Lindsay Robbins reported that "my children were forced from me by constables."[86] A police sergeant from Baltimore's western district "enticed a boy named Henry Johnson" from his guardian, a freedman named Joseph Richards.[87] After the state's November 1864 emancipation, freed people documented a series of police-sanctioned indignities that enabled the apprenticeship of their children. When a black couple showed up to court to refuse their children's binding to a Calvert County man, the constable on site punched the mother in the face in the presence of the judges. He claimed that her stubborn refusal to consent left him no choice. The court approved the indenture.[88]

With both the courts and police on their side, white people felt free to intimidate black parents bold enough to demand back their children. One Baltimore freedwoman recounted her futile attempt to bring her granddaughter home from Towson. When she showed up at the girl's new home, the resident householder "ordered me out of the house, at the time threatening to place me in jail if I did not leave."[89] White people were also comfortable threatening personal violence. Lavina Brooks traveled thirteen miles from her home in the city to plead with Orville McGill for her child, but she "had not been on the above place five minutes, not even seeing my child, when I was ordered off with a threat that if I ever set my foot on his place again he would shoot me."[90] Another black woman related how her children's unlawful keeper "threatened to chain me down to the floor and whip me, if I asked him for my children anymore."[91] Rebecca Sales arrived at a Baltimore residence searching for her daughter before the home owner threw her out, locked the door, and proclaimed that the child was never going to live with her.[92] Black men confronted such hostility, too: one father approached the Pratt Street home of his daughter's guardian only to be driven away and threatened.[93] Sometimes white guardians forcefully resisted black parents' authority outside of the law, such as the time a white woman burned a court order stipulating that she relinquish an apprenticed child.[94] Other times potential white guardians bullied black parents in a courtroom, such as when a former slave master warned a protesting mother in open court that he would "break her d——d head" if she did not stop talking.[95] But whatever the threat and wherever its forum, white intransigence had its desired effect. Black parents knew that if they attempted to claim their children in person, there would be "consequences." As a result, many never even tried.[96]

All black parents could do, and what many eventually did do, was look to familiar allies for help. U.S. Army officials were the first to answer the call. In 1864, Lew Wallace, the Baltimore-based commander of the Eighth Army Corps, received numerous complaints about the apprenticeship of black children and responded by placing all freed slaves under special military protection. He also directed the state's myriad orphans courts to halt their actions at once. Many judges, though not all, complied. Later, in May 1865, Unionist attorneys like Henry Winter Davis, Henry Stockbridge, and Archibald Stirling Jr. took up the cause as well. These white men began bringing apprenticeship cases before the Baltimore City Court, which at the time was presided over by the Radical Republican Hugh Lennox Bond. Bond, in Gregory's words, "stood like a wall between the colored people and their oppressors," remanding almost all of the black children brought before his court to the custody of their parents.[97] But these maneuvers were too limited to make an appreciable difference for many desperate parents. Wallace's order did nothing for those children already bound out.[98] Bond, for his part, never heard enough cases to lower the total number of apprenticed children significantly, largely because the state legislature, still controlled by pro-slavery Marylanders, restricted his power to issue writs of habeas corpus to Baltimore City. He was unable to subpoena white guardians from the state's southern reaches.[99]

In the end, it was the Freedmen's Bureau that proved to be black parents' best ally. The office's complaints division worked primarily and sometimes exclusively on the tidal wave of apprenticeship cases brought forward by freed people. At the end of 1866, Assistant Commissioner Gregory remarked that the number of formal complaints received by his office was actually growing, and "a majority of them are from parents wishing to obtain their children who have been illegally bound under the apprenticeship law of the state."[100] In response, his officers did what they could to curb "the unprincipled practices" of those courts, constables, and citizens who detained black people's children for their own.[101] The standard tactic was a letter. "The Assistant Commissioner directs me to inform you that Mrs. Caroline Anderson has entered complaint against you at this office of your keeping her son Charles Anderson illegally, not having received the consent of his mother as prescribed by law for cases of binding over," read one characteristic piece of correspondence.[102] When on those rare occasions the defendant lived in Baltimore, the bureau demanded a meeting in person, too.[103] Either way, the inquiry was intended to warn the recipient that he or she should resolve the matter quickly and quietly; otherwise the bureau would pursue litigation.

Federal officials believed strongly in the need for freed people to establish their own households, and when black men were not present to head those households, they stepped in for them. It was not uncommon for black soldiers to solicit the bureau's help in reclaiming their children while they were detained from home performing their duties in the South. "Wm. Henry Wilson (col'd) late of the U.S.C. troops complains that while he was away from home, in the service of the U.S., you forcibly took his son . . . from his mother, and had him bound to you without the consent of either of his parents," wrote one agent to a Queenstown white man.[104] In other instances the bureau paid the legal fees for black householders too poor to do so themselves; serving a writ of habeas corpus cost money.[105] But mostly federal officers provided legal services "without charge to the parties concerned" in the hope that householders would be able to support their dependents once the children were safely home.[106]

To realize these patriarchal hopes, the opponents of forced apprenticeship needed white guardians to cooperate — or at least concede. At first, few did. The fight against apprenticeship began to gain traction only after Congress approved the Civil Rights Act of 1866. In late July 1866, the radical attorney William Daniel argued before the Baltimore City Court that the federal legislation nullified all "oppressive bindings" in Maryland because it gave black people "the equal benefit of all laws for the security of persons and property" while overturning any statute that did not do the same. According to Daniel, Maryland's apprenticeship law absolutely failed to give black children the same benefits as it did white children, instead making distinctions between them. More practically, some orphans courts were ignoring parental consent.[107] Presiding judge Hugh Bond agreed. He began overturning indentures on the grounds that they violated the equal protection principle of the Civil Rights Act.[108] Federal agents, meanwhile, began targeting offending white guardians with the confidence of federal law. If a white holder of a black indenture refused to comply, the bureau's agents would bring him or her before Baltimore's criminal court and allow Bond to free the child. Field agents across the state proved far more able to initiate successful cases than did the city's handful of radical lawyers, and in time the number of black children coercively indentured to white masters began to decline.

The biggest boost to the cause came from Salmon P. Chase, the chief justice of the U.S. Supreme Court. While on circuit duty in Baltimore in 1867, Chase agreed to hear a petition for writ of habeas corpus from Elizabeth Turner, a black apprentice. Turner, a former slave, had been indentured against her parents' will on November 3, 1864, two days after the new constitution went into operation. The arguments before Chase were the same as those Bond had been hearing for a year: that the apprenticeship sections of the Maryland Code of Public General Laws violated both federal and constitutional law. And like Bond, Chase concurred. After hearing testimony, he ruled that the laws relating to black apprentices manifestly differed from the laws relating to white apprentices. Not only did the state's statutes compel a master to educate only his white apprentices, and not only did they permit a master to reassign only his black apprentices, but state law, Chase observed, also described the authority of the black apprentice's master as a "property and interest." It made no such description for a white apprentice's relation. Chase proceeded to declare black apprenticeship in Maryland a form of involuntary servitude, a designation that rendered it in violation of both the Thirteenth Amendment and the Civil Rights Act of 1866. As the presiding judge of the Baltimore City Court, Hugh Bond had already liberated quite a few black children. Many other black apprentices had seen their masters cancel their indentures "under the influence of the Bureau, or upon being notified by parties that the court would be appealed to if they refused." Now Chase dealt the fatal blow. The effect of his decision, according to the *Baltimore Sun*, was "to discharge nearly all the colored minors indentured by the Orphans Courts, &c., of the several counties and the city of Baltimore."[109]

Federal agents spent the next eight months forcing intransigent planters to relinquish control of their black apprentices, and by the summer of 1868 the number of outstanding complaints from black parents had dropped into the lower hundreds. One September 1868 bureau report counted 128 unresolved cases, a tally that signaled a precipitous drop from the nearly 2,300 unresolved cases from eighteen months earlier.[110] A combination of black and white activism, along with federal assistance from a variety of milieus, finally destroyed the backbone of one of slavery's most pernicious institutional holdovers. Although black apprenticeship did not vanish completely — complaints about the practice persisted into the 1870s — the liberation of the vast majority of indentured black children in Maryland constituted a very real and very meaningful achievement for opponents of slavery. It especially represented a victory for freed people. Ex-slaves demanded the right to their own households as a condition of their emancipation. After substantial effort and several grueling years, many of them attained that right.

Building the New Order

Slavery's demise in Maryland was both gradual and real. Even as many former masters yearned to return to the days of old and many other white people lamented how they would never now become slave owners, slavery died a legal death. In many ways, the 1864 constitution that formally emancipated the state's eighty-seven thousand slaves was a mere part of a larger process that involved black and white activists, northerners and locals, lawyers and laypeople alike. The constitution also benefited from federal legislation enacted irrespective of events unfolding at home. The Civil Rights Act of 1866 provided radical judges and lawyers in Baltimore (and eventually the chief justice of the U.S. Supreme Court) with the authority to upend an apprenticeship system that had ensnared thousands of black children after their formal liberation. Antislavery activists in and around Baltimore established black freedom out of the rights of *all* men. During the 1860s, a deracialized order took shape.

The Civil Rights Act built upon a liberal ideology that had been growing for decades. Intended to elaborate upon the Thirteenth Amendment — and to demolish southern states' black codes in particular — the law clarified precisely what freedom meant in the postwar United States. "Citizens, of every race and color," read the first section of the act, "shall have the same right in every State and Territory" to make and enforce contracts, sue and be sued, give evidence in court, and inherit, purchase, lease, sell, hold, and convey property.[111] By no means did the Civil Rights Act create the liberal ideals it espoused; considering the fact that white men in places like Baltimore had enjoyed property rights for many decades, there was, in fact, little original in the way it defined freedom for the city's postwar order. What was so new was the act's assurance that the federal government would protect black men in their quests to contract for wages and to head households, too.[112]

In both state and city, then, the latter half of the 1860s witnessed important legal changes. Not only apprenticeship fell. In April 1867, legislators in Annapolis repealed the law authorizing criminal courts to sell black petty criminals into term slavery.[113] Later that year, Marylanders wrote and ratified another constitution, this one specifying the precise rights of emancipation that federal officials, white radicals, and freedmen had been fighting to implement for years. The new constitution's Declaration of Rights guaranteed that "every man, for any injury done to him in his person or property, ought to have remedy by the course of the Law of the Land, and ought to have justice and right, freely without sale, fully without any denial, and speedily without delay."[114] Those words essentially echoed the Civil Rights Act's prohibition "of any law, statute, ordinance, regulation, or custom" that deprived a man of his property rights and reiterated the widespread belief among local antislavery activists that all black men deserved protection under the law.[115] The post-emancipation order that arose in 1860s Maryland was predicated upon the protection of all men's rights, whatever their race.

Such emphasis upon the rights of primarily men was intentional. Black women in the post-emancipation order, much like white women in the pre-emancipation order, were not to enjoy a full array of property rights. As wives, as daughters, even as widows: they remained, in some ways, dependents, often more analogous to the property that men were to possess than to the property holders whom men were to embody. Neither Republican lawmakers in Congress nor Unionist activists in Baltimore ever intended to emancipate the wife along with the slave. "If you do discriminate," one supporter of the Civil Rights Act explained during the bill's debate, "it must not be on account of race, color, or former condition of slavery." One could still, however, discriminate on account of gender, and that was because the antislavery program defined black freedom almost solely in male terms. Like other men, black men were to have a property right in their households. To strip them of that right and convert the wife into an autonomous, contracting, rights-bearing individual was to undermine the entire project of emancipation.[116]

The new order's male accent materialized in Baltimore in several subtle ways. Freedmen, for one thing, had an easier time keeping their households intact than did freedwomen, as white guardians were more likely to indenture orphans and children of single mothers than they were to seize children claimed by fathers or both parents together. In fact, one of the factors that prompted illegal apprenticeship to explode in the first place was the absence of black men during the war; a large number of them were in the army.[117] Nor did it help matters when a sizable minority of those men failed to come home at all. Federal officials often involved themselves precisely where freedmen were missing, providing, in essence, the very stabilizing force for black households that night watchmen and policemen had provided for white households during the prewar decades. Single black women, opined one sympathetic white observer, had "nothing but the military to look up to for protection."[118]

Black men were also more legally equipped than black women to lay claim to their children's wages. One freedman collected redress from a white lawyer after that lawyer's apprentice slashed his son with a knife. The victim, Daniel Murray, was laid up for two weeks, costing his household the money he would have otherwise earned if healthy. The Freedmen's Bureau compelled the white man in charge of the assailant to pay Murray's father, the householder, eight dollars in damages.[119] To federal officials, the incident between two boys was actually an incident between two men: the patriarch whose household suffered and the guardian whose apprentice inflicted the suffering. But what if a woman had headed the victimized household instead? Redress was less likely. Or what if, to take another example, a black mother wanted custody of her children when their father was the signatory of their indenture? Joanna Brown's example suggested that such a mother was out of luck. A Baltimorean, Brown wanted her young daughter and son to come home despite the fact that her husband had consented to their apprenticeship in Sussex County, Virginia. Because it recognized freedmen as having a stake in their families, there was nothing the office could do. The bureau was captive to its very ethos: its officers had no choice but to allow a black father to determine the fate of his children.[120]

In this way it was primarily freedmen, not freedwomen, who escaped the dependency of bondage for the independence of freedom. Yet racial egalitarianism in law did not always translate into racial egalitarianism in practice, even for black men. At every turn white supremacists resisted federal, radical, and black efforts to cleanse Maryland's books of racial distinctions. Once the Baltimore City Court emerged as a credible threat to the apprenticeship system, for instance, legislators in Annapolis restricted Judge Hugh Bond's power to issue writs of habeas corpus beyond the city's limits. Lawmakers also used the same session to incentivize judges monetarily to resist the federal Civil Rights Act.[121] The state's 1867 constitution effectively ended these reactionary efforts to maintain the older racial order, but that document too left a cautionary tale. It was, explained one Freedmen's Bureau report, the result of "a severe struggle with the old slave owners."[122] The white supremacists lost that struggle, yet in political terms the Republicans' victory was Pyrrhic; by the end of the year, conservative Democrats who opposed black equality (if not emancipation altogether) had regained power in both Annapolis and Baltimore. With palpable sadness, Edgar Gregory reported "the complete triumph for the party opposed to the political and educational advancement of the colored people." Bemoaning the "few champions of right and equal justice remaining among the judicial officers of the state," he concluded that "impartial justice to freedmen will not be obtained until the inauguration of a great and radical change on the political system of the state."[123]

Gregory was mostly, though not entirely, correct. As the old order gave way to the new, racial animus endured in spirit if not in law. The Republican Party's impotence in Annapolis, together with the continuing "abuses . . . in the administering of equal justice" that so frustrated the proponents of emancipation, suggested slavery might simply have survived under a different name.[124] Such impotence, and such abuses, also suggested that the freedmen's goal to "secure their righteous claims as Citizens of the Republic" was perhaps futile without deeper political change.[125] But we should hesitate before interpreting the persistence of racism as a return to the old. Legal change was change nonetheless, no matter the tenacity of white racism and resistance. Formerly enslaved black men really did acquire certain rights during the post-emancipation years that they previously could not have enjoyed: working for wages, heading households, and performing a variety of other acts theretofore unavailable to them, such as voting (after 1870), testifying, and walking streets and roads without papers.

Legal changes unquestionably counted in certain instances. Before 1864, black victims of white assault would have been subject to the 1717 statute that rendered them legally incompetent "where any white person is concerned." A black victim would have had no ability to prosecute his or her attacker without a white witness. Emancipation changed all of that. Not only did the state's 1864 constitution declare that "all persons held to service or labor, as slaves, are hereby declared free," but also within another year the General Assembly repealed the entire black code so as to lend legal credibility to the liberation principle. All laws relating to "slaves," "Manumission," "immigration," "Vagrancies," "Tumultuous Assemblages," "Incendiary Publications," "Navigation of Vessels by Negroes," "Licenses to Keep Dog or Gun," "Dealings with Free Negroes," "Contracts of Hire by the Free Negroes," and "Petitions for Freedom" disappeared from Maryland's books, "placing negroes and mulattoes, under the same laws with white persons." By the mid-1860s, state law indeed judged a black person competent to bear witness against a white assailant. There was, as a result, a much greater likelihood for black victims to receive at least some minimal amount of justice.[126]

Without overstating the progress of racial equality after slavery, it is possible to recognize the substantial changes in black Marylanders' legal condition during the latter half of the 1860s. Racism survived the decade, but racial slavery did not. And that mattered. It mattered to black workers who earned wages for labor that under exhaustive duress and threat of violence they had previously performed for free. It mattered to black parents whose children had never before legally belonged to them. It mattered to black people across the state and throughout the city — people who hoped to use the meager resources at their disposal to make something of their new lives in a new world under new laws. However impoverished, curtailed, and insecure, freedom was still fundamentally different, and still fundamentally preferable, to slavery.

Legal changes also mattered to white Marylanders, albeit for different reasons. Rather than give birth to a new form of slavery, the post-emancipation order produced, in essence, a new set of expectations. There flourished among white locals a conviction that newly freed black people needed to be self-sufficient, and that black men especially needed to work hard for wages and head respectable households without any outside assistance. Conservatives like President Johnson could thus demand that freedmen show "they are self-sustaining and capable of selecting their own employment and their own places of abode," while his enemies in Congress could proclaim that every freedman "has a right to support himself."[127] Such expectations, whether uttered by close friends or dubious allies, built black freedom out of the rights of black men. In short, the events of the 1860s codified white hopes for black male self-sufficiency. For three years, federal officers in Maryland operated in conjunction with local activists and civilians to secure economic and household autonomy for black men. And, in white minds anyway, those years marked a tremendous achievement: many freed people finally began working for wages, and apprenticeship fitfully began to disappear. In reality, of course, the results both in and outside of Baltimore were more mixed. Although, yes, many freed slaves did begin working for wages, few acquired real capital, most possessed little in the way of property, and all confronted bleak prospects in the labor market, be it in the city or countryside. And although, yes, apprenticeship mostly vanished, black households rarely resembled the privatized, patriarchal domesticities that constituted the respectable ideal. No matter: as white onlookers saw it, the lawbooks were now free of racial distinctions, and the more obvious roadblocks for black autonomy were now gone. By the time the Freedmen's Bureau shuttered its Baltimore office in late 1868, emancipation looked to many liberals like a brilliant success.

Chapter Seven

THE CRIME OF FREEDOM

◆

OMENTOUS LEGAL CHANGE came to Maryland during the 1860s. At the start of the decade, most of the state's citizens worried about emancipation, and certain men among them even debated "re-enslaving" free people of color, a population they deemed incorrigible and dangerous. But then the war came. Engulfing the nation, the Civil War and its chaotic aftermath provided both impetus and legal cover for the creation of a new order in Maryland, one predicated upon the property rights of all men, white and black alike. By 1870, there was no more talk of re-enslavement.

Emancipation represented an enormous, even revolutionary victory for black people, and for black men especially. Although encumbered by the white terrorism that everywhere in the South threatened to undo the statutory, material, and political gains made by freed people, an interracial coalition of antislavery activists in Maryland successfully upended the slave order that theretofore defined state law. The new regime these activists introduced guaranteed all men, regardless of race, the right to control and govern their own properties, built black freedom out of the responsibilities of industry and the duties of manhood, and promised to protect all men as property-owning, rights-bearing individuals. Baltimore's post-emancipation legal order built black freedom out of black men's potential for wage independence and household autonomy. During the 1860s, slavery perished as a lawful institution in Baltimore, and liberal reformers built a contract regime uninhibited by racial distinctions in its stead.

Among the many changes triggered by the upheaval of the 1860s, the demise of ordinary vigilantism counted as one of the more visible. The story of the antebellum era had been a story of shared policing burdens. A slave code had empowered the white majority to police the black minority in a variety of ways on a variety of sites, from the streets on which black people walked to the worksites and homes in which they worked and slept. If anything, Baltimore's introduction of a professional police force and reformative penal system strengthened the ordinary citizen's police power over free African Americans. It was not solely the newly dressed policemen who followed black Baltimoreans into stores and onto the streets, who chased them away from the docks and invaded their homes, who protected and punished them. It was all white men, ordinary and official alike, who did those things. Yet if policing free black people in a society with slaves had been the ordinary citizen's responsibility, after emancipation such vigilantism became a crime. He who chased a black worker out of a shipyard was a potential assailant. He who invaded a black patriarch's home was a potential burglar. He who seized a black father's son was a potential kidnapper. Beyond the platitudes of white conservatives who grudgingly pledged support for black property rights and beyond the arcane abstractions of laws themselves were new wages and new households and new police protections, all of which made a meaningful difference in black lives. Emancipation and its subsequent legal fallout mattered a great deal.

But new freedoms also brought new forms of compulsion.[1] The Civil War's slave emancipation represented one of the most important moments in the history of the United States, if not of the modern world. It ended what was then the world's biggest slave regime, helped usher the United States into an era of enormous economic expansion, and brought that nation, the world's first constitutional republic, into much closer accordance with the universalist principles its founding documents had espoused nearly a century before. In many senses of the term, emancipation was revolutionary.[2] But this was also a liberal revolution, and for black people in places like Baltimore, liberal ideals conferred a mixed blessing. The trouble with the new order was that it placed the onus of success upon the individual in a society that presumed the individuals primarily capable of success were white. An interracial coalition of activists in Maryland destroyed slavery, repealed the state's black codes, and wrote new, racially unmarked laws, but many white Baltimoreans continued to take for granted that black men were poor candidates to abide by those laws. The result was a growing number of black arrests on Baltimore's streets, pervasive incarceration of black men in Baltimore's prisons, and occasional police brutality directed at black Baltimoreans.

In postbellum Baltimore, in this skeptical world, black men's acquisition of labor and household power had the perverse effect of bringing them into greater conflict with the formal police institutions of state power. Police officers increasingly arrested them; without re-enslavement as an option, judges and juries sent them to prison at growing rates; and over time, penal populations grew ever more black. The new order codified a number of hard-fought victories for black Baltimoreans, and for black men in particular, yet the acquisition of full property rights in a legal culture that treated black autonomy as criminal brought those men in far greater numbers to prison, where they began to bear a new stigma. Racial coercion outlived racial slavery. What most changed was the official status of the white men who inflicted it.

Freedom's Caveat

To understand the changes in Baltimore's system of racial policing, one must first look closely at the terms of emancipation. Black freedom arrived with a caveat. The Thirteenth Amendment expressed this caveat succinctly: "Neither slavery nor involuntary servitude, except as a punishment for crime whereof the party shall have been duly convicted, shall exist within the United States."[3] The Civil Rights Act of 1866 was no less explicit: "Citizens, of every race and color, without regard to any previous condition of slavery or involuntary servitude, except as a punishment for crime whereof the party shall have been duly convicted, shall have the same right" as everyone else to make contracts, possess property, and enjoy equal protection under the law.[4] It was almost axiomatic among antislavery activists, including northern-educated black activists like Henry Highland Garnet, that all men should be free except for criminals. "Involuntary bondage shall not exist," preached Garnet amid the state's November 1864 celebrations, "except for crime."[5] The crime caveat was an articulation of the limits of black freedom itself.

Reformers had long argued that the state should strip any citizen who committed a crime of both his or her rights and freedom, and emancipation did nothing to discourage this belief. If anything, liberals' faith in formal state power to incarcerate probably grew after the Civil War. "Punishment of crime is the only effectual mode of suppressing it," wrote several members of Baltimore's merchant class to the governor.[6] That was because the authorities, through incarceration, forced prisoners to work. One postbellum report of the city jail stated that "the effect of employment is salutary in itself," and so long as prisoners were "subjected to it, who doubts that when they are restored again to society, after the full period of their imprisonment, that to say the least, the chances of their being reformed, would be . . . encouraging."[7] Other penal officers agreed. The jail's physician urged, for instance, "the absolute importance of labor of some kind for the many able bodied men and women who are confined here from year to year."[8] Unfreedom and coercion survived the Civil War in the form of criminal punishment. In Baltimore, the state continued to arrest, incarcerate, and compel labor from free people who broke the law.

Freed people's dilemma was that white people tended to associate blackness with indolence, licentiousness, and lawlessness, which lent the crime caveat enormous importance. The association was not new, of course. Lawmakers before the war had treated most autonomous black behavior as criminal. In addition to labeling runaway slaves "fugitive" and treating every free person of color as a possible runaway, both state and municipal law had barred all black people, whether free or enslaved, from holding political office or voting, testifying against white people in court, traveling within the city after 10:00 p.m., trading in certain commodities, or holding a proprietary right in their own children. Lawmakers during the mid-1860s struck down those laws and in the process perversely heightened white disdain for black agency. Confronting a future with neither slavery nor racially restrictive lawbooks, white men from across the state's political spectrum worried that emancipation was liberating not autonomous individuals but lawless criminals.

The loudest group of skeptics consisted of slavery's supporters. Hailing from the more rural parts of the state, the unrepentant foes of black liberty spent the late 1850s trying to re-enslave free people of color and the early 1860s trying to halt the progress of emancipation. In that time most never wavered from the conviction that black freedom begat crime. "The avoidance of the moderate labor required of [free black people], to habits of theft and to dissatisfaction with their condition," reported the state's slaveholders' convention in 1859, were endemic.[9] When "you declare them free and then attempt to control them, they cannot and will not reconcile their freedom with your restraints by law." By this logic, emancipation invited not salvation but crime. Its effects, however unintentional, would be to "fill our jails and penitentiary, and load us with taxes to pay court charges for their criminal outrages upon our peace and property."[10] "Take off from the negro the discipline and moral restraints of slavery," concluded Curtis Jacobs, the state's most vocal advocate of re-enslavement, "and they have invariably gone back into vice, indolence, and heathenism."[11] The re-enslavement campaign failed, to be sure, but failure did not dissuade its advocates from the wisdom of their words. Five years later opponents of the 1864 constitution articulated an almost identical argument. Charles County's Richard Edelen expressed terror at the possibility of nearly ninety thousand freed people, most of them possessing a "natural aversion to labor," who would find in "the jails, almshouses, and penitentiaries . . . their only refuge from starvation."[12] Others at the convention maintained that emancipation would leave freed people "dead on the dunghill or confined in the penitentiary for crime." The consequences of emancipation, speculated Kent County's Ezekiel Chambers, would be "further degradation, the perpetration of further crime and every sort of vice."[13]

Various conservative, antislavery whites also worried that freed people would be too lazy to follow the law. Colonizationists, for instance, had made a cottage industry of describing free persons of color as stuck "between the irresponsible slave of the South, and the aspiring free white help of the North," and of arguing that black individuals constituted "an inferior class" who "must be considered . . . more indolent and licentious than the whites."[14] Instead of praising black lawfulness, colonizationists and their friends had usually couched their condemnations of slavery in aspirations for white workers. Facing, in 1864, the abrupt prospect of emancipation, the House Committee on the Colored Population thus asserted that slavery's demise made it "the bounden duty of the General Assembly not to throw stumbling blocks in the way of white labor." Emancipation counted among those stumbling blocks. "The undersigned have no faith in the dogma of social equality for the negro race here in the United States," their report concluded. And black vagrancy, property crime, and vice — the supposedly inevitable results of any policy presumptive of "social equality" between the races — would undermine the prosperity of white wageworkers.[15]

It is, perhaps, unsurprising that advocates of re-enslavement and colonization mistrusted black people to abide by the laws of freedom. What may be more surprising is that it was not just they who harbored such doubts. Many of freed people's closest white friends also worried about their propensities to follow the law. Although more hopeful than white conservatives, white radicals frequently expressed concern that a lifetime of slavery had taught freed people that solely the slave master's lash — as opposed to the personal will — should compel hard work. Many of them called for good schooling to counter the bad education of slavery. A different type of education could teach freed people to "feel that it is a reproach and scandal to steal, and be idle, worthless, vagabonds."[16] And, "in so far as public education tends to diminish crime," wrote one Baltimore school superintendent, "no good reason can be given why the good of society will be less advanced by instructing the colored than the white race."[17] Admittedly, the advocacy of black public education was itself a controversial position to hold during the 1860s, a decade when tens of thousands of white Marylanders vigorously opposed black education at all. Yet for freed people these positions also foretold trouble. Even their most trusted white allies worried that they were culturally predisposed to break the law.[18]

White radicals expressed their anxiety about black self-sufficiency all the time. Hugh Bond, the Radical Republican judge of the city's criminal court, worried, for instance, that if left to their own devices black people would "grow more vicious till their presence is intolerable and requires ten times the pecuniary expense in police regulations that their education would require." A board member for the Baltimore Association for the Moral and Educational Improvement of the Colored People likewise deemed the freedman "a more dangerous element as a free man" than as a slave. "He is without the wonted restraint," continued J. F. W. Ware. "He is ignorant, he may become a vagabond, and then vicious, and then — why, danger — new laws, new jails, new police." There was a hint of cynicism to these pleas; white radicals had an agenda, after all: they wanted to build new schools for the children of freed people. But there was a hint of sincerity as well. Ware was no doubt trafficking in well-worn stereotypes when he invoked "the horde of ignorant, unrestrained men, women, and children [who] will be upon you — your city will be the charnel house of vagabondism, vice, and crime."[19]

Many radicals saw their mission toward black Baltimoreans in paternalistic terms. They believed that without institutional intervention, without either schools *or* prisons, black people would succumb to the "vagabondism, vice and criminality to which they are liable."[20] Such a scenario was frightening because of demography. By the end of the 1860s, some twelve thousand more black people lived in the city than had lived there at the decade's start, an increase that grew the total number of black residents to about forty thousand. A majority of these new arrivals appeared after 1864, as emancipation had lifted the restraints upon black freedom of movement and inspired thousands to seek family members and jobs in the state's largest city. During the latter half of the 1860s, the number of black households in Baltimore tripled, going from four thousand to twelve thousand. Although the 1870 black population still represented less than 20 percent of Baltimore's total population, forty thousand was a large number of people if nearly all of them acted lawlessly.[21]

The upshot of so much white anxiety and black demographic growth was distressingly predictable: white Baltimoreans saw illicit behavior almost everywhere they saw black people. For instance, they began to notice black indolence no sooner than emancipation had gone into effect. Black men, the *Baltimore Sun* reported in 1865, "are now loafing about the wharves, acquiring vicious habits, or obtaining the means of a precarious existence only by the few jobs they procure."[22] A year later the editors sounded a similar alarm, remarking that "another not only useless but dangerous class of persons whose presence could be profitably dispensed with is the large number of worthless colored persons that circumstances have forced upon the community. 'They toil not, neither do they spin,' but in many instances this class has been detected in cases of larceny."[23] According to white observers, black Baltimoreans were so "dangerous" and "worthless" because they lacked the "aptitude in acquiring a knowledge of the mechanical branches of industry."[24] Freedom, basically, made them a nuisance. Rather than liberating them, it left them to "depend on what they can pick up to satisfy the demands of hunger, and seek shelter at night in the police stations."[25]

White commentators also despaired over freed people's households. Black men, they alleged, were too lecherous to be respectable patriarchs. Tales of black rapists peppered the dailies, leaving readers to imagine dozens if not hundreds of perpetrators prowling the city like John Smith, a black man charged with "attempting to commit an outrage on the person of Mrs. Henrietta Long."[26] White alarmists also recoiled from the specter of "amalgamation," the interracial couplings between black men and white women that so many feared would be the real outcome of emancipation. Interracial marriages squandered white women, a few of them "quite prepossessing," who both suffered the indignity of being black men's wives and, on occasion, became the victims of violently jealous black women who wanted their troubled men for themselves.[27] Nor was it a surprise to learn that a black man reacted wantonly, emotionally, badly, to disappointment. If, for example, he wanted to marry a girl who did not want to marry him, a typical black man in a typical newspaper account might respond the way John Langford responded: Anna Davy had rejected Langford's proposal, and he had attempted to shoot her, "determining that she should not marry anyone else either." Newspaper readers, always assumed to be white, were schooled to believe that this was how free black men behaved.[28]

When not decrying the lewd, reckless behavior of black patriarchs, white Baltimoreans were complaining about their absence. Slavery's demise corresponded with a rise in reports about "juvenile colored persons who are arrested for petty offenses."[29] Much as they had in the 1850s, reformers during the late 1860s criticized boys' pervasive presence on the streets as well as in the city's jail — only now the boys in question were black. "Another subject to which the Visitors referred in their last report is worthy of your most serious consideration," reported the jail's Board of Visitors. "We allude to the evil of incarcerating colored children in the jail."[30] For years, white Baltimoreans had endured "noisy and boisterous demonstrations by boys" and dealt with them through the growing penal system.[31] "Why then should we not provide the same for *colored* juveniles?" the board asked.[32] Why not indeed. Emancipation had liberated not just black men but also their sons, and the result seemed to be a growing number of black juveniles who appeared "helpless, ignorant, unprovided for" and who ended up "committed to jail frequently for slight misdemeanors."[33] The dysfunction of black households seemed responsible for the newly "growing evil" of bad black boys.

Emancipation convinced white commentators that black crime was ubiquitous in Baltimore. "The sudden revolution made in the condition of the negro race has thrown upon the city many of the most undesirable of that unfortunate people," wrote an exasperated Mayor Banks in January 1869. In addition to swelling "the daily calendar of crime in the country," that revolution had increased "to a much larger extent proportionally the numbers committed to our city prison for minor offense."[34] The *Baltimore Gazette* spoke for many of its readers when it labeled the "shiftless and desultory" freedman "an annoyance to the community in which he resides in consequence of his idle ways and of those habits of petty larceny to which so many of the race seem naturally addicted."[35] Visitors to the state's penitentiary likewise disparaged the "vast numbers of idle or unemployed blacks, who have been thrown upon the public by the events of the past two or three years, and the application to them of a penal code made for a different order of society." Gustave de Beaumont and Alexis de Tocqueville's prophecy had apparently come true: having been either enslaved or legally checked for so long, black people, black men in particular, were now free and ignorant "of the proper relations of things."[36] "Where masters formerly punished their servants for petty crimes," sardonically rationalized the prison's warden in late 1866, black men "are now, under existing laws, carried to the Criminal Courts, and punished by sentence to this Institution."[37]

White concerns over freed people's criminality were so exaggerated that Baltimore's leading black pastors began to ask "as to whether crime was on the increase among the colored people or not."[38] But in reality, what whites feared and what they saw aligned exclusively in their minds. Insofar as they observed anything at all — aside from their own fantastical projections, anyway — they were likely observing the material effects of slavery. Most black Baltimoreans were still poor, only more so now than before. The vast majority of freed people who made their way to the city after the war were especially poor. In 1864, more than four out of five black householders qualified as unskilled laborers — around 82 percent. In 1871 that number climbed to nearly 88 percent. And those were just the householders. Free black Baltimoreans had labored predominantly in domestic service work, laundering, and day laboring before the war, and the ensuing influx of freed people after emancipation drove up the supply and drove down the price of unskilled black labor still further.[39] It was in this desperate context that the Freedmen's Bureau diligently sought to find work for their charges anywhere they could, usually outside of the state.[40] Black Baltimoreans were not lazier than white Baltimoreans. Their poverty was proof that there were not enough jobs and that what jobs there were paid too little.

Similarly, when white people saw disorderly black households, they were observing the ravages that financial hardship inflicted upon freed people's domestic lives. Many freed people either found homes with white people (usually working as domestic servants) or assembled in cellars and alleyway apartments. During the late 1860s, already crowded black residences became more congested still, making bad situations even worse. It was almost always out of economic necessity that black Baltimoreans established unconventional households: they congregated in cramped, cold, and squalid rooms; they took in the children of friends and family members who died; they performed, however inconsistently, outwork; they depended upon all able-bodied members of the household to work, whatever their ages; and they sometimes rented out a small corner of their overcrowded rooms to other black people who somehow seemed even worse off than they were.[41] Not all black Baltimoreans lived in these wretched environments, but many did. And white neighbors took notice. During a cholera outbreak, the city's health commissioner called upon "the infected district" of Elbow Alley and described the black households he witnessed there as being "in a state of indescribable filth." He was bewildered by how so many people could live in such awful circumstances and was especially appalled at how in one home more than eighty black people dwelled together with "no adequate means of ventilation or cleanliness."[42]

White Baltimoreans who saw indolence in poverty and disorder in desperation also usually ignored how the war itself had hindered black men's attempts to head well-ordered households. Quite a few black soldiers never came home at all. "Thousands of women and children (many of the women who are soldiers['] wives) have been thrown out of homes and are now very destitute," observed a group of sympathetic white people in 1864. "We find more suffering than we are able to alleviate."[43] Andrew Meurhead, a member of the Friends Association in Aid of Freedmen, wrote that he too confronted "many calls from women with children, and not a few of these are soldiers['] widows." Meurhead did what he could for the women, "but I have had more calls than I can supply and have been obliged to find shelter for several houseless, homeless, friendless females, who in this unfriendly weather have neither food nor shelter, and must be provided for."[44]

Circumstantial, structural, and otherwise external causes of black poverty did not much matter to most white Baltimoreans. Really, none of those causes had ever mattered to them. When during the antebellum decades free people of color had struggled to escape slavery's incomprehensible shadow, white Baltimoreans had ignored the context and blamed the victim. Now they did the same, only with more gusto. Although certain individuals like Meurhead considered themselves friends to the new arrivals and wanted mostly to help, the majority of white Baltimoreans saw simple failure in the black hardship that increasingly overwhelmed their streets. They saw confirmation that black men were indolent, that black households were disorderly, and that black crime was endemic. They saw nothing but the chilling spectacle of a black mob run amok — nothing, that is, but the "lawless and disorderly," "improper, disrespectful and insulting," "murderous and dastardly" behavior of a liberated people unable to control themselves.[45]

Which brings us back to freedom's caveat: in a climate where white Baltimoreans were wont to see crime wherever they saw black freedom, no matter the circumstances and no matter the reasons, any clause that excluded criminals from emancipation's liberating fruits was no caveat at all. It was a mandate. True, emancipation unshackled black Baltimoreans from the myriad legal burdens of racial slavery — without question, a revolutionary development — but its parameters also inspired the public authorities to police those black Baltimoreans who failed to obey the law. Intentionally or not, freedom's caveat foretold a bleak future for black people in Maryland's largest city, promising not only individual empowerment but also public policing. In the process, it built upon principles developed simultaneously in the name of freedom and under slavery.

New Vigilantes

During the antebellum years, the many advantages that white men enjoyed while policing black Baltimoreans owed primarily to the existence of racial slavery. Not only did the institution write nearly ninety thousand black Marylanders out of legal personhood entirely, keeping many in chains, but it also underwrote a series of laws that obscured the legal distinctions between enslaved and free black people. By constraining free people of color, the law also empowered white people — and white men in particular. For decades white male Baltimoreans had vigilantly monitored, chased, arrested, protected, and whipped black people on the city's streets. Ordinary citizens had also assisted official law enforcement officers in a variety of respects, rendering differences between the vigilante and the policeman sometimes negligible. The weaker and more vulnerable the law made black Baltimoreans, the more it empowered white male Baltimoreans to police them.

White male vigilantism endured beyond November 1, 1864. White men occasionally chased suspected black thieves.[46] Other times they attempted to arrest black shooters.[47] More often they joined policemen already in pursuit of a black suspect.[48] White men and policemen even sporadically fought alleged black rioters side by side, such as in 1870 when "several citizens" joined a group of policemen in quelling a "crowd of colored people" angered by the recent arrest of a black man. In that particular incident, official and unofficial policemen were together able to arrest nearly a dozen black rioters despite injuries sustained by all sides.[49] In fact, it was not uncommon in the aftermath of emancipation for white citizens to stand alongside their police officers in the face of black "crime," whatever its form.[50] So long as lawmakers presumed black men were indolent, disorderly, and riotous, the "good citizens" of the city were available to assist the authorities, and sometimes to act in their place.[51]

Racial vigilantism occasionally morphed into racial violence during the post-emancipation era as well. Perhaps the most egregious incident erupted late in the summer of 1866 at an interracial religious revival just outside the city limits. Trouble started when a drunken group of white men approached the black section of the campground and began taunting the people there by "throwing watermelon rinds, clapping of hands, &c." One witness related that "several of the colored men, who, it was known, had early in the evening armed themselves with heavy clubs cut from the woods, became angry." When one of the white harassers struck a black woman with a stone, that anger found expression in the form of a gun. A black man fired a pistol, scattering the whites "towards the preacher's stand, where large numbers were engaged in devotional exercises." Amid the ensuing tumult, someone — it was unclear who — shot a white revivalist named Milton Benson in the neck as he was rising from the mourners' bench, and that, in turn, provoked "a party of the whites [to take] possession of the tents of the colored people and set them on fire, destroying the contents, consisting of clothing, etc." Almost as a footnote, the witness mentioned that three black people were also shot.[52]

Baltimore in 1866 was not, however, Baltimore in 1861, and for all of the persistence of white vigilantism and violence, change was also perceptible. The decade's legal revolution demanded at least some modification to the city's police system, if not a wholesale rethinking. For one thing, the destruction of slavery removed the most obvious form of racial policing and punishment. Whites who were previously slave owners could no longer enlist the authorities to track down fugitives, regulate their workforces with impunity, or whip their bondsmen. The deracialization of the legal code meanwhile stripped ordinary white men of most of their advantages in rights, limiting their ability to police black people as if they were police officers too. Black men acquired the full rights to earn wages for their labor, head households of their own, vote, testify, move around without restriction, and otherwise behave as free men were supposed to do. Such changes were not merely nominal: they made a meaningful difference in black lives and, in a more general respect, in how the city was policed.

Black Baltimoreans' acquisition of the right to bear witness against white people was perhaps the most important change. Before the war, a black victim of a white assault would have been subject to the 1717 statute that left him or her legally incompetent "where any white person is concerned." That black victim would have had no ability to prosecute his or her attacker without a white witness. Emancipation changed that. The state's wartime constitution asserted that "all persons held to service or labor, as slaves, are hereby declared free," and within another year the General Assembly repealed the entire black code so as to lend legal credibility to the liberation principle. Among those laws was the ban on black testimony. By the mid-1860s, state law indeed judged a black person competent to testify against a white assailant. So when, in 1866, a white man accused of assault protested that the warrant for his arrest was issued without the authority of law — because his victim and accuser was black — the judge overruled his motion and remanded the white man to jail. Whatever the disparity between the law on the books and the law in action, black victims were better equipped to prevail in court against white attackers. White men could go to jail for racial violence. Sometimes, white men *did* go to jail for racial violence.[53]

But if emancipation changed the nature of racial policing and punishment in Baltimore, it did not change the rationale. In the eyes of many white Baltimoreans, black autonomy remained dangerous. If anything, emancipation made it more dangerous. Not only had the new constitution liberated tens of thousands of seemingly unrestrained people, but, by eradicating the law's racial distinctions, state lawmakers also stripped white men of considerable legal power. This two-pronged transformation left Baltimore's white citizenry both frustrated and fearful. It also left them with a single option, one neither preordained nor necessarily self-evident: to turn for help to the very institution they had originally built as an extension of their own power — the police force. Policemen, in turn, would prove equal to the task of checking black freedom.

The suppression of the city's black militia was emblematic of the citizenry's growing reliance upon policemen to constrain the autonomy of free black Baltimoreans. The sight of black troops, either in official Union army garb or in local militia regalia, terrified many white city dwellers. When they imagined uniformed black men, they saw armed and uncontrollable men, probably "under the influence of liquor," who were both lawlessly and violently unpredictable.[54] The white population at first attempted to deal with the matter as it had always done. During the year or so that followed the end of the war, many citizens simply attacked the black troops who crossed their paths. In one instance, "pistols were drawn and bricks thrown, and the negroes, except one, named Stephen Tucker, driven off." Tucker was then "surrounded and beaten severely about the head with billies, and his pistol taken from him."[55] Gradually, however, policemen began to intervene in these fights. Sometimes they arrested both white and black parties for fighting.[56] Mostly, though, they arrested just the black parties, erasing all

traces of white violence from their accounts and blaming the affairs entirely
upon black aggressors.

The ugliest example occurred in mid-October 1867, when a "riot" erupted
"between a colored military organization and a number of white people."
Earlier in the evening the black militia unit known as the Lincoln Zouaves
had marched up Howard Street. Black men and women lined the streets as
they did. All of a sudden, however, "some ten or twelve shots were fired by the
colored men in line, one shot taking fatal effect on a white lad, aged about 18
years, named Chas. A. Ellermeyer." Or so white witnesses claimed. Neither
the local newspapers nor the municipal authorities mentioned the white
attack upon the black militiamen that precipitated the shots. Nor did any
of those witnesses mention the "dense crowd of white men" who drove the
militiamen out of the city limits and into the county. White violence disappeared from the official report, leaving only the black reaction it provoked
to account for the riot. And so, when "the police authorities were promptly
notified, and the whole police force were at once ordered to the spot," policemen arrested solely black men.[57] Shortly afterward, citing safety concerns,
the city revoked the black militia's right to parade at all.[58]

The criminalization of the black militia was only the beginning, and by
1870 policemen were arresting black people at a markedly higher rate than
they had been ten years earlier, when an entire citizenry had been mobilized
to stop the crime of black autonomy and prisons had incarcerated primarily
white people. "John Price, colored, was arrested on Tuesday night by policeman Farran," read the usual morning fare.[59] Story after story from the *Sun*'s
"Local Matters" section reiterated variations on this same theme. Policeman Fairbanks arrested "Henry James, colored"; Sergeant Auld and policeman A. J. Stewart arrested "Thomas Weeks and John Davis, colored";
policeman J. T. Baker arrested "George Piatta, colored."[60] Police officers also
arrested black boys, those "colored youth" whose fathers had supposedly
failed them and whose apparitions seemed to haunt every looming shadow
through which a white man passed.[61] "Three colored boys," reported another
story of a recurring type, "were arrested yesterday by policemen Baker and
Kidd."[62]

Each story of arrest suggested a personal tragedy, a heartbreaking instance of desperation wrought by the difficult conditions of black life in
postwar Baltimore. Yet sad as these stories may have been on their own —
and there were thousands of them — each one also reflected the changing
shape of power on the city's turbulent streets. Before emancipation, white

TABLE 7.1. Black proportion of Baltimore city jail commitments by crime type, 1861 and 1870

Year	Property crime (%)	Personal crime (%)	Drunkenness (%)	Vagrancy (%)
1861	27.88	8.82	16.84	1.36
1870	54.35	34.81	29.54	26.19

Source: Calculated from table B in 1861 and 1870 Annual Reports of the Board of Visitors of Baltimore City Jail, Government Publications and Reports, MSA.

vigilantes had imposed summary justice upon the black population, and that justice only sometimes resulted in a formal arrest. Afterward, policemen largely replaced the vigilantes, and the consequences were noticeable immediately. Policemen during the 1860s arrested black people more frequently for every type of crime — from property (that is, theft and larceny) to personal (such as assault) to peace crimes (for example, drunkenness or vagrancy). By 1870, black individuals formed a significant minority of those arrested for assault, public drunkenness, and vagrancy, and a bare majority of those arrested for theft and larceny. That last number was particularly revealing: less than 20 percent of the city's population was charged with more than 50 percent of its property crime.

Insofar as white men continued to exert racial police power on the streets, they did so in subtler, more ancillary ways. Racial conflict continued to erupt among the caulkers, for instance, but white animosity increasingly took the form of protest. In September 1865, white mechanics in east Baltimore walked off their jobs in the hope of forcing a local ship merchant, John J. Abrahams and Son, to fire its seventy-five black caulkers. Resiliently, the black workers continued to work alone at the yards. A few of their members also launched a publicity campaign of their own, publishing an appeal in the city's newspapers on October 2. "Whilst quietly and diligently trying to make an honest livelihood," explained the appeal, "an inhuman and unjust cry is raised: Away with negro caulkers! extermination! annihilation! — and for what? Because God chose to make our skins dark."[63] The white strikers did not dispute the point. "All we ask of our employers is that the white man have the preference," stated a tract from the journeymen shipwrights of east Baltimore. "We will go to work for one or more of our former employers as soon as they accede to our reasonable request, or we are prepared to do the work ourselves and guarantee entire satisfaction."[64] They made good on their word, too, with many either finding new jobs in south Baltimore, in the Federal Hill neighborhood where white laborers already controlled the labor market, or setting out on their own in Canton, to the east. The activism worked. Within a month the east Baltimore shipbuilders yielded, agreeing to allow their contracts with black caulkers to expire and to give preferential treatment to any white man seeking employment in the future.[65]

On November 6, the black caulkers in east Baltimore "quit work in a body, refusing to labor longer." But it was already too late. White workers from south of the basin quickly filled the vacancies, and everything, reported the *Sun*, was proceeding "smoothly" without them.[66] "The days of Negro caulking are virtually over," somberly added a report in Baltimore's *American and Commercial Advertiser*.[67] More than that, the days of skilled black labor were largely over as well. A year after the white caulkers' strike, white laborers throughout the city organized a broader action against anyone who employed black mechanics at all, and it was not long before "the strike threatened to become more general against all colored labor, mechanical or otherwise."[68] Hundreds of skilled black workers lost their jobs during these years, diminishing their number and further widening the city's racial wealth gap. Among those who found themselves newly unemployed were many formerly free black men who had before the war counted among Baltimore's small yet growing black middle class.

Whites did not entirely abandon extralegal violence, but black men's procurement of a property right in their labor power forced many white wage earners to employ new strategies. The antiblack violence that white workers had perpetrated in the late 1850s threatened in the 1860s to bring conflict with the police. And, indeed, when the white caulkers' strike had begun, the black caulkers had continued to work at Abrahams and Son under police protection. Yet for the black workers, such safety came with a price. The very policemen charged with guarding their right to work under contract were also bound to arrest anyone who failed to secure a labor contract at all. As such, the strike's success and the further impoverishment of the black community soon drove many black men into the policemen's orbit, as black caulkers who labored under temporary police protection in 1865 confronted hostile policemen when, a year later, they no longer had jobs. For their part, white workers compensated for the racial authority they had surrendered to the liberal law by relying upon the institutionalized power of the police force.

"Any person may have a negro arrested under the vagrant act," reported one disgusted Republican editor.[69]

White patriarchs employed a similarly subtle strategy to leverage power over black households. Slavery had directly robbed black men of freedom, capital, and dependents; it had indirectly legitimized laws that invited white citizens to invade black homes without fear of reprisal. The post-emancipation movement to seize black children through the apprenticeship system was mostly a desperate attempt to maintain a crucial component of these power relations, and it failed because federal officers and the Baltimore City Court worked together to return black children to their parents. Many a Baltimore City policeman delivered these children safely home. But once again, such security was purchased through policing. Black men's property right in their own households was inviolable only to the nonuniformed masses. In the event that, say, their sons became "outcast children of crime and poverty," black men's households became vulnerable to the very policemen who had helped return their children.[70] Black juvenile arrest totals climbed sharply during the late 1860s.[71]

And it was precisely here, in that moment of juvenile detention, that white patriarchs involved themselves in black households. Once upon a time, a white man might have seized black dependents for his own, doing so either himself or with the help of a local orphans court. After emancipation, however, that man was more likely to call upon the police to "investigate cases of petty larceny perpetrated by colored boys and girls."[72] Black juvenile arrests rose after the war largely because of white men's fears and complaints. White male Baltimoreans also regularly employed black mothers in their homes as domestic servants, cooks, nurses, and caregivers, effectively redirecting those women's labor away from their own families and toward white ones. Black men and women's necessary absence from home for economic reasons further encouraged the white conviction that black children were as wild as their parents were wanton. Black men's acquired right to household autonomy thus did little to undermine the considerable power white men exerted over them as patriarchs. The Baltimore policemen who arrested hundreds of (allegedly) unattended criminal black children during the late 1860s merely personified that power in a new form.

In a way, policemen were the new vigilantes, and like their predecessors they occasionally used brute force. One particular case stands out. Eliza Murray was a twenty-eight-year-old black woman who had a fight with her husband on the 1867 night a Baltimore policeman shot her in the head. Her cries amid the domestic dispute had provoked the interest of a passing officer, and once at the house the policeman had attempted to arrest Eliza, leading to a struggle. "Mr. Police, don't take her, she hasn't done anything," begged Murray's husband, Jordan.[73] Soon, more officers arrived. So too did a few of the Murrays' neighbors. What happened next therefore happened in front of a sizable audience. "When the police attempted to arrest both the man & wife," wrote the commander of the Maryland and Delaware District of the Freedmen's Bureau, Edgar Gregory, "the neighbors interfered, and begged for a cessation of hostilities, which was replied to by blows from their clubs & pistols upon the head of the husband." At that point, "one of the officers named Frey drew his revolver & pointed at the woman, when her husband begged him not to shoot, even one of his brother officers told him not to shoot, but he fired and shot the woman through the head, killing her instantly, she falling dead in her husband's arms." Nor was Frey finished. He fired again, this time "shooting the husband through the arm." Jordan Murray had been cradling his dead wife in his arms, but upon being hit with Frey's final shot he dropped her and was "seized & beaten over the head with clubs & pistols and taken to the station house where he was detained."[74] Later, Jordan Murray testified that on the walk to the southern district police station, one of the other officers "beat me with his spantoon [sic] over the head, cutting my head and nose, and he punched me in the side."[75]

Gotlieb Frey shot and killed Eliza Murray in cold blood, and the local prosecutor issued a warrant for his arrest the very next day. Police Marshal Farlow dutifully surrendered Frey into custody, but within forty-eight hours the coroner's report exonerated him, calling the act a "shooting by an officer of the Police force, while being resisted in the discharge of his duty."[76] Judge Hugh Bond, still in charge of the criminal court in 1867, was understandably appalled by the report and sent Frey to jail anyway, ordering him to await action from the grand jury. But Bond's effort to secure justice for Eliza Murray also failed. The grand jury refused to indict a white policeman for murdering a black woman. In his report, Gregory called the incident an illustration of "the manner in which Justice before the law is meted out in this city."[77]

Indeed it was: the events of this case, from Eliza Murray's murder to Gotlieb Frey's exoneration, speak to the ways that racial violence survived under the liberal logic of the new order. One of the more striking characteristics of the affair was the demonstration of black rights. Various black civilians attempted to interfere during the melee, with some individuals going so far as to demand that the police stand down. A large crowd also gathered outside the southern district police station afterward, forcing the coroner's jury inquest off-site. More significant, both Eliza's grieving husband and her brother (Grafton Taylor) gave statements that resulted in a warrant being issued for Frey's arrest. And Frey himself appears not to have remained on the force, though the reasons why are unclear: city directories during the 1880s and 1890s listed a number of occupations for a fifty-something Gottlieb Frey — messenger, contractor, clerk — none of which was policeman.[78] But black rights did not prevent the violence, either, and that matters. The crowd of onlookers was unable to stop a policeman from shooting a black woman. Black testimony might have triggered Frey's arrest but not his conviction. And while Frey might have lost his job, Jordan Murray lost his wife. Tellingly, one of the justifications that the policemen gave for entering the Murray home was that it was "a very disorderly one." Officers testified that they had "often heard girls coming out of the house use language indicating that it was used for bawdy purposes." According to one deponent at the coroner's inquest, one of these girls had been Eliza Murray.[79]

Jordan Murray had served in the U.S. Navy, enjoyed citizenship under the state's recent constitution, and possessed a full array of property rights that entitled him and his dependents to municipal protection.[80] But in the end those very attributes opened him up to accusations of crime — to running a "bawdy" house, in this case — that in turn empowered a white man wearing a uniform to enter his home and kill his wife. The man who pulled the trigger was no vigilante. He was in uniform, acting "in the discharge of his duty." Jordan Murray may not have been able to tell the difference.

Black Incarceration in the Age of Emancipation

The policeman's replacement of the vigilante also had significant ramifications for the penal system. Whereas before emancipation ordinary citizens policed the city's black minority and the authorities often sold free black people into slavery or let them go altogether, afterward police officers simply did what they were empowered to do: imprisoned their charges to await trial. The results were immediate. As police officers arrested black people at growing rates, and as judges sent black convicts to the city's various asylums instead of to nearby slave plantations, Baltimore's prison populations grew larger and blacker. The progressively violent police work of the post-emancipation city thus left an indelible mark upon the penal system, one that simultaneously defined emancipation and circumscribed its possibilities. Although now free, many black Baltimoreans went to prison. And although now empowered with property rights, many black men submitted to a form of punishment designed to strip them of their property.

Changes were immediately evident in the jail's population. Black Baltimoreans had always represented a small minority of the people charged with and committed for crimes, usually on par with their proportion to the city's population as a whole. In 1861, for instance, a black population that represented anywhere from 15 to 17 percent of Baltimore's general population produced around 17 percent of the total number of people consigned to its jail. But over the course of the 1860s, that proportion began to climb. In 1865 black arrestees accounted for more than 22 percent of all jail commitments; in 1870, more than 34 percent. Black men formed the majority of this upsurge. In 1861 they represented under 12 percent of all jail commitments, but by the end of the decade that percentage had more than doubled. All told, in 1870 black people were twice as likely to be jailed than they had been a mere decade earlier. Although still not accounting for more than one in five Baltimoreans, black people were soon significantly overrepresented in the city's jail (see table 7.2)

The jail's demographic makeover anticipated similar transformations in the city's other penal institutions. The penitentiary's population converted from majority white to majority black within two years of emancipation and then kept growing still blacker over time. Black inmates went from representing less than 30 percent of the prison population to more than 70 percent of it in under a decade. In fact, there were almost three and a half times the number of black inmates in the Maryland Penitentiary in 1872 than there had been a decade earlier. Once again, the basis for such a demographic shift lay specifically with a dramatic rise of black male prisoners. Black men in 1863 accounted for under a quarter of all of the institution's inmates; in 1872 they accounted for more than three-fifths of them. Despite representing a small minority in both Baltimore and Maryland, overall black men soon formed a majority of the penitentiary's prisoners (see table 7.3).

The almshouse also underwent a shift, albeit not on the same scale as those of the jail and penitentiary. White residents had historically dominated the almshouse's commitment logs. They formed a sizable majority of the region's population, and in any event, most officials had had little appetite for granting poor relief to people of color. During the 1830s, when the black share of the population crested in Baltimore, black residency at the almshouse never crossed the 25 percent threshold despite the free black community being

TABLE 7.2. Black Baltimore city jail commitments, mid-nineteenth century

Year	Total jail commitments	Black men committed	Percentage black	Percentage black male
1861	7,452	865	17.28	11.61
1865	5,614	766	22.14	13.64
1870	8,214	1,961	34.09	23.87

Source: Calculated from table B in 1861, 1865, and 1870 Annual Reports of the Board of Visitors of Baltimore City Jail, Government Publications and Reports, MSA.

TABLE 7.3. Black male Maryland Penitentiary population, mid-nineteenth century

Year	Total inmates	Percentage black	Percentage black male
1863	411	29.7	23.1
1864	387	33.3	23.8
1865	432	45.1	31.9
1866	636	51.9	40.6
1867	679	57.1	46.4
1868	629	65.3	55.0
1869	687	67.1	59.4
1870	669	67.6	59.6
1871	669	68.8	61.0
1872	598	70.7	62.0

Source: Calculated from 1863–72 Annual Reports of the Maryland Penitentiary, Government Publications and Reports, MSA.

so overwhelmingly poor. But black people's relative underrepresentation in the institution did not last. Almshouse administrators admitted nearly eight times as many black people in 1869 as they had four years earlier, and a population that had made up less than 10 percent of the admitted residents soon counted for over 25 percent. A majority of the institution's inmates remained

TABLE 7.4. Black Baltimore almshouse admissions,
mid-nineteenth century

Year	Total admitted	Percentage black
1865	122	9.0
1867	273	23.4
1869	333	25.5

Source: Calculated from 1865, 1867, and 1869 Reports of the Trustees for the Poor,
appendices to the Ordinances of the Mayor and City Council of Baltimore, DLR.

white, but by 1870 the number of black residents in the almshouse more appropriately measured their regional presence (see table 7.4).

The coup de grace of the state's post-emancipation move to incarcerate
African Americans was the confinement of black boys. Those boys' white
analogues already had their own institution, and in the minds of many liberal reformers, the House of Refuge had been an unmistakable success. Now
reformers called for a similar institution for the black population. "The in-
stituting of the 'House of Refuge' for reception of juvenile infractors of the
law, has, doubtless, operated to prevent the increase of white convicts," con-
fidently speculated one set of penal directors in early 1868. "If similar provision should be made for offending juvenile colored persons, much crime in
the future might be averted." The problem, a familiar one, was that the "con-
signments to the Penitentiary for petty criminal offences upon the part of
these" boys was too severe a sentence, but turning the boys loose "with their
proclivities unbridled" guaranteed that in the long run they would "become
in many cases hardened adepts in crime, and . . . find ultimately their way to
the Penitentiary."[81] Officials concluded that the "new condition of the black
population of the State" made necessary "the erection of a proper reformatory for the reception of these youthful violators of law." Such a house would
be good for both property holders and the boys themselves, who otherwise
would be "schooled on all kinds of vice."[82]

In the name of saving black boys from "irretrievable ruin," the state of
Maryland introduced in 1874 a House of Reformation and Instruction for
Colored Children on a farm in Prince George's County, some forty-five miles
from Baltimore.[83] Despite gender-neutral language, this new institution,

like the House of Refuge before it, primarily served to help boys "become useful men and citizens." House managers similarly insisted that they were not wardens but fathers. "There is no semblance of prison life," assured the institution's first annual report; "a home is provided where no bolts or bars confine the inmates, either by day or night." Bars or not, most boys reached the institution after receiving a criminal sentence; one had to break the law in order to end up there at all. Part school and part prison, the house, like other asylums, sought "to elevate the individual in sentiment and feeling, 'to win him from vice and attach him to virtue,'" through forced labor. Inmates worked "in squads under the supervision of one of their own number," in preparation, the directors hoped, for being "able to furnish the farming interest of our State with a good class of laborers."[84]

African Americans' rising incarceration rates propelled a broader upsurge in penal populations that penal reformers called "*suggestive*, if not *startling*."[85] This was certainly true in the jail. There, the inmate population almost doubled within five years of the war's end and had more than doubled within ten. Administrators decried these growing tallies and focused in particular upon the dramatic increase of paupers under their care. "The accused remain in jail one or two weeks and be discharged, and in twenty-four hours the same individual will be again committed on like charge," complained one of the institution's post-emancipation reports. "After a few hours outside the prison walls, spent in drunkenness and debauchery, these worthless vagabonds are arrested and sent to jail."[86] Not coincidentally, it was at this very moment—the early 1870s—when black vagrants began to appear in the jail's dockets at an exaggerated rate. Arrested hardly at all for vagrancy in 1861, black Baltimoreans made up almost 30 percent of those arrested for the "crime" in 1870.[87]

The penitentiary experienced even more demographic growth than the jail, and many inmates suffered because of it. As early as 1867, the number of inmates in the state's prison had reached 679, a 75 percent increase from three years earlier. Officials labored under no allusion as to why their number had risen so rapidly: "There were but thirty-one white persons more in the Institution at the end of the present fiscal year than there were five years since," explained the director of the institution in January 1868, "whilst the number of black prisoners has been more than quadrupled within the same period and nearly doubled within the last two years." The influx of new black prisoners posed a material problem, if only because the dormitory "properly contains but 320 cells, each one of which is just of sufficient capacity for a 'single bed,' and sixty-four of these being located on the ground floor are unsuited for the purpose designed." So onerous was the challenge of housing 679 prisoners in the aging building that the warden felt compelled "to lodge 160 of the colored prisoners in a room less than 50 feet each way."[88]

Penal authorities blamed their swelling inmate populations on black people for two reasons. Not only did black incarceration rates grow during the aftermath of emancipation, but white incarceration rates also fell, broader demographic trends notwithstanding. A few possibilities may help explain why. The crackdown on black freedom — or "crime," as the authorities saw it — most obviously diverted the police's attention and resources away from white suspects. But white people also began to enter private facilities whenever possible.[89] Moreover, between 1867 and 1871 the state's governors pardoned an unusually large number of prisoners in the penitentiary, the vast majority of whom were white (see table 7.5). As a result, white men began to fade from prison roll calls at the very moment black men began dominating them, a trend that encouraged the impression that the "demoralization amongst the colored population" was concurrent with a "diminution of crime among the white population."[90]

White declension was evident across the penal system, but the penitentiary witnessed the starkest decline in white prisoners. White inmates represented more than three-quarters of the prison's population at the start of the Civil War; by the end of the decade, they represented just over a third. Put another way, the percentage of white prisoners in the penitentiary was soon cut in half. In the city's jail and almshouse, meanwhile, white admissions continued to outpace black admissions, though to a decreasing extent over time. In 1861 the overwhelming percentage of commitments to the jail and admissions to the almshouse was white. By 1870, those tallies had fallen significantly (see table 7.6).

So many black inmates overwhelmed the authorities, just as Beaumont and Tocqueville had long ago predicted they would. "With this state of things staring you in the face," asked a clearly frustrated warden John Horn in 1867, "how is it possible for the Maryland Penitentiary to become a reformatory school?"[91] The question was rhetorical. Accommodating the sheer number of black prisoners then residing in prison was hard enough without also worrying about how to make such a group penitent. "The construction of our buildings will not admit of isolation," sighed another visitor to the prison in 1874.[92] Labor, at least as a constructive tool of reform, was also becoming pointless for another reason. Under slavery, black people had worked

TABLE 7.5. White percentage of total Maryland gubernatorial pardons, mid-nineteenth century

Year	Average annual total	Percentage white
1860–66	~31	~88
1867–71	~108	~77

Source: Compiled from Pardon Record, Secretary of State, 1839–1941, S1108, MSA.

TABLE 7.6. White proportion of total Baltimore asylum populations, 1861 and 1870

Year	Maryland Penitentiary (%)	Jail commitments (%)	Almshouse admissions (%)
1861	76.2	82.7	87.2
1870	36.2	65.9	74.5

Sources: Calculated from 1861 and 1870 Annual Reports of the Maryland Penitentiary, Government Publications and Reports, MSA; table B in 1861 and 1870 Annual Reports of the Board of Visitors of Baltimore City Jail, ibid.; and 1861 and 1869 Reports of the Trustees for the Poor, appendices to the Ordinances of the Mayor and City Council of Baltimore, DLR.

around the clock, adding value only to the coffers of their owners and not, as it were, to their own lives. After slavery, penal officials expressed doubts that prison labor would have the same rehabilitative effect upon black inmates that it allegedly had had upon whites. "Comparing the capability of the black and the white man, I find that . . . where the employment is so varied as to require judgment, thought, skill or ingenuity, [the black man] is inferior," Warden Mark C. Thompson noted in his 1866 report.[93] The president of the penitentiary's Board of Visitors made the same observation two years later. Black inmates, he argued in 1868, "have not the same aptitude in acquiring a knowledge of the mechanical branches of industry" as white inmates.[94]

Saddled with too many prisoners and convinced that black inmates were beyond redemption, the directors of the Maryland Penitentiary began leasing out inmates' labor during the late 1860s. The older system had brought the employers inside the prison's walls and into its silent, closely monitored

workshops, where prison architecture was geared toward the reconstitu-
tion of souls. The new system sent the prisoners to the employers, a group
interested in little else but profit. The authorities quickly discovered that
convict leasing was enormously lucrative. Thomas Wilkinson, the warden,
proclaimed in 1872 that the arrangement was "more profitable to the State
than any other system which could be adopted" and urged lawmakers to
expand and make it permanent.[95] A year later, he made the same recommen-
dation.[96] Surpluses became such a recurring trend in the prison's financial
reports, in fact, that not even the Panic of 1873 was able to push the institution's finances into the red.[97] In an important sense, the Maryland Penitentiary began to convert the labor of its largely black inmates into profits for
white men.

It is tempting to conclude that a post-emancipation carceral state aimed
primarily at African Americans served simply to check the progress of black
freedom in the aftermath of emancipation. That is, it is tempting to conclude
that black policing and imprisonment represented little more than racist
whites' reactionary response to the revolutionary legal changes enacted
throughout the decade and that the explosion of black arrest rates, together
with the growing number of black inmates in the city's various penal asylums, was Baltimore's version of the Klan. But that interpretation, though
convenient, obscures the extent to which black incarceration (and, implicitly, racial policing) was endemic to the larger project of emancipation. Antislavery white activists worked from the outset not only to help black men
stand on their own but also to build penal institutions for when they failed
to stand. Edgar Gregory had barely established his Freedmen's Bureau office
in Baltimore before Oliver Otis Howard, the bureau head in Washington, was
sending him funds "for rental and repairs of school buildings and asylums
in your State."[98] "The principal portion of the disbursements has been made
for schools and asylums," read another piece of federal correspondence.[99]
If federal agents could not "make these people take care of themselves," as
was often the case with aging and impoverished former slaves, they worked
instead "to get these into the county Poor House" or "a Hospital" for the insane.[100] Gregory himself anticipated pleas for a black house of reformation
by calling in 1867 for a "Colored Orphans Asylum" for black boys.[101]

Also important was this fact: it was not only proslavery reactionaries and
reluctant emancipationists who believed that black incarceration would
grow under the new order. The freed people's most prominent white ally in
Baltimore was Hugh Bond. During the mid-1860s, Bond proved vital to the

campaigns to destroy apprenticeship, secure black male suffrage, and build black schools. He worked tirelessly — and as far as the opponents of emancipation were concerned, notoriously — to fight for freed people. And yet, like so many of the white activists who worked in the antislavery struggle, Bond opposed any charity "which does not tend to make the colored man feel his duty and capacity to support himself" and beseeched any black man who would listen that "upon you is the ... responsibility of demonstrating ... your fitness."[102] Hopeful for the possibilities of black liberation, Bond was comfortable with the consequences of black failure. After all, he presided over the Baltimore Criminal Court at precisely the moment when the criminal justice system was beginning to confine black men en masse.

The liberal project of emancipation proved in the end to be a double-edged sword. A popular presumption that black freedom would beget crime saddled black men's postwar acquisition of rights with a set of responsibilities that many whites believed they were incapable of shouldering. Governor Thomas Swann saw no contradiction when in 1868 he celebrated black men's new "rights of person and property," all the while calling them "a distinct and peculiar people."[103] Swann's successor Oden Bowie encountered no dissonance either when in his inaugural address he proclaimed that the black man "should be, as he is, protected in all his rights. But he should not, as he never will, be made the equal of or the ruler over the white man."[104] To many white proponents of the inviolability of property, black emancipation and the liberalization of the law were necessary to freedom's progress. Indeed it was vital to the creation of a legal order that realized the Lockean tenets of life, liberty, and property. But black freedom, however central to white Americans' metanarratives, also made state policing and punishment all the more imperative as well.

One may still reasonably ask why. Why, if radical reformers were so dedicated to black emancipation, were so many of them also complicit in black policing? Why was black incarceration consistent with the broader project of emancipation? And why did a carceral state aimed especially at African Americans emerge only in the late 1860s, in the wake of slavery's demise and the law's liberalization? One may reasonably ask why the new order's architects decided to enshrine a new form of black compulsion in their post-slavery society.

Any answer to these questions demands an engagement with the tortured historical relationship between blackness and freedom. That relationship had been forged under slavery. Liberal reformers had built their police force and penal system to protect property at a historical moment when mainstream political and economic thought defined most black bodies as property, and whatever legal changes emancipation wrought, the stigma of criminality persisted. Whether conservative or radical, federal or local, ostensibly friendly or overtly hostile, many of the white men who governed post-emancipation Baltimore never stopped believing that black men made poor candidates for freedom — they never stopped seeing black male autonomy as criminal — which operated, perversely, to condemn black men for the very legal victories they fought so hard to earn. In some ways, the fate of freedmen had been foreshadowed by the fate of free black men in the late 1850s, whose presence had so worried liberal reformers. Popular wisdom castigated both groups as criminal, as "the ignorant and the vicious," and white onlookers had obstinately refused to consider either group capable of industriously working for wages, maintaining respectable households, or comporting themselves lawfully. Black freedom thus "imperil[ed] the rights of persons and property."[105] Once slavery was gone, however, the lawbooks condemned the black man to suffer at the whims of the official white policeman, not of the ordinary white citizen, and sent him not to a plantation as a term slave but to a prison as a convict. Rather than undermining white male supremacy, emancipation merely shifted the locus of racial police power from the amateur to the professional.

None of this is to doubt the revolutionary nature of emancipation, nor is it to deny the imperative of establishing the principle of equal rights before the law. Slavery was, of course, insidiously evil. Equal protection remains, as ever, unequivocally good. My goal here is instead to grapple with the remarkable fact that mass black policing and incarceration developed most fully under the *new* order and not before. In a world that judged black freedom as criminal, emancipation forced lawmakers to confront the fears they had long held at bay. The effect was to liberate freed people into a society already convinced of their failure. And that the postwar legal order posed little existential threat to white male supremacy was a detail white liberals were only too happy to tout. "Because I think myself either by the gift of God or accidental circumstances superior to the Darks it is no reason that I should stop the avenues of their egress," reasoned Hugh Bond. He later asked, rhetorically, "If a man can beat another in a race, why insist on tying a weight to the legs of his competitor?"[106] Even some of their professed friends believed that black Baltimoreans would fail to "win the race"— that they would rarely work hard, seldom head respectable homes, and too infrequently follow the law. White men like Bond never wavered in their adherence to white supremacy, earnestly trusting that freedmen would end up in prison anyway, chained not by masters but as a consequence of their own consent.

All of which is to say that Reconstruction in Baltimore ushered in significant change that cut two ways. Slavery disappeared from the law on the books as well as from the law in practice, and what replaced it was a deracialized system predicated upon the rights of all men to earn wages and head households. Black men's subsequent mass policing and incarceration unfolded under that new order.[107] White lawmakers built a carceral state aimed primarily at black men in response to those men's acquisition of property rights. It is true that those rights constituted one of the great successes of emancipation, something that would demand reclamation many more times again in the years to come. We would do well to recall the bloody work that produced them. But living, as we do now, in a time when mass black policing and incarceration both thrive under a supposedly "post-racial" legal system, we would also do well to consider the awesome and terrifying response that those rights provoked when black men acquired them during the 1860s. The tragedy defines us still.

EPILOGUE

♦

FOR LARGE SWATHS of U.S. history, the extension of black rights and freedom has been inseparable from a rise in racial policing. This was never truer than during the late 1860s. When black men in post-emancipation Baltimore seized labor and household power, they did so in a society whose most liberal legal minds doubted their willingness to work industriously and head well-ordered households without compulsion. Such skepticism of black nature reflected a long-standing view among white people that black freedom would beget crime. Black men's acquisition of the rights to earn wages and head households consequently had the perverse effect of inserting state police power over black lives in a new way, as the public authorities began arresting and incarcerating black people — and black men especially — for being criminals. Having built a police force and penal system to safeguard their property rights, white men looked to these same policemen and prisons for protection from the indolent, lecherous, and lawless freedmen of their fevered imaginations. By 1870, a carceral state aimed primarily at African American men had arisen in Baltimore.

All of this arresting, all of this imprisonment, and all of this violence were the result of liberal freedom's peculiar development in a slave society. Nineteenth-century liberals believed that liberty demanded both personal autonomy and responsibility; they believed, that is, that the free individual not only deserved protection for his rights but also required punishment if he abused those rights. The "his" and "he" in that sentence are intentional, too: classical theorists and the legal reformers they inspired each imagined the liberal subject as a man. And in this, they were almost always explicit. But implicitly they also imagined that subject as a *white* man. Such gender and racial coding ultimately left white men as uniquely positioned to claim the protections of property ownership as it did black men to suffer punishment for property's acquisition. The logic of liberal freedom amplified scrutiny upon the very individuals who, through real industry and against remarkable hurdles, lifted themselves up from slavery.

Whatever the revolutionary merits of emancipation — and it was unquestionably a radically and profoundly progressive event — it did not destroy white male power, black oppression, or racial violence. It mostly transformed their shapes. Among historians, it has become common to suggest that we cannot tell the triumphant history of American freedom without also telling the concurrent stories of inequality, coercion, and oppression. This book stands the truism on its head, suggesting that we cannot fully understand the story of American racism without first understanding the disquieting story of liberal freedom. The black carceral state arose in freedom's name, not in opposition to it.

We are left with important questions of causation and continuity. To compare the black policing of 1860 with the black policing of 1870, as if the latter followed directly from the former — racial oppression before emancipation and racial oppression afterward — is to imply that postwar policing and punishment was an extension of slavery under a new guise. Only in the broadest sense was this true. During the antebellum years, many municipal law officers, be they night watchmen or, later, professional policemen, did in fact behave like slave catchers, and a policeman's arrest of a black person during the late 1860s could not help but seem like a familiar application of an older form of white supremacy. At the same time, both the antebellum plantation and postbellum prison were sites of coerced labor, strict discipline, and race control, and they especially began to bear similarities once the convict-lease system became popular in the South. Whatever the differences between them, the effects of racial slavery and liberal policing were similar: each constrained black freedom. The state took over where the vigilantes, slave patrols, and plantation overseers left off.[1]

And yet the story is not quite so simple. One danger of likening the carceral state to the slave state is that it obscures the fact that postwar racial oppression was reconstructed under purportedly liberal, and often race-less, legislation. In Baltimore, the legal order that dated to the antebellum years relied upon explicit limitations of black rights, particularly in the economic and domestic spheres. This is not to say that black people possessed no property rights; as I have striven to make clear, antebellum free black Baltimoreans earned wages and headed households despite the many obstacles they confronted, with many of them creating meaningfully free lives for themselves and their families. It is simply to point out that they did not possess all rights. A combination of municipal and state statutes mandated special permits for certain black purchases, inhibited black people from trading certain commodities, levied a black curfew after certain hours, and imposed a bevy of restrictions upon certain black contracts. The antebellum legal code also curbed black people's right to assemble in black households, compelled impoverished black parents to apprentice their children to white masters, and undermined black householders' rights to protect their dependents from white invaders or assailants. Most seriously, the legal system empowered white vigilantes to attack, arrest, and punish free people of color who were doing little more than behaving like free people. The majority of black Baltimoreans may not have been enslaved, but every one of them suffered the indignities of a discriminatory legal culture that owed its existence to racial slavery.

Emancipation's lawbooks were different. There was the liberation of eighty-seven thousand black Marylanders, of course, but there was also the liberalization of the law on a wide scale, which affected greater numbers of people than just former slaves. Black and white antislavery activists, some of them local and some of them not, successfully worked during the mid-1860s to secure the rights of all men, regardless of race. In particular, they ensured the sanctity of labor contracts between thousands of white employers and black wageworkers; they destroyed an apprenticeship system that former slaveholders were using to rebind the children of former slaves; and they repealed a litany of laws that had remained on the books after the 1864 state constitution ended slavery, such as the restriction of black voting, the ban on black testimony, and the mandate that all black people, no matter their status, carry free papers on their persons at all times. Few would confuse Baltimore's 1870 legal culture with a racial utopia, but few too would deny that the system of race control that the new order replaced was far more explicit, and far more illiberal, than the one it inaugurated. As any post-emancipation-era black person who bore witness against a white assailant would admit, the changes in the law were very real indeed.

What makes the black men's post-emancipation arrest and imprisonment rates so difficult to explain is also what makes them so concerning: they occurred under the aegis of the new legal order, not the old one. It is far simpler, not to mention comforting, to blame racial oppression upon a system that was justified in the name of racial caste rather than upon the system that overtly aimed to erase racial caste from the law. Had the old order simply survived in modified form, then all that would have remained to do was expunge its remnants. But slavery and its attendant legal system did perish during the 1860s, and the system that lawmakers put in their place guaranteed the wage-earning and householding rights of all men, be they black or white or something else. It is thus vitally important for us to understand not only why so much policing and incarceration of black men occurred after this happened but also how such policing and incarceration constituted one of emancipation's most original creations.

To accept that racial oppression thrived under liberal logic is to accept that the work of fighting white supremacy could not be over, and would never be over, with the deracialization of the legal code alone. For white supremacy was never confined to slavery, let alone legalized racism. The struggles of both free black Baltimoreans during the antebellum years and freed people during the city's postbellum years each suggest, albeit in different forms, that one of the primary means by which white supremacy in America flourished was through the criminalization of black *freedom*. So long as black freedom was itself the crime — so long as lawmakers, law enforcers, jurists, commentators, and theorists viewed the liberal subject not just as a man but in particular as a white man — black people's liberation was destined to invite some sort of racial policing. During the antebellum years, that policing took the form of white vigilantism. During the postbellum years, it materialized in the persons of policemen and within the structures of prisons. The violence continued nonetheless. Creating a race-less state constitution reconstituted white racial power rather than destroying it.

There is thus a second, related danger to likening the racial policing and incarceration of the late 1860s to slavery: it undersells the insidious flexibility of white supremacy. As the historical Baltimore example suggests, extending a full array of labor and domestic rights to black men failed to eradicate the racial violence that had for decades thrived in freedom's name. This was not because, as many white contemporaries believed, black men were ill equipped to possess those rights, but rather because white doubts about black nature were endemic to the very system that white men had built to police freedom. The lesson, then as now, is that the expansion of political borders was not enough to curb white supremacy. Indeed, white men in nineteenth-century America enjoyed the remarkable power that they did, inequality took the shape that it did, and the post-emancipation world looked the way that it did because the mere extendsion of rights to black people was never enough.

This is a lesson well worth heeding today. At least two narratives have characterized black life in postbellum America. One is the story of progress, of civil rights and political inclusion and the election of a black president. It is a story of hope, and it is both real and inspiring. The other account follows a much darker trajectory. As I write these words, black arrest rates dwarf white arrest rates and the various governments of the United States are now incarcerating more black people than slave masters owned slaves in 1861.[2] No less real, such numbers chronicle a story of despair. This book argues that these two narratives are not unrelated, and that African Americans' very success in overcoming the legal and political vicissitudes of institutionalized racism is one of the primary explanations for the state's scrutiny.

One can most clearly see the tenacious persistence of white supremacy in the brutal violence that black people regularly endure at the hands of police officers, and in the ways that that violence is frequently explained away as a consequence of black agency. Every year in the United States, law enforcement officers kill a disproportionate number of black men and women in the line of duty. But whether the black victims at the time of their assaults are fumbling for a driver's license, playing in a gazebo, or walking on a city street, both the officers and their allies tend to justify police violence by dwelling on the victims' culpability — that is, black people's tacit consent to be harmed. Sometimes reports rationalize how black individuals deserved their fates — the routine traffic stop escalated because the driver grabbed a taser; the boy playing in the gazebo reached for a gun; the man walking on the street started, inexplicably, to run — while other times officials disclose irrelevant evidence of a criminal past. Black victims of police violence are almost always doing something all free people do, but when black people drive, play, or run, they look like criminals. It is the very expression of their autonomy, of freedom itself, that invites the police's scrutiny in the first place.[3]

Modern black Americans who suffer injuries at the hands of policemen cannot be easily compared to antebellum free black people who lived in the shadow of slavery, nor can they be equated with freed people who seized rights after emancipation. There is too much history in between. Their brutal experiences are nevertheless reminiscent of a type of violence that befell those older actors, and as such they reveal something profound about the nature of freedom that has endured to the present day. If Americans are to overcome the white supremacy intrinsic to their policing practices — if they wish to break the centuries-old relationship between ordinary white men and official police institutions — they must first sever the centuries-old association of black freedom with criminality. Only then will freedom's protectors begin to live up to their name, and only then will black Americans truly enjoy the fruits of their rights without being punished for having them.

ACKNOWLEDGMENTS

WHERE WOULD WE BE without our friends and family? Some other place, surely, but certainly also in dire straits. And this is especially true for writers, even of the academic kind. Fortunately for me, I am blessed to have had many wonderful people help me with this project along the way, and I owe all of them the deepest gratitude. It's nice to finish something with the knowledge that others have believed in you. Hell, it's nice to finish something at all, and I would never have finished this without substantial help.

I am remarkably indebted to Stephen Kantrowitz, who has read so many of my words and offered tough but invaluable feedback throughout the years. His advice, which is always considered, has helped me turn words and thoughts into chapters and arguments; his keen eye has kept my commas in place and sentences flowing; and his resistance to my ever-persistent desire to float high up in the clouds of abstraction has kept my feet planted firmly on historical (and empirical) ground, where they undoubtedly belong. Steve is a tremendous academic and a remarkably good mentor, which I hope he knows. James Sweet has offered guidance, assistance, and friendship — and some beer — to help me along my wayward path. He is one of the smartest people in the world, and his approach to history has left a profound impact upon the way I see my own role as a historian. Jennifer Ratner-Rosenhagen, Karl Shoemaker, and Susan Zaeske all ushered this book along at a crucial stage in its development and in the process helped to elucidate the problems as well as the merits long before I could have done so myself. I also want to acknowledge my debt to Jeanne Boydston, a historian of the first order who would have had many smart and incisive things to say about this book had she lived to see it through. She once told me to follow the silences, and I wish she were here to read the culmination of that advice.

There are numerous people who have read portions of this manuscript and shared their thoughts. I thank David Gilbert and Jennifer Hull for reading very early versions of the first two chapters, Josh Rothman for reading a slightly less-early version of chapter 2, Susan Cahn for offering up incredibly helpful comments on chapters 3 and 4, and Carole Emberton, Hal Langfur, Ndubueze Mbah, Erik Seeman, Kristin Stapleton, Tamara Thornton, and Victoria Woolcott for helping me to rethink and reframe chapter 3. Stephen Mihm has read several versions of the book's first few chapters and offered great advice as well as considerable encouragement. His belief in the merits of this project has sustained me more than he might realize. Patient and knowledgeable archivists have helped me throughout this process, especially at the Baltimore City Archives, the Maryland Hall of Records, and the Maryland Historical Society. Astute audiences, such as those at the conferences for the Organization of American Historians and the Society of Historians of the Early American Republic, have aided me in countless ways. A subvention from the Julian Park Fund helped pay for an indexer, and I am deeply grateful. Thanks also to the Humanities Institute at the University at Buffalo, which provided both time to flesh out my thinking about riots and democracy and a wonderful community of cross-disciplinary conversation. Erik Seeman and Libby Otto are awesome. And finally, thanks to Cathy Kelly of the *Journal of the Early Republic* and the excellent cadre of anonymous reviewers she assembled on my behalf.

I am very much indebted to the University of North Carolina Press. Without Brandon Proia, I am not sure where I would be. He not only rescued this project at a low moment but has always provided me with gracious and thoughtful counsel as I have struggled to make sense of nineteenth-century Baltimore. That he secured two superb anonymous reviewers who helped make this book much better than it otherwise would have been is only the cherry. Mary Caviness has been patient with my many queries and occasional panic over citations, while Julie Bush did excellent work copyediting. Any mistakes in the final text are mine, and mine alone. I am truly grateful to have the opportunity to publish with UNC Press and owe much to the excellent staff that keeps the house in good working order.

Broader communities of friendship have sustained me through the decade-long process of writing this book. Since I arrived in Buffalo almost six years ago, Susan Cahn and David Herzberg in particular have reinforced my belief in both the project and myself and have lent me the emotional support I needed when I needed it — which has been often. Not only has David Alff, who is both generous and brilliant, shared my time as a Humanities Institute Fellow, but he, Katie Rowan-Alff, and Lewis Powell have also helped make Buffalo a lovely place to live. Scott Burkhardt, Mark Goldberg, Ethan

Katz, Neil Kodesh, Nicole Kvale, Tim Lenoch, Dan Magaziner, Adam Mandelman, Maia Surdam, Zoe Van Orsdal, and Tom Yoshikami have all, in a variety of ways, been there for me when I needed them to be. Meghan Greeley and Kristi Thane kindly opened up their home to me in Baltimore and patiently endured my moods as I went through the challenging process of doing research in a city where I knew no one. I hope they are doing well. Jarred Abel, Nell Burger, Christine Hodgdon, William Kirst, and Sarah Rothman have each lent me their homes when I was traveling to, from, or within Maryland and are all the best. Ryan Quintana has commented on large portions of this work through the years, has talked through innumerable ideas and roadblocks with me, and is one of my closest friends to boot. It's hard to imagine where I would be, or where this book would be, without Ryan. Finally, Keith Woodhouse has always been ready to entertain an idle thought or listen to a new idea or simply endure another round of self-doubt. His thoughts on liberalism have led me to think more deeply about its ramifications for the nineteenth-century world. I am deeply indebted to all of these friends, and many more besides, without whom I would be far less of the scholar and person I am today.

During the past decade my family has patiently and lovingly sustained me through the highs and lows of academe. While I have toiled away in the various regions of the frigid North, my sister, Jaclyn, has grown up to become a lovely young woman whose respect means the world to me. My parents, Bernard and Ellen Malka, have also been amazing. They never once wavered in their belief that I could (and would) finish this thing and were always available to talk me off the ledge when the going seemed to get too rough. Words cannot express my gratitude to them.

And then there is Jennifer. It is no exaggeration to say that she is the reason there is a book at all. I am not the easiest person to live with, and I cannot imagine any person being as patient, considerate, and supportive as my loving partner has been during the past few years. Even as she has had to contend with her own challenging work schedule, our two-body problem, and, during this final push to publication, a pregnancy, she has been there for me every morning, afternoon, and night — and almost always with a smile on her face. She is the love of my life and the reason I managed to do what ultimately needed to be done to finish. This book is for her.

NOTES

Abbreviations

BCA   Baltimore City Archives
DLR   Department of Legislative Reference, City Hall, Baltimore
EPFL   Enoch Pratt Free Library, Baltimore
MHS   Maryland Historical Society, Baltimore
MSA   Maryland State Archives, Annapolis
RFO   Records of the Field Offices for the States of Maryland and Delaware
         (M1906), Bureau of Refugees, Freedmen, and Abandoned Land (RG 105).
         Housed at the National Archives, Washington, D.C.

Introduction

1. Calculated from table B in the 1861 and 1870 Annual Reports of the Board of Visitors of Baltimore City Jail, appendices to the Ordinances of the Mayor and City Council of Baltimore, DLR.

2. 1867 Annual Report of the Maryland Penitentiary, Government Publications and Reports, MSA.

3. Table 1, 1876 Annual Report of the Maryland Penitentiary, ibid.

4. Const. of Maryland, 1864, art. 1, Declaration of Rights; Fields, *Slavery and Freedom on the Middle Ground*, 153.

5. Const. of Maryland, 1867, art. 1, Declaration of Rights.

6. Bowie, "Inaugural Address of Gov. Oden Bowie."

7. For a great example of the latter, see Tarter and Bell, *Buried Lives*.

8. "No behavior is in itself criminal," writes historian Drew Gilpin Faust. "It is, rather, interpreted as such by a social group exercising power in this very act of definition." Faust, "Southern Violence Revisited," 208.

9. For decades, historians have emphasized the ways that both police professionalization and reformative punishment have reinforced class inequities. See, for one classic example, Montgomery, *Citizen Worker*, 52–114. Also see Friedman, *Crime and Punishment in American History*, 61–124; and Walker, *Popular Justice*, 47–111. Others have emphasized the ways that the state (as well as vigilantes under the aegis of the state) policed ethnicity in the nineteenth century. For one good example, see Jacobson, *Whiteness of a Different Color*, 15–90. Still other historians have argued that nineteenth-century municipalities increasingly policed sex outside of marriage. See

Lyons, *Sex among the Rabble*, 309–92. Historian Jennifer Manion meanwhile argues that women, and black women in particular, suffered considerably as the early Republic's criminal justice system professionalized. See Manion, *Liberty's Prisoners*.

10. But it is to take white male power seriously, and to see the lives of black people in the age of slavery as "powerfully conditioned by, but not reducible to, their slavery." For that quote, as well as for his broader reconsideration of agency, see W. Johnson, "On Agency," 116. The literature on urban slavery and free black communities is voluminous. For the classic texts on each, see, respectively, Wade, *Slavery in the Cities*; and Berlin, *Slaves without Masters*. For studies of northern free black people, both men and women, see Dunbar, *A Fragile Freedom*; Horton and Horton, *In Hope of Liberty*; and Myers, *Forging Freedom*. Both Baltimore's black community and the role of slavery in shaping black life in that city have garnered considerable scholarly attention. In addition to Barbara Fields's aforementioned *Slavery and Freedom on the Middle Ground*, see Graham, *Baltimore*; Phillips, *Freedom's Port*; Whitman, *Price of Freedom*; Townsend, *Tales of Two Cities*; and Rockman, *Scraping By*.

11. The idea that the state monopolized legitimate force owes to Max Weber's formulation: "The modern state," Weber wrote almost a century ago, "is a compulsory association which organizes domination. It has been successful in seeking to monopolize the legitimate use of physical force as a means of domination within a territory. To this end the state has combined the material means of organization in the hands of its leaders, and it has expropriated all autonomous functionaries of estates who formerly controlled these means in their own right. The state has taken their positions and now stands in the top place." Weber's conception of the state as "a compulsory association" aligns with Ernst Freund's seminal description of the police power as "the power of promoting the public welfare by restraining and regulating the use of liberty and property." See, respectively, Weber, *Essays in Sociology*, 82–83; and Freund, *Police Power*, iii. For a contemporary application of this argument that frames police reform as the replacement of the posse with the police, see K. Smith, *Dominion of Voice*, 80–81.

12. For a famous example of American jurists struggling to define the term, see *Slaughter-House Cases*. Also see Hockheimer, "Police Power," 158.

13. Foucault, *"Omnes et Singulatim,"* 249. Foucault, in his discussion, relies heavily upon the 1722 *Traité de la police* (Treatise on police) by Nicolas de la Mare. For a broad history of the police power in America, see Dubber, *Police Power*. Also see Tomlins, "Supreme Sovereignty of the State," 33–53.

14. Historian William Novak, for instance, argues that "police power has little to do with our modern notion of a municipal police force." Historian Christopher Tomlins, by contrast, argues that the actions of police officers, and their protection of property rights specifically, became the primary function of the police power during the first half of the nineteenth century. See Novak, *People's Welfare*, 13; and Tomlins, *Law, Labor, and Ideology*, 61–97.

15. In this book I treat incarceration as something like a by-product of policing, as a rough reflection of trends begun on the streets. But I should also be careful to note that the history of incarceration did not precisely mirror that of policing.

To imply it did risks obscuring the adjudication process that occupied the moment between arrest and imprisonment — it risks erasing the history of Baltimore's court system, in other words. And that is problematic if only because, as legal historians have recently made clear, the courts often operated under a different logic than did police officers and vigilantes, to say nothing of penitentiaries and almshouses. The regime assessed in this book is ultimately, then, that of the streets, not the courts. Likewise, the manifestation of white supremacy it assesses is more the racial animus of individuals than the structural racism of the broader criminal justice system. A complete history of the latter would necessitate a closer inspection of what lawyers, juries, and judges thought and how they either contributed to or hindered white supremacy. For examples of how court participants, particularly at the local level, saw their interests in competition with white supremacy, see Edwards, *People and Their Peace*; and Greene, "*State v. Mann* Exhumed," 701–55.

16. My argument here owes much to the work of British political historian Patrick Joyce. Borrowing from Michel Foucault's theory of governmentality, Joyce asserts that "nineteenth-century liberal governance" emphasized "seeing, knowing and securing this 'society' as the free play of things, information and persons." See Joyce, *Rule of Freedom*, 62.

17. See especially Falk, *Law as Process*, 10–12.

18. For the importance of the wage and marriage contracts to nineteenth-century conceptions of freedom, and to understandings of property in particular, see Stanley, *From Bondage to Contract*, 1–59.

19. For his discussion of the "tyranny of the majority," see Tocqueville, *Democracy in America*, chaps. 7 and 8. He cites the 1812 Baltimore riot in chap. 7, on 252. For a fuller context in which he recorded his thoughts, see Pierson, *Tocqueville and Beaumont in America*, 504–8.

20. Graham, *Baltimore*. For the numbers, see table A-7 and table A-8 in L. Curry, *Free Black in Urban America*, 250–51.

21. There are some excellent new works chronicling the criminalization of blackness in the early national United States. See, especially, DeLombard, *In the Shadows of the Gallows*; and Manion, *Liberty's Prisoners*, 120–52.

22. For antiblack paramilitary violence in the New South, see Rable, *But There Was No Peace*; Brundage, *Under Sentence of Death*; and Pfeifer, *Rough Justice*. For black incarceration rates in the postbellum South, see Ayers, *Vengeance and Justice*; Oshinsky, "*Worse Than Slavery*"; and Lichtenstein, *Twice the Work of Free Labor*. For the most innovative recent work on Jim Crow–era black incarceration, which centers on black women, see LeFlouria, *Chained in Silence*; and Haley, *No Mercy Here*.

23. In recent years, historians have compiled an impressive library of work that details the close relationship between slavery and capitalism. For three of the most exhaustive treatments, see W. Johnson, *River of Dark Dreams*; Baptist, *Half Has Never Been Told*; and Beckert, *Empire of Cotton*.

24. For police departments, see Lane, *Policing the City*; Richardson, *The New York Police*; Schneider, *Detroit and the Problem of Order*; and Ethington, "Vigilantes and the Police." Also see synthetic treatments, which naturalize policing as a northern

phenomenon, such as Richardson, *Urban Police in the United States*; S. Walker, *Critical History of Police Reform*; and Monkkonen, *Police in Urban America*. For the rise of penal asylums, see D. Rothman, *Discovery of the Asylum*; Hirsch, *Rise of the Penitentiary Prisons*; Meranze, *Laboratories of Virtue*; N. Johnson, *Forms of Constraint*; and McLennan, *Crisis of Imprisonment*. Finally, for histories of the federal state, see Bensel, *Yankee Leviathan*; Formisano, "State Development in the Early Republic"; and Orren and Skowronek, *Search for American Political Development*, 87–88.

25. For the peculiarity of southern policing, the role of vigilantism in southern policing, and southern skepticism of formal law and state power, see Hindus, *Prison and Plantation*; Wyatt-Brown, *Southern Honor*; Ayers, *Vengeance and Justice*; Waldrep, *Roots of Disorder*; and Dray, *At the Hands of Persons Unknown*. For the importance of the slave patrol in southern governance, policing, and power, see the excellent Hadden, *Slave Patrols*. Other works smartly emphasize the modern nature of the South's racist criminal justice system: see Lichtenstein, *Twice the Work of Free Labor*; Rousey, *Policing the Southern City*; and Curtin, *Black Prisoners and Their World*.

26. Other scholars have questioned the presumed antagonism between state power and ordinary white violence in other milieus. For example, historian Diana Paton contests the notion that "slavery, private penal power, and flogging line up on one side of a set of contrasts whose opposites are free labor, state authority to punish, and imprisonment." See Paton, *No Bond but the Law*, 6.

27. W. Johnson, "Slavery, Reparations, and the Mythic March of Freedom," 44.

28. A tidal wave of new works in Civil War studies has begun to challenge the metanarrative of "freedom" that so frequently organizes the history of emancipation. For the seminal articulation of the freedom narrative, see E. Foner, *Reconstruction*. For a discussion of how this new work is challenging Foner's thesis and reframing our understanding of the Civil War and emancipation, see Emberton, "Unwriting the Freedom Narrative." For one of the best challenges to the freedom narrative and a look at how northern black activists fought and failed to overthrow the "bare liberal freedoms" of whites, see Kantrowitz, *More than Freedom*.

29. For the original thesis, see Hartz, *Liberal Tradition in America*. For updates, see Boorstin, *Genius of American Politics*; Appleby, *Capitalism and a New Social Order*; and Diggins, *Lost Soul of American Politics*. Also see the more critical Greenstone, *Lincoln Persuasion*. For a synthetic treatment of liberalism, republicanism, and Protestantism, see Kloppenberg, "Virtues of Liberalism." For more recent work that incorporates scholarly challenges to liberalism's hegemony, see the essays in Ericson and Green, *Liberal Tradition in American Politics*.

30. For republicanism, see Shalhope, "Toward a Republican Synthesis"; Bailyn, *Ideological Origins of the American Revolution*; Wood, *Creation of the American Republic*; Pocock, *Machiavellian Moment*; and Rodgers, "Republicanism." For the police power, see Novak, *People's Welfare*; Dubber, *The Police Power*; and Balogh, *Government Out of Sight*. And for racism — or what he calls "ascriptivism"— see especially R. Smith, *Civic Ideals*.

31. To be sure, some have, and they have done so powerfully. For a broad elaboration on the coherence between classical liberal thought and systems of power and inequality, see Losurdo, *Liberalism*. For a brilliant discussion of how liberal narratives of the American Revolution helped legitimate slavery, see Furstenberg, "Beyond Freedom and Slavery." And for how the extension of rights in the early U.S. Republic perpetuated violence against those without rights, see Edwards, *People and Their Peace*, especially 223–27. Much of my thinking about liberalism as coercion comes from Joyce, *Rule of Freedom*.

32. In various forms, the argument that the extension of rights buttressed white male supremacy originated in feminist history and theory several decades ago. Such theorists have focused especially upon the gendering of the concept "citizen." See Smith-Rosenberg, "Discovering the Subject of the 'Great Constitutional Discussion'"; Grunderson, "Independence, Citizenship and the American Revolution"; Bloch, "Gendered Meanings of Virtue in Revolutionary America"; and Fraser and Gordon, "Civil Citizenship against Social Citizenship?" Critical race theorists have focused as well upon the racial implications of the universalist language of liberalism. For two examples, see Gotanda, "Critique of 'Our Constitution Is Color-Blind'"; and P. Williams, *Alchemy of Race and Rights*. Other scholars have argued that the Framers' orientation toward property rights made inequality both a presumption of and an object of protection of the Constitution. See especially Nedelsky, *Private Property and the Limits of American Constitutionalism*. For a thorough examination of how the triumph of liberal conceptions of law provided a framework for "the realization of private power and domination," see Tomlins, *Law, Labor, and Ideology*, xv.

Chapter One

1. A few words on pardons, as well as other types of petitions. Petitions are crucial to my efforts to reconstruct policing practices in Baltimore, especially for the years before city officials introduced a professional police force. The people writing petitions used their letters to persuade. Pardon petitioners were particularly likely to present the accused or guilty inmate in highly gendered terms — either as a good child led astray by someone else, or as an adult (usually a man) who strayed while trying to support a family. As a result, many petitions were formulaic, a genre, perhaps even a type of "fiction." Recognizing, then, Hayden White's warning that the world does not "present itself to perception in the form of well-made stories," I have endeavored to deploy petitions, and pardon petitions especially, as texts that gesture at a specific person's point of view, often qualifying the words and even occasionally pointing out their bias. Perhaps most often, I employ petitions as evidence of an ideology — as discourse, in other words, that reveals plausible narratives in the broader political and legal culture. That said, I also want to acknowledge Seth Rockman's approach to many of the same sources used here. Rockman describes petitions as indispensable sources that "offer a chance to hear marginal people represent themselves in their own words." To that end, I also strive to read

petitions for details that cannot be fully contained by the purpose of the writer, whether it was to solicit protection or earn a pardon. See White, *Content of Form*, 24; and Rockman, *Scraping By*, 350. For more on the narrativity of pardon petitions, see N. Z. Davis, *Fiction in the Archives*. For an analysis of early national pardon petitions in Maryland, see Whitman, "'I Have Got the Gun and Will Do as I Please with Her.'"

2. Olson, *Baltimore*, 1.

3. For Baltimore's demographic and economic changes, see Brugger, *Maryland*, 773; Browne, *Baltimore in the Nation*, 87; and Rockman, *Scraping By*, 18.

4. For Baltimore's early economic developments, see Gould, "Economic Causes of the Rise of Baltimore"; Steffen, *Mechanics of Baltimore*, 6–9; and Rockman, *Scraping By*, 16–25.

5. Steffen, *Mechanics of Baltimore*, 4.

6. Semmes, *Baltimore*, 81.

7. For the size of Baltimore's free and enslaved black population, see Wade, *Slavery in the Cities*, 325; Steffen, *Mechanics of Baltimore*, 6; Fields, *Slavery and Freedom on the Middle Ground*, 13; and Rockman, *Scraping By*, 33–35.

8. See Whitman, *Price of Freedom*, 61–118.

9. Steffen, *Mechanics of Baltimore*, 6.

10. Ibid., 3–26. Steffen relies upon Lakin, *Baltimore Directory and Register for 1814–15*.

11. WPA No. 553, box 40, S 1, RG 16, City Council Records (1830), BCA.

12. David Roediger, in his seminal work on working-class culture and identity in the antebellum North, argues that many laboring whites, especially Irish Catholics, embraced racism and perpetrated significant racial violence in order to reaffirm their own whiteness. In other words: if the Irish were not *always* white, they became so by juxtaposing themselves with black people. Roediger labels this process of becoming "the wages of whiteness." In chapter 3, I will explore how policing presented one such way certain laborers embraced a white identity. See Roediger, *Wages of Whiteness*. For W. E. B. Du Bois's original argument that white skin color provided a "public and psychological wage," from which Roediger derives his title, see Du Bois, *Black Reconstruction in the United States*, 700.

13. The term "police" derives from the Latin term *politia*, itself a latinization of the Greek term *politeia*, and in ancient Greece *politeia* signified both the grants and privileges of citizenship as well as the administrative end of government to ensure the public's welfare. For more on the etymology of the term, see Tomlins, *Law, Labor, and Ideology*, 35–59; and Dubber, *Police Power*, 3–80.

14. During the early 1830s, the most frequent "crime" committed by residents of the Baltimore city jail was indebtedness. The next most popular crime was an inability to provide "security to keep the peace." And after that came larceny and assault. City officials charged Baltimoreans for no other crimes in anywhere near these numbers. See Document B, "Report of the Visitors and Governors of the Jail of Baltimore County," appendix to the Ordinances of the Mayor and City Council of Baltimore, passed at the Session of 1832, 9–61, DLR.

15. WPA No. 452, box 67, S 1, RG 16, City Council Records (1841), BCA.

16. See WPA No. 531, box 90, S 1, RG 16, City Council Records (1851), BCA; and "Still Another," *Baltimore Sun*, June 20, 1838, 2.

17. *Review of the Correspondence between the Archbishop and Mayor of Baltimore*, 2–3.

18. "Another Outrage," *Baltimore Sun*, August 31, 1838, 2.

19. Emphasis in original. "Street Insults to Ladies," ibid., December 28, 1840, 2.

20. Novak, "Legal Transformation of Citizenship."

21. "Law Intelligence, Kidnapping," *Niles' Weekly Register* (Baltimore), July 10, 1819, 322–23.

22. "Insults to Females," *Baltimore Sun*, May 26, 1838, 2; "Corner Loungers," ibid., August 25, 1838, 4.

23. "Yet Another," ibid., May 24, 1838, 2.

24. "Street Insults to Ladies," ibid., December 28, 1840, 2.

25. "Insulting Ladies in the Streets," ibid., January 4, 1841, 2.

26. "A Ruffian Knocked Down and Punished," ibid., February 13, 1857, 1.

27. "James R. Jackson," ibid., January 14, 1839, 1.

28. "Deserved Chastisement," ibid., July 20, 1838, 2.

29. A. Robinson to James McHenry, January 5, 1813, folder Robinson A. to James McHenry, 1812–1813, War of 1812 Collection, MHS.

30. Case of John Mallory, folder 50, S1061-25 (1825), Pardon Papers (Governor and Council), MSA.

31. "Mail Robbers," *Niles' Weekly Register*, December 2, 1820, 209.

32. "Mail Robbers," ibid., February 13, 1819, 464.

33. Ward, *American Trenck*, 63.

34. "Mail Robberies," *Niles' Weekly Register*, April 1, 1820, 81.

35. Hutton, *Life and Confession of Peregrine Hutton*, 11.

36. For a good discussion of the two men's public personas during the days before their execution, see Rockman, "Saving Morris Hull."

37. WPA No. 553, box 40, S 1, RG 16, City Council Records (1830), BCA.

38. Hill, *Sermon on the Subject of Temperance*, 9.

39. For a general description of the police work done by constables and watchmen, see Friedman, *Crime and Punishment in American History*, 67–68; and Walker, *Popular Justice*, 25–28. For early Baltimore's municipal crime control apparatus, see Browne, *Baltimore in the Nation*, 47–48 and 155–58.

40. For the establishment of the 1788 criminal court, see Scharf, *Chronicles of Baltimore*, 249; for the 1794 court of oyer and terminer, see chap. 65, Session Laws 1794, Laws of Maryland, MSA; for the 1816 abolition of the court of oyer and terminer and establishment of the Baltimore City Court, see chap. 193, Session Laws 1816, Laws of Maryland, MSA. For a more general history of the Baltimore court system, see Byrnes, *Histories of the Bench and Bar of Baltimore City*, 1–52.

41. For Lightner, see A Gentleman of the Bar, *Trial of William Stewart*, 8–9; for Wiley, see ibid., 9–10; for Chariton, see ibid., 10; and for Hooper, see ibid., 12.

42. For Drake, see ibid., 23; for Thomas Stewart, see ibid., 47–48.

43. For a thorough description of private prosecutions, see Steinberg, *Transformation of Criminal Justice*, 37–115.

44. Ibid., 54.

45. Case of James Johnston, folder 51, S1061-36 (1834), Pardon Papers (Governor and Council), MSA.

46. See case of Catherine Stewart, folder 59, ibid.

47. Case of Richard Collier, folder 19, ibid.

48. Case of John Hughes, folder 18, S1031-11 (1852), Pardon Papers (Secretary of State), MSA.

49. Case of Henry Smith, folder 36, S1031-13 (1854), ibid.

50. Case of Francis Metz, folder 6, ibid.

51. Case of James Karr, folder 27, S1031-14 (1855), ibid.

52. For a sample of the early municipality's voracious appetite for lawmaking, see Ordinances of the Corporation of the City of Baltimore, 1813–1827, BCA. Historian William Novak argues that on the local level, the early Republic's legal-political tradition was as characterized by "the full, coercive, and regulatory powers of law and government" as it was by "rights to property, contract, mobility, privacy, and bodily integrity." See Novak, *People's Welfare*, 16–17.

53. For a good general synopsis of the precarious balance between liberty and power, see Watson, *Liberty and Power*, especially 42–72.

54. For London police, see Critchley, *History of Police in England and Wales*, chap. 2; for a good comparison of the British and American systems, as well as an assessment of how the latter drew on yet also departed from the former, see Miller, *Cops and Bobbies*.

55. Quoted from Friedman, *Crime and Punishment in American History*, 69.

56. "Resistance to Officers," *Baltimore Sun*, May 12, 1841, 2.

57. See "Constables," ibid., December 16, 1837, 2.

58. Emphasis in original. See WPA No. 995, box 56, S 1, RG 16, City Council Records (1837), BCA.

59. "Written Opinion of the Court in the Case of Captain Mullen and James Dukes," *Baltimore Sun*, April 9, 1838, 1.

60. "Charge of Assault and False Imprisonment," ibid., December 30, 1840, 2.

61. WPA No. 390, box 10, S 2, RG 9, Mayor's Office (1833), BCA.

62. WPA No. 391, ibid.

63. WPA No. 1091, box 8, ibid. (1832). Even the deputy high constable came under suspicion for assaulting a woman. For that example, see his two letters of defense: WPA No. 444, box 67, S 1, RG 16, City Council Records (1841), BCA.

64. 1838 Petition of Rufus Eachus, to the Honorable N. Brice, Chief Justice of Baltimore City Court, William Preston Papers, MHS.

65. For 1833 expenses, see WPA No. 396, box 10, S 2, RG 9, Mayor's Office (1833), BCA; for the Western Watch House, see WPA No. 755a, box 46, S 1, RG 16, City Council Records (1833), BCA.

66. WPA No. 755a, box 46, S 1, RG 16, City Council Records (1833), BCA.

67. For the 1850 petition as well as the committee's minority dissent, see WPA No. 873, box 87, ibid. (1850).

68. WPA No. 1083, box 8, S 2, RG 9, Mayor's Office (1832), BCA.

69. Not all of these other "jobs" were legal, either. As Seth Rockman notes, many impoverished Baltimoreans entered underground economies to provide for their families. For his treatment of watchmen's wages and desperation, see Rockman, *Scraping By*, 188, 253–54.

70. WPA No. 617, box 35, S 1, RG 16, City Council Records (1828), BCA.

71. WPA No. 534, box 65, S 2, ibid. (1840).

72. WPA No. 699, box 50, S 1, ibid. (1835).

73. WPA No. 349, box 65, ibid. (1840).

74. WPA No. 408, box 76, ibid. (1846).

75. For watchmen's scant compensation while wounded, see WPA No. 1107, box 37, ibid. (1828); and the aforementioned 1840 appeal, WPA No. 349, box 65, ibid. (1840); for Watchman Cowman, see WPA No. 815, box 101, ibid. (1854); for Stone, see WPA No. 1077, box 102, ibid. (1854); for Watchman Miller, see WPA No. 658, box 106, ibid. (1856); for Watchman Hugarth, see WPA No. 724, box 106, ibid. (1856); and for an additional pay raise petition, see WPA No. 549, box 79, ibid. (1847).

76. WPA No. 427, box 7, S 2, RG 9, Mayor's Office (1831), BCA.

77. WPA No. 574, box 58, S 1, RG 16, City Council Records (1838), BCA.

78. WPA No. 725, box 61, ibid. (1839).

79. For Mayor Leakin's support of the new police bill, see WPA No. 856, box 62, ibid. (1839); for the council's rejection of that bill, see WPA No. 1090–91, ibid. (1839).

80. See WPA No. 593, box 73, ibid. (1844).

81. See WPA No. 446, box 74a, ibid. (1845).

82. See the 1854 report issued by the Joint Committee on Police, WPA No. 764, box 101, ibid. (1854).

83. For criticism of the watch hours, or rather the lack thereof, see WPA No. 531, box 3, S 2, RG 9, Mayor's Office (1823), BCA; and "Arrest of Bad Boys," *Baltimore Sun*, February 28, 1850, 2.

84. WPA No. 781, box 51, S 1, RG 16, City Council Records (1835), BCA.

85. "*State v. Harvey Hevener*" and "*Thomas Stubbins*," *Baltimore Sun*, October 17, 1844, 1.

86. "*State v. Thomas Mortimer*," ibid., October 19, 1844, 4.

87. "*State v. Samuel Jones*," ibid., November 27, 1844, 1. For other cases, see "Disorderly," ibid., December 19, 1849, 1; "Assault on a Watchman," ibid., January 26, 1850, 1; and "Charge of Rescuing a Prisoner," ibid., April 19, 1850, 2; and for a watchman beaten by "a mob," see "A Street Fight," ibid., August 15, 1840, 2.

88. "Powers of Arrest," ibid., November 6, 1838, 1.

89. "An Outrageous Fellow," ibid., November 11, 1840, 2.

90. "Burglary—the Robbers Caught," ibid., March 12, 1844, 2.

91. "Arrest," ibid., June 14, 1841, 2.

92. WPA No. 334, box 13, S 2, RG 9, Mayor's Office (1835), BCA.

93. WPA No. 458, box 68, S 1, RG 16, City Council Records (1842), BCA.

94. Ordinances of the Corporation of the City of Baltimore, 1823–1827, No. 11, 1817, BCA.

95. Ibid., No. 20, 1820.

96. For the creation of the bailiff system, see ibid., No. 46, 1826; and for the anti-gambling ordinance, see ibid., No. 48, 1826.

97. WPA No. 1024, box 5, S 2, RG 9, Mayor's Office (1827), BCA.

98. WPA No. 567, box 40, S 1, RG 16, City Council Records (1830), BCA.

99. WPA No. 1096, box 56, ibid. (1837); also see WPA No. 821, box 83, ibid. (1848), for another, similar example.

100. "Still Another," *Baltimore Sun*, June 20, 1838, 2.

101. WPA No. 630R, box 60, S 2, RG 16, City Council Records (1839), BCA.

102. WPA No. 311, box 24, S 2, RG 9, Mayor's Office (1844), BCA.

103. WPA No. 722, box 75, S 1, RG 16, City Council Records (1845), BCA.

104. See, for instance, "Robbery of Mr. Morrison," *Baltimore Sun*, February 1, 1850, 2.

105. Richardson, *Urban Police in the United States*, 4–5, 22.

106. WPA No. 505, box 79, S 1, RG 16, City Council Records (1847), BCA.

107. For Zell's petition, see WPA No. 655, box 82, ibid. (1848); for the granting of his payment, see WPA No. 821, box 83, ibid.

108. For more on herrenvolk democracy in the United States, see Frederickson, *Black Image in the White Mind*, 90–94. For a revision of Frederickson's thesis, see Roediger, *Wages of Whiteness*, 59–60.

109. Semmes, *Baltimore*, 40–42.

110. Gilje, "Baltimore Riot of 1812." Other good accounts of the riot include Royster, *Light-Horse Harry Lee*, 156–68; Hickey, *War of 1812*, 52–72; and Wilentz, *Rise of American Democracy*, 141–78.

111. Deposition of Peter White in Gwynn and Stone, *Report of the Committee of Grievances*, 66. For a similar account, see deposition of Nixon Wilson in ibid., 150.

112. For a similar summary of municipal acquiescence to the mob, see Royster, *Light-Horse Harry Lee*, 163.

113. "Narrative of John Hall," *Interesting Papers Relative to the Recent Riots at Baltimore*, 58.

114. Quoted in Pierson, *Tocqueville and Beaumont in America*, 505.

115. Emphasis in original. Quoted in ibid., 507.

116. Tocqueville, *Democracy in America*, 95–96.

117. Ibid., 252.

118. August 17, 1835, entry, "James Gordon's Diary," cited in Grimsted, "Democratic Rioting," 172.

119. Deposition of William Read, Joint Committee on the Baltimore Riots, *Report of and Testimony Taken*, 7. See also deposition of James Blair, ibid., 49.

120. William Bartlett to Edward Stabler, August 8, 1835, MHS.

121. For "simultaneous action," see deposition of James Blair, Joint Committee on the Baltimore Riots, *Report of and Testimony Taken*, 53; for "unanimous turn out," see deposition of Henry Sanderson, ibid., 72; for "quelled by citizens," see deposition of Joshua Vansant, ibid., 69; and for "No body knew where the mob was," see "Junius," *Baltimore Republican*, March 5, 1836. Historian Robert Shalhope makes good use of the staunchly antibank "Junius" in his *Baltimore Bank Riot*.

122. J. Morris, *Memorial to the Legislature of Maryland*, 11–12.

123. Deposition of Jacob Deems, Joint Committee on the Baltimore Riots, *Report of and Testimony Taken*, 70.

124. Deposition of Anthony Miltenberger, ibid., 57.

125. Deposition of Henry Sanderson, ibid., 72.

126. Deposition of James Mullen, ibid., 78.

127. Deposition of James Hayman, ibid., 65.

Chapter Two

1. Patrick Joyce makes this point (although about cartography) in nineteenth-century Britain: "If not blind, the state — itself a problematic concept — felt its way into the future, and . . . seeing like a state, to adopt James Scott's term, was a haphazard affair. Rather than being the source of the knowledge it operated through, it might be nearer the mark to say that the state was in important measure the outcome of this knowledge." See Joyce, *Rule of Freedom*, 23; and Scott, *Seeing Like a State*.

2. See especially Larson, "'Bind the Republic Together'"; and Quintana, "Planners, Planters, and Slaves."

3. The "individual" was (and remains) a political construct, and scholars have used a range of terms to describe it. In using the term here, I refer specifically to the idea of the free, self-owning, sovereign subject who during the seventy-five years after American independence claimed a place of great importance in American political and legal thought. For a recent definition, see Welke's definition of "personhood" in *Law and the Borders of Belonging*, 3. For a review of the philosophical underpinnings of the liberal individual, also see MacPherson, *Political Theory of Possessive Individualism*.

4. For Baltimore's demographic and economic changes, see Brugger, *Maryland*, 773; and Browne, *Baltimore in the Nation*, 87. On the fears and anxieties born out of population growth, see D. Rothman, *Discovery of the Asylum*, chap. 3; Halttunen, *Confidence Men and Painted Women*, 1–55; and Lofland, *World of Strangers*, chap. 3.

5. Young, *Lecture on the Increase of Crime*, 6–8.

6. For general accounts of the larger economic changes that transformed social life in the early U.S. Republic, see Sellers, *Market Revolution*; and Howe, *What Hath God Wrought*. For general accounts of the democratization that transformed the political culture of the early U.S. Republic, see Watson, *Liberty and Power*; and Wilentz, *Rise of American Democracy*.

7. WPA No. 435, box 17, S 2, RG 9, Mayor's Office (1837), BCA.

8. WPA No. 397, box 10, ibid. (1833).

9. WPA No. 428, box 17, ibid. (1837).

10. For south Baltimore and "valuable property," see WPA No. 572, box 58, S 1, RG 16, City Council Records (1838), BCA; for west Baltimore and "additional watchman," see WPA No. 725, box 61, ibid. (1839); for west Baltimore and "such other relief," see WPA No. 574, box 58, ibid. (1838); and for east Baltimore, see WPA No. 856, box 62, ibid. (1839).

11. WPA No. 421, box 7, S 2, RG 9, Mayor's Office (1831), BCA.

12. WPA No. 258, box 29, ibid. (1857).

13. WPA No. 398, box 68, S 1, RG 16, City Council Records (1842), BCA.

14. WPA No. 397, ibid.

15. WPA No. 252, box 26, S 2, RG 9, Mayor's Office (1846), BCA.

16. WPA No. 544, box 36, S 1, RG 16, City Council Records (1829), BCA.

17. WPA No. 386, box 10, S 2, RG 9, Mayor's Office (1833), BCA.

18. Case of Bartholomew Manning, folder 2, S1061-25 (1825), Pardon Papers (Governor and Council), MSA.

19. WPA No. 410, box 6, S 2, RG 9, Mayor's Office (1831), BCA.

20. WPA No. 178, box 16, ibid. (1836).

21. WPA No. 437, box 17, ibid. (1837).

22. WPA No. 1291, box 19, ibid. (1838).

23. Case of Thomas Williams, folder 48, S1061-25 (1825), Pardon Papers (Governor and Council), MSA.

24. For the legislature's reasoning, see Joint Committee on the Baltimore Riots, *Report of and Testimony Taken*, 4–5. For more on the bill, see Davies, "Maryland Indemnity Bill of 1836," MHS.

25. WPA No. 602, box 83, S 1, RG 16, City Council Records (1849), BCA.

26. R. Johnson, *The Memorial of Reverdy Johnson*, 6.

27. Ibid., 11–12.

28. Ibid., 15–16.

29. Ibid., 17.

30. "Another Disgraceful Riot," *Baltimore Sun*, November 4, 1840, 2.

31. WPA No. 642, box 82, S 1, RG 16, City Council Records (1848), BCA.

32. WPA No. 861, box 88, ibid. (1850).

33. WPA No. 778, ibid.

34. "Another!," *Baltimore Sun*, January 18, 1838, 2.

35. For a thorough treatment of the economic changes that confronted skilled labor and the political fallout from their economic alienation, see the excellent Towers, *Urban South and the Coming of the Civil War*, 37–108. Towers makes the point that the sectional crisis over slavery, while not unimportant in the urban South's political history, was not the only factor in the dissolution of the Second Party System there.

36. Ibid., 92. Also see Browne, *Baltimore in the Nation*, 210.

37. See Monkkonen, *Police in Urban America*, 49–58. Monkkonen relies upon Rogers, *Diffusion of Innovations*, 21–56.

38. WPA No. 778, box 88, S 1, RG 16, City Council Records (1850), BCA.

39. Hewitt, *Shadows on the Wall*.

40. See Joyce, *Rule of Freedom*, 85–88.

41. "Law and Order Synonymous with National Greatness," *Baltimore Sun*, November 20, 1858, 2.

42. See Ordinance No. 4 (Establish a Police), passed at Special Session, 1856, the Ordinances of the Mayor and City Council of Baltimore, passed at the Session of 1857, DLR (hereafter "1856 Police Bill"). For numbers, see 1856 Police Bill, sections 14–15.

43. For a synopsis of these changes, see "The New Police System," *Baltimore Sun*,

April 14, 1857, 1; for the laws themselves, see 1856 Police Bill, especially sections 1, 2, 4, 5, 6, 7, 8, and 15.

44. For one example, see that of George Sutton: "Riotous Proceedings, " *Baltimore Sun*, May 29, 1857, 1; also see "Strict Discipline," ibid., July 2, 1857, 1; and "The New Police Arrangement," ibid., November 23, 1857, 1.

45. See David R. Johnson's discussion of new police uniforms in *Policing the Urban Underworld*, 96–97. For a description of the uniform, see "The New Police Uniform," *Baltimore Sun*, February 6, 1857, 1.

46. For the new salary structure, including that which denied a policeman the ability to collect money as an informer, see 1856 Police Bill, section 16; and for the city council's repudiation of officers' claims to rewards, see "Not Entitled to Rewards," *Baltimore Sun*, February 20, 1858, 1.

47. Gerard, *London and New York*, 1.

48. WPA No. 47, box 30, S 2, RG 9, Mayor's Office (1861), BCA.

49. WPA No. 43, ibid.

50. WPA No. 55, ibid.

51. "The Philadelphia Riots," *Baltimore Sun*, July 11, 1844, 2. For a good summary of the antidemocratic sentiment behind police reform, see K. Smith, *Dominion of Voice*, 79–82. Also see L. Keller, *Triumph of Order*. For a more classic Marxist interpretation of this thesis, see Montgomery, *Citizen Worker*, 52–114.

52. For a great example of two watchmen calling the other a criminal, see the case of Joseph Pierson, folder 8, S1031-11 (1852), Pardon Papers (Secretary of State), MSA.

53. WPA No. 764, box 101, S 1, RG 16, City Council Records (1854), BCA.

54. 1856 Police Bill, section 14.

55. Case of Harriett Woods, folder 66, S1061-26 (1826), Pardon Papers (Governor and Council), MSA.

56. "Police Operations," *Baltimore Sun*, June 23, 1858, 1.

57. Report, Baltimore City Board of Police, House and Senate Documents 1861D, Government Publications and Reports, MSA.

58. "The Majesty of the Law!," *Baltimore Sun*, April 9, 1858, 2.

59. See Browne, *Baltimore in the Nation*, 202–3.

60. See 1859 Report of the Board of Visitors of the Baltimore City Jail, appendices to the Ordinances of the Mayor and City Council of Baltimore, DLR.

61. Table B, 1861 Report of the Board of Visitors of the Baltimore City Jail, ibid.

62. For comparison, the city's population in 1860 (212,418) was just 25 percent higher than what it was in 1850 (169,054). See table 1, Phillips, *Freedom's Port*, 15. Also see Fields, *Slavery and Freedom on the Middle Ground*, 70.

63. WPA No. 736, box 101, S 1, RG 16, City Council Records (1854), BCA.

64. Beccaria, *On Crimes and Punishments*.

65. I lean heavily here upon Rice, "'This Province, So Meanly and Thinly Inhabited,'" 22–23. Also see Hay, "Property, Authority, and the Criminal Law"; and Innes and Styles, "Crime Wave."

66. Emphasis in original. "Executive Clemency Again," *Baltimore Sun*, July 30, 1852, 2.

67. For a thorough discussion of Rush's thinking, see Frank, *Constituent Moments*, 101–27. Also see Sullivan, "Birth of the Prison"; and Meranze, *Laboratories of Virtue*, 120–26.

68. For early failures, see D. Rothman, *Discovery of the Asylum*, 90–93; for the competition between the Auburn and Philadelphia prison models, see Meranze, *Laboratories of Virtue*, 254–56.

69. Beaumont and Tocqueville, *On the Penitentiary System*, 58. In this claim, I am following in the footsteps of Michael Meranze, whose excellent study of early Republic penal reform in Philadelphia argues that discipline was not contrary to liberalism but central to it. Meranze juxtaposes his argument with David Rothman's earlier claim that penal reformers were nostalgic in their attempts to cope with rapid industrial change and modern social disorder. In fact, Meranze claims, discipline was analogous to liberal capitalism. Capitalism liberated workers from paternalistic social relations — from "extra-economic ties and practices"— only to subject them to the coercions of the market, while penal discipline liberated prisoners' bodies from the violence of authority only to expand that authority's ability to oversee and regulate them. See Meranze, *Laboratories of Virtue*, 13–14; and D. Rothman, *Discovery of the Asylum*, 69–71, 108.

70. Board of Inspectors, *Acts of Assembly*, 5–43.

71. Letter from H. Niles, Maryland Penitentiary, House and Senate Documents 1830, Government Publications and Reports, MSA.

72. Board of Inspectors, *Acts of Assembly*, 43.

73. Case of Charles the Slave, S1107-5 (1828), Pardon Record, MSA.

74. 1854 Annual Report of the Maryland Penitentiary, Government Publications and Reports, MSA. In her study of punishment in nineteenth-century Jamaica, historian Diana Paton notes that many scholars have simply adopted the abolitionists' juxtaposition of slavery and incarceration, obscuring some of their connections. As the Maryland example shows, she is quite correct. Slaves did enter the penitentiary. But the directors' desire to cleanse the institution of enslaved people was also quite telling: it betrayed their desire to make the prison a detention center for the exclusively free. See Paton, *No Bond but the Law*, 6.

75. See Pitt, *Report of the Committee Appointed to Inspect the Situation of the Maryland Penitentiary*, 17 and 14, respectively. Also see Maryland General Assembly, *Depositions Taken at the Penitentiary*.

76. Case of John Sanders, folder 21, S1061-24 (1824), Pardon Papers (Governor and Council), MSA.

77. Letter from H. Niles, Maryland Penitentiary, House and Senate Documents 1830, Government Publications and Reports, MSA.

78. Maryland Penitentiary, *Report of the Committee Appointed . . . to Visit the Penitentiaries and Prisons*, 23–26.

79. Emphasis in original. For "the juvenile," see Maryland Governor, *Document No. 11*, 8; for "original disadvantages," see Maryland Penitentiary, *Report of the Committee Appointed . . . to Visit the Penitentiaries and Prisons*, 23–26.

80. Joint Committee on the Penitentiary, *Testimony Taken before the Joint Committee of the Legislature of Maryland on the Penitentiary*, 10.

81. Maryland Penitentiary, *Report of the Committee Appointed . . . to Visit the Penitentiaries and Prisons*, 15–26.

82. Baxley, White, and Proud, *Report of the Committee of Directors.*

83. For a short summary of the construction, as well as for "complete occupation throughout," see Joint Committee on the Penitentiary, *Testimony Taken before the Joint Committee of the Legislature of Maryland on the Penitentiary*, 12; for the architectural layouts and all other quotes, see Baxley, White, and Proud, *Report of the Committee of Directors.* This architectural model, which was embraced by most American penal reformers in this period, adapted the institutional design of Jeremy Bentham's panopticon. For the seminal discussion of how the panopticon prison represented a new way of thinking about society, see Foucault, *Discipline and Punish.*

84. 1851 Annual Report of the Maryland Penitentiary, Government Publications and Reports, MSA.

85. For "paupers" and a description of the inmates at the almshouse, see the 1827 Report of the Trustees of the Almshouse for Baltimore City and County, EPFL; for the reasoning behind an insane asylum to alleviate the problems at the almshouse, see Collins, *Report on Pauper Insanity*; and for the reasoning behind the refuge, see House of Refuge, *Report and Proceedings on the Subject of a House of Refuge.*

86. WPA No. 632, box 53, S 1, RG 16, City Council Records (1836), BCA.

87. Seth Rockman makes the point that the public welfare regime was "an indivisible fabric" that combined social discipline with elite benevolence and pauper agency. See Rockman, *Scraping By*, chap. 7.

88. See the Report of the Joint Committee on the Alms House: WPA No. 557, box 71, S 1, RG 16, City Council Records (1843), BCA.

89. According to a committee of Philadelphia relief officials, "The Shower bath is a small apartment or case, to the back of which slats are nailed in such a manner as to form nearly a semicircle, and a corresponding semicircular frame is attached to the inside door; so, as when shut, to completely inclose the sufferer, and keep him in a perpendicular position. Above, a barrel is fixed, with small holes in the bottom of it, and is so managed, that either the whole quantity of water may descend at once, or drip very slowly. This last is considered the most effectual mode of punishing, and is quite severe." Quote from Rockman, *Scraping By*, 227–28.

90. WPA No. 737, box 73, S 1, RG 16, City Council Records (1844), BCA.

91. House of Refuge, *Report and Proceedings on the Subject of a House of Refuge*, 4.

92. Raymond, *Elements of Political Economy*, 421.

93. "Juvenile Offenders," *Baltimore Sun*, January 30, 1841, 2.

94. WPA No. 736, box 101, S 1, RG 16, City Council Records (1854), BCA.

95. Examples of this type of logic and language are almost too numerous to note. By the late 1830s, almost all Joint Committee reports on the city jail and annual reports from the state penitentiary argued for a House of Refuge by citing the inability of penal officials to segregate the young. For one great example, see the 1844 Joint Committee Report on the Jail, WPA No. 669, box 73, S 1, RG 16, City Council Records (1844), BCA. Also see a related report from a specially appointed Joint Committee

that, in response, looked into the expediency of enlarging the jail's structures: WPA No. 689, box 75, ibid. (1845).

96. "Juvenile Delinquents," *Baltimore Sun*, August 30, 1838, 2.

97. "Asylum for Juvenile Delinquents," ibid., November 10, 1837, 2.

98. WPA No. 1031, box 42, S 1, RG 16, City Council Records (1831), BCA; also see WPA No. 977, box 56, ibid. (1837).

99. Emphasis in original. For "remedial," see House of Refuge, *Report and Proceedings on the Subject of a House of Refuge*, 4; for "moral good," see Second Annual Report of the Managers of the House of Refuge, 6–8, EPFL.

100. For "germ of crime," see Mayer, *Laying of the Corner Stone of the Baltimore House of Refuge*, 9–10. For "all such children," see House of Refuge, *Act of Incorporation and By-Laws*, 6–7.

101. For "parental sway," see Mayer, *Laying of the Corner Stone of the Baltimore House of Refuge*, 13; and for "repulsive appearance," see First Annual Report of the Managers of the House of Refuge, 4–5, EPFL.

102. First Annual Report of the Managers of the House of Refuge, 4–5, EPFL.

103. Sixth Annual Report of the Managers of the House of Refuge, 12–14, ibid.

104. Mayer, *Laying of the Corner Stone of the Baltimore House of Refuge*, 10.

105. "Lawlessness," *Baltimore Sun*, February 18, 1858, 2.

106. Beaumont and Tocqueville, *On the Penitentiary System*, 79.

107. One historian calls the introduction of police forces "a landmark in the long, slow retreat of lay justice." See Friedman, *Crime and Punishment in American History*, 67.

108. Dubber, "Criminal Police and Criminal Law in the Rechtsstaat," 95–98.

109. Malka, "'The Open Violence of Desperate Men.'"

110. For "ill treatment," see WPA No. 339, box 29, S 2, RG 9, Mayor's Office (1857), BCA; for "the police beat me," see WPA No. 282, ibid. For a broader discussion of this partisan warfare, see Towers, *Urban South and the Coming of the Civil War*, 119–22; and Melton, *Hanging Henry Gambrill*.

111. "Outrages at the Polls," *Baltimore Sun*, November 3, 1859, 1.

112. Ibid.

113. WPA No. 354, box 109, S 1, RG 16, City Council Records (1858), BCA.

114. WPA No. 529, box 120, ibid. (1861).

115. Quoted in Towers, *Urban South and the Coming of the Civil War*, 121.

116. WPA No. 634, box 120, S 1, RG 16, City Council Records (1861), BCA. For a broader discussion of the local context, see Towers, *Urban South and the Coming of the Civil War*, 149–82 and 156–59 especially. The city's Know-Nothing administration, in particular Mayor Thomas Swann, refused to recognize the new police force as legitimate. See Report, Baltimore City Board of Police, House and Senate Documents 1861, Government Publications and Reports, MSA.

117. "The Troops Reach the Camden Railroad Station," *Baltimore Sun*, April 20, 1861, 1. For more thorough discussions of the riot, see C. Clark, "Baltimore and the Attack on the Sixth Massachusetts Regiment"; Towers, "'Vociferous Army of Howling Wolves'"; and Ezratty, *Baltimore in the Civil War*.

118. See Baltimore Police Commissioners, *Report of the Police Commissioners of Baltimore City*, 32–33; also see "Intense Excitement in Baltimore," *Baltimore Sun*, April 22, 1861, 1.

119. See Brown, *Baltimore and the Nineteenth of April, 1861*, 63.

120. Towers, *Urban South and the Coming of the Civil War*, 130.

121. *Baltimore Clipper*, April 17, 1857. Also quoted in Towers, *Urban South and the Coming of the Civil War*, 131.

122. "Meeting in Monument Square," *Baltimore Sun*, April 20, 1861, 1.

123. Towers, *Urban South and the Coming of the Civil War*, 127–28.

Chapter Three

1. For two excellent discussions of the violence that plagued Baltimore's antebellum streets, see A. Greenberg, *Cause for Alarm*, 84–94; and Towers, *Urban South and the Coming of the Civil War*, 149–82. Towers also treats the race riots that erupted on Baltimore's late-1850s docks specifically in an article from the *Journal of Southern History*. That insightful piece suggests that the race riots in Baltimore contradict the two traditional explanations for white-on-black "job busting": that white rioters used the secession crisis to further their economic agendas and that immigrant rioters attacked black workingmen to stake a claim on their whiteness. In the case of Baltimore, Towers shows, the rowdies were often native-born and unionist, and the riots they provoked represented an example of their power within the city's municipal government, which was a developing political machine. My argument in this chapter does not seek to undermine this important point. My goal, instead, is to investigate the ways that liberal and racial ideology together contributed to white workingmen's power over black workingmen as well. See Towers, "Job Busting at Baltimore's Shipyards."

2. "Highhanded Proceedings," *Baltimore Sun*, June 28, 1859, 1.

3. "Miscellaneous," ibid., February 18, 1860, 4.

4. "Highhanded Proceedings," ibid., June 28, 1859, 1.

5. *Niles' Weekly Register* (Baltimore), June 13, 1835.

6. See, respectively, "Laborers' Wages," *Hartford Times*, March 14, 1840, 2; and "Treatise on Money," *New Bedford (Mass.) Mercury*, February 20, 1857, 2.

7. "The Labor Question," *Morning Oregonian* (Portland), January 18, 1869, 2.

8. Seth Rockman makes this same point in his *Scraping By*, 241–46. Also see Glickstein, *Concepts of Free Labor*; and Stanley, *From Bondage to Contract*.

9. "Laborers' Wages," *Hartford Times*, March 14, 1840, 2.

10. For a broader discussion of republican political economy, see McCoy, *Elusive Republic*.

11. For more on the rise of industrial wage work in Baltimore, see Muller and Groves, "Emergence of Industrial Districts"; and Towers, "African-American Baltimore in the Era of Frederick Douglass."

12. Quote from Montgomery, *Citizen Worker*, 14. For the original, see Tuckerman, *Essay on the Wages Paid to Females for Their Labour*, 8.

13. For more on the disappearance of "bound" wage labor in the United States and the legal history of free labor, see Salinger, *"To Serve Well and Faithfully"*; Steinfeld, *Invention of Free Labor* and *Coercion, Contract, and Free Labor in the Nineteenth Century*; Montgomery, *Citizen Worker*, 13–51; Kahana, "Master and Servant in the Early Republic"; and Schmidt, *Free to Work*. Other scholars have argued that while the political rhetoric of the nineteenth century castigated bound wage labor as a relic of the Old World, American courts did not. Instead, they infused the law with a form of "belated feudalism." See Orren, *Belated Feudalism*; and Tomlins, *Law, Labor, and Ideology*, 223–93. Quotes appear in Montgomery, *Citizen Worker*, 25 (Hewitt) and 36 (federal judge).

14. A. Smith, *Inquiry into the Nature and Causes of the Wealth of Nations*, 41.

15. Mill, *Principles of Political Economy*, 243.

16. Both Smith and Mill are also quoted in Stanley, *From Bondage to Contract*, 145.

17. My analysis here owes much to Jeanne Boydston's history of the political economy and pastoralization of housework. See Boydston, *Home and Work*. Both examples are on 151.

18. "Strikes," *Baltimore Sun*, October 13, 1843, 2.

19. Advertisement, ibid., April 13, 1844, 4.

20. "At a Meeting of the Journeymen Caulkers," ibid., February 19, 1844, 1.

21. "To the Master Shipwrights," ibid., April 5, 1853, 2.

22. "Letter to the Editor," ibid., May 17, 1841, 3.

23. For "combined to prevent," see "Destitution and Superabundance," ibid., October 9, 1843, 2; for an "honorable sustenance," see "Workingmen's Meeting," ibid., April 9, 1861, 1.

24. "The Strike of the Workmen," ibid., February 12, 1853, 2.

25. For "America," see "The Sailors Strike," ibid., September 22, 1843, 2; for "beggars," see "Workingmen's Meeting," ibid., April 9, 1861, 1.

26. Case of Margaret McNichols, folder 20, S1031-17 (1858), Pardon Papers (Secretary of State), MSA.

27. Rockman, *Scraping By*, 135.

28. For the wages of teachers, see Townsend, *Tales of Two Cities*, 165; for the paltry wages of seamstresses, see Rockman, *Scraping By*, 142–43 and 154–57. Rockman notes that there were a few scattered voices in support of wage equality in Baltimore. For his more general treatment of the issue, see 132–57.

29. Boydston, *Home and Work*, 156–57.

30. Historians have debated the economic ideology of early Republic evangelical Protestantism for many decades. They have divided between two camps: one side interprets evangelical awakening as a middle-class phenomenon that helped mitigate worker militancy, while the other side sees many direct connections between evangelical ideals and workers' 1830s anticapitalist activism. For the former interpretation, see P. Johnson, *Shopkeeper's Millennium*. For the latter interpretation, see Sellers, *Market Revolution*, 202–36. The middle ground I chart in this paragraph (as well as in the paragraphs that follow) takes inspiration from William Sutton's analysis of evangelical artisans in Baltimore. Sutton, while highly dismissive of

Johnson's argument that the Second Great Awakening cultivated "pious docility" among workers and, thus, liberal hegemony, concedes that evangelical activism was also not "working class radicalism unleashed." In his view, labor militancy among evangelical Baltimoreans was "gradually replaced by the messages of alternative community, individual transcendence, and self-help." See Sutton, *Journeymen for Jesus*, 217–18 ("working class radicalism unleashed") and 258 ("gradually replaced").

31. Sutton, *Journeymen for Jesus*, 215–40, quote on 215–16.

32. Advertisement, *Baltimore Republican*, September 14, 1835. Also see Sutton, *Journeymen for Jesus*, 239.

33. Sutton, *Journeymen for Jesus*, 240–58.

34. A. Smith, *Inquiry into the Nature and Causes of the Wealth of Nations*, 41. Later in his inquiry, Smith makes clear this definition of slavery when he compares the "slave" to "one absolutely dependent on us for immediate subsistence." See ibid., 44.

35. Sellers most explicitly makes this argument in his *Market Revolution*. For a similar argument that focuses upon Baltimore mechanics, see Sutton, *Journeymen for Jesus*. For the demise of these ideals among Baltimore mechanics, see Towers, *Urban South and the Coming of the Civil War*, 37–71.

36. Roediger, *Wages of Whiteness*, 71–80.

37. Montgomery, *Citizen Worker*, 33–36; Steinfeld, *Invention of Free Labor*, 166–68 and 246–47. For more on the company's inability to coerce its workers to stay, as well as its violent attempts to stop them from organizing, see Way, "Shovel and Shamrock."

38. Emphasis in original. Douglass, *My Bondage and My Freedom*, 233.

39. Ibid.

40. Emphasis in original. Ibid., 237.

41. *Maryland Colonization Journal* 10, no. 9 (February 1860): 138, MHS.

42. Phillips, *Freedom's Port*, 122–23, 140.

43. See Fields, *Slavery and Freedom on the Middle Ground*, 40–62; and Phillips, *Freedom's Port*, 58–60.

44. Andrews, *Slavery and the Domestic Slave-Trade in the United States*, 51.

45. Seth Rockman argues that "the capitalists who owned most of Baltimore's productive resources were pleased to see a competitive, open, and diverse labor market." See Rockman, *Scraping By*, 43.

46. For a more thorough discussion of the various types of labor that black Baltimoreans performed, see Phillips, *Freedom's Port*, 74–77.

47. Ibid., 68 and 78.

48. *Josiah Hughes v. Samuel Jackson*. For a good discussion of how *Hughes* undercuts Roger Taney's claim in *Dred Scott* that free black people "had no rights which the white man was bound to respect," see Jones, "*Hughes v. Jackson*."

49. Jones, "Leave of Court."

50. "Order the Security of Labor," *Baltimore Sun*, November 18, 1857, 2.

51. Quoted in Stansell, *City of Women*, 35.

52. "The Poor Association — House of Industry Project," *Baltimore Sun*, March 22, 1859, 1.

53. "Vagrants," ibid., January 20, 1844, 2.

54. For quote, see *Report of the Select Committee to Whom Was Referred the Order of the House*. For the specter of the con man, see Halttunen, *Confidence Men and Painted Women*.

55. "Alms House," *Baltimore Sun*, February 1, 1841, 2.

56. WPA No. 557, box 71, S 1, RG 16, City Council Records (1843), BCA.

57. WPA No. 737, box 73, ibid. (1844).

58. WPA No. 684, box 101, ibid. (1854).

59. WPA No. 737, box 73, ibid. (1844).

60. Case of John Campbell, folder 34, S1061-26 (1826), Pardon Papers (Governor and Council), MSA.

61. All of these cases come from S1061-26 (1826), Pardon Papers (Governor and Council), MSA: case of James Curtain, folder 38; case of James B. Manner, folder 50; case of Richard McLean, folder 51; case of Frederick Kines, folder 62; case of Henry Williams, folder 69; and case of John Thompson, folder 75. The "subsistence" quote comes from McLean's folder.

62. WPA No. 737, box 73, S 1, RG 16, City Council Records (1844), BCA.

63. WPA No. 674, box 44, ibid. (1832).

64. For "paupers or such persons," see WPA No. 805, box 36, ibid. (1828); and for "Emigrants of bad character," see WPA No. 1089, box 56, ibid. (1837).

65. WPA No. 1089, box 56, ibid. (1837).

66. Emphasis in original. "Mitigation of Slavery," No. 8, *Niles' Weekly Register*, August 21, 1819, 409–10.

67. "Mitigation of Slavery," No. 5, ibid., June 26, 1819, 292–94.

68. "Mitigation of Slavery," No. 3, ibid., May 22, 1819, 211–13.

69. "Mitigation of Slavery," No. 8, ibid., August 21, 1819, 409–10.

70. "Baltimore," ibid., September 15, 1832, 39–40.

71. Raymond, *Elements of Political Economy*, 419–20.

72. Tyson, *Farewell Address of Elisha Tyson*, 8–9.

73. Quoted in Whitman, *Price of Freedom*, 155. For original, see *Genius of Universal Emancipation* (Baltimore), September 12, 1825.

74. Board of Managers for Removing the Free People of Color, *Colonization of the Free Colored Population of Maryland*, 4.

75. WPA No. 515, box 3, S 2, RG 9, Mayor's Office (1823), BCA.

76. WPA No. 831, box 4, ibid. (1824).

77. For black loafers, see "Loafers and Vagrants," *Baltimore Sun*, March 30, 1861, 1; for black gamblers, see "Descent on a Gambling House," ibid., April 10, 1861, 1.

78. Letter from "A Colored Baltimorean," *Genius of Universal Emancipation*, January 12, 1828.

79. See, for one example, "African M. E. Conference — Sixth Day," *Baltimore Sun*, May 6, 1859, 1.

80. *Maryland Colonization Journal* 10, no. 9 (February 1860): 137–45, MHS.

81. Case of James Garrison, folder 4, S1031-13 (1854), Pardon Papers (Secretary of State), MSA.

82. J. Wright, *Free Negro in Maryland*, 185. Bettye Jane Gardner argues that white

Baltimoreans' per capita holding was closer to $600. Still, she argues, "the black property holder was caught up in an economic system over which he as a black worker had no control." See Gardner, "Free Blacks in Baltimore," 165–66.

83. See L. Curry, *Free Black in Urban America*, 40–41 and 267–68; and Phillips, *Freedom's Port*, 155.

84. The best treatment of slavery's economic cost on black freedom in Maryland is Whitman, *Price of Freedom*.

85. N. Davis, *Narrative of the Life of Rev. Noah Davis*, 42.

86. Ibid., 56–57.

87. Ibid., 27.

88. Phillips, *Freedom's Port*, 107–12 (quote on 108). Also see Steffen, *Mechanics of Baltimore*.

89. Andrews, *Slavery and the Domestic Slave-Trade in the United States*, 73.

90. Carey, *Slavery in Maryland*, 39.

91. Steuart, *Letter to John L. Carey on the Subject of Slavery*, 10.

92. Latrobe, *Colonization*, 18.

93. Gardner, "Free Blacks in Baltimore," 137–44.

94. Carey, *Some Thoughts Concerning Domestic Slavery*, 21.

95. Andrews, *Slavery and the Domestic Slave-Trade in the United States*, 73.

96. Quoted in Phillips, *Freedom's Port*, 186. For original see *American and Commercial Daily Advertiser* (Baltimore), January 30, 1821.

97. These laws can all be found in Latrobe, *Justices Practice*, 6th ed., 259–79. Also see Brackett, *Negro in Maryland*, 26–174; J. Wright, *Free Negro in Maryland*, 268–70; and Phillips, *Freedom's Port*, 192–93.

98. R. Morris, "Labor Controls in Maryland in the Nineteenth Century," 392–93.

99. For the broader problem of stripping free black people of their freedom, see Berlin, *Slaves without Masters*, 316–40. For Baltimore and Maryland in particular, see Fields, *Slavery and Freedom on the Middle Ground*, 63–89; Jones, "Leave of Court," 55–60; Jones, "*Hughes v. Jackson*," 1777–79; and Diemer, *Politics of Black Citizenship*, 54–55 and 65–66.

100. "The Free Colored Population of Maryland," *Baltimore Sun*, February 14, 1844, 1.

101. Nicholas Brice to Joseph Kent, December 11, 1827, *Genius of Universal Emancipation*, March 1, 1828.

102. "Maryland State Colonization Convention," *Baltimore Sun*, June 11, 1841, 1.

103. For original quotes, see "Slaveholders Convention," *Maryland Colonization Journal* 10, no. 2 (July 1859): 24, MHS. Also quoted in Pennington, "Self-Redeeming Power of the Colored Races of the World," 319–20.

104. Rockman, *Scraping By*.

105. Frank Towers provides excellent political context for the close relationship between Baltimore's native-born white workingmen and the city's new policemen. See Towers, *Urban South and the Coming of the Civil War*, 136–38 and 155. For the Seal Strike, see "The Strike on the Baltimore and Ohio Railroad," *Baltimore Sun*, May 2, 1857, 1; "The Strike and Riot upon the Baltimore and Ohio Railroad," *Baltimore Sun*, May 4, 1857, 1; "The Strike and Riot on the Baltimore and Ohio Railroad," *Daily and*

National Intelligencer, May 6, 1857, 2; and "Baltimore and Ohio Difficulties," *Daily and National Intelligencer*, May 4, 1857, 3. For the 1859 strike, see "Trouble on the City Railway," *Baltimore Sun*, June 3, 1859, 1; "The City Railway Trouble," *Baltimore Sun*, June 4, 1859, 1; and "The City Railway Trouble," *Baltimore Sun*, June 7, 1859, 1.

106. "Workingmen's Meeting," *Baltimore Sun*, April 9, 1861, 1.

107. Advertisement, *Baltimore Republican*, September 14, 1835.

108. Olson, *Baltimore*, 98–99. For quote, see *Niles' Weekly Register*, February 1, 1834. Also see *Niles' Weekly Register*, March 14, 1835.

109. Douglass, *My Bondage and My Freedom*, 225.

110. Ibid., 227–29.

111. Ibid., 229–30.

112. Various historians of Baltimore have chronicled the violence in the workplace during the late 1850s. See Gardner, "Free Blacks in Baltimore," 152–54; Phillips, *Freedom's Port*, 201–2; and Towers, *Urban South and the Coming of the Civil War*, 139–42.

113. "Trouble among the Brickmakers," *Baltimore Sun*, May 18, 1858, 1; and "The Trouble among the Brick Makers," ibid., May 19, 1858, 1.

114. Advertisement, ibid., May 31, 1858, 2. Also see Fardy's ad in ibid., May 18, 1858, 2.

115. "Lawless Proceedings Again," ibid., June 10, 1858, 1.

116. Ibid.

117. Towers, *Urban South and the Coming of the Civil War*, 139–40.

118. "The Disturbances among the Ship-Yards," *Baltimore Sun*, June 11, 1858, 1.

119. "The War among the Caulkers," ibid., July 3, 1858, 1.

120. "The Disturbances among the Caulkers," ibid., July 5, 1858, 1.

121. Towers, *Urban South and the Coming of the Civil War*, 140.

122. Della, "The Problem of Negro Labor in the 1850s," 28.

123. Ibid.; Phillips, *Freedom's Port*, 203.

124. "The Appeal of the Colored Caulkers of Baltimore to the Merchants and Businessmen of Baltimore City and State of Maryland," *Baltimore Sun*, October 2, 1865, 2.

125. "Mitigation of Slavery," No. 8, *Niles' Weekly Register*, August 21, 1819, 409–10.

Chapter Four

1. Jacobs, *Free Negro Question in Maryland*, 20.

2. Rhetorical note: typically, "householder" has two definitions. In one sense it means, quite literally, a person who holds a legal title to the house. In another sense it connotes the head of a family or household, and it is in this vein that I use it in this chapter. The repeated use of "household head," etc., is just too clunky and confusing.

3. Blackstone, *Commentaries on the Laws of England*, 2:442.

4. Stanley, *From Bondage to Contract*, 16.

5. Blackstone, *Commentaries on the Laws of England*, 2:2.

6. Grimké, "Appeal to the Christian Women of the South."

7. See "The Address of Southern Delegates in Congress to their Constituents" in P. Foner, *Life and Writings of Frederick Douglass*, 358.

8. For "compelled to toil without wages," see "Our Paper and Its Prospects" in ibid., 280. For "husband, powerless," see "An Appeal to the British People" in ibid., 158.

9. This is an adaptation of the argument in McCurry, "Two Faces of Republicanism."

10. This larger point about the gendered definition of freedom owes primarily to Amy Dru Stanley's magisterial work on contract freedom in the age of abolition, *From Bondage to Contract.* See especially 20–59.

11. See Boydston, *Home and Work,* 43–44. For a treatment of this fantasy in the North, see Cott, *Bonds of Womanhood.* For a treatment in the South, see McCurry, *Masters of Small Worlds.* The centrality of (economic) independence to early American citizenship owed primarily to republican thought, which among other things reinvigorated traditional Euro-American patriarchalism. For a few works that discuss the importance of republican thought in the political and cultural formation of the American Republic, see Bailyn, *Ideological Origins of the American Revolution;* Wood, *Creation of the American Republic;* Pocock, "Virtue and Commerce in the Eighteenth Century"; Shalhope, "Republicanism and Early American Historiography"; and Wilentz, *Chants Democratic,* 23–103. For the ways republican thought was gendered, see Kerber, *Women of the Republic.*

12. See Boydston, *Home and Work,* 30–55.

13. Cott, *Public Vows,* 7.

14. Phillips, *Freedom's Port,* 91–93. For the family structures of Philadelphia's black community, see Hershberg, "Free Blacks in Antebellum Philadelphia." For the significance with which black Americans viewed kinship ties, see the classic Gutman, *Black Family in Slavery and Freedom.*

15. Phillips, *Freedom's Port,* 123.

16. See ibid., 154, 97–98; and Browne, *Baltimore in the Nation,* 288–89.

17. J. Wright, *Free Negro in Maryland,* 184.

18. "Bent on Destruction," *Baltimore Sun,* December 16, 1857, 1.

19. "The Outrage on William French," ibid., January 13, 1859, 1.

20. "Arrest of Federal Policemen," ibid., September 12, 1861, 1.

21. "Another Marriage in Jail," ibid., June 19, 1858, 1.

22. Board of Inspectors, *Acts of Assembly,* act 26.

23. Ibid., rule 12.

24. Ibid., rule 14.

25. Joint Committee on the Penitentiary, *Testimony Taken before the Joint Committee of the Legislature of Maryland on the Penitentiary,* 22.

26. Prison officials took great pride in their institution's financial self-dependence. See, for example, Maryland Penitentiary, *Report of the Committee on Prison Manufacturers.* Also see Crawford, *Report of William Crawford, on the Penitentiaries of the United States,* 22.

27. Girls became better represented in the refuge over time. In late 1858 boys outnumbered them by a more than 14 to 1 margin; in 1861 that ratio was down to under 8 to 1. Compare each table 2 in the Superintendent's Report, respectively, in the Eighth and Tenth Annual Reports of the Managers of the House of Refuge, EPFL.

28. Each annual report included separate reports from the boys' and girls' schools.

29. For a discussion on the construction of the female dormitory, see Eighth Annual Report of the Managers of the House of Refuge, 12, EPFL.

30. Table 7, ibid.

31. Ninth Annual Report of the Managers of the House of Refuge, 7, EPFL.

32. Ibid., 14, EPFL.

33. See letter from G. W. F., Tenth Annual Report of the Managers of the House of Refuge, 51, EPFL.

34. See, respectively, table D, Superintendent's Report, Fifth (1855) Annual Report of the Managers of the House of Refuge, EPFL; and table 2, Superintendent's Report, Sixth (1856) Annual Report of the Managers of the House of Refuge, EPFL.

35. Case of Frederick Warner, folder 45, S1031-6 (1848), Pardon Papers (Secretary of State), MSA.

36. Case of Stephen Deaver, folder 28, S1061-28 (1827), Pardon Papers (Governor and Council), MSA.

37. Case of David Holmes, folder 38, ibid.

38. Case of William Wilkinson, folder 3, S1061-31 (1829), ibid.

39. Emphasis in original. Case of Charles Torrey, folder 5, S1031-5 (1842–47), Pardon Papers (Secretary of State), MSA.

40. Emphasis in original. "Delinquencies," *Baltimore Sun*, February 15, 1838, 2.

41. For the quote, see Dubber, *Police Power*, 43. For the growing power of patriarchs under a rights regime, see Edwards, *People and Their Peace*. British political historian Patrick Joyce has also made the interesting observation that mid-nineteenth-century maps rendered cities and urban spaces more visible than ever, but with one critical exception: they did not reveal the inside of homes. "In not penetrating the home," Joyce writes, "the gaze of the map sanctioned it as a sphere of privacy, and of intimacy — it was off limits to this form of the public gaze." See Joyce, *Rule of Freedom*, 52–53.

42. Beaumont and Tocqueville, *On the Penitentiary System*, 71–72.

43. "Richard Pearce," *Baltimore Sun*, May 4, 1840, 1.

44. See table B in 1856, 1857, 1858, and 1859 Reports of the Board of Visitors of the Baltimore City Jail, appendices to the Ordinances of the Mayor and City Council of Baltimore, DLR. It is possible that abusive husbands were getting tried for assault, as the courts did occasionally arraign men for domestic abuse. See "Whipping His Wife," *Baltimore Sun*, April 9, 1850, 2; "Assaulting His Wife" and "Shameful Conduct," *Baltimore Sun*, August 2, 1852, 1; and "Whipping His Wives," *Baltimore Sun*, November 16, 1856, 1. For the liberal law's protection of domestic abuse, see Bloch, "American Revolution, Wife Beating, and the Emergent Value of Privacy." Also see Siegel, "'Rule of Love'"; and Pleck, *Domestic Tyranny*.

45. "More Outrages by Bad Boys," *Baltimore Sun*, March 16, 1850, 2.

46. "Look Out for Burglars!," ibid., August 26, 1840, 2.

47. "William Robinson," ibid., June 7, 1841, 4. Also see "A Desperate Pair of Rowdies," ibid., August 26, 1845, 2.

48. "Attempted Robbery," ibid., April 3, 1843, 2.

49. For an example of a vigilant shopkeeper, see "Juvenile Offenders," ibid., January 30, 1841, 2.

50. "Assault upon a Public House," ibid., March 4, 1857, 1.

51. Case of Richard Wheeler, folder 10, S1061-27 (1826–27), Pardon Papers (Governor and Council), MSA.

52. Yellott, *Argument of Coleman Yellott*, 3–4 and 10–11.

53. Ibid., 12–13.

54. The number of white juvenile jail commitments began to outpace the number of black juvenile jail commitments beginning in the mid-1840s, and for the rest of the antebellum period the trend persisted. In 1845, for instance, 83 of the 122 boys sent to jail were white; in 1852, 106 of the 125 boys processed were white; and in 1859, 103 out of 138 male juvenile commitments were white. See 1845, 1852, and 1859 Reports of the Board of Visitors of the Baltimore City Jail, appendices to the Ordinances of the Mayor and City Council of Baltimore, DLR.

55. Case of John Garrettson, folder 16, S1031-11 (1852), Pardon Papers (Secretary of State), MSA.

56. "A Colored Baltimorean," *Genius of Universal Emancipation*, November 27, 1829. The first part of this quote ("Why should we abandon our firesides") appears in a number of secondary works: Berlin, *Slaves without Masters*, 204; Phillips, *Freedom's Port*, 221; and E. Clark, *By the Rivers of Water*, 63. For Watkins's household information, see William Watkins, Biographical Series, MSA.

57. Case of Samuel Crapins, folder 22, S1031-11 (1852), Pardon Papers (Secretary of State), MSA.

58. Labor historians have meticulously shown that the households at the center of working-class and lower-class cultures rarely reproduced the domestic arrangements that constituted bourgeois ideals. See especially Seth Rockman's discussion of the instability of working-class households in early Republican Baltimore in *Scraping By*, 160–73. Also see Stansell, *City of Women*, 41–62; and Bradbury, *Working Families*. For a good discussion of poverty's influence over family formation in Europe during the same period, see Fuchs, *Gender and Poverty in Nineteenth-Century Europe*.

59. Stansell, *City of Women*, 49–50; Rockman, *Scraping By*, 168.

60. WPA No. 435, box 17, S 2, RG 9, Mayor's Office (1837), BCA.

61. "Bad Boys," *Baltimore Sun*, May 10, 1848, 2.

62. "Bad Boys," ibid., February 9, 1841, 2.

63. For the mud, see the aforementioned "Bad Boys," ibid., February 9, 1841, 2; for the "blasphemous oaths," see "Juvenile Profanity," ibid., January 30, 1841, 2; for stealing clothes and throwing stones, see "Bad Boys — House of Refuge Wanted," ibid., June 18, 1845, 2; and for the fire starters, see "Bonfire and False Alarm," ibid., August 30, 1850, 1.

64. "Thieving Rascals," ibid., November 1, 1838, 2.

65. For "young men," see WPA No. 477, box 7, S 2, RG 9, Mayor's Office (1831), BCA; for "Boys and Lads nearly grown up," see WPA No. 367, box 10, ibid. (1833); for "Boys from 14 to 19 years of age," see WPA No. 439, box 17, ibid. (1837); for the "large number of grown boys," see WPA No. 1251, box 19, ibid. (1838); and for "from their appearance," see "Letter to the Editors," *Baltimore Sun*, May 16, 1838, 1.

66. WPA No. 995, box 56, S 1, RG 16, City Council Records (1837), BCA.

67. WPA No. 737, box 73, ibid. (1844).

68. "A Lesson for Boys," *Baltimore Gazette*, October 9, 1834, 2.

69. "Execution," *Baltimore Sun*, November 30, 1858, 1.

70. WPA No. 728, box 59, S 1, RG 16, City Council Records (1838), BCA.

71. "Decay of Parental Discipline," *Baltimore Sun*, January 4, 1858, 2.

72. "'Boys' Meetings,'" ibid., February 2, 1858, 2.

73. Baltimore Ministry at Large, *Home Mission*, 9.

74. Baltimore City Mission of the Protestant Episcopal Church, *First Report of the Baltimore City Mission of the Protestant Episcopal Church*, 9–10.

75. Tenth Annual Report of the Managers of the House of Refuge, 8–9, EPFL.

76. Eighth Annual Report of the Managers of the House of Refuge, 7–8, EPFL.

77. House of Refuge, *Report and Proceedings on the Subject of a House of Refuge*, 13.

78. "The Education of Boys," *Baltimore Sun*, July 17, 1857, 1.

79. Baltimore Ministry at Large, *Home Mission*, 5.

80. First Annual Report of the Managers of the House of Refuge, 14–15, EPFL.

81. "Riotous Boys," *Baltimore Sun*, May 16, 1838, 2.

82. WPA No. 288, box 24, S 2, RG 9, Mayor's Office (1844), BCA.

83. Table 5, Superintendent's Report, Seventh Annual Report of the Managers of the House of Refuge, EPFL.

84. J. Wright, *Free Negro in Maryland*, 184.

85. Phillips, *Freedom's Port*, 180–81.

86. For quote, which Phillips also cites, see Buckler, *History of Epidemic Cholera*, 31.

87. "Burned Out," *Baltimore Sun*, May 25, 1849, 2.

88. See Phillips, *Freedom's Port*, 100–102; and L. Curry, *Free Black in Urban America*, 53.

89. Eighteenth- and early nineteenth-century white Americans had a tendency to see rape as a black-on-white crime. See Block, *Rape and Sexual Power in Early America*, 163–209. There is some debate over when precisely the myth of the black rapist emerged in American culture. For a sampling, see Jordan, *White over Black*, 151–54; Slotkin, "Narratives of Negro Crime in New England"; J. D. Hall, "'The Mind That Burns in Each Body'"; Bardaglio, *Reconstructing the Household*, 37–78; and Cohen, "Social Injustice, Sexual Violence, Spiritual Transcendence." For an argument that positions the rise of the black rapist myth after the Civil War — at least in the South — see Hodes, *White Women, Black Men*.

90. "Mitigation of Slavery," No. 3, *Niles' Weekly Register* (Baltimore), May 22, 1819, 211–13.

91. WPA No. 485, box 7, S 2, RG 9, Mayor's Office (1831), BCA.

92. "Beggars," *Baltimore Sun*, November 18, 1844, 2.

93. "Attempt to Poison!," ibid., May 31, 1838, 2.

94. For Ross, see WPA No. 1221, box 19, S 1, RG 9, Mayor's Office (1838), BCA; for Kobourn, see WPA No. 1223, ibid.; for Grayson, see WPA No. 1227, ibid.; for Hamer, see WPA No. 1231, ibid.; for Williams, see WPA No. 328, box 20, S 2, ibid. (1839); and for Coalman, see WPA No. 334, box 20, S 2, ibid. (1839).

95. See Latrobe, *Justices Practice*, 6th ed., 246. Also see Phillips, *Freedom's Port*, 193; and Gardner, "Free Blacks in Baltimore," 129–32.

96. "Maryland Free Colored People's Convention, July 27–28, 1852," in Foner and Walker, *Proceeding of the Black State Convention*, 2:48–49. For "they were men," see "Colored Colonization Convention," *Baltimore Sun*, July 27, 1852, 1.

97. I found Cook in the proceedings from the Baltimore City Orphans Court's 1850 December term, when Lynch transferred his guardianship to another white farmer. See Orphans Court Proceedings (Baltimore City), Register of Wills, CR 288-2, CM208, MSA.

98. For more on the practice, see Phillips, *Freedom's Port*, 158–59.

99. I came up with the figure twenty simply by counting the number of indentures in two different terms during the early 1850s. During the December term of 1850, Baltimore City's orphans court apprenticed twenty-one "orphans." During the February term of 1851, the judges apprenticed twenty-two "orphans." The court did not note race, but almost two-thirds of the children I counted were apprenticed to guardians with the same surname, suggesting they went to a family relation. See Orphans Court Proceedings (Baltimore City), Register of Wills, CR 288-2, CM208, MSA.

100. *Josiah Hughes v. Samuel Jackson.*

101. Jones, *"Hughes v. Jackson,"* 1779–82.

102. *Josiah Hughes v. Samuel Jackson.*

103. See "Another Alleged Kidnapping Case," *Baltimore Sun*, August 17, 1860, 1; "The Sanders Kidnapping Case," ibid., August 20, 1860, 1; "The Sanders Kidnapping Case Sent to the Grand Jury," ibid., August 21, 1860, 1; and "Orphans Court," ibid., August 24, 1860, 1. For the court hearings, which occurred in mid-August and early September, see Orphans Court Proceedings (Baltimore City), Register of Wills, CR 290-1, CM208, MSA.

104. "Assaults," *Baltimore Sun*, May 21, 1860, 1.

105. Case of Theodore Denny, folder 84, S1061-31 (1830), Pardon Papers (Governor and Council), MSA.

106. "State v. Thomas Harris," *Baltimore Sun*, October 30, 1844, 4.

107. Case of D. S. Sweaney, folder 20, S1031-11 (1852), Pardon Papers (Secretary of State), MSA.

108. "Severe Assault," *Baltimore Sun*, January 1, 1850, 1.

109. WPA No. 195, box 12, S 2, RG 9, Mayor's Office (1834), BCA.

110. J. Hall, "Address to the Free People of Color of the State of Maryland," 2.

111. "A Colored Baltimorean," *Genius of Universal Emancipation*, November 27, 1829.

112. See *Maryland Colonization Journal* 10, no. 9 (February 1860): 138, MHS. For more on the Maryland Colonization Society, see Stopak, "Maryland State Colonization Society." For black Baltimoreans' strenuous (and successful) efforts to counter the colonization movement, see Diemer, *Politics of Black Citizenship*.

113. WPA No. 291, box 24, S 2, RG 9, Mayor's Office (1844), BCA.

114. Case of John Garrettson, folder 16, S1031-11 (1852), Pardon Papers (Secretary of State), MSA.

115. Douglass, "Abolition Fanaticism in New York."

116. "Mob and Riot," *Baltimore Sun*, August 28, 1838, 2.

117. WPA No. 402, box 17, S 2, RG 9, Mayor's Office (1837), BCA. Also see "Reward for Rioters," *Baltimore Sun*, September 1, 1838, 2.

118. "Mob and Riot," *Baltimore Sun*, August 28, 1838, 2. Also see "The Riot at the African Church," ibid., August 30, 1838, 2.

119. There was, in fact, another large riot during this same period where groups

of Protestants laid siege to the Carmelite Convent on Asquith Street. The flight of a nun precipitated the event. For documents pertaining to the case, see Breckinridge, *Tracts to Vindicate Religion and Liberty*; and *Review of the Correspondence between the Archbishop and Mayor of Baltimore*. For a discussion that places the Carmelite Convent riot in a larger nativist context, see Mannard, "The 1839 Baltimore Nunnery Riot."

Chapter Five

1. For more on the intimate association of blackness with criminality during the age of slavery, see DeLombard, *In the Shadows of the Gallows*. Also see Melish, *Disowning Slavery*; and Manion, *Liberty's Prisoners*, 120–52. For the ways that the association took new shape during the late nineteenth and early twentieth centuries, see Muhammad, *The Condemnation of Blackness*.

2. Historians have long argued over the origins of racism, from where it happened to why it happened to when it happened. Some three-quarters of a century ago, Eric Williams wrote that "slavery was not born of racism; rather, racism was the consequence of slavery." In subtle ways many historians of North American slavery have reinforced this assumption, primary among them Ira Berlin, whose analysis of "Atlantic Creoles" and the "Charter Generation" of North American slaves assumes a flexible pre-nineteenth-century definition of "race" that hardened because of the slave society's rise. See E. Williams, *Capitalism and Slavery*, 7; Berlin, "From Creole to African"; and Berlin, *Many Thousands Gone*. However, other historians, especially those who specialize in a broader African diaspora, have argued that racial thought solidified much earlier than U.S. historians assume. For these, see especially Jordan, *White over Black*; J. H. Sweet, "Iberian Roots of American Racist Thought"; Eltis, *Rise of African Slavery in the Americas*, chap. 3; and D. Davis, *Inhuman Bondage*, chap. 3.

3. Historians have long argued that antislavery whites were as likely as conservatives to stigmatize free black behavior as criminal. One of the ways they did so was by playing such a critical role in building prisons. See D. Davis, *Problem of Slavery in the Age of Revolution*, 242; Paton, *No Bond but the Law*; and Manion, *Liberty's Prisoners*, 120–52.

4. Phillips, *Freedom's Port*, 145.

5. Ibid., 171–75. Many of these lodges belonged to the masons. For a great discussion of the importance of freemasonry to free black leaders and activists, see Kantrowitz, "'Intended for the Better Government of Man.'"

6. Douglass, *My Bondage and My Freedom*, 145–46.

7. Phillips, *Freedom's Port*, 167–68.

8. See Watkins, "Address Delivered before the Moral Reform Society," 166. Also see Gardner, "Ante-bellum Black Education in Baltimore."

9. Novak, "Legal Transformation of Citizenship."

10. For the 1842 recommendations, see Committee on the Colored Population, *Report of the Committee on the Colored Population*. For the fight against those recommendations, see Diemer, *Politics of Black Citizenship*, 117–18. In his book, Diemer

compares the political behavior of black Baltimoreans with that of black Philadelphians, arguing that both communities cultivated white allies and used them to great effect. Black Philadelphians in particular capitalized on "what they saw as the latent sympathy for limited black citizenship rights." See Diemer, *Politics of Black Citizenship*, 120.

11. Diemer, *Politics of Black Citizenship*, 147–48 and 175–77. For more on the failed re-enslavement campaign in Maryland, see Phillips, *Freedom's Port*, 206–10 and 232–34; and Freehling, *Road to Disunion*, 185–201. For Jacobs's quote, see Jacobs, *Speech of Col. Curtis M. Jacobs*, 7. For additional rationale for re-enslavement, see "Slaveholder's Convention," *Maryland Colonization Journal* 10, no. 2 (July 1859): 17–40, MHS.

12. Quoted in Gardner, "Free Blacks in Baltimore," 146.

13. Case of William Hamilton, folder 2, S1031-5 (1842–47), Pardon Papers (Secretary of State), MSA.

14. Harper, *Letter from Gen. Harper*.

15. "Persons of Color," *Niles' Weekly Register* (Baltimore), April 16, 1825, 100.

16. Hersey, *Appeal to Christians on the Subject of Slavery*, 88–89.

17. Harper, *Letter from Gen. Harper*.

18. "Persons of Color," *Niles' Weekly Register*, April 16, 1825, 100.

19. *Debates of the Constitutional Convention of the State of Maryland*, 578–79, MSA.

20. Carey, *Some Thoughts Concerning Domestic Slavery*, 21.

21. Quoted in DeLombard, *In the Shadows of the Gallows*, 223–24 (N.Y. convention) and figure 14, 242 (criminologist).

22. Historian Christopher Phillips called this the "street corner telegraph." He uses both quotes as well. See Phillips, *Freedom's Port*, 150. For originals, see Semmes, *Baltimore*, 166–67 and 157, respectively.

23. WPA No. 515, box 3, S 2, RG 9, Mayor's Office (1823), BCA.

24. WPA No. 831, box 4, ibid. (1824).

25. "Rioting," *Baltimore Sun*, September 26, 1840, 2.

26. Phillips, *Freedom's Port*, 117–44.

27. WPA No. 475, box 7, S 2, RG 9, Mayor's Office (1831), BCA.

28. Emphasis in original. Quoted in Graham, *Baltimore*, 148. For original, see *Baltimore Clipper*, June 17, 1840, 2.

29. For "a watchman named Lawton," see "Watch Returns," *Baltimore Sun*, August 29, 1838, 4. For the clarification, see "The Riot at the African Church," ibid., August 30, 1838, 2.

30. Aristotle, *Politics*, 1252a and 1253b. My argument here builds on Jeannine DeLombard's brilliant point that "crime shaped evocations of black personhood in [early] American print culture" and that slaves in particular were "consistently recognized as persons for the purposes of criminal law." See DeLombard, *In the Shadows of the Gallows*, 6 and 11, respectively.

31. *Cong. Globe*, 38th Cong., 2nd Sess., 120 (January 5, 1865).

32. *John M. Burke v. Negro Joe*.

33. Andrews, *Slavery and the Domestic Slave-Trade in the United States*, 88–89. Christopher Phillips cites this same passage to emphasize how black ministers were

able to draw from shared experiences with their black audiences and therefore communicate the gospel more easily than could their white counterparts. See Phillips, *Freedom's Port*, 142–43.

34. Andrews, *Slavery and the Domestic Slave-Trade in the United States*, 53 (first and second quotes) and 37 (third quote).

35. U.S. Bureau of the Census, *Eighth Census of the United States, 1860*.

36. Committee on the Colored Population, *Report of the Committee on the Colored Population*, 3.

37. "The Free Colored Population of Maryland," *Baltimore Sun*, February 14, 1844, 1.

38. For the story of Nat Turner, see Oates, *Fires of Jubilee*; for the remarkably contested history of the rebellion, see K. Greenberg, *Nat Turner*.

39. See WPA No. 464, box 7, S 2, RG 9, Mayor's Office (1831), BCA.

40. See WPA No. 463, ibid. For a discussion of these letters, as well as of the aforementioned Saratoga Street letter, see Katz, "Rumors of Rebellion."

41. Latrobe, *Justices Practice*, 4th ed., 205.

42. Phillips, *Freedom's Port*, 182.

43. WPA No. 922, box 45, S 1, RG 16, City Council Records (1832), BCA.

44. Hambleton, *Report of the Committee on the Coloured Population*, 3.

45. Diemer, *Politics of Black Citizenship*, 78. For the seminal explication of the idea that legal behavior differs from jurisprudence, see Pound, "Law in Books and Law in Action."

46. See, for instance, "The Law in Relation to Free Colored Persons," *Baltimore Sun*, March 19, 1861, 1.

47. Later, in 1843, the state banned explicitly "secret associations of negroes." For the city council's "zealous" support of this bill, in particular so that it could dissolve a black Masonic Lodge, see WPA No. 634, box 71, S 1, RG 16, City Council Records (1843), BCA.

48. WPA No. 709, box 75, ibid. (1845).

49. For Basil Savoy, see WPA No. 1228, box 19, S 1, RG 9, Mayor's Office (1838), BCA; for Enols Chase, see WPA No. 1229, ibid.; and for Samuel Grayson, see WPA No. 1227, ibid.

50. Historian Jennifer Manion argues that the association of black people with crime "served to justify the extreme regulation of black public and social spaces." By "extreme regulation," she means violence. See *Liberty's Prisoners*, 147.

51. "Shooting of a Woman," *Baltimore Sun*, July 19, 1844, 2.

52. For an example of a white man's pardon — after he killed a black man and admitted to it — see case of James Love, S1108-2 (1850), Pardon Record, MSA.

53. "Another Assault," *Baltimore Sun*, January 22, 1841, 2.

54. "Cases of Aggravated Assault," ibid., February 2, 1860, 1.

55. "Colored Colonization Convention," ibid., July 27, 1852, 1. For a transcript, see "Maryland Free Colored People's Convention, July 27–28, 1852," in Foner and Walker, *Proceeding of the Black State Convention*, 2:48–49. Also see Diemer, *Politics of Black Citizenship*, 155–57.

56. "Assault," *Baltimore Sun*, June 17, 1841, 1.

57. "Negro Outrages," ibid., November 2, 1837, 2. Also printed as "Negro Outrages," *Baltimore Gazette and Daily Advertiser*, November 2, 1837, 2.

58. Case of James Tighlman, folder 16, S1031-13 (1854), Pardon Papers (Secretary of State), MSA.

59. *"John Fields," Baltimore Sun*, February 2, 1841, 1.

60. "Rowdyism," ibid., January 24, 1844, 2.

61. "Wanton Assault," ibid., May 13, 1841, 2.

62. "Desperate Fight with a Poultry Thief," ibid., March 2, 1861, 1.

63. WPA No. 253, box 64, S 2, RG 16, City Council Records (1839), BCA.

64. WPA No. 468, box 87, S 1, ibid. (1850).

65. WPA No. 306, box 109, ibid. (1858).

66. A city council subcommittee went so far as to reject outright any consideration that watchmen, constables, or bailiffs receive part of the fines the city levied from informants. Its reasoning: it would wreak havoc. See WPA No. 664, box 73, ibid. (1844).

67. WPA No. 418, box 89, ibid. (1851).

68. Emphasis in original. WPA No. 264, box 27, S 2, RG 9, Mayor's Office (1851), BCA.

69. WPA No. 709, box 75, S 1, RG 16, City Council Records (1845), BCA.

70. To be precise, whereas in 1850 free black people represented 13.8 percent of Baltimore County's population, in 1860 they represented 12.1 percent of Baltimore City's population. Overall free black population declension was therefore nowhere near as great as the relative decline of black inmates in the city's jail.

71. As historian Christopher Phillips notes, it was precisely during the tumultuous 1850s that Baltimore's "racial middle ground . . . all but vanished." Phillips, *Freedom's Port*, 194.

72. Coates, "On the Effects of Secluded and Gloomy Imprisonment," 96. Also quoted in DeLombard, *In the Shadows of the Gallows*, 104; and C. Smith, *Prison and the American Imagination*, 105.

73. "Governor's Message," *Baltimore Sun*, January 8, 1858, 1.

74. "Highly Colored," ibid., August 31, 1857, 1.

75. "Watch Returns," ibid., February 17, 1841, 2.

76. See, for instance, the 1860 Report of the Marshal of Police, appendix to the Ordinances of the Mayor and City Council of Baltimore, 351–56, DLR.

77. "Watch Returns," *Baltimore Sun*, April 27, 1838, 2.

78. "Released from Jail," ibid., February 9, 1858, 1.

79. "Watch Returns," ibid., August 21, 1838, 4.

80. Emphasis in original. "Watch Returns," ibid., September 12, 1838, 4.

81. Emphasis in original. "Watch Returns," ibid., September 26, 1838, 1.

82. "Watch Returns — *Monday, Aug. 20*," ibid., August 29, 1838, 4.

83. "Watch Returns — *Thursday, August 23*," ibid.

84. For "nine and thirty lashes," see "William Guyle," ibid., June 19, 1838, 1; for "thirty lashes," see case of Charles the Slave, S1107-5 (1828), Pardon Record, MSA; and for "twenty stripes," see case of Cecelia Martin, S1107-5 (1831), Pardon Record, MSA.

85. Emphasis in original. "Whipping at the Stake," *Baltimore Sun*, October 12, 1838, 2.

86. "Watch Returns," ibid., September 26, 1838, 1.

87. Emphasis in original. "Whipping at the Stake," ibid., October 12, 1838, 2.

88. *Report of the Select Committee . . . Respecting the Maryland Penitentiary*, 4.

89. For 1836 law, see Maryland Acts of Assembly, December Session 1835, chapter 200, section 3; for 1858 law, see Maryland Acts of Assembly, 1858, chapter 324.

90. Calculated from table B in 1850 Report of the Board of Visitors of the Baltimore City Jail, appendix to the Ordinances of the Mayor and City Council of Baltimore, DLR.

91. Joint Committee on the Penitentiary, *Testimony Taken before the Joint Committee of the Legislature of Maryland on the Penitentiary*, 66–67.

92. See "*State v. James Peters*," "*State v. Philip Frisby*," and "*State v. James Henry Williams*," *Baltimore Sun*, February 10, 1844, 4.

93. "*James Buffalo*" and "*Charlotte Williams*," ibid., June 11, 1838, 1.

94. See, respectively, "*Alexander Wilson*," ibid., June 23, 1838, 1; "*State v. Maria Matthews*" and "*State v. Eliza Smith*," ibid., February 16, 1844, 2; and "*Hyson Williams*," ibid., November 4, 1840, 4.

95. *Thomas M. Watkins (Free Negro) v. The State*.

96. 1845 Annual Report of the Maryland Penitentiary, Government Publications and Reports, MSA.

97. Case of James Tighlman, folder 16, S1031-13 (1854), Pardon Papers (Secretary of State), MSA.

98. Maryland Penitentiary, *Report of the Committee on Prison Manufacturers*, 6.

99. "Warden's Report," 1849 Annual Report of the Maryland Penitentiary, Government Publications and Reports, MSA.

100. In his work on poverty and wage labor in Baltimore, Seth Rockman also notes "the underrepresentation of free people of color in the Almshouse relative to their actual need," but he explains this "noteworthy" fact by pointing to the reluctance among white ward managers to bestow *relief* upon black people. I would simply add that there was also a reluctance to impose the institution's *discipline* upon them. See Rockman, *Scraping By*, 210.

101. Sixth Annual Report of the Managers of the House of Refuge, 12–14, EPFL.

102. Table D, Superintendent's Report, Fifth Annual Report of the Managers of the House of Refuge, EPFL.

103. Ninth Annual Report of the Managers of the House of Refuge, 7, EPFL.

104. Sixth Annual Report of the Managers of the House of Refuge, 12–14, EPFL.

105. A forceful and eloquent discussion of this trend is Alexander, *New Jim Crow*. Also see Thompson, "Why Incarceration Matters"; and the articles in the special edition on the carceral state in *Journal of American History* 102, no. 1 (June 2015). For a challenge to the standard thesis that the drug war is to blame for mass black incarceration, see Pfaff, *Locked In*.

106. Ayers, *Vengeance and Justice*, 295n57.

107. U.S. Bureau of the Census, *Eighth Census of the United States, 1860*.

108. Beaumont and Tocqueville, *On the Penitentiary System*, 93–94.

Chapter Six

1. "Celebrating the Day," *American and Commercial Advertiser* (Baltimore), November 1, 1864, 1. Also see Wagandt, *Mighty Revolution*, chap. 14; and Fuke, *Imperfect Equality*, 1.

2. Clarke, *Speech*, 13.

3. *Debates of the Constitutional Convention of the State of Maryland*, 579, MSA.

4. Ibid., 583.

5. Ibid., 577–79.

6. Pugh, *Speech*, 12.

7. *Debates of the Constitutional Convention of the State of Maryland*, 577, MSA.

8. Letters Sent, Office of the Assistant Commissioner, Roll 1, RFO.

9. No. 81, Letters Sent, ibid.

10. Office of the Assistant Commissioner, Reports, Roll 5, RFO.

11. Quoted in Fuke, *Imperfect Equality*, 117.

12. Quoted in ibid., 118.

13. "The Civil Rights Bill," *American and Commercial Advertiser*, April 3, 1866, 2.

14. "The Education of the African in Our Midst," *Annapolis Gazette*, September 28, 1865, 2.

15. "Public Schools for Colored Children," *Baltimore Sun*, April 16, 1868, 1.

16. "Colored Celebration in Honor of Free Maryland," *Liberator* 34, no. 48 (November 24, 1864): 190.

17. Report—July 11, 1867, Assistant Commissioner's Quarterly Reports of Operations, Roll 5, RFO.

18. "Colored Celebration in Honor of Free Maryland," *Liberator* 34, no. 48 (November 24, 1864): 190.

19. "Hiring of the Freedmen," *American and Commercial Advertiser*, December 16, 1865, 4.

20. Report—July 11, 1867, Assistant Commissioner's Quarterly Reports of Operations, Roll 5, RFO.

21. Emphasis in original. "The Civil Rights Bill," *American and Commercial Advertiser*, April 3, 1866, 2.

22. "Colored Educational Meeting," ibid., August 27, 1867, 4.

23. "Meeting of Colored Persons," *Baltimore Sun*, July 20, 1869, 1.

24. Fields, *Slavery and Freedom on the Middle Ground*, 152–53.

25. Message of Governor Swann to the General Assembly of Maryland at Its Regular Session (1867), Senate Journal and Documents, Government Publications and Reports, MSA.

26. Report—November 1866, Assistant Commissioner's Quarterly Reports of Operations, Roll 5, RFO.

27. Fields, *Slavery and Freedom on the Middle Ground*, 138.

28. For both quote and further analysis, see Fuke, *Imperfect Equality*, 27.

29. Knower to Cunningham, Letters Sent, Office of the Assistant Commissioner, Roll 1, RFO.

30. Wiegel to Parkes, December 1, 1866, ibid.

31. No. 5, Wiegel to Watts, January 4, 1867, ibid.

32. No. 46, Knower to Bain, February 4, 1867, ibid.

33. Office of Assistant Commissioner to Abraham Baldwin, July 10, 1866, ibid.

34. No. 46, Knower to Bain, February 4, 1867, ibid.

35. Major General Lew Wallace, "Communication on Freedmen's Bureau," House Journal and Documents 1865J, Government Publications and Reports, MSA.

36. Preface, Roll 1, RFO.

37. General Orders No. 112, "Communication on Freedmen's Bureau," House Journal and Documents 1865J, Government Publications and Reports, MSA.

38. Bolemius to Maxwell, October 1866, Letters Sent, Office of the Assistant Commissioner, Roll 1, RFO.

39. Preface, Roll 1, RFO.

40. John Wyatt — July 7, 1866, Registers of Complaints, Volume 1 (17), Complaint Division, Roll 37, RFO.

41. No. 52, July 18, 1866, Letters Sent, Office of the Assistant Commissioner, Roll 1, RFO.

42. No. 46, July 18, 1866, ibid.

43. No. 280, December 20, 1866, ibid.

44. For "prevent suffering," see No. 52, July 18, 1866, ibid; for "gain a support," see No. 32, January 24, 1867, ibid.

45. No. 60, February 20, 1867, ibid.

46. Howard to Gregory, January 24, 1867, Letters Received (A–F), Roll 2, RFO.

47. Assistant Commissioner's Quarterly Reports of Operations, Roll 5, RFO.

48. Report — November 1866, ibid.

49. Anthony Armstrong — July 27, 1866, Registers of Complaints, Volume 1 (17), Complaint Division, Roll 37, RFO.

50. Maria Hamilton — February 28, 1867, ibid.

51. Phillis Jones — January 4, 1867, ibid.

52. Nathan [?]aldin — December 28, 1866, ibid.

53. No. 60, Amie Augustus — February 15, 1868, Registers of Complaints, Volume 2 (18), ibid.

54. No. 31, Jessie W. Ames — March 7, 1868, ibid.

55. Hannah Snow — August 12, 1867, Registers of Complaints, Volume 1 (17), ibid.

56. See, respectively, Charles Williams — October 19, 1866, ibid.; No. 144, Robert Prackston — April 15, 1868, Registers of Complaints, Volume 2 (18), ibid.; No. 145, Jane Gardner — April 15, 1868, Registers of Complaints, Volume 2 (18), ibid.; No. 187, John Whitney — May 11, 1868, Registers of Complaints, Volume 2 (18), ibid.; and No. 209, John H. Butler — May 25, 1868, Registers of Complaints, Volume 2 (18), ibid.

57. See, respectively, Harriett Whittington — January 31, 1867, Registers of Complaints, Volume 1 (17), ibid.; Louisa George — April 29, 1867, ibid.; Indy Jones — February 4, 1867, ibid.; Amanda Buchanan — October 16, 1867, ibid.; No. 42, Lydia Duvall — March 20, 1868, Registers of Complaints, Volume 2 (18), ibid.; and No. 107, Sarah Nichols — March 18, 1868, Registers of Complaints, Volume 2 (18), ibid.

58. No. 94, Rebecca Parmelia — March 10, 1868, Registers of Complaints, Volume 2 (18), ibid.

59. Report — July 11, 1867, Assistant Commissioner's Quarterly Reports of Operations, Roll 5, RFO.

60. Rutherford to Howard, October 27, 1866, Letters Sent, Volume 53, Roll 41, RFO.

61. Quoted in Fuke, *Imperfect Equality*, 38.

62. See Fields, *Slavery and Freedom on the Middle Ground*, 156–66.

63. "Day Break in Maryland," *Easton (Md.) Gazette*, February 25, 1865, 2.

64. "Colored Educational Meeting," *American and Commercial Advertiser*, August 27, 1867, 4.

65. *Cong. Globe*, 38th Cong., 2nd Sess., 120 (January 5, 1865).

66. Thomas Bishop, Co. T. 7th, Anna, wife — July 12, 1866, Registers of Complaints, Volume 1 (17), Complaint Division, Roll 37, RFO.

67. For one example, see John Gross, Co. T. 4th, Maria Widow — June 29, 1868, ibid.

68. Petition of Elizabeth Kenard, "Communication on Freedmen's Bureau," House Journal and Documents 1865J, Government Publications and Reports, MSA.

69. Petition of Robert Wilson, ibid.

70. Petition of Lucy Lee, ibid.

71. Report of Bartus Trew, ibid.

72. Jane Wright — July 10, 1866, Registers of Complaints, Volume 1 (17), Complaint Division, Roll 37, RFO.

73. Petition of E. T. Hall, "Communication on Freedmen's Bureau," House Journal and Documents 1865J, Government Publications and Reports, MSA.

74. Quoted in Fuke, *Imperfect Equality*, 76–77.

75. Petition of George F. Curry, "Communication on Freedmen's Bureau," House Journal and Documents 1865J, Government Publications and Reports, MSA.

76. For "ox-cart loads," see "Communication on Freedmen's Bureau," ibid.; for "wagonloads," see "Condition of the Freed Negroes in Kent County," *American and Commercial Advertiser*, December 13, 1864, 4.

77. Report — November 1866, Assistant Commissioner's Quarterly Reports of Operations, Roll 5, RFO.

78. Report — October 16, 1867, Letters Sent, Office of the Assistant Commissioner, Roll 1, RFO.

79. Petition of John Dennis, "Communication on Freedmen's Bureau," House Journal and Documents 1865J, Government Publications and Reports, MSA.

80. I am counting Baltimore City here as a county. For the numbers, see Ketchum Report — March 11, 1867, Letters Sent, Office of the Assistant Commissioner, Roll 1, RFO.

81. Some 249 signatures were attached to the petition. See "From Maryland Blacks" in Bergron, *Papers of Andrew Johnson*, 266.

82. The following can be found in Registers of Complaints, Volume 1 (17), Complaint Division, Roll 37, RFO: Martha Brown — July 2, 1866; Lydia Garret — June 30, 1866; Mrs. Hill — June 28, 1866; Ann Jones — June 18, 1866; Edward Dorsey — July 14, 1866; Caroline Anderson — July 20, 1866; Henrietta Wright — August 13, 1866; and

Mary Bacon — November 12, 1867. The following can be found in Registers of Complaints, Volume 2 (18), Complaint Division, Roll 37, RFO: No. 184, Ann Broome — May 8, 1868; No. 192, Harriet Mason — May 19, 1868; No. 193, Mary E. Darr — May 19, 1868; Nos. 201 and 202, A. Mason — May 21, 1868; No. 298, Stephen Wright — July 28, 1868; No. 324, Annie Cornish — August 29, 1868; and No. 331, Sarah Harris — September 10, 1868.

83. M. Nichols to O. O. Howard, October 11, 1866, Letters Received, Roll 3, RFO.

84. Report — October 11, 1867, Letters Sent, Office of the Assistant Commissioner, Roll 1, RFO.

85. Petition of Lucy Lee, "Communication on Freedmen's Bureau," House Journal and Documents 1865J, Government Publications and Reports, MSA.

86. Petition of Lindsay Robbins, ibid.

87. Joseph Richards — November 30, 1866, Registers of Complaints, Volume 1 (17), Complaint Division, Roll 37, RFO.

88. Fuke, *Imperfect Equality*, 75.

89. Petition of Hester Hall, "Communication on Freedmen's Bureau," House Journal and Documents 1865J, Government Publications and Reports, MSA.

90. Petition of Lavina Brooks, ibid.

91. Petition of Louisa Foster, ibid.

92. Petition of Rebecca Sales, ibid.

93. Petition of Soloman Banks, ibid.

94. Ross to Lawrence, January 20, 1865, ibid.

95. For quote, see Fields, *Slavery and Freedom on the Middle Ground*, 140.

96. Petition of Harriet A. Connaway, "Communication on Freedmen's Bureau," House Journal and Documents 1865J, Government Publications and Reports, MSA.

97. Report — April 11, 1867, Assistant Commissioner's Quarterly Reports of Operations, Roll 5, RFO.

98. Fuke, *Imperfect Equality*, 78–79.

99. Report — July 11, 1867, Assistant Commissioner's Quarterly Reports of Operations, Roll 5, RFO.

100. Report — December 31, 1866, ibid.

101. Report — June 30, 1868, ibid.

102. No. 57, Knower to Faithful — July 1, 1866, Letters Sent, Office of the Assistant Commissioner, Roll 1, RFO.

103. No. 252, Wiegel to Passans — December 7, 1866, ibid.

104. Knower to Hurgenvater [?], November 16, 1866, ibid.

105. No. 34, Gregory to Ketchum, January 24, 1867, ibid.

106. Howard to Gregory, January 24, 1867, Letters Received (A–F), Roll 2, RFO.

107. "Habeas Corpus Case under the Civil Rights Bill," *American and Commercial Advertiser*, July 31, 1866, 4.

108. "Habeas Corpus Case under the Civil Rights Bill," ibid., August 14, 1866, 4.

109. "Before the Chief Justice Chase," *Baltimore Sun*, October 17, 1867, 1.

110. Report from Baltimore Field Office — September 14, 1868, Register of Complaints of Illegal Apprenticeships, Roll 6, RFO.

111. Civil Rights Act of 1866, chap. 31, sec. 1.

112. My argument here relies heavily upon Amy Dru Stanley's brilliant discussion of contract freedom in *From Bondage to Contract*, 1–59.

113. Report — April 11, 1867, Assistant Commissioner's Quarterly Reports of Operations, Roll 5, RFO.

114. Article 19, Declaration of Rights, Constitution of Maryland, 1867.

115. Civil Rights Act of 1866, chap. 31, sec. 2.

116. See Stanley, *From Bondage to Contract*, 55–59, quote on 58.

117. Fuke, *Imperfect Equality*, 72–73.

118. Petition of E. T. Hall, "Communication on Freedmen's Bureau," House Journal and Documents 1865J, Government Publications and Reports, MSA.

119. George Murray — May 9, 1867, Registers of Complaints, Volume 1 (17), Complaint Division, Roll 37, RFO.

120. No. 62, Joanna Brown — February 17, 1868, Registers of Complaints, Volume 2 (18), ibid.

121. Report — April 11, 1867, Assistant Commissioner's Quarterly Reports of Operations, Roll 5, RFO.

122. Report — October 16, 1867, Letters Sent, Office of the Assistant Commissioner, Roll 1, RFO.

123. Report — January 10, 1868, ibid.

124. Report — October 16, 1867, ibid.

125. Report — January 10, 1868, ibid.

126. Miscellaneous Reports and Papers, Roll 6, RFO.

127. See, respectively, "Veto of the Freedmen's Bureau Bill," in Foster, *Andrew Johnson, His Life and Speeches*; and *Cong. Globe*, 39th Cong., 1st Sess. (1866), 768.

Chapter Seven

1. Stanley, "Beggars Can't Be Choosers."

2. See the seminal E. Foner, *Reconstruction*. For the black political struggles that made Reconstruction such a revolution in the first place, see Hahn, *Nation under Our Feet*.

3. U.S. Const., amend. XIII, sec. 1.

4. Civil Rights Act of 1866, chap. 31, sec. 1.

5. "Colored Celebration in Honor of Free Maryland," *Liberator* 34, no. 48 (November 24, 1864): 190.

6. Cases of J. E. Stockdale, et al., folder 43, box 62, S1031-24 (1866–68), Pardon Papers (Secretary of State), MSA.

7. 1870 Annual Report of the Board of Visitors of Baltimore City Jail, 478, Government Publications and Reports, MSA.

8. 1871 Annual Report of the Board of Visitors of Baltimore City Jail, 964, ibid.

9. "Slaveholders Convention," *Maryland Colonization Journal* 10, no. 2 (1859): 24, MHS.

10. Jacobs, *Free Negro Question in Maryland*, 18–19.

11. "Slaveholders Convention," *Maryland Colonization Journal* 10, no. 2 (1859): 34, MHS.

12. *Debates of the Constitutional Convention of the State of Maryland*, 577, MSA.

13. Ibid., 735.

14. *Maryland Colonization Journal* 10, no. 9 (1860): 139, MHS.

15. Report and Bill, Committee on the Colored Population, House Journal and Documents 1864, Government Publications and Reports, MSA.

16. "The Education of the African in Our Midst," *Annapolis Gazette*, September 28, 1865, 2.

17. "Thirty-Ninth Annual Report of the Board of Commissioners of Public Schools to the Mayor and City Council of Baltimore," Ordinances of the Mayor and City Council of Baltimore, 1868, 193, DLR.

18. Scholars have emphatically demonstrated that there were conservative limits to Radical Republican ideology. My discussion here builds heavily upon Fuke, "Hugh Lennox Bond and Radical Republican Ideology."

19. For Bond, see "Rooms of the Baltimore Association for the Moral and Educational Improvement of the Colored People," *Easton (Md.) Gazette*, January 7, 1865, 1. For Ware, see "The Freemen in Our Midst," *American and Commercial Advertiser* (Baltimore), March 15, 1865, 2.

20. "The Freemen in Our Midst," *American and Commercial Advertiser*, March 15, 1865, 2.

21. Fuke, *Imperfect Equality*, 112–13.

22. "The Labor Question," *Baltimore Sun*, August 9, 1865, 1.

23. "A Timely Order," ibid., September 24, 1866, 4.

24. 1868 Annual Report of the Maryland Penitentiary, Government Publications and Reports, MSA.

25. Quoted in Fuke, *Imperfect Equality*, 115. For original, see *Baltimore Gazette*, June 2, 1866.

26. "An Alleged Outrage," *Baltimore Sun*, January 25, 1869, 1.

27. "A Case of Amalgamation," ibid., January 13, 1869, 1.

28. "Shooting Affray," ibid., November 29, 1869, 1.

29. Report, Board of Police Commissioners for Baltimore City, Senate Journal and Documents 1867I, Government Publications and Reports, MSA.

30. 1869 Annual Report of the Board of Visitors of Baltimore City Jail, Government Publications and Reports, MSA.

31. "Disorderly Party of Boys," *Baltimore Sun*, April 3, 1872, 1.

32. 1869 Annual Report of the Board of Visitors of Baltimore City Jail, Government Publications and Reports, MSA.

33. For "helpless," see "Juvenile Negro Offenders," *Baltimore Sun*, March 13, 1867, 2; for "committed to jail," see "Affairs of the City, Message of the Mayor of Baltimore," ibid., January 20, 1869, 1.

34. "Affairs of the City, Message of the Mayor of Baltimore," ibid., January 20, 1869, 1.

35. Quoted in Fuke, *Imperfect Equality*, 128. For original, see the *Baltimore Gazette*, November 3, 1865.

36. All quotes from "The Maryland Penitentiary," *Baltimore Sun*, February 21, 1867, 2. For the prophecy, see Beaumont and Tocqueville, *On the Penitentiary System*, 93–94.

37. 1866 Annual Report of the Maryland Penitentiary, Government Publications and Reports, MSA.

38. "Meeting of Colored Pastors," *Baltimore Sun*, February 11, 1869, 1.

39. See Fuke, *Imperfect Equality*, 119–21.

40. For an example, see case of Mary Jane Wesley, Letters Received (A–F), Roll 2, RFO.

41. Fuke, *Imperfect Equality*, 196–99.

42. "The Health of the City," *Baltimore Sun*, October 15, 1866, 4.

43. Baynes et al. to Ross, in Major General Lew Wallace, "Communication on Freedmen's Bureau," House Journal and Documents 1865J, Government Publications and Reports, MSA.

44. Meurhead to Ross, in Major Gen. Lew Wallace, "Communication on Freedmen's Bureau," ibid.

45. For "lawless and disorderly," see "Trouble with Freedmen in Georgia," *Baltimore Sun*, November 23, 1865, 4; for "improper, disrespectful and insulting," see "Excitement at Piscataway," ibid., January 22, 1870, 4; and for "murderous and dastardly," see "Another Terrible Episode — A Whole Family Fired Upon," ibid., August 5, 1872, 4.

46. "Store Robbed," ibid., January 6, 1868, 1.

47. "Desperate Shooting Affray," ibid., November 8, 1872, 4.

48. "Dangerously Injured," ibid., April 25, 1867, 1.

49. "Riotous Proceedings," ibid., June 10, 1870, 1.

50. For another example of a white citizen attempting to assist an officer, see "Resisting an Officer and Gross Assault," ibid., December 27, 1865, 1.

51. Report, Board of Police Commissioners for Baltimore City, Senate Journal and Documents 1867I, Government Publications and Reports, MSA.

52. "Exciting Affray at a Camp Meeting," *Baltimore Sun*, September 1, 1866, 4.

53. Miscellaneous Reports and Papers, Roll 6, RFO.

54. For one example of white fears of black soldiers, see "Exciting Shooting Affray — A Colored Soldier Shoots Two White Men," *Baltimore Sun*, January 20, 1865, 1.

55. "Shooting Affray," ibid., January 18, 1866, 1.

56. "Street Fight between Whites and Blacks," ibid., May 10, 1866, 1.

57. For the *Sun*'s description of the story, from which all the quotes are taken, see "Fatal Shooting from a Colored Military Organization," *Baltimore Sun*, October 18, 1867, 1. Also see "Riot and Loss of Life," *Cincinnati Daily Inquirer*," October 18, 1867, 3. For a more balanced account, see "Different Reports about Impeachment," *Washington News*, October 19, 1867, 1.

58. Report — January 10, 1868, Letters Sent, Office of the Assistant Commissioner, Roll 1, RFO.

59. "Charged with Larceny," *Baltimore Sun*, January 9, 1868, 4.

60. For James, see "Larceny," ibid., January 17, 1868, 1; for Weeks and Davis, see "Robbery of Clothing," ibid., January 27, 1868, 1; and for Piatta, see "Wholesale Robbery of Vessels," ibid., May 4, 1868, 1.

61. "Juvenile Negro Offenders," ibid., March 13, 1867, 2.

62. "Destroying Private Property," ibid., March 30, 1869, 1.

63. "The Appeal of the Colored Caulkers of Baltimore to the Merchants and Businessmen of Baltimore City and State of Maryland," ibid., October 2, 1865, 2.

64. "The Trouble among the Mechanics," ibid., October 7, 1865, 2.

65. "The Strike at an End," ibid., October 28, 1865, 1.

66. "The Colored Caulkers," ibid., November 6, 1865, 1.

67. Quoted in Fuke, *Imperfect Equality*, 134.

68. "Condition of the Colored People," *New York Tribune*, September 1, 1870, 2.

69. "Conservative View of the Civil Rights Bill," *Easton Gazette*, April 14, 1866, 2.

70. 1869 Annual Report, Home of the Friendless of the City of Baltimore, MHS.

71. The jail stopped reporting the number of juvenile commitments in 1860, but the institution's annual reports regularly complained of the high number of black juveniles committed for trial. The 1868 report, for example, called "attention to the increasing evil of committing colored children to jail. They are sent there in great numbers, and many of them at very tender years." See "Report of the Visitors of Jail," *Baltimore Sun*, February 4, 1868, 1.

72. "The Maryland Penitentiary," ibid., December 28, 1867, 1.

73. "A Colored Woman Killed by a Policeman," *American and Commercial Advertiser*, September 23, 1867, 4.

74. Report — October 11, 1867, Letters Sent, Office of the Assistant Commissioner, Roll 1, RFO.

75. "A Colored Woman Killed by a Policeman," *American and Commercial Advertiser*, September 23, 1867, 4.

76. "The South Baltimore Homicide," ibid., September 24, 1867, 4; and "The South Baltimore Homicide — Verdict of the Jury," ibid., September 26, 1867, 4.

77. Report — October 11, 1867, Letters Sent, Office of the Assistant Commissioner, Roll 1, RFO.

78. Gotlieb Frey, Baltimore City Directory, 1886 (messenger), 1892 (contractor), 1898 (clerk), Ancestry.com, U.S. City Directories, 1822–1995.

79. "The South Baltimore Homicide — Verdict of the Jury," *American and Commercial Advertiser*, September 26, 1867, 4.

80. For Murray's service as a landsman during the Civil War, see Jordan Murray, National Park Service, Ancestry.com, African American Civil War Sailor Index, 1861–1865.

81. 1867 Annual Report of the Maryland Penitentiary, Government Publications and Reports, MSA.

82. For "new condition," see ibid. For "erection," see 1868 Annual Report of the Maryland Penitentiary, ibid. For "schooled on all kinds of vice," see 1871 Annual Report of the Maryland Penitentiary, ibid.

83. For "irretrievable ruin," see 1871 Annual Report of the Maryland Penitentiary, ibid.

84. 1874 Annual Report of the House of Reformation and Instruction for Colored Children, ibid.

85. Emphasis in original. See 1867 Annual Report of the Maryland Penitentiary, ibid.

86. 1872 Annual Report of the Board of Visitors of Baltimore City Jail, ibid.

87. 1861 and 1870 Annual Reports of the Board of Visitors of Baltimore City Jail, ibid.

88. 1867 Annual Report of the Maryland Penitentiary, ibid.

89. See additional discussion in Fuke, *Imperfect Equality*, 200–201.

90. For "diminution," see 1868 Annual Report of the Maryland Penitentiary, ibid.

91. 1867 Annual Report of the Maryland Penitentiary, ibid.

92. 1874 Annual Report of the Maryland Penitentiary, ibid.

93. 1866 Annual Report of the Maryland Penitentiary, ibid.

94. 1868 Annual Report of the Maryland Penitentiary, ibid.

95. 1872 Annual Report of the Maryland Penitentiary, ibid.

96. 1873 Annual Report of the Maryland Penitentiary, ibid.

97. 1874 Annual Report of the Maryland Penitentiary, ibid.

98. Howard to Gregory, November 26, 1866, Office of the Assistant Commissioner Reports, Roll 2, RFO.

99. Office of the Assistant Commissioner Reports, Roll 5, RFO.

100. Report—August 31, 1866, Reports Received from the Shenandoah Division, Roll 6, RFO.

101. No. 121, Gregory to Howard, April 11, 1867, Letters Sent, Office of the Assistant Commissioner, Roll 1, RFO.

102. Quoted in Fuke, *Imperfect Equality*, xx.

103. Swann, "Message of Governor Swann to the General Assembly of Maryland."

104. Bowie, "Inaugural Address of Gov. Oden Bowie."

105. Bowie, "Message of Gov. Oden Bowie to the General Assembly of Maryland."

106. Quoted in Fuke, *Imperfect Equality*, 230.

107. For an excellent discussion of how the perpetuation of racial discrimination survived under the post-racial logic of the criminal code, see Holloway, *Living in Infamy.*

Epilogue

1. Historians rarely liken policemen to slave patrollers if only because their analyses are typically demarcated by geography, as I noted in the introduction. Slavery's police regimes are more commonly understood to have given way to post-emancipation systems of vigilantism and lynching. See, for example, Waldrep, *Roots of Disorder.* For a contemporary (and popular) discussion of the policeman as a type of slave patroller, see Carter, "Policing and Oppression Have a Long History." For a good

example of an argument that characterizes prison labor as a reconstituted form of slave labor, see Blackmon, *Slavery by Another Name*. Finally, for an analysis that places the modern penitentiary on a continuum of race control regimes that only began with slavery, see Wacquant, "From Slavery to Mass Incarceration."

2. There is so much recent writing on black policing and incarceration that it is impossible to cite it all. I will therefore just cite two local investigations. For an excellent study of young black men in Philadelphia who confront constant police harassment, see Goffman, *On the Run*. For a brilliant examination of mass black incarceration in California after 1980, see Gilmore, *Golden Gulag*.

3. The three incidents to which I am alluding are the murders of Walter Scott (Charleston), Tamir Rice (Cleveland), and Freddie Gray (Baltimore). For a brief but illuminating discussion on how officials attack black victims' characters, see Carimah Townes, "The Character Assassination of Freddie Gray," *Think Progress*, April 30, 2015, https://thinkprogress.org/the-character-assassination-of-freddie-gray-833fa5 92f0f6. For a discussion of recent instances of police brutality, see Hill, *Nobody*. For more historical treatments of the subject, see Nelson, *Police Brutality*, and K. Williams, *Our Enemies in Blue*.

BIBLIOGRAPHY

Archival and Manuscript Collections

Annapolis, Maryland
  Maryland State Archives
    Biographical Series
      William Watkins, http://msa.maryland.gov/megafile/msa/speccol/sc5400
        /sc5496/002500/002535/html/002535bio.html (accessed
        March 2, 2017)
      The Debates of the Constitutional Convention of the State of Maryland,
        Assembled at the City of Annapolis, Wednesday, April 27, 1864. Vol. 1.
        Annapolis, Md.: Richard P. Bayly, 1864.
    Government Publications and Reports
      House and Senate Documents
      House Journal and Documents
      Reports of the Board of Visitors of Baltimore City Jail
      Reports of the House of Reformation and Instruction for Colored Children
      Reports of the Maryland Penitentiary
      Senate Journal and Documents
    Laws of Maryland
      Chapter 65, Session Laws 1794
      Chapter 193, Session Laws 1816
    Orphans Court Proceedings (Baltimore City)
    Pardon Papers
      Governor and Council, 1775–1836
      Secretary of State, 1837–1947
    Pardon Record
      Secretary of State, 1839–1941
Baltimore, Maryland
  Baltimore City Archives
    City Council Records, 1797–present (Record Group 16)
    Mayor's Office, 1797–present (Record Group 9)
    Ordinances of the Corporation of the City of Baltimore, 1813–1827
  Department of Legislative Reference, City Hall
    Ordinances of the Mayor and City Council of Baltimore, 1832–1870
  Enoch Pratt Free Library

Annual Reports of the Managers of the House of Refuge
Report of the Trustees of the Almshouse for Baltimore City and County, 1827
Maryland Historical Society
    Annual Reports of the Home of the Friendless of the City of Baltimore, 1869
    Allyson Davies, "The Maryland Indemnity Bill of 1836: Development of a
        Political Issue," 1969
    Maryland Colonization Journal, 1859–60
    War of 1812 Collection
    William Bartlett to Edward Stabler, August 8, 1835
    William Preston Papers
Washington, D.C.
    National Archives
        Records of the Field Offices for the States of Maryland and Delaware (M1906),
            Bureau of Refugees, Freedmen, and Abandoned Land (Record Group
            105)

Government and Legal Records

1794 Md. Laws Acts of 1794, Chapter 57
1816 Md. Laws 193
1864 Maryland Constitution
1867 Maryland Constitution
Civil Rights Act of 1866, 14 Stat. 27–30
Congressional Globe
Dred Scott v. Sandford, 60 U.S. 393 (1857)
John M. Burke v. Negro Joe, Court of Appeals of Maryland, 6 G. & J. Md. 136
    (1834)
Josiah Hughes v. Samuel Jackson, Court of Appeals of Maryland, 12 Md. 450 (1858)
Maryland Acts of Assembly, December Session 1835
Maryland Acts of Assembly, 1858
Slaughter-House Cases, 83 U.S. 36, 49 (1873)
Thomas M. Watkins (Free Negro) v. The State, Court of Appeals of Maryland,
    14 Md. 412 (1859)
U.S. Bureau of the Census, *Eighth Census of the United States, 1860: Population*
    (Washington: Government Printing Office, 1864)
U.S. Constitution

Newspapers

American and Commercial Advertiser (Baltimore), 1864–67
American and Commercial Daily Advertiser (Baltimore), 1821
Annapolis Gazette, 1865
Baltimore Clipper, 1840, 1857
Baltimore Gazette, 1834, 1866

Baltimore Gazette and Daily Advertiser, 1837

Baltimore Republican, 1835–36

Baltimore Sun, 1837–70

Cincinnati Daily Inquirer, 1867

Daily and National Intelligencer (Washington, D.C.)

Easton (Md.) Gazette, 1865–66

Frederick (Md.) Examiner, 1867

Genius of Universal Emancipation (Baltimore), 1825, 1828, 1829

Hartford Times, 1840

The Liberator (Boston), 1864

Morning Oregonian (Portland), 1869

National Freedman (New York), 1865

New Bedford (Mass.) Mercury, 1857

New York Tribune, 1870

Niles' Weekly Register (Baltimore), 1812–20, 1832–35

Washington News, 1867

Published Primary Sources

Andrews, E. A. *Slavery and the Domestic Slave-Trade in the United States*. Boston: Light and Stearns, 1836.

Baltimore City Mission of the Protestant Episcopal Church. *First Report of the Baltimore City Mission of the Protestant Episcopal Church*. Baltimore: Jos. Robinson, 1854.

Baltimore Ministry at Large. *Home Mission: First Annual Report Addressed to the Trustees and Friends of the Baltimore Ministry at Large, by Their Missionary to the Poor*. Baltimore: John D. Toy, 1843.

Baltimore Police Commissioners. *Report of the Police Commissioners of Baltimore City, with Accompanying Documents*. Annapolis: House of Delegates, 1861.

Baxley, H. Willis, A. White, and John G. Proud. *Report of the Committee of Directors Appointed to Prepare Plans for the New Buildings to Be Erected in the Yard of the Maryland Penitentiary*. Baltimore: Jas. Lucas and E. K. Deaver, 1835.

Beaumont, Gustave de, and Alexis de Tocqueville. *On the Penitentiary System in the United States and Its Application in France*. 1832. Reprint, Carbondale: Southern Illinois University Press, 1964.

Beccaria, Cesare. *On Crimes and Punishments*. 1764. Translated by David Young. Indianapolis: Hackett, 1986.

Bergron, Paul H., ed. *The Papers of Andrew Johnson, February–July 1866*. Knoxville: University of Tennessee Press, 1908.

Blackstone, William. *Commentaries on the Laws of England*. 4 vols. Oxford, 1765–69.

Board of Inspectors. *The Acts of Assembly: Together with the Governor's Proclamations and the Rules and Regulations, Respecting the Penitentiary of Maryland*. Baltimore: J. Robinson, 1819.

Board of Managers for Removing the Free People of Color. *Colonization of the Free Colored Population of Maryland, and of Such Slaves as May Hereafter Become Free.* Baltimore: J. Robinson, 1832.

Bowie, Oden. "Inaugural Address of Gov. Oden Bowie to the General Assembly of Maryland." Document D in *Public Documents of the House of Delegates of Maryland, January Session, 1868.* Annapolis: William Thompson, 1868.

——. "Message of Gov. Oden Bowie to the General Assembly of Maryland, at Its Regular Session, January, 1870." Document A in *House and Senate Documents, 1870.* Annapolis: William Thompson, 1870.

Brackett, Jeffrey. *The Negro in Maryland: A Study of the Institution of Slavery.* Baltimore: Johns Hopkins University, 1889.

Breckinridge, Robert J. *Tracts to Vindicate Religion and Liberty. No. 1. Containing the Review of the Case of Olevia Neal, the Carmelite Nun, and the Review of the Correspondence between the Archbishop and Mayor of Baltimore.* Baltimore: Matchett and Nelson, 1839.

Brown, George William. *Baltimore and the Nineteenth of April, 1861: A Study of the War.* 1887. Reprint, Baltimore: Johns Hopkins University Press, 2001.

Buckler, Thomas H. *A History of Epidemic Cholera, as It Appeared at the Baltimore City and County Almshouse, in the Summer of 1849.* Baltimore: James Lucas, 1851.

Carey, John L. *Slavery in Maryland, Briefly Considered.* Baltimore: John Murphy, 1845.

——. *Some Thoughts Concerning Domestic Slavery, in a Letter to —— Esq. of Baltimore.* Baltimore: John L. Lewis, 1838.

Clarke, Daniel. *Speech of Hon. Daniel Clarke, of Prince George's County, Delivered in the Constitutional Convention of Maryland, in Opposition to the 23rd Article of the Declaration of Rights, Emancipating the Slaves, and Abolishing Slavery in Maryland.* Baltimore: Sherwood and Co., 1864.

Coates, Benjamin H. "On the Effects of Secluded and Gloomy Imprisonment on Individuals of the African Variety of Mankind in the Production of Disease." *Pennsylvania Journal of Prison Discipline and Philanthropy* 1, no. 3 (July 1845): 267–68.

Collins, Stephen. *Report on Pauper Insanity Presented to the City Council of Baltimore.* Baltimore: James Lucas, 1845.

Committee on the Colored Population, House of Delegates, Maryland General Assembly. *Report of the Committee on the Colored Population.* Annapolis, 1842.

Crawford, William. *Report of William Crawford, on the Penitentiaries of the United States; Addressed to His Majesty's Principal Secretary of State for the Home Department.* London, 1835.

Curry, George F. *Communication from Major Gen'l Lew. Wallace, in Relation to the Freedman's Bureau, to the General Assembly of Maryland.* Annapolis: Richard P. Bayly, Printer, 1865.

Davis, Noah. *A Narrative of the Life of Rev. Noah Davis, a Colored Man.* Baltimore: John F. Weishampel Jr., 1859.

de la Mare, Nicolas. *Traité de la Police.* Paris, France: Michel Brunet, 1722.

Douglass, Frederick. "Abolition Fanaticism in New York: Speech of a Runaway Slave from Baltimore at an Abolition Meeting in New York, held May 11, 1847." Baltimore, 1847.

———. *My Bondage and My Freedom.* 1855. Reprint, Los Angeles: Indo-European Publishing, 2012.

———. *Narrative and Life of Frederick Douglass: An American Slave.* 1845. Reprint, New York: Signet Classics, 2005.

Foner, Philip, ed. *The Life and Writings of Frederick Douglass: Early Years, 1817–1849.* New York: International Publishers, 1950.

Foner, Philip S., and George E. Walker, eds. *Proceeding of the Black State Convention, 1840–1865.* 2 vols. Philadelphia: Temple University Press, 1980.

Foster, Lillian, ed. *Andrew Johnson, His Life and Speeches.* New York: Richardson and Co., 1866.

A Gentleman of the Bar. *The Trial of William Stewart for the Murder of His Father, Benjamin Stewart, on the Night of the 21st June, 1838, on Laudenslager's Hill, before Baltimore City Court, October Term, 1838, reported by a Gentleman of the Bar.* Baltimore: Bull and Tuttle, 1838.

Gerard, James. *London and New York: Their Crime and Police.* New York: W. C. Bryant, 1853.

Grimké, Angelina. "Appeal to the Christian Women of the South." *Anti-Slavery Examiner* 1, no. 2 (September 1836): 35–36.

Gwynn, William, and John Stone. *Report of the Committee of Grievances and Courts of Justice of the House of Delegates of Maryland, on the Subject of the Recent Mobs and Riots in the City of Baltimore, Together with the Depositions Taken before the Committee.* Annapolis: Jonas Green, 1813.

Hall, James. "An Address to the Free People of Color of the State of Maryland." Baltimore: J. D. Toy, 1859.

Hambleton, Samuel. *Report of the Committee on the Coloured Population, to Which Was Referred an Order of the House, Directing Them to Enquire into the Expediency of Forcing All the Free People of Colour to Leave This State, within a Certain Period of Time.* Annapolis: Jeremiah Hughes, 1836.

Harper, Robert Goodloe. *Letter from Gen. Harper from Maryland, to Elias B. Caldwell, Esq.: Secretary of the American Society for Colonizing the Free People of Colour.* Baltimore: R. J. Matchett, 1818.

Hawkins, Archibald. *The Life and Times of Hon. Elijah Stansbury, an Old Defender and Ex-Mayor of Baltimore.* Baltimore: John Murphy, 1874.

Hersey, John. *An Appeal to Christians on the Subject of Slavery.* 2nd ed. Baltimore: Armstrong and Plaskitt, 1833.

Hewitt, John Hill. *Shadows on the Wall; or, Glimpses of the Past.* 1877. Reprint, London: Forgotten Books, 2013.

Hill, Stephen P. *Sermon on the Subject of Temperance, Delivered on the 27th Day of December, 1835, in Accordance with the Call Made on the Rev. Clergy, by the Executive Committee of the Maryland State Temperance Society, to Unite in a*

Simultaneous Temperance Effort on That Day; and Published at Its Request.
Baltimore: Sands and Neilson, 1836.

House of Refuge. *Act of Incorporation and By-Laws of the House of Refuge for Juvenile Delinquents with Rules and Regulations for Its Government.* Baltimore: Steam Press, 1855.

———. *Report and Proceedings on the Subject of a House of Refuge at a Meeting of the Citizens of Baltimore Held at the City Hall.* Baltimore: Benjamin Edes, 1830.

Hutton, Peregrine. *The Life and Confession of Peregrine Hutton, Who, with His Companion, Morris N. B. Hull, Was Executed in Baltimore, July 14, 1820; for Robbing the Mail and Murdering the Driver.* Baltimore: Benjamin Edes, 1820.

Interesting Papers Relative to the Recent Riots at Baltimore. Philadelphia, 1812.

Jacobs, C. W. *The Free Negro Question in Maryland.* Baltimore: John W. Woods, 1859.

———. *Speech of Col. Curtis M. Jacobs, on the Free Colored Population of Maryland, Delivered in the House of Delegates, on the 17th of February, 1860.* Annapolis: E. S. Riley, 1860.

Johnson, Reverdy. *The Memorial of Reverdy Johnson, Praying Indemnity for the Destruction of His Property, in the City of Baltimore, by a Mob, in August, 1835.* Annapolis: William M'Neir, 1836.

Joint Committee on the Baltimore Riots. *The Report of and Testimony Taken before the Joint Committee of the Senate and House of Delegates of Maryland, to Which Is Referred the Memorials of John B. Morris, Reverdy Johnson and Others, Praying Indemnity for Losses Sustained by Reason of the Riots in Baltimore, in the Month of August, Eighteen Hundred and Thirty Five.* Annapolis: William M'Neir, 1836.

Joint Committee on the Penitentiary, Maryland General Assembly. *Testimony Taken before the Joint Committee of the Legislature of Maryland on the Penitentiary.* N.p., 1838.

Lakin, James. *Baltimore Directory and Register for 1814–15.* Baltimore: J. C. O'Reilly, 1814.

Latrobe, John H. B. *Colonization: A Notice of Victor Hugo's Views of Slavery in the United States.* Baltimore: John D. Toy, 1851.

———. *The Justices Practice under the Laws of Maryland . . . and an Explanation of Law Terms.* 4th ed. Baltimore: Fielding Lucas, 1847.

———. *The Justices Practice under the Laws of Maryland . . . and an Explanation of Law Terms.* 6th ed. Baltimore: Lucas Brothers, 1861.

Maryland General Assembly. *Depositions Taken at the Penitentiary by the Committee Appointed for That Purpose by the Legislature of Maryland.* Annapolis: J. Hughes, 1823.

Maryland Governor. *Document No. 11: Accompanying the Executive Communication of the 29th December, 1830; Report of the Directors of the Maryland Penitentiary.* Annapolis: Jonas Green, 1830.

Maryland Penitentiary. *Report of the Committee Appointed by the Board of Directors of the Maryland Penitentiary to Visit the Penitentiaries and Prisons in the City of Philadelphia and State of New York.* Baltimore: Lucas and Deaver, 1828.

————. *Report of the Committee on Prison Manufacturers*. Baltimore: Lucas and Deaver, 1842.

Mayer, Charles F. *Laying of the Corner Stone of the Baltimore House of Refuge: And the Address upon the Occasion by the Hon. Charles F. Mayer*. Baltimore: James Lucas, Hoe's Cylinder Press, 1852.

Mill, John Stuart. *Principles of Political Economy with Some of Their Applications to Social Philosophy*. Vol. 2. 1866. Reprint, London: Longmans, Reader, and Dyer, 1866.

Morris, John B. *Memorial to the Legislature of Maryland*. Baltimore: Lucas and Deaver, 1836.

Pennington, J. W. C. "The Self-Redeeming Power of the Colored Races of the World." *Anglo-African Magazine* 1 (1859).

Pitt, John R. *Report of the Committee Appointed to Inspect the Situation of the Maryland Penitentiary*. Annapolis: J. Hughes, 1823.

Public Documents of the House of Delegates of Maryland, January Session, 1868. Annapolis: William Thompson, 1868.

Pugh, Joseph P. *Speech of Hon. Jos. B. Pugh, of Cecil County, Delivered in the Constitutional Convention of Maryland, June 23d, 1864, in Favor of the 23d Article of the Declaration of Rights, Emancipating Slaves and Abolishing Slavery in Maryland*. Baltimore: Sherwood and Co., 1864.

Raymond, Daniel. *The Elements of Political Economy, in Two Parts*. 2nd ed. 1823. Reprint, New York: Augustus M. Kelley, 1964.

Read, William. *Testimony Taken before the Joint Committee of the Senate and House Delegates of Maryland, in Behalf of the Civil Authorities of Baltimore*. Annapolis: William M'Neir, 1836.

Report of the Select Committee . . . Respecting the Maryland Penitentiary. Annapolis: Jeremiah Hughes, 1837.

Report of the Select Committee to Whom Was Referred the Order of the House, Directing an Investigation into the Causes of the Increase of Pauperism, Intemperance and Crime, and Also to Suggest the Best Remedies Thereof. Annapolis: Jeremiah Hughes, 1836.

A Review of the Correspondence between the Archbishop and Mayor of Baltimore. Baltimore, 1839.

Robinson, Alex C. *Report of the Lunatic Department of the Baltimore Alms-House with an Appeal on the Subject of an Asylum for the Insane Poor*. Baltimore: J. Robinson, 1841.

Scharf, J. Thomas. *The Chronicles of Baltimore; Being a Complete History of "Baltimore Town" and Baltimore City from the Earliest Period to the Present Time*. Baltimore: Turnbull Brothers, 1874.

Semmes, Raphael. *Baltimore: As Seen by Visitors, 1783–1860*. Baltimore: Maryland Historical Society, 1953.

Smith, Adam. *An Inquiry into the Nature and Causes of the Wealth of Nations*. Vol. 1. 1776. Reprint, New York: Bantam Classics, 2003.

Steuart, R. S. *Letter to John L. Carey on the Subject of Slavery.* Baltimore: John Murphy, 1845.

Swann, Thomas. "Message of Governor Swann to the General Assembly of Maryland." Document A in *Public Documents of the House of Delegates of Maryland, January Session, 1868.* Annapolis: William Thompson, 1868.

Tocqueville, Alexis de. *Democracy in America.* 1832. Reprint, New York: A. A. Knopf, 1945.

Tuckerman, Joseph. *An Essay on the Wages Paid to Females for Their Labour.* Philadelphia: Carey and Hart, 1830.

Tyson, Elisha. *The Farewell Address of Elisha Tyson, of the City of Baltimore, to the People of Colour, in the United States of America.* Baltimore: William Woody, 1824.

Ward, Thomas. *The American Trenck; or, The Memoirs of Thomas Ward, Now in Confinement in the Baltimore Jail, under a Sentence of Ten Years Imprisonment, for Robbing the U.S. Mail, the 18th of July, 1823.* Baltimore, October 1829.

Watkins, William. "Address Delivered before the Moral Reform Society in Philadelphia, August 8, 1836." In *Early Negro Writing: 1760–1837,* edited by Dorothy Porter, 155–66. 1971. Reprint, Baltimore: Black Classic Press, 1995.

Yellott, Coleman. *Argument of Coleman Yellott, in Defence of John Stump, Indicted for the Murder of Henry L. Hammond.* Baltimore: Bull and Tuttle, 1850.

Young, Harry H. *A Lecture on the Increase of Crime, Delivered before the Monumental Lyceum.* Baltimore: James Young, 1853.

Secondary Sources

Alexander, Michelle. *The New Jim Crow: Mass Incarceration in the Age of Colorblindness.* New York: New Press, 2010.

Appleby, Joyce. *Capitalism and a New Social Order: The Republican Vision of the 1790s.* New York: New York University Press, 1984.

———. "Liberalism and the American Revolution." *New England Quarterly* 49, no. 1 (March 1976): 3–26.

Aristotle. *The Politics.* Edited and translated by Stephen Everson. Cambridge: Cambridge University Press, 1988.

Ayers, Edward L. *Vengeance and Justice: Crime and Punishment in the 19th-Century South.* New York: Oxford University Press, 1984.

Bailyn, Bernard. *Ideological Origins of the American Revolution.* Cambridge, Mass.: Harvard University Press, 1967.

Balogh, Brian. *A Government Out of Sight: The Mystery of National Authority in Nineteenth-Century America.* Cambridge: Cambridge University Press, 2009.

Baptist, Edward E. *The Half Has Never Been Told: Slavery and the Making of American Capitalism.* New York: Basic Books, 2014.

Bardaglio, Peter. *Reconstructing the Household: Families, Sex, and the Law in the Nineteenth-Century South.* Chapel Hill: University of North Carolina Press, 1998.

Basch, Norma. *In the Eyes of the Law: Women, Marriage, and Property in Nineteenth-Century New York.* Ithaca: Cornell University Press, 1982.

Beckert, Sven. *Empire of Cotton: A Global History.* New York: A. A. Knopf, 2014.

Bensel, Richard Franklin. *Yankee Leviathan: The Origins of Central State Authority in America, 1859–1877.* Cambridge: Cambridge University Press, 1990.

Berlin, Ira. "From Creole to African: Atlantic Creoles and the Origins of African-American Society in Mainland North America." *William and Mary Quarterly* 53, no. 2 (April 1996): 251–88.

———. *Many Thousands Gone: The First Two Centuries of Slavery in North America.* Cambridge, Mass.: Harvard University Press, 1998.

———. *Slaves without Masters: The Free Negro in the Antebellum South.* New York: Pantheon Books, 1974.

Blackmon, Douglas A. *Slavery by Another Name: The Re-enslavement of Black Americans from the Civil War to World War II.* New York: Anchor Books, 2008.

Bloch, Ruth H. "The American Revolution, Wife Beating, and the Emergent Value of Privacy." *Early American Studies* 5 (Fall 2007): 223–51.

———. "The Gendered Meanings of Virtue in Revolutionary America." *Signs: Journal of Women in Culture and Society* 13 (1987): 37–58.

Block, Sharon. *Rape and Sexual Power in Early America.* Chapel Hill: University of North Carolina Press, 2006.

Bonner, Robert E. *Mastering America: Southern Slaveholders and the Crisis of American Nationhood.* Cambridge: Cambridge University Press, 2009.

Boorstin, Daniel. *The Genius of American Politics.* Chicago: University of Chicago Press, 1953.

Bordieu, Pierre. *Le sens pratique.* Paris: Minuit, 1980.

Boydston, Jeanne. *Home and Work: Housework, Wages, and the Ideology of Labor in the Early Republic.* New York: Oxford University Press, 1990.

Bradbury, Bettina. *Working Families: Age, Gender, and Daily Survival in Industrializing Montreal.* Toronto: McClelland and Stewart, 1993.

Browne, Gary Lawson. *Baltimore in the Nation, 1789–1861.* Chapel Hill: University of North Carolina Press, 1980.

Brugger, Robert J. *Maryland: A Middle Temperament, 1634–1980.* Baltimore: Johns Hopkins University Press, 1988.

Brundage, W. Fitzhugh. *Under Sentence of Death: Lynching in the South.* Chapel Hill: University of North Carolina Press, 1997.

Byrnes, John Carroll. *Histories of the Bench and Bar of Baltimore City.* Baltimore: Baltimore Courthouse and Law Museum Foundation, 1997.

Carter, Stephen L. "Policing and Oppression Have a Long History." *Bloomberg View*, October 29, 2015. https://www.bloomberg.com/view/articles/2015-10-29/policing-and-oppression-have-a-long-history.

Chaplin, Joyce E. "Slavery and the Principle of Humanity: A Modern Idea in the Early Lower South." *Journal of Social History* 24, no. 2 (Winter 1990): 299–315.

Clark, Charles B. "Baltimore and the Attack on the Sixth Massachusetts Regiment, April 19, 1861." *Maryland Historical Magazine* 56, no. 1 (1961): 39–71.

Clark, Erskine. *By the Rivers of Water: A Nineteenth-Century Atlantic Odyssey.* New York: Basic Books, 2013.

Cohen, Daniel A. "Social Injustice, Sexual Violence, Spiritual Transcendence: Constructions of Interracial Rape in Early American Crime Literature, 1767–1817." *William and Mary Quarterly* 56, no. 3 (July 1999): 481–526.

Cott, Nancy. *The Bonds of Womanhood: "Woman's Sphere" in New England, 1780–1835.* New Haven: Yale University Press, 1977.

———. *Public Vows: A History of Marriage and the Nation.* Cambridge, Mass.: Harvard University Press, 2000.

Critchley, T. A. *A History of Police in England and Wales.* Rev. ed. Montclair, N.J.: Patterson Smith, 1972.

Curry, Leonard. *The Free Black in Urban America, 1800–1850: The Shadow of a Dream.* Chicago: University of Chicago Press, 1981.

Curtin, Mary Ellen. *Black Prisoners and Their World: Alabama, 1865–1900.* Charlottesville: University of Virginia Press, 2000.

Davis, David Brion. *Inhuman Bondage: The Rise and Fall of Slavery in the New World.* New York: Oxford University Press, 2006.

———. *The Problem of Slavery in the Age of Revolution, 1770–1823.* Ithaca: Cornell University Press, 1975.

Davis, Natalie Zemon. *Fiction in the Archives: Pardon Tales and Their Tellers in Sixteenth-Century France.* Stanford: Stanford University Press, 1987.

Della, Ray. "The Problem of Negro Labor in the 1850s." *Maryland Historical Magazine* 66, no. 1 (Spring 1971): 14–32.

DeLombard, Jeannine Marie. *In the Shadows of the Gallows: Race, Crime, and American Civic Identity.* Philadelphia: University of Pennsylvania Press, 2012.

Diemer, Andrew K. *The Politics of Black Citizenship: Free African Americans in the Mid-Atlantic Borderland, 1817–1863.* Athens: University of Georgia Press, 2016.

Diggins, John P. *The Lost Soul of American Politics: Virtue, Self-Interest, and the Foundations of Liberalism.* New York: HarperCollins, 1984.

Dray, Philip. *At the Hands of Persons Unknown: The Lynching of Black America.* New York: Random House, 2002.

Dubber, Markus Dirk. "Criminal Police and Criminal Law in the Rechtsstaat." In *Police and the Liberal State,* edited by Markus D. Dubber and Mariana Valverde, 92–109. Stanford: Stanford University Press, 2008.

———. *The Police Power: Patriarchy and the Foundations of American Government.* New York: Columbia University Press, 2005.

Du Bois, W. E. B. *Black Reconstruction in the United States, 1860–1880.* 1935. Reprint, New York: Free Press, 1998.

Dumm, Thomas L. *Democracy and Punishment: Disciplinary Origins of the United States.* Madison: University of Wisconsin Press, 1987.

Dunbar, Erica Armstrong. *A Fragile Freedom.* New Haven: Yale University Press, 2008.

Edwards, Laura. *The People and Their Peace: Legal Culture and the Transformation of Inequality in the Post-Revolutionary South.* Chapel Hill: University of North Carolina Press, 2009.

Einhorn, Robin. *American Slavery, American Taxation*. Chicago: University of Chicago Press, 2008.

Eltis, David. *The Rise of African Slavery in the Americas*. Cambridge: Cambridge University Press, 2000.

Emberton, Carole. "Unwriting the Freedom Narrative: A Review Essay." *Journal of Southern History* 82, no. 2 (May 2016): 377–94.

Ericson, David F. *Slavery in the American Republic: Developing the Federal Government, 1791–1861*. Lawrence: University of Kansas Press, 2011.

Ericson, David F., and Louisa Bertch Green, eds. *The Liberal Tradition in American Politics: Reassessing the Legacy of American Liberalism*. New York: Routledge, 1999.

Ethington, Philip. *The Public City: The Political Construction of Urban Life in San Francisco, 1850–1900*. New York: Cambridge University Press, 1994.

———. "Vigilantes and the Police: The Creation of a Professional Police Bureaucracy in San Francisco, 1847–1900." *Journal of Social History* 21, no. 2 (Winter 1987): 197–227.

Ezratty, Harry. *Baltimore in the Civil War: The Pratt Street Riot and a City Occupied*. Charleston, S.C.: History Press, 2010.

Falk, Sally Moore. *Law as Process: An Anthropological Approach*. Boston: Routledge and Kegan Paul Books, 1978.

Faust, Drew Gilpin. "Southern Violence Revisited." *Reviews in American History* 13, no. 2 (June 1985): 205–10.

Fields, Barbara. *Slavery and Freedom on the Middle Ground: Maryland during the Nineteenth Century*. New Haven: Yale University Press, 1985.

Foner, Eric. *Reconstruction: America's Unfinished Revolution, 1863–1877*. New York: Harper and Row, 1988.

Formisano, Ronald. "State Development in the Early Republic: Substance and Structure." In *Contesting Democracy: Substance and Structure in American Political History, 1775–2000*, edited by Bryon E. Schafer and Anthony J. Badger, 7–35. Lawrence: University of Kansas Press, 2001.

Foucault, Michel. *Discipline and Punish: The Birth of the Prison*. Translated by Alan Sheridan. New York: Vintage, 1979.

———. *Madness and Civilization: A History of Insanity in the Age of Reason*. New York: Random House, 1965.

———. "*Omnes et Singulatim*: Towards a Criticism of 'Political Reason.'" In *The Tanner Lectures on Human Values*, edited by Sterling M. McMurrin, 225–54. Vol. 2. Stanford: Stanford University Press, 1979.

Frank, Jason. *Constituent Moments: Enacting the People in Postrevolutionary America*. Durham: Duke University Press, 2010.

Fraser, Nancy. *Unruly Practices: Power, Discourse and Gender in Contemporary Social Theory*. Minneapolis: University of Minnesota Press, 1989.

Fraser, Nancy, and Linda Gordon. "Civil Citizenship against Social Citizenship? On the Ideology of Contract-versus-Charity." In *The Condition of Citizenship*, edited by Bart van Steenburgen, 90–107. Thousand Oaks, Calif.: Sage, 1994.

Frederickson, George. *The Black Image in the White Mind: The Debate on Afro-American Character and Destiny, 1817–1914*. New York: Harper and Row, 1971.

Freehling, William. *The Road to Disunion, Volume II: Secessionists Triumphant, 1854–1861*. Oxford: Oxford University Press, 2007.

Freund, Ernst. *The Police Power: Public Policy and Constitutional Rights*. Chicago: University of Chicago Press, 1904.

Friedman, Lawrence M. *Crime and Punishment in American History*. New York: Basic Books, 1993.

Fuchs, Rachel G. *Gender and Poverty in Nineteenth-Century Europe*. New York: Cambridge University Press, 2005.

Fuke, Richard Paul. "Hugh Lennox Bond and Radical Republican Ideology." *Journal of Southern History* 45, no. 4 (November 1979): 569–86.

———. *Imperfect Equality: African Americans and the Confines of White Racial Attitudes in Post-emancipation Maryland*. New York: Fordham University Press, 1999.

Furstenberg, François. "Beyond Freedom and Slavery: Autonomy, Virtue, and Resistance in Early American Political Discourse." *Journal of American History* 89, no. 4 (2003): 1295–1330.

Gardner, Bettye Jane. "Ante-bellum Black Education in Baltimore." *Maryland Historical Magazine* 71, no. 3 (1976): 360–66.

———. "Free Blacks in Baltimore, 1800–1860." PhD diss., George Washington University, 1974.

Gilje, Paul. "The Baltimore Riot of 1812 and the Breakdown of the Anglo-American Mob Tradition." *Journal of Social History* 13 (Summer 1980): 547–64.

———. *Rioting in America*. Bloomington: Indiana University Press, 1996.

———. *Road to Mobocracy: Popular Disorder in New York City, 1763–1834*. Chapel Hill: University of North Carolina Press, 1987.

Gilmore, Ruth Wilson. *Golden Gulag: Prisons, Surplus, Crisis, and Opposition in Globalizing California*. Berkeley: University of California Press, 2007.

Glenn, Evelyn Nakano. *Unequal Freedom: How Race and Gender Shaped American Citizenship and Labor*. Cambridge, Mass.: Harvard University Press, 2002.

Glickstein, Jonathan. *Concepts of Free Labor in Antebellum America*. New Haven, Conn.: Yale University Press, 1991.

Goffman, Alice. *On the Run: Fugitive Life in an American City*. Chicago: University of Chicago Press, 2014.

Goodman, Paul. *Of One Blood: Abolitionism and the Origins of Racial Equality*. Berkeley: University of California Press, 1998.

Gotanda, Neil. "A Critique of 'Our Constitution Is Color-Blind.'" *Stanford Law Review* 44 (November 1991): 1–68.

Gould, Clarence. "The Economic Causes of the Rise of Baltimore." In *Essays in Colonial History Presented to Charles McLean Andrews by His Students*, 225–51. New Haven: Yale University Press, 1931.

Graham, Leroy. *Baltimore: The Nineteenth Century Black Capital*. Lanham, Md.: University Press of America, 1982.

Greenberg, Amy. *Cause for Alarm: The Volunteer Fire Department in the Antebellum City*. Princeton: Princeton University Press, 1998.

Greenberg, Kenneth S., ed. *Nat Turner: A Slave Rebellion in History and Memory*. New York: Oxford University Press, 2003.

Greene, Sally. "*State v. Mann* Exhumed." *North Carolina Law Review* 87, no. 3 (March 2009): 701–75.

Greenstone, J. David. *The Lincoln Persuasion: Remaking American Liberalism*. Princeton: Princeton University Press, 1993.

Grimsted, David. *American Mobbing: Toward Civil War, 1828–1861*. New York: Oxford University Press, 1998.

———. "Democratic Rioting: A Case Study of the Baltimore Bank Mob of 1835." In *Insights and Parallels*, edited by William L. O'Neill, 125–91. Minneapolis: Burgess, 1973.

Gross, Kali N. *Colored Amazons: Crime, Violence, and Black Women in the City of Brotherly Love, 1880–1910*. Durham: Duke University Press, 2006.

Grossberg, Michael. *Governing the Hearth: Law and the Family in Nineteenth-Century America*. Chapel Hill: University of North Carolina Press, 1985.

Gundersen, Joan R. "Independence, Citizenship and the American Revolution." *Signs: Journal of Women in Culture and Society* 13 (1987): 59–77.

Gutman, Herbert G. *The Black Family in Slavery and Freedom, 1750–1925*. New York: Random House, 1976.

Hadden, Sally E. *Slave Patrols: Law and Violence in Virginia and the Carolinas*. Cambridge, Mass.: Harvard University Press, 2001.

Hahn, Steven. *A Nation under Our Feet: Black Political Struggles in the Rural South from Slavery to the Great Migration*. Cambridge, Mass.: Harvard University Press, 2003.

Haley, Sarah. *No Mercy Here: Gender, Punishment, and the Making of Jim Crow Modernity*. Chapel Hill: University of North Carolina Press, 2016.

Hall, Jacquelyn Dowd. "'The Mind That Burns in Each Body': Women, Rape, and Racial Violence." In *Powers of Desire: The Politics of Sexuality*, edited by Ann Snitow, Christine Stansell, and Sharon Thompson, 328–49. New York: New Feminist Library, 1983.

Halttunen, Karen. *Confidence Men and Painted Women*. New Haven: Yale University Press, 1982.

Harris, Leslie. *In the Shadow of Slavery: African Americans in New York City, 1626–1863*. Chicago: University of Chicago Press, 2003.

Hartog, Hendrik. *Man and Wife in America: A History*. Cambridge, Mass.: Harvard University Press, 2000.

Hartz, Louis. *The Liberal Tradition in America: An Interpretation of American Political Thought since the Revolution*. New York: Harcourt, Brace, 1955.

Hay, Douglas. "Property, Authority, and the Criminal Law." In *Albion's Fatal Tree: Crime and Society in Eighteenth-Century England*, edited by Douglas Hay et al., 17–64. New York: Allen Lane, 1975.

Hershberg, Theodore. "Free Blacks in Antebellum Philadelphia: A Study of

Ex-slaves, Freeborn and Socio-economic Decline." *Journal of Social History* 5, no. 2 (Spring 1972): 183–209.

Hickey, Donald. *The War of 1812: A Forgotten Conflict.* Urbana: University of Illinois Press, 1990.

Hill, Marc Lamont. *Nobody: Casualties of America's War on the Vulnerable, from Ferguson to Flint and Beyond.* New York: Atria, 2016.

Hindus, Michael Stephen. *Prison and Plantation: Crime, Justice, and Authority in Massachusetts and South Carolina, 1767–1878.* Chapel Hill: University of North Carolina Press, 1980.

Hirsch, Adam J. *The Rise of the Penitentiary Prisons and Punishment in Early America.* New Haven: Yale University Press, 1992.

Hockheimer, Lewis. "Police Power." *Central Law Journal* 44 (1897): 158–62.

Hodes, Martha. *White Women, Black Men: Illicit Sex in the Nineteenth-Century South.* New Haven: Yale University Press, 1997.

Holloway, Pippa. *Living in Infamy: Felon Disfranchisement and the History of American Citizenship.* New York: Oxford University Press, 2014.

Horowitz, Morton J. *The Transformation of American Law, 1780–1860.* Cambridge, Mass.: Harvard University Press, 1977.

Horton, James Oliver, and Louis E. Horton. *In Hope of Liberty: Culture, Community and Protest among Northern Free Blacks, 1700–1860.* New York: Oxford University Press, 1997.

Howe, Daniel Walker. *What Hath God Wrought: The Transformation of America, 1815–1848.* New York: Oxford University Press, 2007.

Hurst, James Willard. *Law and the Conditions of Freedom in the Nineteenth-Century United States.* Madison: University of Wisconsin Press, 1956.

Huston, James L. *Calculating the Value of the Union: Slavery, Property Rights, and the Economic Origins of the Civil War.* Chapel Hill: University of North Carolina Press, 2002.

Innes, Joanna, and John Styles. "The Crime Wave: Recent Writing on Crime and Criminal Justice in Eighteenth-Century England." *Journal of British Studies* 25 (October 1986): 380–435.

Jacobson, Matthew Frye. *Whiteness of a Different Color: European Immigrants and the Alchemy of Race.* Cambridge, Mass.: Harvard University Press, 1998.

Johnson, David R. *Policing the Urban Underworld: The Impact of Crime on the Development of the American Police, 1800–1887.* Philadelphia: Temple University Press, 1979.

Johnson, Norman. *Forms of Constraint: A History of Prison Architecture.* Urbana: University of Illinois Press, 2000.

Johnson, Paul. *A Shopkeeper's Millennium: Society and Revivals in Rochester, New York, 1815–1837.* New York: Hill and Wang, 1978.

Johnson, Walter. *The Chattel Principle: The Internal Slave Trade in the Americas.* New Haven: Yale University Press, 2004.

———. "On Agency." *Journal of Social History* 37, no. 1 (Autumn 2003): 113–24.

———. *River of Dark Dreams: Slavery and Empire in the Cotton Kingdom*. Cambridge, Mass.: Belknap Press, 2013.

———. "Slavery, Reparations, and the Mythic March of Freedom." *Raritan* 27, no. 2 (Fall 2007): 41–67.

———. *Soul by Soul: Life inside the Antebellum Slave Market*. Cambridge, Mass.: Harvard University Press, 1999.

Jones, Martha S. "*Hughes v. Jackson*: Race and Rights beyond *Dred Scott*." *North Carolina Law Review* 91, no. 5 (2013): 1757–84.

———. "Leave of Court." In *Contested Democracy: Freedom, Race, and Power in American History*, edited by Manisha Sinha and Penny Von Eschen, 54–74. New York: Cambridge University Press, 2007.

Jordan, Winthrop. *White over Black: American Attitudes towards the Negro, 1550–1812*. Chapel Hill: University of North Carolina Press, 1968.

Joyce, Patrick. *The Rule of Freedom: Liberalism and the Modern City*. London: Verso, 2003.

Kahana, Jeffrey S. "Master and Servant in the Early Republic, 1780–1830." *Journal of the Early Republic* 20 (Spring 2000): 27–57.

Kalyvas, Andreas, and Ira Katznelson. *Liberal Beginnings: Making a Republic for the Moderns*. Cambridge: Cambridge University Press, 2008.

Kann, Mark E. *Punishment, Prisons, and Patriarchy: Liberty and Power in the Early American Republic*. New York: New York University Press, 2005.

Kantrowitz, Stephen. "'Intended for the Better Government of Man': The Political History of African American Freemasonry in the Era of Emancipation." *Journal of American History* 96, no. 4 (March 2010): 1001–26.

———. *More Than Freedom: Fighting for Black Citizenship in a White Republic, 1829–1889*. New York: Penguin, 2012.

———. "One Man's Mob Is Another Man's Militia: Violence, Manhood, and Authority in Reconstruction South Carolina." In *Jumpin' Jim Crow: Southern Politics from Civil War to Civil Rights*, edited by Jane Elizabeth Dailey, Glenda Elizabeth Gilmore, and Bryant Simon, 67–87. Princeton: Princeton University Press, 2000.

Katz, Sarah. "Rumors of Rebellion: Fear of a Slave Uprising in Post–Nat Turner Baltimore." *Maryland Historical Magazine* 89 (Fall 1994): 328–33.

Keller, Lisa. *Triumph of Order: Democracy and Public Space in New York and London*. New York: Columbia University Press, 1999.

Keller, Morton. *America's Three Regimes: A New Political History*. New York: Oxford University Press, 2007.

Kerber, Linda. "Can a Woman Be an Individual? The Discourse of Self-Reliance." In *Toward an Intellectual History of Women: Essays by Linda K. Kerber*, 200–223. Chapel Hill: University of North Carolina Press, 1997.

———. *No Constitutional Right to Be Ladies: Women and the Obligations of Citizenship*. New York: Hill and Wang, 1998.

———. *Women of the Republic: Intellect and Ideology in Revolutionary America*. Chapel Hill: University of North Carolina Press, 1980.

Keyssar, Alexander. *The Right to Vote: The Contested History of Democracy in the United States.* New York: Basic Books, 2000.

Kloppenberg, James. "The Virtues of Liberalism: Christianity, Republicanism, and Ethics in Early American Political Discourse." *Journal of American History* 74 (June 1987): 9–33.

Lane, Roger. *Policing the City: Boston, 1822–1885.* Cambridge, Mass.: Harvard University Press, 1967.

Larson, John Lauritz. "'Bind the Republic Together': The National Union and the Struggle for a System of Internal Improvements." *Journal of American History* 74 (September 1987): 363–87.

LeFlouria, Talitha L. *Chained in Silence: Black Women and Convict Labor in the New South.* Chapel Hill: University of North Carolina Press, 2015.

Lichtenstein, Alex. *Twice the Work of Free Labor: The Political Economy of Convict Labor in the New South.* London: Verso, 1996.

Lofland, Lyn A. *A World of Strangers: Order and Action in Urban Public Space.* Prospect Heights, Ill.: Waveland Press, 1973.

Losurdo, Domenico. *Liberalism: A Counter-History.* London: Verso, 2011.

Lyons, Clare A. *Sex among the Rabble: An Intimate History of Gender and Power in the Age of Revolution, 1730–1830.* Chapel Hill: University of North Carolina Press, 2006.

MacPherson, C. B. *The Political Theory of Possessive Individualism: Hobbes to Locke.* New York: Oxford University Press, 1962.

Malka, Adam. "'The Open Violence of Desperate Men': Rethinking Property and Power in the 1835 Baltimore Bank Riot." *Journal of the Early Republic* 37, no. 2 (Summer 2017): 193–223.

Manion, Jennifer. *Liberty's Prisoners: Carceral Culture in Early America.* Philadelphia: University of Pennsylvania Press, 2015.

Mannard, Joseph G. "The 1839 Baltimore Nunnery Riot: An Episode in Jacksonian Nativism and Social Violence." *Maryland Historian* 11 (Spring 1980): 13–27.

McCoy, Drew. *The Elusive Republic: Political Economy in Jeffersonian America.* Chapel Hill: University of North Carolina Press, 1980.

McCurry, Stephanie. *Masters of Small Worlds.* New York: Oxford University Press, 1995.

———. "The Two Faces of Republicanism: Gender and Proslavery Politics in Antebellum South Carolina." *Journal of American History* 78, no. 4 (March 1992): 1245–64.

McGlynn, Frank, and Seymour Drescher, eds. *The Meaning of Freedom: Economics, Politics, and Culture after Slavery.* Pittsburgh: University of Pittsburgh Press, 1992.

McLennan, Rebecca M. *The Crisis of Imprisonment: Protest, Politics, and the Making of the American Penal State, 1776–1941.* Cambridge: Cambridge University Press, 2008.

Melish, Joanne Pope. *Disowning Slavery: Gradual Emancipation and Race in New England, 1780–1860.* Ithaca: Cornell University Press, 1998.

Melton, Tracy Matthew. *Hanging Henry Gambrill: The Violent Career of Baltimore's Plug Uglies*. Baltimore: Maryland Historical Society, 2006.

Meranze, Michael. *Laboratories of Virtue: Punishment, Revolution, and Authority in Philadelphia, 1760–1835*. Chapel Hill: University of North Carolina Press, 1996.

Miller, Wilbur R. *Cops and Bobbies: Police Authority in New York and London, 1830–1870*. Chicago: University of Chicago Press, 1977.

Monkkonen, Eric H. *Police in Urban America, 1860–1920*. Cambridge: Cambridge University Press, 1981.

Montgomery, David. *Citizen Worker: The Experience of Workers in the United States with Democracy and the Free Market during the Nineteenth Century*. Cambridge: Cambridge University Press, 1993.

Morgan, Edmund. *American Slavery, American Freedom*. New York: W. W. Norton, 1975.

Morris, Richard B. "Labor Controls in Maryland in the Nineteenth Century." *Journal of Southern History* 14 (August 1948): 385–400.

Muhammad, Khalil Gibran. *The Condemnation of Blackness: Race, Crime, and the Making of Modern Urban America*. Cambridge, Mass.: Harvard University Press, 2010.

Muller, Edward K., and Paul A. Groves. "The Emergence of Industrial Districts in Mid-Nineteenth Century Baltimore." *Geographical Review* 69, no. 2 (April 1969): 159–78.

Myers, Amrita Chakrabarti. *Forging Freedom: Black Women and the Pursuit of Liberty in Antebellum Charleston*. Chapel Hill: University of North Carolina Press, 2011.

Nash, Gary, and Jean Soderlund. *Freedom by Degrees: Emancipation in Pennsylvania and Its Aftermath*. New York: Oxford University Press, 1991.

Nedelsky, Jennifer. *Private Property and the Limits of American Constitutionalism: The Madisonian Framework and Its Legacy*. Chicago: University of Chicago Press, 1990.

Nelson, Jill, ed. *Police Brutality: An Anthology*. New York: W. W. Norton, 2000.

Newman, Simon. *Parades and the Politics of the Street: Festive Culture in the Early American Republic*. Philadelphia: University of Pennsylvania Press, 1997.

Novak, William J. "The Legal Transformation of Citizenship in Nineteenth-Century America." In *The Democratic Experiment: New Directions in American Political History*, edited by Meg Jacobs, William J. Novak, and Julian E. Zelizer, 85–119. Princeton: Princeton University Press, 2003.

———. "The Myth of the 'Weak' American State." *American Historian Review* 113, no. 3 (2008): 752–72.

———. *The People's Welfare: Law and Regulation in Nineteenth-Century America*. Chapel Hill: University of North Carolina Press, 1996.

Oakes, James. *Slavery and Freedom: An Interpretation of the Old South*. New York: A. A. Knopf, 1990.

Oates, Stephen B. *The Fires of Jubilee: Nat Turner's Fierce Rebellion*. New York: Harper and Row, 1975.

Olson, Sherry H. *Baltimore: The Building of an American City*. Baltimore: Johns Hopkins University Press, 1980.

Orren, Karen. *Belated Feudalism: Labor, the Law, and Liberal Development in the United States*. New York: Cambridge University Press, 1991.

Orren, Karen, and Stephen Skowronek. *The Search for American Political Development*. Cambridge: Cambridge University Press, 2004.

Oshinsky, David. *"Worse Than Slavery": Parchman Farm and the Ordeal of Jim Crow Justice*. New York: Free Press, 1996.

Pateman, Carol. *The Sexual Contract*. Palo Alto: Stanford University Press, 1989.

Paton, Diana. *No Bond but the Law: Punishment, Race, and Gender in Jamaican State Formation, 1780–1870*. Durham: Duke University Press, 2004.

Pfaff, John. *Locked In: The True Causes of Mass Incarceration—And How to Achieve Real Reform*. New York: Basic Books, 2017.

Pfeifer, Michael J. *Rough Justice: Lynching and American Society, 1874–1947*. Urbana: University of Illinois Press, 2004.

Phillips, Christopher. *Freedom's Port: The African American Community of Baltimore, 1790–1860*. Urbana: University of Illinois Press, 1997.

Pierson, George Wilson. *Tocqueville and Beaumont in America*. New York: Oxford University Press, 1938.

Pleck, Elizabeth. *Domestic Tyranny: The Making of Social Policy against Family Violence from Colonial Times to the Present*. New York: Oxford University Press, 1987.

Pocock, J. G. A. *The Machiavellian Moment: Florentine Political Thought and the Atlantic Republican Tradition*. Princeton: Princeton University Press, 1975.

———. "Virtue and Commerce in the Eighteenth Century." *Journal of Interdisciplinary History* 3 (1972): 119–34.

Pound, Roscoe. "Law in Books and Law in Action." *American Law Review* 44 (1910): 12–36.

Quintana, Ryan. "Planners, Planters, and Slaves: Producing the State in Early National South Carolina." *Journal of Southern History* 81, no. 1 (February 2015): 79–116.

Rable, George C. *But There Was No Peace: The Role of Violence in the Politics of Reconstruction*. Athens: University of Georgia Press, 1984.

Rice, Jim. "'This Province, So Meanly and Thinly Inhabited': Punishing Maryland's Criminals, 1681–1850." *Journal of the Early Republic* 19 (Spring 1999): 15–42.

Richardson, James. *The New York Police: Colonial Times to 1901*. New York: Oxford University Press, 1970.

———. *Urban Police in the United States*. Port Washington, N.Y.: Kennikat Press, 1974.

Rockman, Seth. "Saving Morris Hull: Capital Punishment and the Court of Public Opinion in Early Republic Baltimore." In *From Mobtown to Charm City: New Perspectives on Baltimore's Past*, edited by Jessica Elfenbein et al., 64–91. Baltimore: Maryland Historical Society, 2002.

———. *Scraping By: Wage Labor, Slavery, and Survival in Early Baltimore*. Baltimore: Johns Hopkins University Press, 2008.

Rodgers, Daniel T. "Republicanism: The Career of a Concept." *Journal of American History* 79, no. 1 (June 1992): 11–38.

Roediger, David. *The Wages of Whiteness: Race and the Making of the American Working Class.* New York: Verso, 1991.

Rogers, Everett M. *Diffusion of Innovations.* New York: Free Press, 1962.

Ross, Ellen. *Love and Toil: Motherhood in Outcast London, 1870–1918.* New York: Oxford University Press, 1993.

Rothman, Adam. *Slave Country: American Expansion and the Origins of the Deep South.* Cambridge, Mass.: Harvard University Press, 2005.

Rothman, David. *The Discovery of the Asylum: Social Order and Disorder in the New Republic.* Rev. ed. Boston: Little, Brown, 1990.

Rothman, Joshua D. *Flush Times and Fever Dreams: A Story of Capitalism and Slavery in the Age of Jackson.* Athens: University of Georgia Press, 2012.

———. "The Hazards of Flush Times: Gambling, Mob Violence, and the Anxieties of America's Market Revolution." *Journal of American History* 95, no. 3 (December 2008): 651–77.

Rousey, Dennis. *Policing the Southern City: New Orleans, 1805–1889.* Baton Rouge: Louisiana State University Press, 1996.

Royster, Charles. *Light-Horse Harry Lee and the Legacy of the American Revolution.* New York: A. A. Knopf, 1981.

Salinger, Sharon. *"To Serve Well and Faithfully": Labor and Indentured Servants in Pennsylvania, 1682–1800.* Cambridge: Cambridge University Press, 1987.

Schlesinger, Arthur. *The Age of Jackson.* New York: Little, Brown, 1945.

Schlossman, Steven L. *Love and the American Delinquent: The Theory and Practice of "Progressive" Juvenile Justice, 1825–1920.* Chicago: University of Chicago Press, 1977.

Schmidt, James D. *Free to Work: Labor Law, Emancipation, and Reconstruction, 1815–1880.* Athens: University of Georgia Press, 1998.

Schneider, John C. *Detroit and the Problem of Order, 1830–1880: A Geography of Crime, Riot, and Policing.* Lincoln: University of Nebraska Press, 1980.

Schoen, Brian. *The Fragile Fabric of Union: Cotton, Federal Politics, and the Global Origins of the Civil War.* Baltimore: Johns Hopkins University Press, 2009.

———. "Positive Goods and Necessary Evils: Commerce, Security, and Slavery in the Lower South, 1787–1837." In *Contesting Slavery: The Politics of Bondage and Freedom in the New American Nation*, edited by John Craig Hammond and Matthew Mason, 161–82. Charlottesville: University of Virginia Press, 2011.

Scott, James C. *Seeing Like a State: How Certain Schemes to Improve the Human Condition Have Failed.* New Haven: Yale University Press, 1998.

Sellers, Charles. *The Market Revolution: Jacksonian America, 1815–1846.* New York: Oxford University Press, 1991.

Shalhope, Robert. *The Baltimore Bank Riot: Political Upheaval in Antebellum Maryland.* Urbana: University of Illinois Press, 2009.

———. "Republicanism and Early American Historiography." *William and Mary Quarterly* 39, no. 2 (April 1982): 334–56.

———. "Toward a Republican Synthesis: The Emergence of an Understanding of Republicanism in American Historiography." *William and Mary Quarterly* 29, no. 1 (January 1972): 49–80.

Shammas, Carole. *A History of Household Government in America.* Charlottesville: University of Virginia Press, 2002.

Siegel, Reva B. "'The Rule of Love': Wife Beating as Prerogative and Privacy." *Yale Law Review* 105 (June 1996): 2117–2207.

Sinha, Manisha. *The Counterrevolution of Slavery: Politics and Ideology in Antebellum South Carolina.* Chapel Hill: University of North Carolina Press, 2000.

Slotkin, Richard. "Narratives of Negro Crime in New England, 1675–1800." *American Quarterly* 25, no. 1 (March 1973): 18–28.

Smith, Caleb. *The Prison and the American Imagination.* New Haven: Yale University Press, 2009.

Smith, Kimberly. *The Dominion of Voice: Riot, Reason, and Romance in Antebellum Politics.* Lawrence: University Press of Kansas, 1999.

Smith, Rogers. *Civic Ideals: Conflicting Visions of U.S. Citizenship in U.S. History.* New Haven: Yale University Press, 1997.

Smith, Susan. *Sick and Tired of Being Sick and Tired: Black Women's Health Activism in America, 1890–1950.* Philadelphia: University of Pennsylvania Press, 1995.

Smith-Rosenberg, Carroll. "Discovering the Subject of the 'Great Constitutional Discussion,' 1786–1789." *Journal of American History* 79 (1992): 841–73.

Stanley, Amy Dru. "Beggars Can't Be Choosers: Compulsion and Contract in Postbellum America." *Journal of American History* 78, no. 4 (March 1992): 1265–93.

———. *From Bondage to Contract: Wage Labor, Marriage, and the Market in the Age of Slave Emancipation.* Cambridge: Cambridge University Press, 1998.

Stansell, Christine. *City of Women: Sex and Class in New York, 1789–1860.* Urbana: University of Illinois Press, 1982.

Steffen, Charles G. *The Mechanics of Baltimore: Workers and Politics in the Age of Revolution, 1763–1812.* Urbana: University of Illinois Press, 1984.

Steinberg, Allen. *The Transformation of Criminal Justice: Philadelphia, 1800–1880.* Chapel Hill: University of North Carolina Press, 1989.

Steinfeld, Robert. *Coercion, Contract, and Free Labor in the Nineteenth Century.* Cambridge: Cambridge University Press, 2001.

———. *The Invention of Free Labor: The Employment Relation in English and American Law and Culture, 1350–1870.* Chapel Hill: University of North Carolina Press, 1991.

Stopak, Aaron. "Maryland State Colonization Society: Independent State Action in the Colonization Movement." *Maryland Historical Magazine* 63, no. 3 (September 1968): 275–98.

Sullivan, Robert R. "The Birth of the Prison: The Case of Benjamin Rush." *Eighteenth-Century Studies* 31, no. 3 (Spring 1998): 333–44.

Sutton, William R. *Journeymen for Jesus: Evangelical Artisans Confront Capitalism in Jacksonian Baltimore*. University Park: Pennsylvania State University Press, 1998.

Sweet, James H. "The Iberian Roots of American Racist Thought." *William and Mary Quarterly* 54 (January 1997): 143–66.

Sweet, John Wood. *Bodies Politic: Negotiating Race in the American North, 1730–1830*. Philadelphia: University of Pennsylvania Press, 2006.

Tarter, Michele Lise, and Richard Bell, eds. *Buried Lives: Incarcerated in Early America*. Athens: University of Georgia Press, 2012.

Thompson, Heather Ann. "Why Incarceration Matters: Rethinking Crisis, Decline, and Transformation in Postwar American History." *Journal of American History* 97, no. 3 (December 2010): 703–34.

Tomlins, Christopher. *Law, Labor, and Ideology in the Early American Republic*. Cambridge: Cambridge University Press, 1993.

———. "Necessities of State: Police, Sovereignty, and the Constitution." *Journal of Police History* 20, no. 1 (2008): 47–63.

———. "The Supreme Sovereignty of the State: A Genealogy of Police in American Constitutional Law, from the Founding Era to *Lochner*." In *Police and the Liberal State*, edited by Markus D. Dubber and Mariana Valverde, 33–53. Palo Alto: Stanford University Press, 2008.

Towers, Frank. "African-American Baltimore in the Era of Frederick Douglass." *ATQ* 9, no. 3 (September 1995): 165–80.

———. "Job Busting at Baltimore's Shipyards: Racial Violence in the Civil War–Era South." *Journal of Southern History* 66, no. 2 (May 2000): 221–56.

———. *The Urban South and the Coming of the Civil War*. Charlottesville: University of Virginia Press, 2004.

———. "'A Vociferous Army of Howling Wolves': Baltimore's Civil War Riot of April 19, 1861." *Maryland Historian* 23, no. 2 (1992): 1–28.

Townsend, Camilla. *Tales of Two Cities: Race and Economic Culture in Early Republican North and South America: Guayaquil, Ecuador, and Baltimore, Maryland*. Austin: University of Texas Press, 2000.

Wacquant, Loïc. "From Slavery to Mass Incarceration: Rethinking the 'Race Question' in the US." In *Race, Law, and Society*, edited by Ian Haney López, 277–94. Burlington, Vt.: Ashgate, 2007.

Wade, Richard. *Slavery in the Cities: The South, 1820–1860*. New York: Oxford University Press, 1964.

Wagandt, Charles L. *The Mighty Revolution: Negro Emancipation in Maryland, 1862–1864*. Baltimore: Maryland Historical Society, 1964.

Waldrep, Christopher. *Roots of Disorder: Race and Criminal Justice in the American South, 1817–80*. Urbana: University of Illinois Press, 1998.

Walker, Samuel. *A Critical History of Police Reform: The Emergence of Professionalism*. Lexington, Mass.: Lexington Books, 1977.

———. *Popular Justice: A History of American Criminal Justice*. 2nd ed. New York: Oxford University Press, 1998.

Warner, Sam Bass, Jr. *The Private City: Philadelphia in Three Periods of Its Growth.* Philadelphia: University of Pennsylvania Press, 1968.

Watson, Harry. *Liberty and Power: The Politics of Jacksonian America.* New York: Hill and Wang, 1990.

Way, Peter. "Shovel and Shamrock: Irish Workers and Labor Violence in the Digging of the Chesapeake and Ohio Canal." *Labor History* 30, no. 4 (Fall 1989): 489–517.

Weber, Max. *Essays in Sociology.* New York: Oxford University Press, 1946.

Welke, Barbara. *Law and the Borders of Belonging in the Long Nineteenth Century United States.* Cambridge: Cambridge University Press, 2010.

Wells, Jonathan Daniel. *The Origins of the Southern Middle Class, 1800–1861.* Chapel Hill: University of North Carolina Press, 2004.

White, Hayden. *The Content of Form: Narrative Discourse and Historical Representation.* Baltimore: Johns Hopkins University Press, 1987.

Whitman, T. Stephen. "'I Have Got the Gun and Will Do as I Please with Her': African Americans and Violence in Maryland, 1782–1830." In *Over the Threshold: Intimate Violence in Early America,* edited by Christine Daniels and Michael V. Kennedy, 254–67. New York: Routledge, 1999.

———. *The Price of Freedom: Slavery and Manumission in Baltimore and Early National Maryland.* Lexington: University Press of Kentucky, 1997.

Wilentz, Sean. *Chants Democratic: New York and the Rise of the American Working Class, 1788–1850.* New York: Oxford University Press, 1984.

———. *The Rise of American Democracy: Jefferson to Lincoln.* New York: Oxford University Press, 2005.

Williams, Eric. *Capitalism and Slavery.* Chapel Hill: University of North Carolina Press, 1944.

Williams, Kristian. *Our Enemies in Blue: Police and Power in America.* New York: South End Press, 2007.

Williams, Patricia J. *Alchemy of Race and Rights: Diary of a Law Professor.* Cambridge, Mass.: Harvard University Press, 1992.

Wolcott, Victoria W. *Remaking Respectability: African American Women in Interwar Detroit.* Chapel Hill: University of North Carolina Press, 2001.

Wood, Gordon S. *The Creation of the American Republic, 1776–1787.* Chapel Hill: University of North Carolina Press, 1969.

———. *The Radicalism of the American Revolution.* New York: A. A. Knopf, 1992.

Wright, Gavin. *Slavery and American Economic Development.* Baton Rouge: Louisiana State University Press, 2006.

Wright, James Martin. *Free Negro in Maryland, 1634–1860.* New York: Columbia University Press, 1921.

Wyatt-Brown, Bertram. *Southern Honor: Ethics and Behavior in the Old South.* New York: Oxford University Press, 1982.

INDEX

Abolitionism, 106, 125, 190, 284n3

Adjudication process, 259n15

African diaspora, 284n2

Alabama, 184

Allright, P., 173

Almshouses: in Baltimore, 53, 75–76, 78, 79; sex segregation in, 76, 182; and "worthy poor," 104; and immigrants, 105; percentage of black Baltimoreans in, 181–82, 183, 236–37, 238, 288n100; percentage of white Baltimoreans in, 182, 183, 185, 236, 237–38, 240, 241; disciplinary program of, 182, 288n100; logic of, 259n15; and public welfare regime, 271n87

Alvord, J. W., 191

Amalgamation, 223

American and Commercial Advertiser, 191–92, 232

American Colonization Society, 160, 168

American Party. *See* Know-Nothing Party

Ames, Jessie W., 199–200

Anderson, Caroline, 206, 208

Anderson, Charles, 208

Andrews, Ethan Allen, 100, 164–65

Annapolis Orphans Court, 204–5

Antislavery activists: and rights of all men, 2, 211, 219, 249; and black poverty, 144, 156; criminality associated with black freedom, 156; and power of industry to uplift freed people, 194, 242–43; and wage contracts, 202, 249; interracial coalition of, 217, 218;

and white supremacy, 244–45. *See also* Abolitionism

Apprenticeship, 93, 145–46, 204–13, 215, 233, 243, 249, 283n99

Aristotle, 163

Armacourt, Joshua, 38

Armstrong, Anthony, 199

Attorneys, 33–36, 59

Auburn Prison, 71, 74, 75

Augustus, Amie, 199

Auld, Hugh, 99, 158

Auld, Sophia, 158

B&O Railroad, 114, 115

Bacon, Mary, 206

Bain, William, 196

Baker, J. T., 230

Baldwin, Abraham, 196

Baltimore: black population of, 1, 9–10, 100, 165, 222–23, 236; street violence in, 9; as Mobtown, 9, 47–48, 89, 90; free black community in, 9–10, 13, 21–23, 24, 90, 100, 157, 165, 167, 175, 287n70; free labor economy of, 10, 20; as port city, 10, 20, 21; and North-South divide, 11–13; mixed-labor economy of, 13, 23–24; race riots in, 14, 273n1; bureaucracy of, 19, 31, 62; harbor of, 20; population growth, 20, 21, 55, 57, 59, 61, 68, 120; and wheat market, 20–21; and tobacco market, 21; population of slave community, 21–22, 23, 100, 108–9; and indentured servant trade, 23; ethnic diversity in,

154, 233; and household autonomy, 133–36; and white vigilantism, 169–71; and emancipation, 250–51
White-on-black "job busting," 273n1
White skilled craftsmen, 91–92, 96, 98
White supremacy: and police professionalization, 6, 7, 10, 11, 12, 13, 248; and prisons, 7, 12; national legacy of, 12; and policing practices, 46, 252; resistance to racial egalitarianism, 213; and emancipation, 244, 250; and criminalization of black freedom, 250; flexibility of, 250; persistence of, 251; structural racism of criminal justice system contrasted with, 259n15; and expansion of property rights, 261n32
White terrorism, 217
White vigilantism: and slavery, 4; racial violence of, 6, 12, 14, 119, 121, 123, 227–28; and police professionalization, 10–11, 54, 57–58, 80, 84, 119, 121, 166, 174, 176, 180, 181, 218, 227, 250; in South, 12; legal cover for, 14; in civil society, 25, 27–28, 37, 45, 46, 47; and mercenary acts, 36–46, 66, 174; and Indemnity Act, 59; and legal discrimination of free black Baltimoreans, 169–76, 185–86, 192–93, 230–31, 249; and protection of free black Baltimoreans, 172; and fears of black crime, 184; demise of, 217–18; endurance of, 227; in post-emancipation era, 227–35; and black militia, 229–30
White workingmen: property rights of, 54, 81, 84, 85; and Know-Nothing Party, 63, 65, 114, 119; and police reform, 84, 85; power over black workingmen, 89–90, 115–21, 231–33, 273n1; alliance with police force, 90, 113, 114–15, 119, 232, 277n105; and strikes, 114, 231, 232; monopolization of trades, 115

Whitney, John, 200
Whittington, Harriett, 200–201
Wiley, Alexander, 31, 32
Wilkins, Bartus, 174
Wilkinson, Thomas, 242
Wilkinson, William, 132
Willar, Frederick, 172–73
Williams, Abraham, 145
Williams, Charles, 200
Williams, Charlotte, 179
Williams, Eric, 284n2
Williams, Henry, 105
Williams, Hyson, 179
Williams, James Henry, 179
Williams, Thomas, 59
Wilson, Alexander, 179
Wilson, Robert, 203–4
Wilson, William Henry, 208–9
Wilson, William P., 197
Women: incarceration of, 13, 75, 130, 133, 136, 137; men's protection of, 26–27; and private defense attorneys, 33–34; assaults on, 38, 264n63; dependency of, 94, 96, 126; household rights of, 95, 138; and wage contracts, 95–96, 126, 196; and "worthy poor," 104; and coverture, 126; girls in House of Refuge, 130, 131, 279n27; and property rights, 212. *See also* Black women
Wright, Alexander, 204
Wright, Henrietta, 206
Wright, James, 132
Wright, Jane, 196, 204
Wright, Stephen, 206
Wyatt, John, 198

Yellott, Coleman, 135–36
Young, Harry H., 55–56
Young, Sarah, 173

Zell, John, 46
Zion Lodge No. 4, 157